KLEZMER!

KLEZMER!

Jewish Music from
Old World to Our World

Henry Sapoznik

Schirmer Books
An Imprint of Macmillan Library Reference USA
NEW YORK

Unless otherwise indicated, all photos and graphics are
from the collection of the author.

SCHIRMER BOOKS
An Imprint of Macmillan Library Reference USA
1633 Broadway
New York, NY 10019

Library of Congress Catalog Card Number: 99-31627
Printed in the United States of America

Printing number
1 2 3 4 5 6 7 8 9 10

Library of Congress Cataloging-in-Publication Data
Sapoznik, Henry.
Klezmer! : Jewish music from old world to our world / Henry Sapoznik.
p.   cm.
Includes bibliographical references and index
ISBN 0-02-864574-X
1. Klezmer music—History and criticism.   2. Jews—Music—
History and criticism.   I. Title.
ML 3528.8.S26 1999
781.62'924—dc21
99-31627
CIP

This paper meets the requirements of ANSI/NISO Z39.48-1992
(Permanence of Paper).

This book is dedicated to my mother,
Pearl Steinberg-Sapoznik, and to the memory of
my *zeyde*, Isaac Steinberg, and my father,
Zindel Sapoznik.

CONTENTS

FOREWORD

IT'S 8:15 P.M. AND WE'RE BACKSTAGE, waiting to
go on. The Yiddish music ensemble Kapelye has attracted a large,
enthusiastic audience, and the house manager is holding the curtain
to accommodate the throng of last-minute arrivals. Extra chairs are
being turned out, with attempts to adhere to the fire code long ago
abandoned.

The members of the band have grown accustomed to strong
American interest in the traditional Yiddish music Kapelye popular-
ized since its inception in 1979. But tonight we are not in America.
The curtain for this performance is being held in Berlin.

Fifty years after the conclusion of World War II, young Germans
have come to embrace and, increasingly, to play Yiddish music. Kids
whose parents and grandparents participated in one of history's
most profound episodes of genocide are filling theaters, clubs, and
festivals to take part in what is arguably history's most dramatic
musical comeback. The musical score of the Yiddish experience is
being championed by people unfamiliar with the language or the
tunes, many of whom have never even met a Jew. It is a living repertoire for a half-phantom audience.

The centuries-old tradition of klezmer, the ebullient, wistful music
that heralded celebrations for European Jews since the Middle Ages,
had been slowly eroded by assimilation-crazy America, the Holocaust, and the rise of Israeli culture. So why now, with the success
of modern Hebrew pop music, electric Hasidic, and sing-along synagogue music, should klezmer find new audience? Why should a
music born and raised in the Yiddish homelands find vitality in
today's overstimulated world music market? How could a musical
genre more than five hundred years old withstand the Holocaust and
Americanization to re-emerge and inspire a new generation of Jews?
And why should a music so deeply identified with the rituals of Yiddish-speaking Jews of Eastern Europe engage passionate non-Jewish
players?

Reasons for the revitalization are as diverse as the people who
have come to this music over the last two decades. For myself, having
grown up with Yiddish music at family gatherings, Catskills hotels,
and Holocaust memorials, what began as a personal quest blossomed
into an international movement dedicated to self-expression, a powerful sense of continuity and community, and great dance music.

Even the old-timers, musicians who loved klezmer music like no one else, never dreamed they would hear these tunes played again.

The capriciousness of the journey is not lost on the members of Kapelye this night in Berlin as we wait to go onstage. Muffled murmurs from our German audience waft backstage, sounding eerily like Yiddish and deepening the bittersweet irony of the moment.

. . .

Somewhere behind Marc Chagall's flying fiddlers exists the true image of the Yiddish musician, the klezmer. In contrast to Chagall's delicately muted colors are the simple monochromes popularly associated with these unschooled players whose "soul music" moved listeners from laughter to tears. It is the bleak color of grinding poverty, compelling klezmorim to travel from town to town, Wandering Jews of the Wandering Jews. The images multiply: the sensual klezmer of novels like Sholem Aleichem's *Stempenyu*, a man ruled by his passion for his violin and for the opposite sex; the shabby vagabonds of the 1938 film *Yidl Mitn Fidl*, happy to earn a few kopeks playing their simple Jewish folk melodies.

To understand the klezmer, though, we must first know the place he inhabited. Though some did live in *shtetlekh*, the small Jewish towns of Eastern Europe, that was by no means the norm. Jewish musicians came from a wide swatch of territories in the Old World: sleepy inland villages, tumultuous port towns, glittering capital cities, ancient walled ghettos. Bearers of musical traditions, klezmorim were also harbingers of new sounds. The diversity of their homelands was reflected in the broad array of music they came in contact with and played.

Literate and intuitive, rowdy and respected, religious and worldly, klezmorim, possessers of a long and hard-won heritage, ran the gamut from rural traveling players to urban *muzikantn* to fantastically garbed Hasidic court musicians. The mix deepened further still, with Jews posing as Gypsies and non-Jews fiddling alongside Jewish musicians.

Klezmer, a Yiddish contraction of the Hebrew words *kley* (instrument) and *zemer* (song), originally defined not the music but the musicians who played it—instruments of song whose diverse experience made them instruments of change. The klezmer's story, then, is Jewish history in miniature, a distilled panorama of growth and

preservation, of triumph over adversity, and of unimagined revitalization and renewal.

So how did such innovative artists—and their art form—become
obscured? Klezmer music has been given short shrift by historians
who dismissed it as lost even during one of its most vibrant
moments. It was romanticized by playwrights and novelists who
used the musicians' lives as the backdrop for overheated melodramas, and even by the klezmorim themselves—who would perform as
Hasidim one day and Cossacks the next if the right situation presented itself. Then there were the Eastern European klezmorim who
made the transition to classical music careers—when allowed. From
amid these personae, the true old-time professional Jewish musician
begins to emerge.

A more accurate image of klezmorim can also be coaxed from the
several excellent scholarly works that have noted them, from ads
and articles in the pages of yellowing Yiddish newspapers that hint
at the ubiquitousness of music in the community's everyday life, and
from the scattered minutes of a now nearly defunct Jewish musicians' protective association that document the struggle to keep
klezmer music alive.

The sound track to this story is provided by the Yiddish 78 RPMs
and recordings of radio broadcasts found in grandparents' closets
and rescued from dumpsters, old-age homes, and flea markets. The
hiss and crackle of these scratched, chipped discs is a sonic sepia
tone of the exuberant adolescence of Yiddish popular music and the
technology that recorded it.

But the story of klezmer music resonates most in the words of the
musicians who lived the life. With European klezmorim gone and
their American-born successors nearly so, these recountings are
indelible testimonies. Undocumented until their twilight years, the
recollections are an amalgam of nostalgia, pride, and awareness of
the importance klezmer had for them and for their audiences. Like
the tunes they played, the stories of who they've met and what
they've learned are a road map of Yiddish culture and history. Their
anecdotes fill the gaps of our understanding of the klezmer—this last
source, the rarest and most powerful of all.

ACKNOWLEDGMENTS

TRADITIONAL HISTORIES OF MUSIC offer little if any information about Jewish music. And most Jewish music histories disregard klezmer music in favor of cantorials, folk songs, and the ritual music of ancient Israel. Luckily for the story of klezmer music, the few remaining veterans of its "golden age" were happy to share with me what they knew—musicians eager to talk and more than slightly amazed that someone, anyone, would show interest decades after the last customer had called to ask if they were available to play a wedding in June. It is to these musicians, as well as to my colleagues and friends, that I am deeply indebted.

Thanks to my editor and old friend Richard Carlin at Schirmer Books, for not only suggesting this book but for his patience and encouragement, and to Carrie Schneider for reading, editing, and making the manuscript fit for publication.

Special thanks to my longtime partner and musical mentor Pete Sokolow, the "Youngest of the Old Guys," who has deepened my understanding of klezmer music and introduced me to his fellow old guys: Sid Beckerman, Howie Leess, the Epstein Brothers (Max, Julie, and the late Willie), Ray Musiker, and Paul Pincus. The members of Kapelye past and present—Michael Alpert, Eric Berman, Lauren Brody, Adrienne Cooper, Ken Maltz, and Zalmen Mlotek—who helped create a twenty-year expression of cutting-edge musical Yiddishkayt. Thanks to Barbara Kirshenblatt-Gimblett, for first introducing me to the wonders of the YIVO archives, and to Lorin Sklamberg, my partner in Living Traditions, who has helped me make KlezKamp: The Yiddish Folk Arts Program a vital part of thousands of lives. For their help on this book I thank klezmer musician and historian Joshua Horowitz, particularly for the use of his original research on Joseph Michael Gusikov; discographer and reissue collaborator Dick Spottswood; YIVO music archivist extraordinaire Chana Mlotek; Berlin-based ethnomusicologist Susan Bauer and bassist Heiko Lehmann; and Library of Congress folklorist David Taylor and Klezmatics fiddler Alicia Svigals. I also owe a great debt to the pioneering Jewish music publisher Velvel Pasternak for putting out my first two klezmer tune books when no one else saw their value.

Thanks to Roberta Newman for helping me over the years to assemble many of the photographs used in this book; to Zachary

Baker, David Goldberg; to ethnomusicologists Mark Slobin and Gila Flam, Klezmer Conservatory Band founder Hankus Netsky and Jim Guttman; and to Nina Warnke, Jeffrey Shandler, Itzik Gottesman, Dan Peck, and Andrea Serota for their helpful comments. Thanks also to Jeff Oboler and Chava Miller, who in the bite-size oasis that was the Martin Steinberg Center gave me the space and encouragement to plant the seeds that have become this book.

For invaluable assistance about the lives of pioneering klezmer greats I am indebted to Doris Kandel-Rothman for materials about her father, Harry Kandel, to Bebe Schwartz for information about her father, Abe Schwartz, and sister Sylvia, and to Estelle Frankel-Drushkin about her father, Joseph Frankel.

Thanks to the Lucius N. Littauer Foundation for providing finishing funds for this book.

The book humbly acknowledges those who gave deeply but cannot share in the *nakhes* of this finished work, the musicians whose voices I am honored to present in the pages of this book: Dave Tarras, Joe Helfenbein, Louis Grupp, Irving Graetz, and Leon Schwartz. Their willingness to share their stories has illuminated and extended this vital branch of Yiddish culture.

Henry Sapoznik
Olive Bridge, New York

ON YIDDISH ROMANIZATION AND CIVILIZATION

LITTLE LANDMINES IN THE FIELD of Yiddish language surround the twin issues of its transcription and transliteration. Newspapers, sheet music, books, records, and articles over the past century exhibit a span of sometimes bewildering anglicizations.

In this book, Yiddish words that have not entered common English usage as heralded by a listing in *Webster's Tenth New Collegiate Dictionary* are spelled according to the *Modern English-Yiddish Yiddish-English Dictionary* (McGraw-Hill, 1968), compiled by the linguist Max Weinreich for the New York-based Jewish research institute *Yiddisher Visnshaftlekher Institut* (YIVO). In a departure from Weinreich's literal rendering of Yiddish, I capitalize initial letters in composition and place name titles. And where appropriate I deviate from Webster's Tenth spellings, as in the case of *gemmorah*, which transmits the sound of Yiddish speakers more accurately than the Israeli-inspired dictionary listing *Gemara*. Astute readers will no doubt find more exceptions peppered throughout the text.

Finally, the term *Yiddish* used adjectively denotes not only the language but the society and culture served by it. *Yiddish music*, then—be it folk songs, theater compositions, the singing of cantors, even instrumental music—refers to what has been recognized as music by *yidishe oyern* (Jewish ears), long the arbiters of what gains entry into the soundscape of *Yiddishkayt*.

Getting It Down

Mr. Abramowitz invites me to sit at his kitchen table, the only unclut-
tered surface in his tiny Brooklyn apartment.

"This is my uncle Beresh," he says, holding up a faded photograph.
Abramowitz is about as old as the man he points to in the picture, but
his clear bright eyes bespeak the vibrancy of his lost youth as a profes-
sional klezmer in the old country. "He had the finest band in Talisk—
the Talisker Kapelye."

The picture shows eight musicians, the older players with large
flowing white beards and yarmulkas seated in front of a row of
younger starry-eyed boys. All hold their instruments as if caught mid-
tune: two fiddles, a wooden flute, rotary trumpets, a clarinet, a drum,
and a double bass.

"My uncle's band traveled all over Poland before the First World
War, and they played for Jews and goyim alike,"Abramowitz tells me.
"Uncle Beresh taught himself to play. He had a God-given ear. He used
to mimic everyone and anything. In those days, you know, being a
Jewish musician was not a respected life. No. You should be either a
rabbi or a merchant. If not that, then you had a poor life, like a shoe-
maker or tailor had. A very hard life. But even still below that was a
klezmer. How many weddings do you think there were in my little town
every year? Maybe two or three? Maybe. You had to travel over terrible
roads, scared for bandits and always depending on the charity of
strangers.

"Uncle Beresh's kapelye played different kinds of music for the dif-
ferent people who hired him. Jewish, goyish, Hasidic, the light clas-
sics. Uncle Beresh wanted us to be able to play everything. But still my
favorite music is Yiddish. We used to play all the big khasenes *around,*
the weddings, so I got plenty of experience for tunes. We played special
dances just for that occasion—like the broyges tants*: you know what*
that is? The mothers of the bridal couple would act out an imaginary
fight. A fight! They'd dance around in a circle; then they'd make up.
We'd play the tune slow for the fight part and then fast at the end. It
was supposed to guard against them fighting after the children were
married. Maybe somewhere it did. I don't know.

"But most of all I enjoyed when Uncle Beresh would play a doina.
For this he was famous. The people would all become still when the
band would play a low single drone note. Suddenly my uncle would
step into the middle of the floor with his fiddle under his chin and
would start to play. Years later, when I got lots of experience playing

with jazz guys, I learned that improvisation was an important thing, but as a kid who knew? It was beautiful. His fingers flew over the fingerboard, making the instrument sing. Yes, sing. When he'd get to a place where the chord would change, he'd play a few special notes and we'd know where to change. And when he stopped, oh, people would be crying, crying.

"In 1902 my uncle Beresh packed up and moved to America. He heard that the streets were lined with gold and that everyone worked. Seventeen months later he was back. Oy, did he complain! 'All the Jews cut off their beards! They go to shows on shabbos!' But most of all I think it was because no one appreciated his small-town playing. In the old country he was somebody; in America he was a griner. He tried playing music, and when that didn't work he went into the needle trades. But he was so outraged at the greedy, bloodthirsty bosses that he left and came back. I remember like it was yesterday.

"When my family was making ready to go to America years later, Uncle Beresh came down to the station to see us off. With tears running down his face he holds my head up and says to me, 'My dear child, whatever you do don't sell your fiddle to the Satan of Jazz.'"

"So, did you sell your fiddle to the Satan of Jazz?" I ask Abramowitz as he gets up to make us some tea.

"No, I never sold it," he says. "But I did rent it occasionally."

～ 1 ～

"In the Beginning ..."
The European Roots of Klezmer Music

MICHAEL JOSEPH GUSIKOV: THE FIRST KLEZMER STAR

HE WAS A SLIGHT, DELICATE MAN, with a fragility intensified by what proved to be a fatal case of tuberculosis. Born into a family of musicians, by age fifteen he was renowned in the Jewish world. At twenty-six he was the toast of the European salon set. At twenty-eight he was dead.

His name was Michael Joseph Gusikov and though he has been all but forgotten, in his day he was considered the equal of Frédéric Chopin, Franz Liszt, and Nicolò Paganini as a performer and musical phenomenon. He is the *zeyde*, the grandfather, of the modern performing klezmer.

Who was this enigmatic Jewish musician? Was he, as some have stated, an illiterate prodigy, a true *klezmer* who made it in the non-Jewish world, or was he an opportunistic self-promoter who played off his "otherness" to fashion an upper-class constituency? He may well have been both. Mystery shrouds the life of this shooting star, whose legend was crafted by hagiographers and codified by subsequent scholars.[1]

Gusikov was born in 1809 in the Polish city of Shklov, into a Hasidic family. He and his older brother were taught flute and violin by their father, himself a professional musician. Like so many of his contemporaries', Gusikov's repertoire included not only Jewish music but Polish, Russian, German, Ukrainian, and French melodies, as well as light classical pieces. He and his father and brother traveled widely, gaining a reputation as far away as Moscow.

In his teens Gusikov began to play the *shtroyfidl*, a set of diatonically arranged solid wooden tubes—he later extended them chro-

Michael Joseph Gusikov. (*Oesterreichische National Bibliothek*)

matically—placed atop a bed of straw and played with small wooden sticks. The instrument, which he began playing at weddings, was described not surprisingly as having a thin and humble sound.

By the time Gusikov was twenty his lungs had begun to fail and he switched to playing the *shtroyfidl* full time. Response was keen in his hometown, and he quickly accumulated invitations to play for local nobility. Eventually, he developed a specific repertoire for the novel, homely instrument and took his show on the road. Since Gusikov's earliest successes in the *shtetlekh*, he had craved entrée to the salons and concert halls patronized by the urban Gentile upper classes. So it was that Gusikov embarked on the first klezmer crossover career.

Starting in 1834 he toured extensively, appearing in cities like Odessa, Kiev, Lemberg (Lvov), and Krakow. But it was Vienna, the musical center of Europe, that drew Gusikov.

He fared well in the Austrian capital. Having honed his parlor skills in the provinces, he crashed the big time and, with the help of some sophisticated advance advertising, perked up the otherwise dull 1836 Viennese summer season in which everyone who was anyone was elsewhere. A series of successful salon recitals led to enthusiastically received concerts at the Theater in der Josephstadt.

Novelty aside, interest in Gusikov and his instrument was helped by the brief period of renown then being enjoyed by the *tsimbl*—his model for the *shtroyfidl*—in European concert halls. In the mid-eighteenth century Leopold Mozart and Antonio Vivaldi, among others, composed works for the instrument—also called "hackbrett" or "cutting board"—and by the time Gusikov started touring, a residue of interest in instruments like it remained.

Gusikov parlayed his "otherness" into a new commodity: the user-friendly, deracinated Jew, amenable to the genteel. And his music stimulated interest in his every aspect, including his appearance; his *peyes*—the ritual sidecurls of Orthodox Jewish men—generated a women's fashion fad in Paris called *coiffure à la Gusikov*.

Eyewitnesses to Gusikov's music included members of the illustrious Mendelssohn family, who heard him play on several occasions. In a letter to his mother in 1836, Felix Mendelssohn wrote:

> I am curious whether you liked Gusikov as much as I did—he is a true phenomenon; a devil whose delivery and adeptness is second to no virtuoso in the world and who for this reason delights me more on his wooden and straw instrument than many do on their pianos because it is so thankless . . . By the way I haven't been so entertained at a concert for such a long time as at this one because he is really a true genius.[2]

Mendelssohn goes on to refer condescendingly to a group of Hasidim attending the concert as "a herd of bearded Polish Jews"—interesting, in that as recently as his father's conversion to Christianity there had been "bearded Jews" in his own family. Felix Mendelssohn's grandfather was Rabbi Moses Mendelssohn, the founder of the late-eighteenth-century Haskalah (Enlightenment) movement, which encouraged Ashkenazim to be a man in the street and a Jew in the home.

The shtroyfidl. (*Oesterreichische National Bibliothek*)

Felix Mendelssohn's sister Fanny also wrote home about Gusikov.

> The rage here is a Polish Jew who is supposed to display
> fantastic virtuosity on an instrument that consists of bun-
> dles of straw and sticks of wood. I would not believe it if
> Felix hadn't written about it. I have seen him and I can
> assure you he is an uncommonly good-looking man. In
> dress and habits he flirts with strict Judaism and seems
> to have great success at court with it.

Fanny astutely noted that Gusikov wasn't as observant as his public
persona indicated. Alternately pictured with and without a yarmulke
and *peyes*, Gusikov had cooled his adherence to Orthodox practices by
this time; his Viennese premiere was on a Saturday during *shabbos*.

A few days after writing her letter, Fanny attended one of
Gusikov's performances and posted this lukewarm review:

> I have heard the phenomenon play and I assure you,
> without being quite as carried away as many others, he
> does turn virtuosity topsy-turvy . . . Very cleverly he has
> [the instrument] put together in front of the audience; he
> seems to be a first-rate fox altogether . . .

Such dismissal aside, Gusikov's reputation was secured, and he set his sights on his next triumph: Paris. But it was not to be. Depleted by the strenuous travel, he died shortly after completing a concert in the German city of Aachen in 1837.

In his progression from wandering klezmer to respected *muzikant*, from local and ethnic folk music to popular classical and salon music, Gusikov helped to pave the way for the popularization of klezmer. By employing local classical musicians and periodically using Jewish repertoire, he made it so non-Jews could accept his domesticated form of the genre, shifting his emphasis from a modal, functional music to a tonal repertoire and altering nonharmonic accompaniment into a style his listeners would understand.

Gusikov's attempts to balance the musical and social desires of the Jewish and non-Jewish communities while feeding his needs as a musician and artist echo throughout the klezmer experience. To appreciate his monumental journey, it is important to understand the forces that combined to create him—forces that also shaped the multilayered life and music of the klezmer.

DA CAPO

There has always been music in Jewish life. *Kinorot, nevelim, ugavim, Khalilim*—the Bible is rich with descriptions of the highly ritualized music played at the Temples in Jerusalem. Huge orchestras comprising mixed strings, winds, percussion—even a massive pipe organ—were organized by the Levites, an elite class of trained Temple musicians. Sadly, we cannot know what the music sounded like; the Levites were literate but had no system of writing music.

With the destruction of the second Temple in 70 C.E. the Jewish people, disowned and dispersed, were plunged into a period of mourning. The Levites' purpose ended, their tradition quickly disappeared and with it the status accorded musicians.

In keeping with Jewish law for times of loss, rabbis decreed that Jews refrain from making instrumental music. The ruling—*ika shira b'pe* (major music by mouth)—spelled the beginning of rabbinic antipathy to instrumental music.

But as the Jewish musicologists A. Z. Idelsohn and Alfred Sendry have documented, instrumental music was never quite eliminated. In abeyance to an edict that weddings must have song and rejoicing, instruments and their players were grudgingly allowed. What emerged was a kind of "necessary evil" status for instrumental music and for the musicians and *badkhonim* (wedding jesters) themselves—a classification that would stay with them throughout the Diaspora.

By the ninth century, when small Jewish communities began appearing on the banks of the river Rhine in the southwestern part of what the book of Genesis called "Ashkenaz"—Germany—the Yiddish language had begun to emerge. A mix of German dialects, Hebrew constructions, and local speech influences, Yiddish evolved along with the culture that grew around it into a distinct presence wherever it existed.

From as early as the fifteenth century, references to klezmer bands can be found in surviving town records and memoirs. (Interestingly, according to Idelsohn, women were active in these medieval bands, as they would not be again until the turn of the twentieth century.) The klezmorim's musical environment was broad and interactive. It is clear from early on that a repertoire of strictly "Jewish" material was a rarity because it was always necessary to meet the musical needs of Jews and non-Jews alike. And the continual back-and-forth among popular local tunes intensified this cross-fertilization.

The richest interaction was between Jews and Gypsies. Whether it is a result of their common outsider and itinerant status or their shared predilection for subtly hued Eastern-influenced melodies and the elegiac, mournful tunes known as *doinas*, the connection between Jews and Gypsies was strong for generations. Jewish musicians, on the periphery of mainstream Jewish life, found wary allies in these similarly marginalized people.

The creator of Gypsy-Hungarian national music, Rozsavölgyi Mark (1787–1848), was in reality Mordchele Rosenthal, whose "Gypsy" orchestra was made up entirely of Jews disguised as Gypsies.[3] (Mark's compositions were used as themes in Franz Liszt's "Hungarian Rhapsodies," composed between 1840 and 1853.)

Jewish bands frequently played at non-Jewish weddings and festivities, providing cheap employment and occasional comic relief. They were sometimes hired to play and entertain for the amusement of the assembled, with the music and musicians ridiculed and demeaned. Bands that endured this kind of baiting came to be known as *Ma Yofusniks* , a rubric derived from the title of a song that was the "Hava Nagila" of its time: "Ma Yofus" (How Beautiful, from Solomon's Song of Songs), later called "Tants, Tants Yiddlekh" and "Reb Dovidl's Nigun."[4]

In many municipalities, Jewish musicians could only ply their trade with the approval of local non-Jewish governments—approval that was not always forthcoming. Restricted as to when they could play and which and how many instruments they could employ, klezmorim had to run a bureaucratic gauntlet to make a living. In the Alsatian city of Metz, for example, three musicians were allowed, while a fourth could only be added for a wedding. In Frankfurt a quartet was permissible, but had to quit by midnight. Some towns even forbade Jewish musicians from playing at Jewish weddings.[5]

Such regulations had long, labyrinthian histories. In 1641 the Archbishop of Prague handed down a ruling that allowed Jews to perform Sundays and holidays at non-Jewish functions, but stiff petitioning from non-Jewish musicians got the ruling revoked. The revocation was quietly rescinded by 1648; then two years later it was reversed. Approval was once again granted klezmorim to play in 1651, but lobbying by the Gentile community led to its being overturned the following year.

Some towns insisted on "quiet" instruments, like flutes and *tsimbls*, and eschewed drums or brass. Never restricted was the fiddle— the cornerstone in Jewish ensembles. (*Yidl mitn fidl*, "the Jew and his fiddle," is an old Yiddish expression that later became the title of a song and film.) The fiddle and its siblings, like viola, cello, and bass, made up the nucleus of early klezmer bands. Other instruments at this time included the *fleyt* (flute), *baraban* (drum), and *tats* (cymbal). What made all these instruments vital to the klezmer ensemble was their role in the local shared repertoire, the ability to be made and/or repaired locally, and their portability.

By the sixteenth century the *tsimbl* (hammered dulcimer) had been introduced in Europe, in the case of Romania by Jewish musicians.[6] A trapezoidal box strung with metal wires played with wooden sticks, the *tsimbl* rested on a stand, or when being played in a procession, hung suspended from the player's neck. (Picture a cigarette girl in a Hollywood movie nightclub scene.)

Someone who played the *tsimbl* was called a *tsimbler*, like the well-known klezmer-cum-classical violinist Efrem Zimbalist. Jewish family names like these reflect former involvement with Yiddish music, as do names like Musiker, Musikant, or even Kunstler (artist). What with increased Russian emigration to New York these days, you can even find a Klezmer or two in the Brooklyn phone book.

Though there was a core of full-time professional klezmorim, very few musicians could subsist on money made from music alone.

"Der Blinder Musikant" (The Blind Musician), a Polish postcard from the 1920s featuring a street fiddler accompanied by his sighted "lead boy"/ singer. (*YIVO Institute for Jewish Research*)

Many were also tailors, cobblers, synagogue handymen, and, in inordinate numbers, barbers.

Though we know which instruments klezmorim played, we know remarkably little about what the music sounded like. Clues can be heard in non-Jewish folk tunes still played throughout Eastern Europe and in the tradition of the *khazonim* (cantors) and their accompanying choirs of apprentices, *meshoyrerim*. Cantorial music, with its rich array of modes and vocalizations, lies at the very heart of what exemplifies the klezmer sound and its ornament vocabulary.

Klezmorim religious and not were familiar with synagogue music and often based their Jewish repertoire performances on its modal and melodic constructions. The omnipresence of cantors, *ba'al tfiles* (readers of the Torah), and other part-time liturgical singers meant that their knowledge of modes was integral to the community's musical awareness.

The influence of the human voice on klezmer music is made clear by the name for its quintessential instrumental ornament: the *krekhts*, which translates literally as "sigh" or "moan," one of several borrowings from the cantorial tradition:

But with no written record of early klezmer, we haven't a clue to the original use of such ornaments or, in fact, to how the music sounded overall. Before the mid-nineteenth century very little was actually notated. Some of the musicians playing klezmer music were unable to read or write music, as evidenced by this description of a klezmer band, made up of two fiddles, a clarinet, a tsimbl, and a 'cello, in a small town in Germany in 1800:

> Only the first violinist played from written music, the others following by ear. The cellist, an old man, played with especial skill. He knew nothing of notes but had an excellent ear, observed each turn of the leading melody and was able to add accompaniments in perfect harmony.[7]

Although there was much social and religious animosity between Jewish and non-Jewish musicians, references to their playing together can be found in Eastern European documents from as early as the Middle Ages. Fiddlers got together to play; clarinetists admired each others' style and repertoire; bands divided their earnings.

Still, klezmorim retained the singularity of their sound. In addition to quasi-liturgical tunes played in the synagogue before *shabbos* and for occasions like the dedication of Torah scrolls, the mainstay of the klezmer repertoire was derived from the wedding, with its rich mix of ritual and processional music: the *mazltov dobriden*, used to greet arriving guests; the *tsu der khupe* and *fun der khupe*, which led the bridal couple to and away from the wedding canopy; and the *a gite nakht*, the slow signature tune that ended the festivities. More important were accompaniments for the dances—the dramatic

broyges tants, a dance of anger and reconciliation between the moth-
ers-in-law; the celebratory *patsh tants* (hand-clapping dance); circle
dances in triple and livelier double meter (*freylekhs*); and the *sher*,
the old-world equivalent of the American square dance. Equally key
were the songs of the *badhkn*, who led the intricate rituals of the
Jewish wedding. Through backing this master of ceremonies, klezmorim derived many of the vocal nuances characteristic of their
music.

The repertoire of Jewish weddings was never solely Jewish, however. Nonritual dances included the *hopak*, and *kozachok*—common
to Gentile neighbors in the Ukraine and Russia, respectively—and
later the polka, mazurka, waltz, and gavotte. And so, from tradition
and experience, the klezmer crafted a musical literature unham-
pered by its lack of notation.

By the end of the century, though, illiterate Jewish musicians
were no longer as pervasive as popular folklore or longlasting preju-
dices would have it. Violinist Louis Grupp (1888–1983), who came
from a long line of klezmorim, received his highly literate musical
education in the Russian Volhynian town of Chudnov, under the
tutelage of his uncle Alter Goyzman (pronounced "Housman"), the
esteemed klezmer fiddler known as Alter Chudnover.

Grupp's mother was instructed to start him on violin at age six.
"When I came home from the *kheyder* (school) my mother met me at
the door," Grupp recalled. "She was beaming. '*Leybele, der feter alter
hut mir tsigezugt dir tsinemen tsim fidl.*' ["Leybl, Uncle Alter told me
to get you started on the fiddle."] She was proud. After all, he was
Alter Goyzman."

From his earliest lessons with Alter Chudnover, Grupp was obliged to learn to read music: if the young fiddler wanted to join his
uncle's orchestra, he would have to read like the other twelve band
members.

"Sure, we read music; he taught us," Grupp said. "We practiced
Kreutzer, Screidek [popular music method books of the day]. My
uncle used to get a sheet like this with a melody and he used to
orchestrate it. He had a brother in America who used to send him
big music, overture selections. My cousin that went to the Conservatory in Warsaw used to send me books."

Another homebred klezmer was the clarinetist Dave Tarras
(1897–1989), born at the close of the nineteenth century in the
Ukrainian *shtetl* of Ternovka. "We were a family of musicians," Tarras said. "We knew we were good musicians. My cousins were, my

Alter Goyzman (Chudnover), fiddler and orchestra leader (*extreme left*); nephew Louis Grupp on fiddle (*seated far right*); Chudnov, Volhyn, c. 1905.

father, my brothers—one was a concertmaster in the Philharmonic; he played in Leningrad by the symphony.

"My grandfather was a fiddler. He was a poor musician, but he was a *badkhn*. I had an uncle, a fiddle player, was one of the greatest. And he had four sons, also good fiddle players, and clarinet— they played all instruments."

Tarras's father, a valve trombonist and *badkhn*, started training Tarras at age nine by teaching him to read and write music. "The first lesson I got was the notes: a, b, c," he said. "We [klezmorim] had no conservatories; we learned in the street. If I wanted a book to study I'd have to send away to Kiev and it cost about two rubles. My father used to tell me, 'You play good without it. Why should you spend two rubles?'"

Tarras began instrumental lessons, first on the balalaika, then on mandolin and flute. "There was a flute player in my father's band, so he started teaching me a little," he recalled. "And then he got himself a girl in town, so he stopped teaching me because he was afraid if he teaches me to be a flute player, he wouldn't have . . ." What he wouldn't have had was a corner on the flute market and a way to support himself and his bride-to-be. What he would have had, and recognized it, was big competition in the talented young Tarras. This incident and the fact that the instrument's sound didn't express his musical ideas caused Tarras, at age thirteen, to become dissatisfied with the flute.

"A certain clarinet player taught me how to play a little bit—just three weeks," he said. "So I come home from the holidays, I went to

Dave Tarras, age nine, pictured with his aunt in Ternovka, Ukraine, in 1906.

play already a *goyishe khasene* [Christian wedding] with my father, me on the clarinet, and then I just picked up by accident a nice tone."

The local Polish nobility knew good music when they heard it, and called upon the services of the Tarras family band. "They had for us the greatest respect," Tarras said. "They used to come with a wagon with four big horses, and give us good seats, and take us. After two or three days [at the wedding] they gave us a sack of potatoes and chickens and bread and brought us back to the door. Maybe they were *anti-semits*, but it never came out. They had respect."

Like the Gusikovs before them, the Tarras family had to develop a broad repertoire that included music shared with the surrounding cultures. "My father kept ten men: two fiddles or three—one was a *secunda* [chord fiddle]—flute, clarinet, trumpet, trombone, tuba, and drums with the *tats* [cymbal] in the right hand, and another played a small drum," Dave Tarras remembered. "We traveled for a hundred miles. Those days landowners, the Poles, *Grafs*—counts, barons—they used to make every time balls, you already had to play different music: waltzes, mazurkas, and once in a while an overture like [von Suppe's] 'Poet and Peasant.' So my relatives were good musicians, and they were prepared."

The family's ability to read music was only required for tunes outside the klezmer repertoire. For Jewish weddings, Tarras said, arrangements were not necessary: "We knew hundreds of waltzes by memory—*shers*, *freylekhs*, and *bulgars*. Each instrument knew exactly what they should do, how to fill in."

Learning tunes by heart was part of the training young musicians were expected to master. Like the *meshoyrerim*, their cantorial cousins, young klezmorim learned the art and repertoire of the *kapelye* (or band) as apprentices. The apprentice was the stopgap in the *kapelye*, filling out the orchestra when times were good to give it a richer, lusher sound, filling in at the last minute if the band was overbooked.

Grupp described a particularly unpleasant example of the latter:

> My first job what I did was an emergency. The citizens of the town of Tranieff were marrying off a girl crippled or blind or something to a boy, and some of my uncle's *kapelye* were going to play for free but something came up. I was around thirteen and played maybe one or two tunes. I also had a cousin my age who played flute and a peasant who used to play the big bass drum. My uncle sent us in their place.

>When they came to get us and saw these young boys, the town was very upset. My uncle told us to tell them that the musicians couldn't come and we boys would do the best we can. If they want, fine. If not, also fine. They couldn't help themselves, so they said already we go. After that the town decided not to allow my uncle or any member of his orchestra to come and play there again.

Being an apprentice was how you learned; as Tarras mentioned, there were no klezmer schools. But there were guilds. Guilds trained future players, protected the musician's territory, and acted as a lobbying mechanism with the authorities.

The first klezmer guild in Prague, founded in 1558, and using the fiddle as its emblem, would have to wait nearly a century to secure the right to play for non-Jews.[8] In addition to their playing for weddings and for market days, guild members would volunteer their services to play in the synagogue on Fridays before *shabbos* or to accompany the rounds of the *shabbos klaper*, who paraded through town reminding women of the approaching sabbath. Membership in the guild had strict requirements: a master musician had to be married, and he and his assistants had to read Torah daily and study the holy books on *shabbos*.

The first guilds formed in Poland, in the seventeenth century, were like modern unions in that they were autonomous organizations dealing with inheritance, health insurance, disability pension, and indemnity. The guild in Jassy, Romania, formed in 1819, had so many members it had its own synagogue, on Pantelimon Street.

When Jewish musicians traveled to a town to play a wedding where local klezmer already existed, the local guild might try to pay compensation to the foreign band to keep them away, or vice versa. If that didn't work, a colleague or a rabbi from a neighboring town was called in to mediate. Beyond that, fistfights were known to break out, as municipal records of the day attest.

The guilds solidified the klezmer community. And that community was codified through *klezmer shprakh* (language), a sort of verbal shorthand among band members. Like in-group lingos employed by everyone from surgeons to short-order cooks, *klezmer shprakh*, with its anagrams, letter inversions, and sly redefinitions of Yiddish, Polish, Hebrew, and German words, was used to keep outsiders out and insiders in. Given the frequent association between klezmer and the Jewish criminal element—musicians and thieves often shared quarters in areas like the Moldovanka section of Odessa—it is not surprising that *klezmer shprakh* sneaked into criminal argot. For example, the word *balen* (playing of tunes) is an inversion of *labern*, itself derived from the Yiddish gangster argot for card-playing. In the early twentieth century European police compiled these words and distributed the lists for use in criminal investigation.[10]

Comprising several hundred words, *klezmer shprakh* included terms for nearly every aspect of musicians' professional lives—their instruments: *foyal* (clarinet), *barok* (cello), and *verbel* (bass); their music: *labushnik* (musician), *krokadil* (dance), from of the dance Quadrille, and *tablatir* (written music), from the medieval predecessor of written music; and their clients: *shmarotsher* (wedding guest), German for parasite.[11]

Several twentieth-century klezmorim, like Dave Tarras and Max Epstein, still knew—and used—the argot. But what doesn't seem to have existed were words dealing with the mechanics of the music itself, the ornaments that characterize it, or the scales and modes. Modern players have added such terms to the lexicon. Contemporary klezmer Lev Liberman's *boyt'tya* describes this important ornament:

And clarinetist Ray Musiker's *tsokhtshes* gives a name to klezmer music's characteristic laughing/crying sound, continuing the evolution of the language of klezmer.

THE VOCAL TRADITION OF INSTRUMENTAL MUSIC

A link between the music of the synagogue and the klezmer was the singing of the *badkhn*, the wedding poet, whose job was to organize the array of dances, ceremonies, elocutions, and honorifics. Also called a *marshalik*, *leyts*, and even *nar* (fool), the *badkhn* moved guests from sequence to sequence, emotion to emotion, by presenting a variety of orations, like the *kale baveynen*, below, sung for an orphaned bride:

Oy kale veyn kale veyn	Oh, bride, cry
Di darfst bald tsi der khipe geyn	You're going to the *khupe*

un dayn mame ligt in drerd	and your dead mother
un ken nit bay dir shteyn.	can't accompany you.

Part of the power of the *badkhn's* rhymes, called *badkhones*, was the subtle give-and-take that went on between the *badkhn* and the lead instrument accompanying him, usually the fiddle. The singer and the instrumentalist blended with and responded to each other, the smooth glissandos of the voice overlapping the melodic bridges the fiddle played between verses.

As the fulcrum on which weddings' time-honored ceremonies turned, the *badkhn* rode herd on everything—from the erudite and slightly risqué rhymes produced at the *khosn's tish* (the groom's assemblage) to the somber and introspective *bazetsn, badekn, bazingen un baveynen di kale* (seating, veiling of, and singing to the bride, wherein she is reminded of the grave responsibility of this change in her life) to the *droshe geshenk*, where the gifts are enumerated to the delight and amusement of the assembled. It wasn't just improvised rhymes. The *badkhn* fiddled, juggled, impersonated a woman in labor, danced, and mimicked an ecstatic Hasid, a circus bear, or a

The Spielman family *kapelye* in Ostrovke, Poland, c. 1905. Note twin brothers Yisroel Leyb (*bass, rear*) and Rivale (*fiddle, seated third from left*). (*YIVO Institute for Jewish Research*)

cruel Cossack. Such carnival-like revelry came to arouse the ire of the stern rabbinate, ever wanting to "erect a fence against hilarity," as the historian I. Z. Idelsohn has noted. Rabbis bristled at what they saw as the *badkhn's* glib, sacrilegious utterances.

The number and chronology of rabbinic injunctions raised against wedding performers—*badkhonim* and klezmorim alike—shows how entertainment, even when tied to a specific requirement, remained suspect in the eyes of the clergy. More important, it indicates how unaccepting the community was of those misgivings. Still, Jewish musicians continued to be governed by edicts, not only from rabbis but from *kehiles* (Jewish town councils), which also had a hand in regulating wedding entertainers.

Minsk town records from 1801 show that the klezmer Isaac began including *badkhones* in his performances at weddings. The *kehile* reacted: "be it resolved that Isaac dare no longer be a *badkhn* at any wedding."[12] It seems the position was already filled: the *badkhn* Mendel would be deprived of his *parnose* (livelihood) if Isaac offered *badkhones*. And Minsk had a second *badkhn*, who had been granted a residency permit to work under the condition that he make Mendel his partner.

After several appeals, in 1805 the Jewish town council acceded to Isaac's desire to act also as *badkhn*:

> Whereas many people have by all means demanded that the musician Isaac who has been previously enjoined from acting as a *badkhn* be allowed to function as a *badkhn* at weddings. This, even if he is engaged as a *badkhn* he should function as a musician also. If the host invites another *badkhn* said Isaac can by no means act as a *badkhn*.

Under the heading "Concerning a brawl among klezmorim," the town council made this pronouncement the following August:

> According to a resolution of the community, the musicians who took part in beating the musician Isaac are excluded from the musicians' guild, for failure to obey the community administration to arbitrate their differences. Instead the musicians went to a non-Jewish court.
>
> Simultaneously, the injured Isaac is also excluded from the musicians' guild, for failure to obey the community administration to arbitrate their differences, instead

going to a non-Jewish court. All the above persons are
barred forever from the calling of musicians and no Jew
is permitted to engage them as such or in the capacity of
badkhn under any circumstances.

Isaac's banishment lasted just about a week. He was reinstated as a
badkhn/musician but only until October 1807, when the following
decree was issued:

It is resolved from this day on to forbid Isaac son of
Shalom to act as a *badkhn* in our city if there is another
badkhn there. Violation of this decision will be
announced in all synagogues and will bar the offender
from functioning as a musician.

Things were hardly better a generation later for the Vilna-born *badkhn* Eliakum Zunser (1836–1913). Zunser's experience underscores
both the difficult life of a wedding poet and the rough nature of his
colleagues, the klezmorim:

In the beginning I earned very little at my new business.
I was only called to poor weddings and was poorly paid,
and second I had to have music to accompany my recita-
tion of my songs and the musicians would take all my
earnings from my pocket. If they could not do this at the
wedding itself, they would fall upon me in the street,
when I was going home from the wedding, push me
against the wall and rob me of my money.[13]

The *badkhn,* so vital in Jewish communities throughout the 1800s,
gradually slipped into disuse by the early 1900s, when *badkhones*
were heard only as parodies recorded on 78s. Today, the only places
to hear them are among the hundreds of Hasidic communities sprin-
kled throught the world—all of which can trace their origins to Eastern Europe.

From their founding in Poland in the eighteenth century, the
Hasidim, followers of the charismatic leader known as the Ba'al
Shem Tov ("Master of the Good Name"), placed high value on music
and dance as augmentation to prayer and study. The ultimate musical
expression was the *nigun,* a wordless song, rendered a cappella.
Nigunim range from the middle tempo *hisvadus* (assemblage) to their

version of the boisterous *freylekh*. There are also *trerediker* (crying) tunes, with their somber and ample use of *krekhts*, the break in the voice. Unlike in non-Hasidic communities, where the word *kapelye* referred to a band, Hasidim called their lush vocal choirs *kapelyes*, like those of the Lubavich Mitler Rebbe or the Gerer Hasidim.

More important than new compositions was the Hasidic tradition of adapting secular songs for religious use. In moving from the inns to the *rebbe's tish* (rabbi's table), tunes got reborn and made pure. In many ways Hasidic tradition has looked upon these "converted" tunes as holier than new ones. So it is not uncommon to find polkas and mazurkas in the *nigunim* of the Polish Ger or waltzes in the music of the Modzitz Hasidim (Modzitzer curiously refer to their *nigunim* as "opera"), and Russian/Ukrainian *karoboshkas* or even a tune called "Napoleon's March," memorializing Bonaparte's advance on Moscow in 1812, in the Lubavitch melodies. Other Hasidim, like those from the towns of Belz, Bobov, or Karlin, didn't borrow tunes but composed *nigunim* unique to them. Regardless, each Hasidic group brought to its music a sense of *kidusha* (piety).

Like a Yiddish Henry Higgins, you can tell where the numerous *nigunim* are from not only by their regional musical characteristics, but by their syllabification. The Modzitzer "bim bom" is as different from the Gerer "yadi yadi" as from the Lubavitch "oy, yoy."

This active mix of "inside" and "outside" tunes resulted in a Hasidic repertoire much richer than the image of insular Hasidic life might suggest. These musicians were a far cry from the fictional Hasidic band that whips itself into a frenzy in American Yiddish humorist Moishe Nadir's playful anti-Hasidic song, "Der Rebbe Elimeylekh," a sort of Yiddish "Old King Cole." The songs they sang spanned the spectrum from introspective to ecstatic.

But just because the overriding Hasidic tradition was vocal doesn't mean there were no Hasidic klezmorim. Clarinetists Dave Tarras and Naftule Brandwein (1884–1963), for example, were descended from Hasidic musical dynasties and maintained elements of the earlier Hasidic material in their repertoires years after they left for America. The klezmer repertoire is rife with tunes strongly influenced by Hasidic style. The most popular was the *khosidl* (Little Hasid), a dance tune attributed to Hasidim characterized by a slow to medium pace that speeds into an enthusiastic finish.

In general, when Hasidic communities wanted klezmer they brought in musicians from outside, especially those who were renowned or admired. Louis Grupp was at one of these jobs in 1903:

I remember this wedding where the rebbe of Krisilev was marrying his daughter and they wanted my uncle. We didn't have no Hasidim [in Chudnov]. I never saw the rabbis with the big fur hats and the white stockings until I played their weddings.

They already had a Jewish orchestra in their town, but they still took my uncle 'cause he had a name. The other orchestra pleaded with the rebbe not to deny them their *parnose*, their living. The rabbi was known as a fair man, and so in order to satisfy everybody they had to negotiate a settlement: They had both orchestras play.

Although most musicians had to travel some to play enough jobs to survive, they usually stayed within a few days from home, marking this as their "territory." Others found it expeditious to travel more widely to destinations like the Black Sea port city of Constantinople.

Once known as the "Vienna of the Balkans," Constantinople housed a cosmopolitan mix including Greeks, Turks, and Ashkenazi Jews—for some of whom the city was a way station en route to the Holy Land—in addition to its long-term Sephardic population. After

This turn-of-the-century Polish-Jewish klezmer band features older, more religious players and their younger colleague dressed in modern Western attire. (*YIVO Institute for Jewish Research*)

the conquest of Constantinople in 1453, the founding of an overland trade route through Poland linked the Ottoman Empire with Central and Western Europe and acted as a highway for Jewish musicians seeking broader venues.

By the mid-nineteenth century Constantinople was home to some five hundred Jewish musicians. The city also had its own Yiddish theater, which in 1875 mounted one of the first Yiddish theater productions, *The Sale of Joseph.*

Despite their considerable presence, Jewish musicians in this cultural crossroads played mostly non-Jewish music. Like their compatriots everywhere, they had to learn the popular urban repertoire and dance music of the surrounding culture. Here, Yiddish music mixed with Greek as well as Turkish styles, an exchange that reverberated into the recording era, when Ashkenazi Jews were intimately involved in the production and distribution of non-Jewish music. As early as 1910, a pair of brothers, Julius and Hermann Blumenthal, ran a music store and recording studio in Istanbul that recorded Turkish art music and even some klezmer. (Columbia absorbed the label in 1925.) This cross-fertilization of influences spread to the new world, when klezmorim who had played in Constantinople, like *tsimblist* Joseph Moscowitz (1879–1953), brought the mix to the shores of America.

In 1876 an outbreak of pan-Slavicism due to the Bulgarian uprising against the Turks brought Russia into a war against the Ottomans. The Romanian city of Jassy, with its direct rail link to Odessa, was the site of the newly established Russian commissariat. It also became the breeding ground of Yiddish theater.[14]

FROM SHTETL TO STAGE

A brief respite from official anti-Semitism in Russia in the late nineteenth century eased the social, cultural, and economic situation for the Jews. Czar Alexander II, who reigned from 1855 to 1881, introduced liberalizing programs at a time of rising nationalism and enlightenment across Europe. For Eastern European Yiddish-speaking Jews, the trend coincided with the rise of the assimilatory Haskalah movement and the ascendancy of socialism, Zionism, and a secular, more worldly culture.

It was now possible for Jewish musicians to enter higher musical study without converting to Christianity, a former requirement in Russia. Among Alexander's acts was the 1868 founding of the St. Petersburg Conservatory, with its open-admission policy for Jews.

The formation of the conservatory was enhanced by the naming of violinist Leopold Auer (1845–1939) as a professor of violin. Auer was the key to a wave of what ethnomusicologist Mark Slobin calls "klezmer kids becoming violin virtuosi."[15]

Another Russian city that served as a hub for the emergence of Jewish cultural life was Odessa, which boasted a Jewish population of 140,000 by 1900 and attracted all sorts of creative and talented Jewish artists. The city was characterized by the more Western outlook of its cultural and social life—the many schools, opera houses, and political organizations that thrived there. Its burgeoning economic development was due in no small part to the marked participation of Jews in each of those areas. This participation was so great that at one point during the 1870s, sixty percent of the student body at the Government College of Music and the Arts was Jewish.

Odessa's culture-rich environment also existed in the less-savory quarter of the city's waterfront Moldovanka district. The Moldovanka was a seething slum of criminals, black marketeers, prostitutes, musicians, and singers, and the numerous wine cellars and cafés they habituated. It was in these venues—and in the homes of more enlightened Jews—that the poet/journalist Abraham Goldfaden (1840–1908) transformed a call for passing entertainment into the long-lived Yiddish theater.

There had been Jewish "theater" going back to the sixteenth century, but it took the shape of *Purim-shpils*—plays depicting the triumph of Mordechai and Esther over the evil Persian Haman. All the roles—including women's—were played by yeshiva boys, who, taking their time-honored skit from house to house, always ended with the rhyme:

Haynt iz purim	Today is Purim
Morgn iz oys	Tomorrow, no more
Git indz a groshn	Give us a penny
un varft indz aroys	And show us the door.

Yet, until the slow rise of wine cellar entertainers like the local Broder Singers and the respected poet/singer Eliakum Zunser, there had never been the idea of an entertainment performed for its own sake, apart from a holiday. By making use of the available performers, including the Broder Singers and various musicians and former *meshoyrerim*, Goldfaden crafted a theater of diverse repertoires.

How this worked is made clear by a look at Goldfaden's audition technique. In his groundbreaking 1982 book *Tenement Songs*, an examination of Yiddish popular song in America, Mark Slobin relates a story about Goldfaden's composing process. When seeing prospective singers for his plays, he would ask them to sing whatever songs they knew best: anything—a Ukrainian lullabye, a Hasidic *nign*, a snatch of a Musaf service, an aria from an opera by Meyerbeer. While they sang, Goldfaden's orchestrator, Arnold Perlmutter, sat in a corner transcribing the melody. Once the decision was made to hire a particular actor, the audition song would be plugged into the play, with new lyrics crafted by Goldfaden. This not only sped the process through which a new show was produced, it quietly but inexorably broadened the musical education of Yiddish-speaking audiences.

But when Goldfaden experienced a resistance to some of his "foreign" inclusions, he decided to try the kind of folk tunes with which Zunser and trained *badkhonim* aroused audiences to high-pitched enthusiasm. This taught him that Yiddish words and characteristic Jewish moods did not always meld easily with German or French operatic airs, but his judicious balancing of these genres made Goldfaden's work resonate in the Jewish community.

Goldfaden came to Odessa after having opened his first Yiddish theater in Jassy during the Russo-Turkish war in 1877, the beginning of the end of the Ottoman empire. Jassy drew scores of grain, flour, and livestock speculators, who sniffed the potential windfall of corruption. The war made a boomtown of Jassy, and the contractors, agents, salesmen, and middlemen growing rich in the Romanian town demanded amusement. Goldfaden, who had come to make a name for himself as a journalist, adjusted slightly and became a playwright.

A Russian-Jewish klezmer band featured in the pages of the *Forverts*, 1920. (*YIVO Institute for Jewish Research*)

He pulled together an assemblage of renegade *badkhonim*, *meshoyrerim*, and klezmorim, cross-bred them with actors and musicians from the non-Jewish theater, and crafted a robust performing troupe. Some of these renegade musicians were the Lemes family, klezmorim who in 1860 led the Romanian National Theater Orchestra.[16] News items from the local press of the time show the close connection between Yiddish theater and klezmer music: "At the Jignitze Theater in Bucharest *Shmendrik* will play; Lemes plays, for the last time, his composition 'National Quadrille,'" *The Daily Yidisher Telegraph* proclaimed on May 21, 1878; and on April 16, 1882, "at the Pomul Verde in Bucharest, the Goldfaden Troupe plays *Di Bobe mitn Eynikl* [The Grandmother with the Grandson], with the collaboration of the orchestra Zelig Itsik Lemes and his son Milo Lemes."

Though there were other competing Yiddish performing companies, Goldfaden outdistanced his competition with more mature writing, flamboyant theatrics, and the ability to spot nascent talent. Some of the talent was female. The law of *kol isha* (Hebrew for "voice of a woman") was long invoked to preclude women from taking an active part in synagogue life or becoming cantors, under the claim that their voices would be "distracting" to the piety of the prayers. The influence of this law and the added stigma of the theater in general kept young women away from the stage. Goldfaden helped change that.

Though Goldfaden allowed women onto the stage, their presence in the orchestra pit was still years off. In Volhyn, klezmer Alter Chudnover had begun the unheard-of practice of teaching his daughters and nieces piano, flute, and violin, though social convention still prevented them from playing music professionally.

At the conclusion of the Russo-Turkish war, Yiddish theater companies made their way back to Odessa to capitalize on what they had started back in Jassy. Almost as soon they began, though, Yiddish and its public presence was outlawed in Russia. The assassination of Alexander II in 1881 and the ascension of his son Alexander III rolled back whatever social gains the late czar had instituted. Yiddish theater took to the provinces, where it would remain until resurging popularity brought it center stage once again in the major cities of Russia.

MARCHING SONGS

Though it was now nearly impossible to ply trades that openly espoused Yiddish culture, Jews did continue to make headway into the mainstream world of classical music. Louis Grupp's uncle Alter Chudnover helped the six-year-old violinist Mischa Elman enter the lofty world of classical music, after Elman's father arranged for an impromptu audition with the klezmer great.

"He just wanted to have my uncle listen to Mischa and give his opinion of what he thought of the child," Grupp said, recalling the visit. "And from then on my uncle took over. Through some politics he knew some lady who was a cousin of the czar—her name was Romanov—and through her he was successful for Mischa to go to Leningrad (Petrograd at that time), where Jews were not allowed. He went to the conservatory, and from then on he started."

Once at the conservatory, Elman found a mentor in Leopold Auer, as did Jascha Heifetz and Efrem Zimbalist. In helping them make the transition from *shtetl* to stage, Auer also imbued the resultant classical music milieu with a sound and aesthetic gleaned from his protégés' earlier exposure to klezmer music. What became popularly regarded as the "Russian" sound—wide vibratos, glissandi, and characteristic ornaments—are all hallmarks of the style of Yiddish fiddle-playing these virtuosos had played back in their hometowns, a sound now appropriated in the hallowed halls of the conservatory.

This tradition was maintained by another transformed klezmer, Pyotr Solomonovich Stolyarsky (1871–1944). Born in the Ukraine into a klezmer family, the young Stolyarsky played at weddings as a child before going on to study violin at the Odessa Conservatory. Named professor of violin there in 1920, he went on to mentor such great instrumentalists as Nathan Milstein and David Oistrakh.

A more severe kind of musical conservatory awaited Jews who found themselves impressed into military service. The record of musicians in the military dates from the seventeenth century. One Chaim Cimbalist served in a Polish military band and died in the War of 1637.[17]

Future American klezmer musicians like Lieutenant Joseph Frankel (who enjoyed military band commissions from both the Russian and American armies), Jake Hoffman, and Harry Kandel gained involuntary experience as band members in the czarist army. Military bands taught musical precision and a more worldly repertoire. The bands also gave rural players a chance to learn on the latest in modern manufactured instruments. Much as southern African-Americans created jazz using the castoff brass and woodwind instruments made for Civil War bands, Jewish musicians returned home with discarded instruments and, applying music lessons learned in uniform, changed forever the older string-oriented band sound.

Mendel Wasserman, a traditional fiddler and *badkhn* from Glovachev, Poland, c. 1920. (*Courtesy Mrs. Lillian Klempner*)

The best account we have of Jewish musicians serving in military bands comes from Dave Tarras. In 1915, the war that was engulfing the whole of Europe reached the doorstep of the eighteen-year-old clarinetist.

"A soldier came from the front, from a music band, and he's looking for musicians," Tarras recalled. "They promised they would let him off [on a pass] if he'll bring musicians. I was already drafted, so when I heard they were forming a band I came there. My father brought me and I said goodbye. The next day I came in by train and I went to play already with the military band at the officers' dinner. I sat down, and they gave me right away to play a clarinet solo, 'Geraldo.' I'll never forget that. I shot it through; I was a good reader. In no time I became the conductor."

Tarras's experience playing mandolin and balalaika also served him well, and because of his status as personal musician to the staff officers, Tarras's proximity to the front—and any real danger—was limited to what the officers felt was good for their own well-being. Tarras's musical talents insulated him from the brutality and dissipation in the czarist army, and in many ways he actually benefited from the experience.

In Russia by the end of the nineteenth century there were an estimated three thousand professional klezmorim, two thousand in the Ukraine alone.[18] By then, klezmer was influenced by music from Moldavia and Romania, which displaced earlier sounds. *Doina*, the rhapsodic form at the core of the klezmer repertoire, came in with this wave of Romanian-style music, replacing *taksim*, its more complex Turkish predecessor.

Another important form was the *bulgar*, which took root in Bessarabia—right next door to Romania—and produced the popular line dance of the same name (from the name *Bulgaresti*, or "in Bulgarian style"). What the *bulgar* actually has to do with Bulgaria is still a matter for speculation; the country's Jewish population was predominantly Sephardic, not Ashkenazic. What may have given rise to the name was the presence of an ethnic Bulgarian population in Bessarabia and Odessa or the heavy interaction between klezmer and Moldavian Gypsy musicians in Northen Bulgaria. In any event, by the end of the nineteenth century, among Jews who had emigrated to the United States "the bulgars" had become the descriptive for a far richer old-time Yiddish dance repertoire that for the moment still flourished throughout Eastern Europe.[19]

ROVNE: MUSICAL CAPITAL OF VOLHYN

The fortress-like Sportova Klub on the main thoroughfare in Rovne, a grim industrial city of one million in the newly emerged Ukraine, gives little hint of its former incarnation. Peer at its cornerstone, though, and you can still make out Hebrew letters nearly obliterated by erosion, bullet holes, and inept postwar cementing. To the Jewish inhabitants of Rovne it was always simply *der Groyser Shil* (the Big Synagogue)—big not only in structure but stature. For at one time Rovne was the "City of Khazonim," the seat of Jewish music in the entire region of Volhyn.

The city itself bears even less trace of its prewar Jewish population, or of the rich center of Jewish life it was a half-century ago. In 1941, of Rovne's thirty thousand inhabitants, twenty-one thousand were Jews. More than one hundred were my family.

Zeyde was my mother's father, Isaac Steinberg. He was a capmaker's apprentice who would later become a house painter and a talented self-taught muralist. He was also mad for music. And Rovne had already long enjoyed a reputation for great Jewish music when Zeyde moved there with his family from the nearby *shtetl* of Azran in 1899.

Cantors were at the core of Rovne's musical renown. The most famous was the *khazn* Jacob Samuel Margovsky or, as he was lovingly known, Zeydl Rovner. It is said that he made *der Groyser Shil* Rovne's cantorial showplace and paved the way for other greats, including the Koussevitsky family.

"*Nisht nor khazonim, ober yo, klezmorim, di beste* [Not just cantors, but the best musicians]": that's what my *zeyde* was always quick to point out. As usual, he was right. *Di Etyitshkes un di Getyetshkes—* all my life I heard about these competing klezmer bands, whose adherents split Rovne right down the middle. Alter Getye, the city's senior fiddler and *badkhn*, formed his band long before Zeyde was born and led it until the outbreak of World War I.

Zeyde recounted a wedding he attended during the sepia-tone days when Alter Getye still led the band:

> When I was sixteen years old a pal of mine got married. The party started nine o'clock on a Saturday night. First they finished playing, dancing and then the *badkhn* stood up on a chair next to a long table; the *badkhn* used to seat the bride and after supper, he used to make an enumeration of the gifts. First the groom's pals: 'Groom's good friend gives a ruble!' And there was a cymbal and he used to give it a whack. Announce the gift and give it a whack. If anyone gave a half a ruble, we used to call it a little ruble. If someone gave a samovar, that was a big

droshe geshenk [presentation of a gift]. It was like twenty rubles. There were things, things, beautiful things: a chandelier, beds, a closet. After that, more dancing. A polka coquette [a single dance], mazurka, *kasatshok*, Russian *sher* for eight pairs, couple dances, called dances. Those who knew the dances didn't need a caller. And it lasted a whole night.

Though Rovne didn't have its own resident theater troupe, it was on the circuit of the many Yiddish theater companies that plied their trade in the provinces in the winter. My grandfather explained:

Troupes used to come in the winter from Vilna and Warsaw. It was really beautiful. Twenty kopeks in the gallery. Down below it cost a half ruble. Up there in the gallery it was tight. To see the stage you had to lean over. In 1908 Yershkowitz from Vilna and Guzik from Warsaw played in our town. Habima also: *Tkias Kaf, Kol Nidre*—in Hebrew.

Summer brought not theater but circuses, from Germany, Russia, and Hungary. While featured performers traveled with the circus, Jewish musicians were hired locally to help flesh out the band. But not someone like Alter Getye; it needed to be someone who read music. Alter Getye died sometime before World War I, and old-style wedding music in the city seemed to die with him.

Volhyn, Podolia, Moldova, Bessarabia: this quadrant of southeastern Europe east and just north of Romania produced the klezmer music that dominated as the century drew to a close. And it was this music—the *bulgars*, the *doinas*—that klezmorim brought with them as they emigrated to America.

～ 2 ～

"Lebn Zol Columbus":
Yiddish Music in the New World

From the ship we walked off I had my clarinet with me in a satchel. They wanted to fumigate and I wanted to tell them that I had a clarinet, but before I started to explain what I want, the clarinet was fumigated and was to pieces."[1]

—DAVE TARRAS ON HIS ARRIVAL AT ELLIS ISLAND (1923)

BY THE TIME DAVE TARRAS'S SHIP steamed into Ellis Island, America had been the port of choice for generations of Jews. Sephardic refugees from Recife, Brazil, landed in New Amsterdam—New York City—and Newport, Rhode Island, as early as the mid-seventeenth century.

But these Sephardim, descendants of Jews expelled from Spain in 1492, would soon be outnumbered by the coming wave of Ashkenazim, the majority at first German (*yehudim*), who arrived between 1840 and 1870. German Jews, many of them followers of the Haskalah, or Jewish enlightenment movement, had discarded traditional religious practices in an attempt to conform with modern Western culture. There is little evidence that the klezmer tradition was still active in Germany by the time these émigrés arrived in the States.

Proud of their own ascendancy in the emerging economy of America's post–Civil War era, German Jews—known derisively by Yiddish-speaking Jews as *yekes*—were concerned by the flood of Yiddish speakers from Eastern Europe. They established philanthropic organizations both to fulfill the long-respected role of community charity and to speed the westernization of their less acculturated cousins. In terms of preserving aspects of *Yiddishkayt* that had its

31

roots in Eastern Europe, the newcomers were left to organize that for themselves. But first they would have to run the gauntlet of American popular culture.

"I LANDED AND BECAME A VAUDEVILLE MUSICIAN"

If the Boston Tea Party signaled the revolution against British political domination, the Astor Place Riots in 1849, precipitated by anti-English sentiment among immigrant Irish theatergoers, heralded a backlash against Anglophile theater in America in favor of more "native" entertainment. The seed had already been planted.[2]

The minstrel show, by 1830 a staple in New York, established a canon of theatrical representations of the "other" that prevailed into the next century. White performers greased in burnt cork and equipped with broad "darky" accents, banjos, and fiddles created a mythic and infantalizing portrayal of American blacks. This branch of American theater would prove the professional stepping stone for future generations of minority performers.

As the receptacle of such a wide swatch of émigrés, the depiction of "types" became a popular form of grassroots theater. The desire for a purely American art form inspired performers to look at the assortment of regional characters populating the United States and helped to create ethnic depiction theaters, which followed the massive immigration of Irish and Germans (called "Dutch" in the corruption of the word *deutsch*—German) and, eventually, Yiddish-speaking Jews.

No group was immune from portrayal on the stages of American vaudeville theaters. For every authentic ethnic performer, like Irish singing star Maggie Cline or Harrigan and Hart, there were a dozen ethnic impersonators from the "Dutch" comedians Weber and Fields to the still-popular blackface comics. Sometimes these minority groups would be combined to create a weird pastiche of ethnicities, as in a 1905 program from Harlem's Keith and Proctor's 125th St. Theater that featured "Matthew and Ashley in their Hebrew Comedy: 'A Smash-Up in Chinatown.'"[3]

With the decline of German and the concomitant rise of Eastern European Jewish emigration in the 1880s, the once popular "Dutch" comedy was subtly retooled to fit the new foreign group. The malapropistic language was recycled, and in place of corpulent, pilsner-imbibing burghers came scurrying, derby-hatted, arson-for-profit

An American postcard from around World War I featuring a group of comics backstage prior to a "Best Hebe" contest, a popular entertainment of its time.

secondhand-clothing dealers—the Yiddish-speaking Jews. So émigré Jews moved into American popular culture much as they did into the hand-me-down tenement apartments and theaters they inherited when they arrived. For immigrant performers and their children, the lesson learned from this parade of ethnic pictorializations was that the way to ascend the ladder of entertainment success was to portray someone farther down that ladder—the route of performers like Isidore Itzkowitz (Eddie Cantor), Asa Yoelson (Al Jolson), Fanny Borach (Fanny Brice), Sonia Kalish (Sophie Tucker), and George Jessel, who parlayed blackface performances into mainstream careers.

By the early years of the twentieth century vaudeville had established itself as the leading form of popular entertainment in America.[4] The typical vaudeville show was a crazy quilt of acrobats, animal acts, Zouaves executing precision drills, knockabout comics of all stripes, and of course, music, the spectrum of which was dizzying: ragtime played by everything from solo five-string banjo to mighty mandolin orchestras; hoary heart songs; ballads about mother, home, and hearth; virtuoso trumpet players demonstrating endless complex variations on popular melodies; rousing jingoistic anthems; and not least, humorous ditties about the picturesque underclasses. Though the affordable and energetic form was a popular amusement, not everyone was amused.

In 1922 Patterson James, a reviewer for *Billboard*—and a favorite in the pages of Henry Ford's weekly publication *The Dearborn Independent*—went "a-slumming" with an "esthetic young Jew" to a vaudeville house to uncover the pernicious Jewish influence in American society:

> The afternoon was a succession of shocks. . . . The theater was dirty, but the show began. [The orchestra leader] Julius Something-or-other . . . entertained the audience with gyrations on his fiddle. . . . Whenever the performer on the stage seemed in danger of securing the undivided attention of the audience, Julius did a neck spin on the bridge of his violin to show he was still leading the orchestra.
>
> Then appeared a stripling with well-oiled head and a most extraordinary suit of clothes [who] uttered some cabalistic words in Yiddish . . . warbled a dismal ditty about nothing at all in particular. . . .
>
> Arrived "America's Celebrated Singing Comedienne," . . . a rotund lady with a very short skirt. . . . The going was very bad for "America's Celebrated Singing Comedienne," so she emitted a sentence or two of Yiddish to indicate that she and her greased pianist were Jewish and that if there were any other Jewish people in the audience they should right away come to the assistance of two Yiddish performers trying to get along and were not being applauded by the Gentiles. . . . ([T]he esthetic one with me foamed with rage at what he called "Kike race appeals."[5]

Ford's dislike of what he considered Jewish-influenced American popular song didn't keep him from becoming the subject of one himself. After a libel suit was brought against him in 1927—buttressed by the Anti-Defamation League—Ford was made to retract his anti-Semitic pronouncements and fold his weekly paper. (His resulting apology quickly spawned the comic "hebe" ditty "Since Henry Ford

Apologized to Me," by showman Billy Rose, which proclaims that, with all now forgiven, "if he runs for President/ I wouldn't charge a single cent/I'd cast my ballot absolutely free."

In "The Popular Song," a 1903 verse printed in *Taylor's Popular Recitations*, the author tells prospective composers how to get themselves in print:

> A Sheeny to publish your song is superior
> He'll force himself where a white man will duck
> No thin cuticle mars a Hebrew's exterior
> He's got nerve and the devil's own luck.[6]

Jewish-born composers who found themselves in the roil of Tin Pan Alley knew that in order to make it they would have to write songs reflecting popular taste. So it was that composers like Harry Von Tilzer, Abe Holtzman, and Charles K. Harris absorbed the language of popular culture and repackaged it for a willing and enthusiastic audience. For example, when Harris—best known for his 1892 hit "After the Ball"—attuned his songwriting to Jewish themes, it emerged first as "Bake That Matza Pie" (c. 1880) and later as "A Rabbi's Daughter" (1898), a melodramatic potboiler about the unhappy offspring, who, denied her Gentile lover, dies of a broken heart—a cautionary tale for an assimilationist time.

> You are a Rabbi's daughter, and as such you must obey
> Your father you must honor unto his dying day
> If you a Christian marry, your old father's
> heart you'll break
> You are a Rabbi's daughter, and must leave
> him for my sake.[7]

The most famous of these composers, Irving Berlin (born Yisroel Baline), was the most prolific in writing songs about the group from which he had come. Like his colleagues in the Yiddish theater, Berlin was a cantor's son and a trained *meshoyrer*, but when it came to writing songs with Jewish subjects, his characters fit squarely into the accepted stereotype of the time: avaricious, sensual, socially maladroit. No entity in the history of American popular music portrayed Jews as perennial outsiders so adeptly as the one-man composition factory of Irving Berlin.

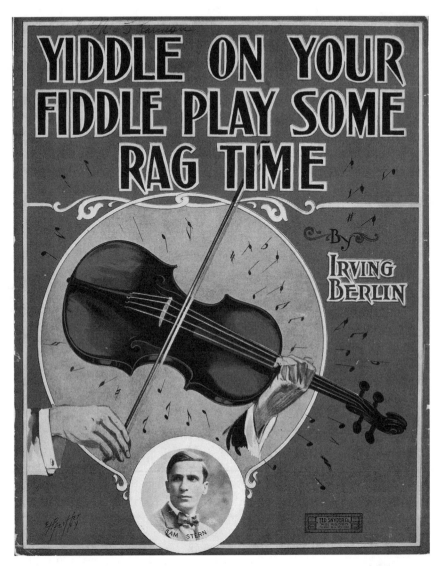

Sheet music cover for the popular Irving Berlin novelty song "Yiddle on Your Fiddle Play Some Rag Time," 1909.

Within a decade he churned out a phalanx of "hebe" songs, including "Yiddle on Your Fiddle Play Some Rag Time" (1909); "Yiddisha Eyes" and "That Kazzatzky Dance" (1910); "Yiddisha Nightingale" (1911); "The Yiddisha Professor: Cohen the Piano Teacher" (1912); and "Cohen Owes Me Ninety-Seven Dollars" (1915), in which the protagonist is miraculously cured on his deathbed when repaid the $97 in question. Though the works were minor in the corpus of compositions Berlin created over his long career—and while such songs were never as popular as "blackface" or "coon" songs of the same period—it is nonetheless telling that the author of such profoundly representative Christian anthems as "White Christmas" and "Easter Parade" never turned his pen to the creation of an

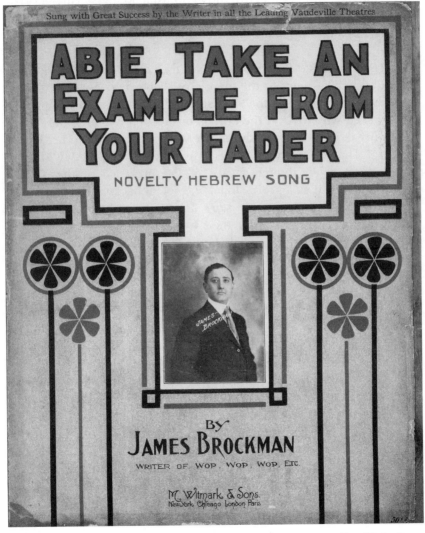

Sheet music cover for one of the many "novelty hebrew songs" published during Tin Pan Alley's adolescence. The composer James Brockman, we are helpfully reminded, also penned the song "Wop, Wop, Wop."

uplifting Jewish-themed song. Berlin was by no means alone in the ethnic depiction industry. Other tunes gracing the shelves of music stores across America that same decade had titles like "When Mose With His Nose Leads the Band" or "Yonkel the Cow-Boy Jew."

The fad continued throughout the teens, with other songs like "Yiddisher Tango Ball," "The Yiddisher Baseball Game," "That Yiddisher Tango" (1914); "At That Yiddish Society Ball," "Yidisher Irish Baby," "My Yiddisher Romeo"(1915); "My Yiddisha Matinee Girl" (1916); "My Yiddish Butterfly" (1917); and "A Yiddisha Soldier Man," "My Yankee Yiddisha Boy," and "My Yiddisher Vampire" (1918).

Shortly before his death, Joe Smith, of the celebrated vaudeville duo Smith and Dale (heirs to the mantle of Weber and Fields's "Dutch" comedy and the models for Neil Simon's *Sunshine Boys*) remarked, when asked why he trod the boards on Second Avenue, that "wanting to break into the Yiddish theater was like wanting to break into prison."[8] That feeling was common to the majority of Jewish-born entertainers, who, though aware of the presence of the Yiddish stage, regarded it as a professional and social backwater.

This was true not only for stars on the stage, but for musicians toiling in the orchestra pit at their feet. The pull of vaudeville was strong, even for klezmer fiddler Louis Grupp. "I tried to get experience from working in different types of places," Grupp recalled. "Different types of joints and restaurants and movies, until I finally landed and became a vaudevillian musician. Played in mostly every house in New York City. Everything and anything."[9]

Over in Brooklyn, another young Jewish musician was cutting his teeth on the professional music circuit. Also from a musical family— his grandfather had taught himself to play the fiddle—Max Epstein (b. 1912) was inspired to continue the tradition. A brilliant violin student, he took his first job in 1924, when he was just twelve years old. Epstein dropped out of high school to play in New York's then ubiquitous vaudeville houses, including the Pitkin Theater in the Brownsville section of Brooklyn. An agile reader and player, he soon excelled at playing in these live forums. But for Epstein and other pit musicians of his day, the prevalence and modernity of the movie house was a strong draw.

Upper-echelon vaudeville was tightly controlled by the old boys of the Keith-Orpheum Circuit, but movies were a ground-floor business with no history, and from the start Jews found themselves attracted to the running of nickelodeons showing the new phenomenon. As movies evolved quickly from single-customer peep shows to mass-audience spectacles, live music became a necessary element. One of Grupp's first non-Jewish jobs in New York was playing movie houses on Rivington Street. "There was a little theater for movies called the Waco Theater," he said. "I played there and that's how I got my experience."

By 1908 the Waco was one of forty-two theaters on the Lower East Side out of 123 citywide.[10] Amid westerns and drawing room dramas, Jewish musicians occasionally played for films that depicted Jewish life—sometimes quite accurately. Grupp recalled that one of his first jobs at the Waco was playing for *The Black Hundred*, a film based on a contemporary Russian case in which the Jewish Mendele Beilis was falsely accused of the ritual murder of a Christian boy. "We came from Russia, from the pogroms, and here we were in a theater playing the music for a pogrom," he said. "My father never could get over it."

Grupp also had the distinction of being in the orchestra for the New York premiere of *Humoresque*, the 1920 film adaption of Fanny Hurst's melodrama of life on the Lower East Side. This American take on *Stempenyu*, Sholem Aleichem's lusty novel about a Svengali-like klezmer violinist, tells of a young man whose fiddle was his ticket out of the slum into which he was born.

"So there's a scene in the movie when the young man is playing a concert for the Jews in the old neighborhood," Grupp explained. "I was in the first violin chair, so I naturally played the violin solo. The title card described it as 'Kol Nidre.' Sure, for the first few times I played Kol Nidre, but after that, *doinas, bulgars*. The other guys in the pit—Jewish—got a kick out of it. Maybe some of the audience did, too."

Small theaters like the Waco or the Emmanuel Theater in the Williamsburg section of Brooklyn—where Max Epstein came to play—didn't rate the printed scores that accompanied the films. Instead musicians played from a book of appropriately themed music (i.e., chase, orientala, wedding) provided by the film company. These bite-size musical lessons taught Epstein and other Jewish professionals how to mix and match ideas to fit a variety of situations. [11]

THE RISE OF YIDDISH POPULAR CULTURE

Of the twenty-five thousand Jews who answered the 1890 Baron de Hirsh survey of Jewish occupations on the Lower East Side, only sixty-seven listed "musician" as their occupation.[12] That number would explode with the increase of émigrés in the years to follow. Some musicians were able to apply their music skills upon arrival; others had to find creative ways to introduce their music, as this December 23, 1912, article in *The New York Times* illustrates:

FIDDLING COBBLER WINS

Drives Out All Competitors in Pitt Street with His Charms of Music

This is the story of the Musical Cobbler of Pitt Street— Pitt Street, the tenement-lined thoroughfare that stretches from Division Street on to East Houston. His name is Schmerle Burstein, and his shop is in the basement of the building at 46 Pitt. . . .

He began to win his customers by throwing in a mandolin solo with every tapped pair of Pitt Street shoes. Then he found that they liked his violin playing and his old fiddle was taken from the closet. The trade increased by leaps and bounds till finally, Burstein engaged one of his thwarted competitors as assistant and let him do the cobbling while he, the proprietor, filled the little shop with melody.

During the last few days he has added a truly wonderful hand-walking act to the diversions of the basement, and he is brushing up his forgotten knowledge of the simpler tricks of magic. So far as is known Pitt Street is the only street in all the five boroughs which has a shop with a cabaret.

Well beyond shoe stores, however, a vast array of outlets for music awaited musicians arriving in turn-of-the-century New York. Among these players, it was the more flexible "go-getters" who eased the transition into mainstream culture, because their new audiences wanted to hear a mix of familiar, homey tunes and a more American sound.

Grupp's father and brothers—including the eighteen-year-old Louis—came to America in 1907. Grupp, fiddle under his arm, had completed his apprenticeship with his uncle Alter and was now ready to be an American musician. "After the pogroms in 1905 my father decided we must come here, so we came," he said. "From then on I didn't take no more lessons."

Grupp describes a world at whose center was the *landsmanshaft*, a self-help organization made up of émigrés from the same town.

Part social circle, part social service, the *landsmanshaft* (in his case "The Chudnover Benevolent and Protective Society") also acted as a clearinghouse for *simkhes* (celebrations) in the expatriate Chudnover world. Alter's reputation held the Grupp family in good stead here and made the weddings and parties easier to find.

"My father used to get the job," Grupp said. "I went along and my young brothers who didn't play yet did, too, although they studied music. And they would engage two or three more men and go and play the wedding, and from that wedding someone would recommend another wedding, and that's how we got along for years."

Weddings were still the backbone of professional musicians' jobs, and every small *shul* (synagogue) had its share. The recent vintage of many émigrés meant that old traditions like the *badkhn*, or wedding poet, could still be found, although in rapidly decreasing measure. In his 1902 book *Spirit of the Ghetto*, an unusually sympathetic study of Lower East Side Jews, Hutchins Hapsgood describes the famed *badkhn* Eliakum Zunser reduced to running a small print shop on the Lower East Side, due to the decline of interest in his once popular *badkhones*.[13]

While *badkhones* may have been eclipsed, weddings were still celebrated with the same fervor and pomp. The major change was the depth and newness of the ancillary repertoires needed to reflect the cultures surrounding the Jewish communities, calling in far greater measure for the sort of adaptability musicians had exhibited in the old country. Ritual dances, like the *broyges* and *mitzve tantsn*, were tossed overboard on the transatlantic voyage in favor of the Turkey Trot, the Hesitation Waltz, and the One Step. These new dances, while devoid of ritual meaning, played as important a role in the émigré Jewish world: they were rites of acculturation, arrival, and modernity. The transformation of these dances was very much in keeping with Jews' ongoing tradition of being a part of and apart from the dominant Gentile culture.

Restaurants, cafés, roof gardens, wine cellars—and even some cobbler shops—competed for the leisure time of Jewish workers at the turn of the century. The Lower East Side was full of such places, tucked into basement entryways and street-level storefronts. And the flavor of these wine cellars is nowhere better captured than in Michael Gold's *Jews Without Money* (1930), in which he describes one run by *tsimblist* Joseph Moscowitz in 1914:

> There were dozens of Russian and Roumanian wine cellars on the East Side. They were crowded with family

parties after the day's work. People talked, laughed, drank wine, listened to music. That was all, no one smashed chairs about in the Christian manner, or cursed or fought or slobbered.

Moscowitz runs a famous restaurant now on Second Avenue. In those years he kept a wine cellar on Rivington Street. It was popular among Roumanian immigrants, including my father and his friends. Moscowitz was, and is, a remarkable performer on the Roumanian gypsy cymbalom.

I remember his place. It was a long narrow basement lit by gas-lamps hanging like white balloons. Between the lamps grew clusters of artificial grapes and autumn leaves. There were many mirrors, and on them a forgotten artist had painted scenes from Roumanian life—shepherds and sheep, a peasant, a horse fair, peasants shocking wheat, a wedding.

At one end of the room, under a big American flag, hung a chromo showing Roosevelt charging up San Juan Hill. At the other end hung a Jewish Zionist flag—blue and white bars and star of David. It draped a crayon portrait of Dr. Theodore Herzl, the Zionist leader, with his pale, proud face, black beard and burning eyes. To one side was an open charcoal fire, where lamb scallops and steaks grilled on a spit. Near this, on a small platform, Moscowitz sat with his cymbalom. Strings of red peppers dried in festoons on the wall behind him. A jug of wine stood at his elbow and after every song he poured himself a drink. . . .

As Moscowitz played, his head moved lower and lower over the cymbalom. At the crescendo one could not see his face, only his bald head gleaming like a hand-mirror. Then, with a sudden upward flourish of his arms, the music ended. One saw his shy, lean face again, with its gray moustache. Everyone cheered, applauded and whistled. Moscowitz drank off his wine, and smiling shyly, played an encore. (Moscowitz is a real artist, after twenty years he still makes restaurant music with his heart, and has never saved any money.)

A hundred Jews in a basement blue as sea-fog with tobacco smoke. The men wore their derby hats. Some were bearded, some loud, sporty and young, some brown as nuts. The women were fat and sweated happily, and smacked their children. Moscowitz played. The waiters buzzed like crazy bees. A jug of good red Roumanian wine decorated the oilcloth on every table. The cash register rang; Mrs. Moscowitz was making change. The artificial grapes swung from the ceiling. Teddy Roosevelt, with bared teeth, frightened the Spaniards. Moscowitz played a sad and beautiful peasant ballad. A little blubber-faced man with a red beard beat his glass on the table, wept and sang. Others joined him. The whole room sang. . . .

I could not take my eyes off the gleaming bald head of Moscowitz the musician.

"Pop, what song is he playing now?" I asked.

"Don't you know?" my father asked in real surprise.

"No."

"Yi! Yi! Yi!" my father sighed, sentimentally. "I see, Mechel, you have really become an American. That is the song, Mechel, the shepherds play on their flutes in Roumania when they are watching their sheep. It is a *doina*. How many summer days have I heard it in the fields!"

"It is better than your American ragtime," said Mottke severely. "It is music—not this pah-pah-pah ragtime."

"Music of the soul," said my father sentimentally.

"Pah-pah-pah" did appeal to Joseph Moscowitz, however. When he entered recording studios for the first time, in 1916, in addition to the *doinas, khosidls,* and *czardases* he recorded were "Operatic Rag" and "Panama Pacific Drag"—two popular ragtime compositions.

Meanwhile, alongside wine cellars, a new phenomenon, the catering hall, arose to accommodate increasingly lavish Jewish weddings. Venues like New York's Pythagoras Hall began as small storefronts and, through careful attention to the efficient mounting and clockwork precision of party making, mushroomed into a big business well suited to new consumerism.

New facilities demanded new rituals. Where the *badkhn* once commanded the sequence of rituals and dances, it was now the caterer. Why bother with a *badkhn* when the caterer saw to it that the cake-cutting ceremony was carried out according to form? Manhattan's Victoria Hall, in keeping with the latest rage of electricity, got rid of its old-fashioned cloth *khupe* and introduced in its stead the "electric *khupe*," consisting of dozens of lightbulbs.[14]

The explosion of interest in "affairs" was fueled by the modern bar mitzvah. If the traditional wedding had over the years carefully nurtured the specific ritual dances associated with it, the bar mitzvah had none of these. It had never been any more involved than the family of the bar mitzvah hosting a modest *kiddush* for the congregation in their home or in the synagogue basement. After making the blessings over challah and wine in honor of this newest member of the adult community, the congregation would sample herring, gefilte fish, chopped liver, and maybe a schnapps or two. Almost overnight, it seems, it was agreed that these modest parties would no longer do. Now bar mitzvahs were racing to match the by then de rigueur lavishness of Jewish weddings.

Musicians responded by meeting patrons' new musical requests. Slipping away were the older dances, the quirky tunes that might have made sense back in their hometowns but here were out of step. Though foxtrots were beginning to make inroads against *freylekhs*, people still wanted *shers*, *bulgars*, and the latest hits coming out of the Yiddish theater.

Among prayer shawls, feather beds, and prized heirlooms, émigré Jews unpacked a passion for the stage. On the Lower East Side, theaters, lecture halls, and cafés previous populations had abandoned for greener pastures became great venues for Jewish self-expression. Each area of the "Jewish" Lower East Side was distinct: Hester and Forsythe streets were for pushcarts, Delancey and Canal housed shops and light manufacturing, and the Bowery was its theater district. By 1910 there were thirteen Yiddish theaters on the Lower East Side, most of them vaudeville houses. The number would continue to grow, shifting in predominance to Second Avenue.[15]

It is no coincidence that theater and synagogue shared more than just the patrons who occupied their seats. Virtually every major composer who wrote for the Yiddish theater had studied as a *meshoyrer*—an apprentice cantor or *khazn*—and knowingly employed modes and scales used in the time-honored cantorial tradition, cementing an instant familiarity between audience and song.

Boris Thomashefsky understood all that. Thomashefsky (1867–1939), the first American Yiddish theater superstar, was famous for his grand personage, living as if he were onstage twenty-four hours a day. At the height of his career, he sported a silk top hat and cape, rolled up to his theater in a chauffeur-driven limousine,

Boris Thomashefsky, c. 1921

and took his pay in gold, which he kept in a money belt around his sizable waist.

Thomashefsky's grandfather was a *khazn* in his hometown of Asitniatchka (near Kiev), where the boy soprano trained as a *meshoyrer* before going on to sing in Berditchev, then the center of Jewish music liturgy in Russia. There Thomashefsky studied with the great cantor Nissi Belzer and became a local celebrity when he drew applause for a solo during High Holiday service. Emigrating with his family to New York's Lower East Side in 1881, the young Thomashefsky found work singing in the Henry Street Synagogue choir. His introduction to Yiddish theater came via a saloon keeper and synagogue trustee named Frank Wolf, who financed a visit from a Yiddish troupe from London.

The following year Thomashefsky managed to work his way up from a job in a cigar factory to coproducing and acting in one of the first American Yiddish productions, Goldfaden's *Di Kishefmakhern* (The Sorceress), in Manhattan's Turnverein Hall on East Fourth Street off Second Avenue. An unmitigated disaster—when the prima donna didn't show up, Thomashefksy, in the grand theater tradition, did the role in drag—the show nevertheless convinced him his future lay in the Yiddish theater. Within a decade he was proved right.

Meanwhile, more—and more kinds of—Yiddish companies rose up in response to the growing appetite for theater. In an attempt to "raise" the level of the theater, some playwrights produced works spoken in *daytshmerish*, an affected Yiddish/German blend that strived to imitate German vocabulary and syntax. Thomashefsky correctly gauged the emerging tastes of the Jewish audience and presented them with what they wanted: broad, lively theater featuring recognizable music and larger-than-life heroes who delivered their dialogue in *daytshmerish*, setting them apart from less exalted characters. His formula, the exemplar of what was later referred to as *shund* (trash), caught on.

In 1887 the author of Thomashefsky's premiere play, the preeminent Yiddish playwright/director/composer Abraham Goldfaden, arrived in the United States, an "old-country" bumpkin whelmed by New York's fast-paced, intense environment. He was chagrined to find that theaters were staging his plays without permission—or payment—and that his star had been eclipsed by his former players, who had ridden the coattails of his groundbreaking work.

Returning to Europe a year later after failing to gain a foothold in America, Goldfaden felt lost between two worlds and headed back to New York in 1903. Revered but ignored, Goldfaden watched his plays attain the success he could not. Scraping by on charity extended by loyal artists who owed him their start, of the Jewish community Goldfaden once remarked: "I wish they would give me the price of the tombstone which they will erect in my memory. Then I should be able to delay its erection."

In 1886 one of Goldfaden's competitors from Europe also landed in New York: the enigmatic "Professor" Moishe Hurwitz. "Professor" Hurwitz was born in 1844 in Stanislav, eastern Galicia into a religious home. At the age of eighteen he left for Jassy, Romania, where he applied his early religious training to become a Hebrew teacher, and from there traveled to Bucharest. He claimed to have been a professor of geography at the University there, hence his "academic" title. Although that claim is not documented, what is known is that after being dismissed as director of a Jewish school in the Romanian capital, Hurwitz, possibly out of spite or economic motives, converted to Christianity.

Rebuffed by Goldfaden in 1877, Hurwitz set himself up as one of Goldfaden's most dogged competitors. His troupe produced Yiddish plays in Bucharest and elsewhere in Rumania for several years. In 1886 he emigrated to the United States, and there wrote opportunistic, fire-breathing playlets, earning him the mantle of godfather of low-rent *shund* theater.

Hurwitz's first play, produced at the Romanian Opera House in New York in 1889, was *Tisa Eslar, oder, Di Farshverung*, which he had written while still in Romania. The subject of the play was a notorious blood libel trial that had taken place in the Hungarian town of Tisza-eszlar just a few years earlier. Despite his having penned sequels, and several other works over the next fifteen years, "Professor" Hurwitz's fame declined and he died a pauper in New York in 1910.

During the period of Goldfaden's return to Europe, yet another rival for the attention of the Jewish audiences arrived. The playwright and theater impresario Jacob Gordin (1853–1909) championed Yiddish art theater, a higher form of theater for Jews in America. Advocating *kunst*—"art"—he became a firebrand for better-quality performances that would use realism instead of romanticism to raise the masses. In addition to his own highly literate works, Shakespeare, Gorky, and Ostrovsky were all grist for Gordin's elevation mill, as evidenced by one of his earliest successes, *The Jewish King Lear*. Finding devotees—most notably actor Jacob P. Adler—and writing plays like *God, Man and Devil* (a Yiddish spin on the Faust legend), Gordin promoted *kunst* over *shund* or musical/comedy theater, and the use of plain Yiddish over *dayt-shmerish*, setting the stage for world-class dramatic offerings.

Yet despite his powerful presence in the Yiddish theater, Gordin's failure in the management of his own theater presaged his greater failure in finding a long-term mass audience that wanted to be "elevated." Gordin may have captured the minds of theatergoers, but that was not the body part settling into loge seats. People liked musicals.

If Gordin lacked real mass appeal, Jacob P. Adler had no such problem. Adler, who unlike his colleagues in the Yiddish theater was

Jacob P. Adler, as he was c. 1915.

no *meshoyrer*, had become interested in drama and literature back in Russia. In 1879 he joined Goldfaden's troupe. Forced to flee Russia when the Yiddish theater was banned, he made it to London, where he suffered one professional setback after another before being brought to America.

Arriving in New York in 1887, Adler made a much-publicized but ultimately disastrous debut—the audience, expecting a drama, was served a comedy—and was soon forced to pitch his tent in Chicago and await a propitious moment to return and try again in New York.

Like Hasidic rabbis who elicited passionate loyalty from their followers, stars of the Yiddish theater had *patriotn*—fans who would argue and sometimes come to blows over their respective champions. It was not unheard of, for example, for Adler devotees to engage in pitched street battles against admirers of the actor David Kessler.

This powerful sense of ownership—held by everyone from wardrobe mistress to season box holder—gave theater a special place in the lives of its patrons.

Adler's downtown portrayal of Shylock was his ticket to its reprise, in Yiddish, on Broadway in 1903—in an otherwise all-English production of *The Merchant of Venice*. Not to be outdone, Thomashefsky starred in his own overheated adaptation of Harriet Beecher Stowe's novel *Uncle Tom's Cabin*, leading wags in the Yiddish press to bestow upon him the derisive moniker "Uncle Thom."

The banner of a more literary- and art-style Yiddish theater was also raised by the activist offerings of enthusiastic amateurs and their dramatic clubs, a somewhat loftier starting point for Yiddish theater stars. A small New York theater group served that function for the actor Elihu (Elye) Tenenholtz (1890–1971), my great uncle, who went on to perform from Second Avenue to Hollywood.

Born in the hamlet of Azran, on the outskirts of Rovne, Tenenholtz came to America with his family around 1900. Like Thomashefsky before him, young Tenenholtz found employment in a cigar factory and a ready audience in his coworkers, whose approbation urged him on. By 1903, he joined the staunchly amateur Progressive Dramatic Club, a venue for the presentation of literary works from Gordin to George Bernard Shaw. There Tenenholtz originated the idea of staged readings of Sholem Aleichem stories, which were so well received the famous writer thanked him personally.

Tenenholtz wrote, too—drama criticism and humorous feuilletons under the pen-name "Moishe McCarthy" for New York-based Yiddish periodicals like the *Varheit*, for which he also transcribed the memoirs of the Yiddish theater star Bessie Thomashefsky. Tenenholtz's dramatic and literary talents were brought further to the fore through his association with the actor/director Maurice Schwartz (1888–1960).

Schwartz, who was also born in the Ukraine and emigrated at the turn of the century, apprenticed in Yiddish theaters from Cleveland to Philadelphia before getting his break in New York. In 1918 his visionary opportunism led him to grab the reins of power at the faltering Irving Place theater, where together with Tenenholtz, actor/director Jacob Ben-Ami, Jacob P. Adler's daughter Celia, and comic Ludwig Satz, Schwartz founded New York's Yiddish Art Theater. But after only one season of some thirty-five productions, the association dissolved with Ben-Ami opening his higher-minded Jewish Art

Theater and Schwartz continuing to present more pragmatic, mid-dle-road art theater works.

Despite world-class goals every bit as refined as its uptown coun-terparts, Yiddish art theater never found a surefire way to subsidize itself. Of the two art theater factions, Schwartz's populist style won out; the Yiddish Art Theater remained open some thirty years, while Ben Ami's playhouse was shuttered after only two. Ami moved onto to Broadway and off-Broadway, only occasionally venturing back into the Yiddish orbit and only then to take parts with great literary merit.

Still, audiences preferred the song-and-dance performances of comics like Sigmund "Zelig" Mogulesko (1856–1914)—another Goldfaden alumnus—and the rougher-hewn Yiddish vaudeville, some of the first staged Yiddish entertainment in America. Vaude-ville featured such bush-league theater as *Among the Indians*, a playlet by the writer/accountant/publicist and adman Chanan-Yakov Minikes. The crude one-act play featured a crafty Yiddish traveling salesman, ignorant but dangerous Indians, and a broadly played heroine, epitomizing the genre with its racial stereotyping, single-entendre sexual allusions, and perhaps the earliest-known instance of shameless product placement. (One character complains to anoth-er about the high price he paid for his suit. "Start buying from L. Minsky," the hero suggests, "the largest, most up-to-date and cheap-est wholesale dry goods store and manufacturer of clothing, at 55, 57, and 59 Canal Street, New York.")[18]

Minikes's brand of performance was one the father of Yiddish the-ater could not fathom. An uneasy mix of showman, didact, and Zion-ist, Goldfaden believed theater should not only entertain but uplift. His formula, like much of the music he wrote, was to have continued influence on the theater of his creation. Goldfaden's final work, *Ben Ami*, would have remained unproduced in his lifetime if not for the coming together of two leading lights of the theater: Thomashefsky and Mogulesko, who premiered the work in December 1907.

Thomashefsky's offer was a two-edged sword for the ailing play-wright. The young director sought to spruce up the play, a drama, with some comic songs—much to Goldfaden's horror. Noting his displeasure, Thomashefsky merely brought in a composer and insert-ed the songs without Goldfaden's approval. Despite this blow, the playwright attended every performance of the work until his death, the following month.[19] Goldfaden's demise was Yiddish theater's first great loss, and mourners lined the streets to pay their respects at his funeral. As he predicted, he received a fancy tombstone erected by the Jewish community in his memory.

Whether pure or pinioned, the real magnet of Yiddish theater was its veracity. Unlike the uptown theater of the Gentile majority, with its drawing room comedies and escapist and exotic fare, Yiddish theater told stories that could have come from audience members' lives. Uptown audiences wanted to escape from; downtown audiences wanted to escape to. Whether a show was set in the court of Solomon, the steppes of Russia, or a New York City sweatshop, theatergoers absorbed and were absorbed by the drama's contemporary subtext.

Themes of forsaken love, abandoned mothers, *shtetl* weddings, and anti-Semitism were evergreen. Together with old-world musical comedies that cast a Sabbath candle-like glow over the towns these immigrants had left behind, Yiddish theater brought the breadth of Jewish experience to neighborhood playhouses.

Yet for the actors and actresses who presented these stories, the combination of labor disputes, poor working conditions, and low wages created harsher drama backstage than anything played out before the curtain. In the old theater system, for example, actors were paid a share or "mark" rather than an actual salary, with shares divided unevenly among principals and subordinates. Under the guise of cooperative distribution, a weekly share could range from $125 for top performers to $3 for lesser lights.[20]

The Gilded Age, an American era of fierce class consciousness, was also the time that labor unions first started flexing their muscles, and the Jewish community was in the forefront of labor unrest. Inequity in the arts led to the formation of the activist United Hebrew Trades in 1888, with the rise the following year of the Hebrew Actor's Union and a musician's union with the ungainly name of Russian Progressive Musical Union No. 1 of America (RPMU), which supplied music—mostly for free—for Jewish events from picnics to political rallies.[21]

While the RPMU was an open and accessible shop, the Hebrew Actors Union quickly devolved into a protectionist cabal ultimately responsible for choking off the flow of new young talent into the Yiddish theater. The importance of the RPMU and its eventual successor, the Progressive Musicians Benevolent Society, formed in 1903, was ratcheted by the fact that musicians from the Yiddish music world were barred from the American Federation of Musicians (AFM), which came into being in 1896. By 1921, when the AFM started allowing in musicians from the Jewish music professions, the Progressive reformed itself as a *landsmanshaft*, and with that its power waned.

Parallel to the rise of political and labor groups like the RPMU were the worker's choruses and mandolin orchestras. Like their fellow amateur performers in the theater who were serving art, these nonprofessional musicians served the higher goal of commitment to political beliefs.

From Zionists to Communists the choruses sang the anthems—and the praises—of their particular political beliefs. Among the most active people's choruses were those of the militant pro-Soviet Freiheit Gezangs Ferain, the more moderate socialist Arbeiter Ring chorus, and the labor Zionist Paole Zionist Singing Society, which sang in Hebrew. These groups' ability to disseminate their songs to a far-flung constituency was aided by national networks of affiliated chapters.

Mandolin orchestras, meanwhile, modeled themselves after the popular turn-of-the century college, community, and professional vaudeville mandolin groups but eschewed tunes like "Doc Browns Cakewalk" in favor of political and labor songs like "The Internationale," adapted to fit their needs.

BROADSIDES, SHEETS, 78s

Concurrent with the rise of theater's popularity came the dual marketing venues of music publishing and recording. As evidenced by the primacy of Thomashefsky's musicals over Gordin and Adler's intellectual *kunst* dramas, when the curtain fell it was music that people remembered. Music sustained them during the week in their shops, factories, and homes. Familiar yet new, music from the latest shows propelled *patriotn* into stores to buy it—on recordings and on song sheets.

The sheet music industry, which had come into being after the Civil War, blossomed in the last years of the century. Yiddish music began to get printed not only by mainstream Jewish publishers looking to expand their markets but by smaller, newly minted presses eager to capitalize on a perceived market. Prior to the actual printing of Yiddish music, broadsides—topical lyrics set to popular melodies—were sold in the street by the people who sang them.

What helped drive music publishing overall was the boom in pianos, which the Victorian era made a vital part of the cultural and social upbringing of proper young ladies.[22] Nothing better exemplifies

Sheet music cover for Abe Schwartz's "In-Laws' Dance," 1921.

this in the Jewish world than a graphic the Hebrew Publishing Company used for decades on its sheet music covers. The illustration profiles a girl in diaphanous dress seated at the piano while in the background her prominently yarmulked father, white-haired mother, and paramour (sans yarmulke) all beam with pride at the parlor recital. It was the piano that allowed women like Sylvia Schwartz, Beverly

Musiker, and Dora Cherniavsky to find a public place in klezmer ensembles and in Yiddish theater orchestras.

Yiddish music publishers cropped up overnight to fill the need of the sheet music-hungry public, with journeyman publishers like J. Katzenellenbogen and Solomon Schenker joining the fray. Between 1890 and 1910 at least a dozen music publishers had little outlet stores on East Broadway, Canal Street, and over the bridge in Brooklyn.[23] Even theaters got into the act, rushing to print copies of the words and music to their hit show tunes and selling them in the lobby during intermission.

The earliest Yiddish music published in America were 1890 text-only editions by Goldfaden, Mogulesko, and Zunser. By 1894 Yiddish parodies of American popular songs like "Good Old Summertime" and "Meet Me in St. Louis" were for sale. When New York publisher J. Katzenellenbogen began publishing, he hired fledgling Yiddish composers like Louis Gilrod (1879–1930), David Meyerowitz (1867–1943), and Solomon Smulewitz (1868–1943), who created a Yiddish equivalent of the American popular song.[24]

This was the era of singer/composers, and none was more prolific than Solomon Smulewitz, who wrote more than 150 songs. Also calling himself "Small" (which the corpulent Smulewitz certainly was not), he was a triple threat: lyricist, composer, and singer in the mold of his idol, Zunser, whose star he eclipsed. A *meshoyrer, badkhn*, and fiddler, Smulewitz began composing songs at the turn of the century that had the feel of the previous generation's up-to-the-minute broadsides. But unlike the balladeers of an earlier time, who had only the street corner from which to offer their latest creations, Smulewitz benefited from the emerging publishing houses and record labels.

Anyone with a few dollars and the help of a friendly local printer could publish, but recording required the good graces of an amenable record company. Luckily, at this point, there were plenty, and Smulewitz made his way to them all: Lambert, Zonophone, Columbia, and, when it opened for business in 1904, the United Hebrew Disc and Cylinder Record Company.

Smulewitz had the kind of voice made for the early acoustic recording process, which relied so heavily on sheer wind power. His timbre and vibrato found a comfortable place in the register of the clumsy recording horn. A hard worker and dependably accurate, Smulewitz was a regular presence in early recording studios.

In 1908 he scored his greatest success, writing and recording the song "A Brivele der Mamen" (A Little Letter to Mother). This song, about a mother in the old country who dies waiting for word from her son that never arrives, immediately captured the attention—and pocketbooks—of the newly migrated Jewish public, many of whom were no doubt remiss in their own correspondence.

Smulewitz ignited red-hot interest in sentimental mother songs (a currently popular song theme among general and other ethnic composers), resulting in knockoff "brivele" ballads—some even written by other composers. Smulewitz had a sweet tooth for pathos, producing such pieces as "Khorbn Titanic, oder Der Naser Keyver" (The Titanic's Disaster, or The Watery Grave), playing up the Jewish angle in this essentially Gentile event by focusing on the doomed couple Isidore and Ida Straus as "the great ship went down."

Smulewitz continued to record both his own and his colleagues' compositions, in many cases, as was common, re-recording the same songs for different labels. By 1919, just about the time records were starting to become a regular feature in the home, Smulewitz ended his recording career, writing songs others would sing—a wise move, since his barrel-chested style soon passed out of fashion.

Although Smulewitz and his singer/songwriter cohorts dominated Yiddish music publishing catalogs, a small but enthusiastic buying public existed for other kinds of sheets. In 1902 Herman Shapiro arranged traditional wedding music in the anthology *Di Originale Yiddishe Khasene*, scored for piano. The music charts an old-fashioned Jewish wedding, starting with "A Gite Vokh"—the first tune played after the conclusion of the Sabbath, kicking off the weeklong celebration—and ending with "A Gite Nakht" ("Good Night," played at week's end). This anthology remained in the Hebrew Publishing catalog into the 1930s.

Over the next few years other Yiddish composers would also anthologize elements of traditional klezmer music. Joseph Rumshinsky's 1909 *At a Hebrew Wedding Ceremony: Descriptive Fantasia* was released by the tony uptown publisher Theodore Lohr. It's not clear whom this collection was aimed at, with its stilted English titles ("Special Rejoicing Dances for Men, Women and Bridal Relatives") and piano arrangements of old-fashioned dance music.

When composer/comic Sigmund Mogulesko and librettist Joseph Lateiner opened their operetta *Blimele* (Little Flower), in 1909, the show-stopping song "Khosn, Kale Mazl Tov" (Congratulations to the

Bride and Groom) was quickly taken up by Jewish and non-Jewish dance bands. "Khosn, Kale Mazl Tov" soon became one of several token Jewish tunes, and its authorship was quickly forgotten.

Workaday composers of the Yiddish theater all took time out to write songs or tunes reflecting the klezmer tradition. In "Tsu der Khupe Vetshere" (To the Wedding Meal), Smulewitz has one of his musicians speak for musicians for all time: "Let's strike up a merry tune and lead the wedding party to the festive meal. But remember, we musicians also have to eat."

Unlike the publishing of Yiddish songs, recording was largely in the hands of non-Jewish firms. In 1877 Thomas Edison invented the first practical means of recording. Among the challengers to Edison's hegemony was the German-born Jewish inventor Emile Berliner (1851–1929). Whereas Edison developed cylinder recording, Berliner vastly improved on that design by perfecting the flat disc we know today, which revolutionized the recording industry with its ability to reproduce thousands more copies than cylinders could.[25]

Emigrating from Hannover in 1870, Berliner settled in Brooklyn and eventually, Washington, D.C., where he patented his flat shellac disc in 1887.[26] A better inventor than businessman, he entered into a partnership with engineer Eldridge Johnson, organizing a number of companies, including his Berliner Gramophone in 1892, National Gramophone by 1897, and Zon-O-Phone in 1899. After much reorganization, in 1901 Berliner and Johnson founded the Victor Talking Machine Company, which soon became the dominant force in recorded sound.[27]

Berliner did not stay long in the rambunctious record business, instead moving on to the fields of public health and, later, radio.[28] But before exiting the arena, he began augmenting his American offerings with records made at his London-based Gramophone Company, originally known as the Gramophone and Typewriter Company. Many of the earliest foreign recordings the European company issued were overseen by Berliner's young assistant Fred Gaisberg and his associates. On Berliner's orders, Gaisberg headed to London to assume the role of chief recording engineer, and in May 1899 began a series of field trips to the continent to try out the recording equipment under the rigors of field tests. Among the recordings he amassed, the quantity of Jewish and other ethnic records was so great that by December they merited their own sections in the Gramophone catalog.[29]

Cantor G. Sirota.

The famed cantor Gershon Sirota, who died in the liquidation of the Warsaw ghetto in 1943.

Over the next few years Gaisberg supervised recording sessions in European cities—including Breslau, Bucharest, Budapest, Czernowitz, Lemberg (Lvóv), St. Petersburg, and Warsaw—that had large and culturally vibrant Jewish communities. Gramophone signed a span of Jewish musicians from theater to cantorial and, to a lesser extent, klezmer traditions.

The Jewish catalog was anchored by the presence of one performer: cantor Gershon Sirota (1873–1943). Sirota, who made more than 175 records during his career, was the first star of Jewish recording. In an era that venerated singers, he singlehandedly established cantorial music as the equal of other vocal styles. In Warsaw in 1902 he made his first Gramophone recordings, which gained immediate and widespread notice, including that of the prestigious Tlomackie Synagogue, which appointed him cantor in 1905.[30] "Sirota of the Golden Voice"—as he was called by the press—continued to record for Gramophone off and on until 1912.

Sirota was courted by every major and minor label in Europe, as attested to by the voluminous Gramophone correspondence concerning his contract negotiations:

> Riga, November 9, 1911: As you know this artiste is of the utmost importance to us, and we are anxious to see that the Competition do not get any of his records . . . This you know is most important, especially at this moment when we are threatened with the Competition getting on the inside. . . .[31]

As the end of Sirota's contractual period came closer, messages to Gaisberg to re-sign him became shriller: "DO NOT LEAVE UNTIL YOU HAVE DEFINITELY SETTLED RE SIGNING CONTRACT. IMPORTANT."

It made no difference. Lapses between contracts allowed Sirota to record for other companies, including the French Pathé label, Zon-O-Phone, Odeon, Clausophon, Usiba, Scala, United, and the Russian label Favorite. Like Gramophone, which licensed records for release to its American affiliate Victor, Favorite exported Sirota's discs to Columbia, ensuring his standing as the most widely available European Jewish artist on record.

Gaisberg, acting more like an ethnographer than a corporation employee, sometimes located and recorded artists on the spur of the moment, with negative repercussions. Commenting on a field trip Gaisberg took to Warsaw in 1911, a Gramophone associate wrote:

> I am sure that London will greatly object to your having recorded six Jewish records . . . You know very well that London did not authorise us to make such recording and the responsibility for having done so lies entirely with you.

The widespread roamings of Gaisberg and his team of engineers recorded hundreds of klezmorim, *khazonim*, and Yiddish theater singers, a high-tech synthesis of what *klezmorim* traditionally did as they traveled from town to town. From now on, records would go where the performers themselves never had, giving them undreamed-of influence. These recordings also codified the music, making local styles conform to now-standardized versions.

A letter dated June 24, 1904, from Gramophone in Milan to the London office documents the widespread distribution of these records:

> Re: HEBREW SELECTIONS BY CANTOR GERSHON SIROTA:
> We thank you for calling our attention to the records of which we have ordered a complete set from Hannover. In all probability they will be useful to us in our Egyptian trade.

This activity did not go unnoticed by other upstart record labels. As Berliner had challenged Edison's primacy back in the United States, small regional labels confronted Berliner in Europe. Startup companies like Beka, Odeon, Extraphon, and Favorite were stealing the thunder of the omnipotent Gramophone Company, recording regional performers and solidifying their own territorial markets. Though this kind of hot competition was not good for Gramophone, it did create a fertile environment for the widespread recording of numerous Jewish artists who may well have been overlooked by the smugly complacent larger label.

As early as 1911 a disgusted Gramophone employee complained to the field office about the challenge of recording local Jewish performers in the Greek town of Smyrna (now Izmir, Turkey). "The Favorite, when quite a small company, was able to make records in February," he wrote, "whereas we, the great Gramophone company, after some two years are meeting with all kinds of difficulties and unpleasantness."[32]

Another of these upstart companies was Warsaw-based Syrena.[33] Like most labels, Syrena issued primarily classical and popular recordings, but by fall 1910, its director recognized the value of recording ethnic music and selling it back to the communities from which it was gotten. As with all other labels, the label began with cantorial and popular song and, only after establishing a market share, branched out into klezmer music. Recordings of small ensembles featuring fiddle, flute, and *tsimbl*—the last gasps of the klezmer's preindustrial sound—were soon joined by larger bands like the generically titled Russian-Jewish Orchestra and a quirky little ensemble headed by V. Belf.

Who "V. Belf" was is clouded in mystery. But a period publicity piece from the Syrena company sheds some light on its most popular Jewish instrumental artist:

> The artists, surrounded by all comforts and attention and well paid, relate to the work in a totally different manner and think nothing of re-recording a number two or three times if necessary. To be precise I must state that all the business, all the reins of management are concentrated in the hands of chief director Ph. L. Tempel who indeed turns out to be the energetic inspirer of all the projects and a specialist at ferreting out hit numbers. Who would have supposed that a poor Jewish musician, Belf, could have bought himself a house in his home town out of the proceeds which the factory paid him? But who dug up and contracted this Belf? —Tempel. And do you know, readers, how many Belf records the factory sells? Every day not less than two to three thousand items are shipped south, yet new orders pour in endlessly.[34]

Compared to the smooth, familiar style of klezmer played by the likes of Dave Tarras, the rough edginess of these Belf records is striking. The instrumentation was usually a clarinet, a couple of fiddles—one melody, another playing chords, or *secunda*—and the occasional cello and piano. The piano playing gives us a clue to the very recent inclusion of "harmony" instruments in ensembles that had primarily been melodic. The piano is played more for its percussive than harmonic properties, with chords far more approximate than deliberate. The overall effect gives the whole sound an immediacy, as if we have just walked in on a session. The seemingly unbridled feel of the playing, with clarinet and fiddle swooping in and out of each other's way, makes for visceral listening rarely encountered in other studio recordings of klezmer music.

Though listed as "Romanian," the players are most probably from the Ukrainian region of Podolya, near the culturally influencing area of Romania. Inclusion of the word was a marketing ploy, given the popularity of Romanian-style music among East European Jews at the turn of the century. And it paid off; over the next four years the Syrena label issued nearly two hundred klezmer sides.[35]

Despite the large number of recordings made of Yiddish theater singers, cantors, and comics by the various labels, the recording of klezmer music was dramatically underrepresented. Apart from the modest couplings of fiddle and/or flute with *tsimbl* or piano, played by such performers as fiddlers Leon Ahl, Oscar Zehngut, and Jacob Gegna, and flutist Shloimke Kosch, the only larger ensemble recordings issued were Belf's and a couple of other, more generically titled ensembles.

Yet of the hundreds of Yiddish records made in Eastern Europe from the turn of the century until the First World War, only the records of the great Sirota and a tiny handful of theater and klezmer records got exported to the United States; the export of American Jewish recordings to Europe was in far greater numbers. Although Syrena eventually did manage to export a few of its titles to the United States (most notably some of the Belf 78s), they entered the game far too late, cut off by the outbreak of the war.

In response to its growing presence in Eastern Europe, Gramophone opened its first factory in Poland in 1912. At the same time the new factory was being inaugurated a different group of music collectors was at work in another part of Poland. Unlike Gaisberg, these men were armed not with the latest in disc technology but with simple home cylinder machines, and unlike the commercial labels they sought not the latest and greatest singers or hottest songs from the Yiddish stage or synagogue but the most archaic tunes they could find. And finally, unlike commercial labels, these collectors made recordings not for profit but for posterity. This, then, was the first ethnographic expedition to make sound recordings of Jewish folklife in Eastern Europe.

This collecting foray was initiated by the Jewish Historical Ethnographic Society in St. Petersburg in 1911 and continued until the outbreak of World War I. But the idea of conducting the folklore expeditions belonged to the Jewish writer and folklorist known as S. Ansky (Solomon Rappaport, 1863–1920), who, armed with folktales collected on these trips, went on to write the famous Yiddish play *The Dybbuk*.

Besides Ansky, other outstanding representatives of Jewish culture participated in these expeditions in different years, including composer and music expert Joel Engel (1867–1927), folklorist Zinovy Kisselhof (1878–1939), and the artist Solomon Yudovin (1892–1954). Using cameras, notepads, sketchbooks, and cylinder machines, the collectors documented everything from songs to curses and proverbs to children's street games and, of course, as much music as they could find, all the while accumulating ceremonial objects, clothing, and folk crafts from local inhabitants.

During 1912–13 the expedition managed to visit and collect materials in towns and villages in the regions of Volhyn and Podolya, the latter probably not far from where the Belf band originated. Documented on hundreds of fragile and already obsolete cylinders, the materials nonetheless became the core of the Jewish Historical Ethnographic Museum collections that opened in St. Petersburg in 1914.

Taken together, commercial company recordings and those made by Ansky's collectors are a cultural time capsule of Jewish communities—songs both popular and traditional, folk tales, *khazones*, and klezmer tunes. Though some Yiddish records were issued under the Soviets in the 1930s, the modest little period from the turn of the century until World War I was the high point of European Jewish recording.

Back in the United States, Emile Berliner concentrated on discs made in the newly emerging "world city," New York. His first Jewish records were of anonymous singers and date from the early 1890s. But by the turn of the century Berliner was issuing credited Yiddish records, most notably by the magician and singer Frank Seiden.

One of the last of the old-time mountebanks, "Professor" Seiden made himself famous early in his career for his acts of legerdemain and illusion. In his autumn years, he retired to a bar he ran on the Bowery.[36] Teaching many up-and-coming magicians—most notably Malini (Galicia-born Max Katz, himself an avuncular figure to Houdini)—Seiden also found time to saunter over to the fledgling recording studios that had popped up in New York City below Fourteenth Street, making his first record in 1901.

From his earliest known recording for Berliner, "Rozhinkes mit Mandlen" (Raisins and Almonds)—already a standard in every Yiddish performer's repertoire—to forgotten broadside-like pieces recorded for Columbia such as the 1903 "Spanish-Amerikaner Shlakht" and "Kapitan Dreyfus," Seiden's work epitomized the repertoire of turn-of-the-century Yiddish singers. In just five years he produced more than two hundred discs, some of the rarest of all American Jewish recordings.

Kalmen Juvelier (1863–1939) also began his recording career with "Rozhinkes mit Mandlen." Born in Lemberg, Poland, of a poor

Kalmen Juvelier's 1904 78 RPM recording of "Rozhinkes mit Mandlen," produced by United Hebrew Disc and Cylinder Record Company.

family, he studied as a *meshoyrer* but abandoned synagogue for stage, joining the itinerant Broder Singers.[37] He then fell in with a traveling group of actors and singers, and, eventually, into the early companies formed by Goldfaden and Goldfaden's rival from Bucharest, "Professor" Moishe Hurwitz.

In 1880 Juvelier and the Hurwitz troupe emigrated to the United States. It didn't take long for Juvelier to become a leading light in the emerging New York Yiddish theater world. He was soon approached by the start-up record companies and cut his teeth at United Hebrew Disc and Cylinder Record Company (UHD&C), when it opened its doors in 1904.[38]

UHD&C, perhaps the most unusual David to Edison's Goliath, was formed by Pierre Long and managed by H. W. Perlman and S.

Rozansky in response to Jews' growing interest in record buying. Perlman already had a modest business selling Perlman pianos, assembled at his factory at 235 Grand Street on New York's Lower East Side. With the popularity of the phonograph, he correctly reasoned that the newly arrived immigrant community would want records of music familiar to them: why should the only manufacturers be non-Jews? Hanging out its shingle by mid-1904, UHD&C opened its offices in the same building as Perlman's piano factory and began issuing records. "We produce recordings of an exclusively Hebrew nature," a company announcement in the January 15, 1905, issue of *Talking Machine World* ballyhooed, introducing the first ethnic-owned, operated, and targeted record company in America.[39]

In 1905 the Yiddish newspaper *Di Amerikaner Froyen Zhurnal un Kompanyon* proclaimed that the UHD&C had arranged to record "Abraham Golfaden interpreting some of his most famous compositions." Sadly, though, those recordings were never made, and Goldfaden's voice is lost to us forever.

UHD&C's entry into recording was its most unusual release and is one of the first documented examples of a pirated Jewish record. Titled "Hashkiveynu" and listed simply as being performed by "Cantor and Choir," the recording was none other than the venerable *khazn* Gershon Sirota performing not "Hashkiveynu" but the retitled "Vehosor Soton." The copy, ineptly transferred from a European Gramophone disc, was issued anonymously to avoid royalty payments.

Located a stone's throw from the Jewish Rialto—Second Avenue—UHD&C brought in the aspiring as well as the newly famous to stand before their recording horns. High-visibility performer/composers like Solomon Smulewitz, Bessie Thomashefsky, and David Kessler and the doyenne Regina Prager sang for UHD&C, as did lesser-known artists like Meyer Goldin and Hyman Shuster, all dipping their ladles into a common pot of songs by Goldfaden, Mogulesko, and Friedsell. Modestly produced, the records most often feature singers accompanied by a lone (Perlman-made?) piano.

UHD&C also recorded bands, like composer Louis Friedsell's stuffy little theater orchestra and a bouncier ensemble led by one A. Golub. Though the majority of pieces these groups recorded were overtures and instrumental versions of the latest theater songs, the 1905 recordings "Popuri," a medley of old-fashioned dance tunes, and "Khosn Kale Mazl Tov," Mogulesko's soon-to-be klezmer standard, are the first "klezmer" pieces recorded in America.

Names unknown and mysterious to us today emerge from the crackly sound of these thick and primitive discs. Spoken introductions precede the performances, announced at a carnival barker's volume: "'March fun Di Tsvey Tanoim,' *geshpilt fun Golub's Band* [March from the Two Seers, played by Golub's band], United Hebrew Record Company."

These intros give us a clue as to how records were made in the days before titles and performers were listed on the cylinders themselves. Unfortunately, UHD&C used the economical but noisy reusable wax cylinder to make the masters for its discs. These recycled cylinders produced a seriously inferior product in which the noisy cylinder can be heard clattering. Though not all UHD&C discs suffered that fate, enough did to sour even the most enthusiastic consumer. Despite this drawback, the company managed to produce some 150 discs in the three years it was in operation. It would be another forty years before a Jewish-owned record company would issue discs for the Jewish listening audience.

By 1909 more than twenty-seven million discs and cylinders had been manufactured in the United States.[40] And though the vast majority were American mainstream and classical recordings, Jewish music was part of the equation.

In the heady days before the First World War, Jewish artists whose names are largely forgotten—William Dory, Hyman Corenfeld, and Hyman Adler—recorded for also-forgotten labels like U.S. Everlasting, Lambert, or Busy Bee. When the dust settled around the various large and small record companies, only two emerged as leaders: the aptly named Victor and slightly more poverty-row Columbia, with Edison the distant third. This situation remained until after World War I.

Victor had claimed the high ground with its superior pressings, prestigious artists, and tony Red Seal label, which featured the records of Gershon Sirota. Though Victor had taken an early interest in Jewish artists, they haughtily hove to their recording of classical and popular artists. It was up to the hungrier Columbia label to carve out a niche by recording less high-toned acts.

Originally a distribution arm of the Edison company, Columbia broke away to take part in the disc revolution Berliner had initiated.[41] Locked out of the high road of name artists, Columbia saw the ethnic market as wholly worth its while. By 1908, the year Columbia issued the first double-sided discs, it had also introduced its new discrete

record series "A," for general popular, and "E," for foreign.[42] These
"E" series records, identified by their distinctive pale green labels,
became a kind of multi-ethnic recording neighborhood. Here, the
various foreign culture groups Columbia recorded lived peacefully
alongside one another, each with its own bilingual catalog.

Record catalogs aimed at Jews talked more about remembering
what was left behind than of a culture emerging in a modern-age
America. A 1914 Columbia Jewish records catalog lured listeners
with this oddly agrarian scenario:

> Long ago, long ago . . . do you remember the time?
> Remember when you lived near the forest of your home
> and birds sang for you throughout the day? And when
> you left home, far, far away you lost the forest and the
> birds? But in your current life the little singers follow
> you regardless of what twists and turns your life takes.
> And now you've made a new better life for yourself and a
> bigger songbird warbles in your home, begs to enter
> your home and to chase away sickness and dispel sad-
> ness, if only you will invite him in. He will sing for your
> little son or daughter the old songs of your town, the
> same ones your mother used to sing to you when you
> were their age. Let the Columbia gramophone do that.
> Let it sing happy songs for you that will make you laugh
> or cry and elicit tears from your eyes. Let the Columbia
> gramophone make you feel calm and lucky once again as
> it used to be long ago when you first listened to the song-
> birds in your forsaken home.

Repertoire was another factor in the marketing of Jewish music. A
1921 Columbia catalog lists, in order of implied importance, patriotic songs, Hebrew "hymns" (cantorials), folk songs, comic recitations
and songs, duets, and dance and instrumental music—which included klezmer music. Still not a big-selling item, klezmer music was
recorded by all manner of musicians in all manner of styles. For
example, in Edison's 1908 catalog, under the heading "Hebrew,"
band selections (which include a wooden rendition of Mogulesko's
"Khosn, Kale Mazl Tov") are credited to the Edison Military Band—
presumably the same Edison's Military Band that a few pages earlier
is credited with playing "St. Patrick's Day Is a Bad Day for Coons."

More and more, the influence of songs first heard on the Yiddish
stage, like Mogulesko's hit, affected what klezmer musicians recorded

The Russische-Jüdische Orchestra, headliners in Columbia's 1914 Hebrew-Jewish catalog.

and performed. Another early popular song, "Die Neshome Fun Mayn Folk" (The Soul of My People), composed by the team of Perlmutter and Wohl (with Boris Thomashefsky) in 1911, found its way onto several instrumental records, including a *tsimbl* and accordion disc made in 1913 by Yankowitz and Goldberg, and even as late as 1927, in a souped-up version by Abe Schwartz's orchestra. In 1914 Perlmutter, Wohl, and Thomashefsky had a hit with the popular "Dem Pastukhl's Kholem" (The Shepherd's Dream), recorded by Meyer Kanewsky, Jacob Medvedieff, and Kalmen Juvelier, and turned into a blazing instrumental version by Abe Schwartz in 1928. This kind of easy transition from stage to dance band would continue as long as prolific composers of the Yiddish theater kept coming up with hit songs.

With the outbreak of World War I, Yiddish records made in Eastern Europe became impossible to obtain. The complicated ownership of Gramophone's multinational branches and the shutting down of borders meant many former European partners were now considered "enemy hostiles." Cut off from the rich music preserves of Europe, domestic labels looked more closely at talent available on this side of the Atlantic, and European-made discs slowly started disappearing from American record catalogs. In May 1914 the band selection in Columbia's catalog featured 78s made by the umlauted "Russische-Jüdische Orchester," shown in the accompanying photograph as a group of severe-looking men posed with two clarinets, three fiddles, three trumpets, and two trombones; toward the back of the catalog came the first true large-ensemble klezmer recordings—those of Abe Elenkrig (1878–1965).

Trumpet player/barber Abe Elenkrig's band—listed in Yiddish as A. Elenkrig's Yidisher Orkester and malapropistically mangled in English below as the Hebrew Bulgarian Orchestra (the band played *bulgars*)—was composed of violin, trombone, piano, and drums, delivering a perky, danceable sound. Columbia's marketing of Elenkrig's records reflects the parallels between the Yiddish dance music of the time and its strong connection to Romanian music; several Elenkrig selections were coissued in the Columbia Romanian catalog, with the band appropriately renamed Orchestra Romaneasca.

At about the same time another Jewish performer, Meyer Kanewsky, began recording cantorial pieces at Columbia. Quickly changing hats, he added Yiddish folk and theater songs under the *nom de disque* M. Guttman, and Ukrainian and Russian folk songs as M. Mironenko. The arrangements for recording were so informal that in one case, Kanewsky made recordings in exchange for merchandise.

When Kanewsky left Columbia for Victor in fall 1915, he took Elenkrig with him, directing a more sophisticated session featuring the expanded ensemble (viola, flute, clarinet, drums, two cornets, two violins, piano, and tuba) that resulted in the record "Di Zilberne Khasene/Nit Bay Motyen" (The Silver Wedding/Not By Motye), which achieved near-hit status.[44]

Smarting from the defection and success of this large and robust orchestra sound, Columbia cast around for someone to take the place of the Elenkrig orchestra. It took almost a year, but the label finally found Abe Schwartz, a young fiddle player, who, with his daughter on piano, would comprise the heart of its Jewish catalog for the next decade and a half.

～3～

THE GOLDEN AGE OF YIDDISH POPULAR MUSIC

AMERICA'S RAPID INDUSTRIALIZATION, a response to its entrance into World War I, didn't end with the successful conclusion of the war. Its peacetime mission was to fulfill the needs of a rising leisure class. This increased tide of consumerism created more outlets for America's rising popular culture and especially for the phonograph. Improvements in the quality of recordings and the machines that played them—and their decreasing cost due to the explosion of companies manufacturing them—made owning records more simple. In 1912 there were only three manufacturers of talking machines in the country; four years later there were forty-five.[1]

Though record players were getting cheaper, record prices remained at the relatively high rate of 75¢ for a ten-inch and $1.25 for the tonier twelve-inch disc in Victor's Red Seal series. Despite these costs, a half-day's pay for many laborers, phonographs and records were becoming more common in the homes of working-class families. And a growing number of these Americans were foreign born.

"Sell your foreigners!" blared a headline in the September 1917 issue of *Voice of the Victor*, the in-house organ for Victor record dealers. Enumerating the ethnic selections available on the label, the article exhorts dealers to nail the foreign trade by hiring multilingual assistants. "A good, live, young Hebrew could probably speak most of these languages well enough to get along," it pointed out, "for Jews are good at selling."

For the first time, a broadening repertoire of popular material was being generated almost too fast for record companies to issue and pressing plants to print. Yiddish popular culture, drawn as it was from traditional, classical, and borrowed elements, was producing a new and vibrant music, reaching the community from local theaters and from the horns of phonographs.

Bursting from its ancillary position in earlier general music catalogs, Jewish music had become a growing commodity. Record companies offered a mix of popular songs, folk songs (recorded in arty, nontraditional style), and cantorials—religious singing as popular as recent songs in the Jewish record market. Extracted from the synagogue, *khazones* was turned from prayer into performance. And with the invention of sound recording, novel issues emerged regarding the *khazn's* relationship to his religion, community, and calling.

Traditional Jews questioned the propriety of recorded prayers that could be played out of context in a profane environment, constituting sacrilege. Although it was now possible to play a record of the holiest of prayers, Kol Nidre, on the holiest day of the year, Yom Kippur—its proper ritual occasion—was it permissible? The utterance of God's name out of context was certain sacrilege to observant Jews, which many cantors dealt with by replacing *adoynoy*, God's sacred name, with the desanctified *adoyshem*.

Musical accompaniment, standard in the recording of theater and popular songs, was a vexing issue when applied to *khazones*. Outside of a few early solo discs and the slightly more plentiful a cappella choir accompaniments—how *khazones* were performed in the *shul*—most recordings made in America featured organ or orchestral accompaniments, none of which would be heard at an Orthodox service.

So why would listeners who sought "authentic" representations of this sacred repertoire be satisfied with performances backed by instrumental accompaniment, which was both stylistically and religiously incongruous? Why would people who understood the function of prayer want to hear truncated forms of Sabbath blessings, High Holiday prayers, or festival chants at inappropriate times? The purchaser of a cantorial 78 RPM disc was probably not planning to pray along with it—as a person might buy an instrumental record to dance to it—but sought instead an emotional, not ritual experience.

Recordings elevated the importance of performance in the success of a cantor—the *sheliakh tsibur* (messenger of the people). Yet ultimately, these recordings did offer listeners some of what prayer in the synagogue setting did: a sense of well-being and reaffirmation, not to mention nostalgia for the old country—the raison d'être for most ethnic records. The comfort and familiarity cantorial records imparted, in addition to a thrilling vocal performance, contributed to their continuing popularity for more than half a century.

These records show how many cantors were bitten by the popular-performance bug, which was revealed not only in their arty renditions of cantorial gems but in the expanded material they recorded. While some, like Leib Glantz, Alter Yechiel Karniol, and David Roitman never strayed from the cantorial repertoire, those who veered from *khazones* generally did so in favor of a Yiddish song or two—including Yosele Rosenblatt and Mordechai Hershman, Moishe Oysher, and Berele Chagy. Others, like Meyer Kanewsky, went even farther afield, recording Ukrainian and Russian songs in addition to their Jewish repertoire.

Then there were cantors who dabbled in opera, beginning with Joel David Strashunsky (1816–1850), the first star *khazn* to succumb to the lure of acceptance in the Gentile world. Known as the Vilna Balabesl (the Little Boss of Vilna), the cantor abandoned his synagogue for the opera houses of Vienna, where he died after a short-lived period of popularity.

Half a century later, cantors like Selmar Cerini, Gershon Sirota, Joseph Shlisky, and Zavel Kwartin attempted to cross over into mainstream art song. Though Rosenblatt's voice got him dubbed "the Jewish Caruso," it was Sirota of whom Caruso himself said, "Thank God he has chosen to employ his heavenly gift in a different field and I do not have to compete with such a formidable challenger in opera."[2]

Despite such dalliance with secular repertoire, early-twentieth-century cantors remained rooted in the synagogue. But their apprentices had no such compunction. Some of these new-generation *meshoyrerim*, William Schwartz and Joseph Feldman, left liturgy behind to become actors-singers, harbingers of a novel performing esthetic. Supplanting the theretofore standard repertoire of the Romanian Yiddish theater, they favored more up-to-date songs by young Jewish-American composers.

Gone were the declaimers and wine cellar singers, the rough-hewn performers trained under Goldfaden. These new singers were refining their Yiddish theater skills based on an American prototype. While retaining the modal familiarities of cantorials, the songs they sang followed turn-of-the-century American-style popular music, with its verse and chorus structure.

Listeners were also becoming more sophisticated, like the records and talking machines that played them. No longer satisfied with a singer backed by a lowly tinkling piano, the record-buying public wanted all a phonograph could give—a full brass band. The accompaniments were generally provided by the label's house orchestras, groups of skilled readers on call for a day's work, who played whatever was put before them. At 9:15 A.M. an operatic coloratura might step up to the horn, at 11:00 A.M. a Ruthenian comic duet, and at 3:15 P.M. an Orthodox cantor. The orchestras backed them all.

Under their conductors' direction, these ensembles created a unified label sound, turning out records more efficiently like the industrial assembly lines record companies sought to emulate. A label like Victor, for example, mostly retained conductors who recorded accompaniments for all their performers, Yiddish and otherwise. From 1924 to 1927, Leroy Shield, for example, recorded dozens of accompaniments for Jewish performers like the Yiddish theater star Molly Picon, before going on to create memorable music for the films of The Little Rascals and Laurel and Hardy at the Hal Roach Studios. Other alumni of the system included military band leader/ragtime orchestra conductor Charles Prince and Edward King, the latter known mostly for his work in developing mainstream American orchestras.

Victor also maintained the Shilkret brothers: Lew, Jack, and most important, Nathaniel, who were hired to direct Victor's "light" music in 1915. "Nat" Shilkret's assignment from 1917 until 1925 was to record hundreds of Yiddish song accompaniments for many of the most popular and influential Yiddish singers of the era. Effective, strong, and clear, these arrangements—akin to the earlier military band sound with more contemporary stylistic elements like slide trombones—are characterized by their complete lack of "Jewish" elements. Even Yiddish composer/conductors frowned on musicians inserting any hint of klezmer style, whether in pit orchestras or on recording dates. Clarinetist Paul Pincus, for example, recalls playing under the baton of Sholom Secunda in the 1930s and being chastised for adding klezmer ornaments to the music for a Yiddish show.

OF ARTISTS AND REPERTOIRE

American Yiddish recording artists drew from a refreshed well of singer/composers who succeeded Old World predecessors like Goldfaden and Zunser. Chief among them was Joseph Rumshinsky (1879–1956). Another product of the *meshoyrer* system, Rumshinsky was born in Vilna, where he began his long career making choir arrangements. He arrived in New York in 1903, working as an arranger for the older generation of composers and collaborating with

Yiddish theater composer Joseph Rumshinsky, c. 1912.

these more seasoned veterans (such as Solomon Smulewitz, with whom he published his first piece, the score for a production of *Nathan the Wise*, in 1906). However, his fame soon outstripped theirs.

A harsh and judgmental man, Rumshinsky was known to berate orchestra members loudly on the bandstand. Clarinetist Max Epstein tells the story of playing with him in a theater when a fire broke out. Rumshinsky took off and was halfway out to the street when he heard the orchestra playing "God Bless America," in an effort to restore calm. He rushed back in screaming: "What kind of crappy music are you playing? Play my music! Stop with that crap here!"

Rumshinsky was also an undeniable force in the formative years of Yiddish musical theater—so much that by 1916 Boris Thomashefsky had tapped him as a co-composer. Their first great collaboration, the klezmer-themed musical *Tsebrokhene Fidele* (Broken Fiddle), was premiered that same year. But their equally fiery temperaments caused the relationship to flounder, and by 1919 Rumshinsky went his own way to score even greater triumphs.

Undaunted, Thomashefsky arranged for the importation of a musical comedy performer who would help redefine modern Yiddish popular performance: Aaron Lebedeff (1873–1960). Born in Homel,

Aaron Lebedeff, Yiddish theater's Al Jolson (1929).

White Russia, Lebedeff studied with a local *khazn* and foiled his family's plans for him to enter a trade by running off to join local Yiddish theater troupes.[3] Indefatigable, he continued to appear with groups in cities like Minsk, even opening his own dancing school in his early twenties.

Inducted into the Russian army during the First World War, Lebedeff was stationed in the Far East. He and his wife remained there to entertain Red Cross workers after the Russians pulled out due to the outbreak of the Revolution.[4] In 1920, while performing in Shanghai, Thomashefsky heard of Lebedeff and sent for him to star in a new musical, *Lyovke Molodyets* (Good Guy Liovke). An immediate hit, "Lebby" had a jaunty and athletic demeanor that matched the high-energy pace emerging in the Yiddish theater. In short order he began his successful strut from one hit show to another. Different yet oddly similar, each musical was built around the massive stage presence—and paint-peeling voice—of this star.

Lebedeff was also an immediate hit in the recording studio. A powerful and resonant tenor, he was an inveterate ad-libber and tinkerer with others' music. He also authored his own songs, most notably "Roumania, Roumania," first recorded in 1925 under the title "Der Freylekher Rumeyner" (The Lively Romanian).

The staying power of the song, which Lebedeff continued to polish and rerecord throughout his career, was due to its theatricality and Romanian style, so popular with Jews. Like its inspiration, the *doina*, the piece begins in a slow, relaxed, free-metered tempo building into a faster bridge section and ending in a wild rush of catcalls, mouth-popping, whistles, and Lebedeff's full catalog of sound effects. (His 1942 version of the song may have made recording history as the first record to end with a mechanical fade-out.) It is a testament to the flexibility of the popular Yiddish milieu that a singer from White Russia with the nickname "der Litvak Komiker" (the Lithuanian Comedian) should become famous for singing a song about Romania.

Another performer who defined the modern Yiddish singer was the actress Molly Picon (1898–1992), the first American-born Jewish performer to achieve Yiddish theater fame. As the daughter of a Yiddish theater wardrobe mistress in Philadelphia, young Molly was a thespian from the start. But unlike such other success stories as Jolson, Jessel, and Cantor, Picon cast her lot with Yiddish entertainers. By age twenty-three, she was starring in her first musical comedy, *Yankele* (Little Yankl), the sort of pants role that would stay with her throughout her career. The show, a hit upon its 1921 opening at Kessler's Second Avenue Theater, was scored by the reigning star composer of Yiddish musicals, Joseph Rumshinsky, with lyrics by Picon herself. Her irrepressible zest and high-octane antics were a welcome relief from the histrionics of the more corpulent, forearm-flung-across-the-forehead-style Yiddish actresses then populating the stage.

Molly Picon in a publicity photo from the 1925 play *The Radio Girl*.

Picon's Yiddish also reflected her Philadelphia upbringing. To improve her diction, her husband/manager Jacob Kalich took her on an extended tour of Europe, where she could learn authentic European Yiddish and polish her image to boot. While there she starred in several movies, including the recently restored six-reel silent comedy *East and West*. When she returned to the United States Picon began to exploit her newly buffed image by recording the songs made popular from her last show, *Yankele*, including the title song and "Ikh Hob a Katar in Mayn Noz" (I Have a Cold in My Nose), a comic novelty song of a type popular in vaudeville.

Compared with the voices of Yiddish singers of her day like Nellie Casman, Picon's thin, trilly, fussy soprano sounds weak and inconsequential. Casman (1896–1984)—who had hits with her and Samuel Steinberg's composition "Yosl, Yosl" in 1922, and David Meyerowitz's "Vi Zenen Mayne Zibn Gite Yor" (Where Are My Seven Good Years?), in 1925—was a composer and a robust, lusty singer whose persona was every bit as vital as her material. She specialized in comic material, such as "Epes Is Dermeyer Mit Mir" (Something's Wrong With Me), in which she laments, "I feel a little funny and I'm eating for two," while stumbling around the stage in an obviously pregnant state, and "Mister Malekh Hamoves, Ikh Bin Busy" (Mr. Angel of Death, I'm Busy). She even went on to record some of Picon's songs, including "Molly Dolly" and "Tzipke." But the stronger voice never attained the stardom the lesser one did. Picon's stage mannerisms and easy blend of Yiddish and English made her the audience favorite.

From 1924 to 1932 Picon collaborated with Rumshinsky, producing one hit musical after another. Nineteen twenty-five was particularly productive, yielding three shows: *Shmendrik*, *Dos Tsigayner Meydl*, and *Molly Dolly*. The latter included an uncharacteristic number for Picon, "Vos Zol Ikh Ton Az Ikh Hob Im Lib?" (What Should I Do As I Love Him?), inspired by the 1922 success of Fanny Brice's "My Man." Each song, similar in feel to French chanteuse Edith Piaf's repertoire, features a woman lamenting the cruelty of her lover. It was no surprise that Brice (née Borach) should be emulated by Picon, who some contemporary papers referred to as "The Jewish Fanny Brice."[5]

Brice and Picon were both broad comics whose kinetic styles greatly pleased their audiences. But Brice portrayed an endless series of clumsy, buffoonish Jewish women in a grimacing fashion. Theater critic Brooks Atkinson, a Brice devotee, praised her performance of a

"Yiddishe" Peter Pan for its "broadly Jewish style of grotesque vulgarity."[6] Recordings like "Sheik of Avenue B" (1921), "I'm an Indian" (1922), and "Becky Is Back in the Ballet" (1922) placed Jews in comically incongruous circumstances. Brice's vocals are replete with exaggerated pronunciations and promiscuous "oy, oy, oys." Side one of the two-part Victor record "Mrs. Cohen at the Beach" (1927), a dialect monologue about a Jewish matron taking her family for a day trip to the seaside, concludes with Brice enumerating the delicacies brought along for lunch—"And we've got h-a-a-a-a-am . . ."—a signal to turn that record over.

Unlike her Ziegfeld Follies costar Bert Williams, the talented black singer/comedian who reluctantly donned blackface makeup

Saxophonist Nathan Glantz recorded this 1927 instrumental version of the Billy Rose/Fred Fisher "hebe" novelty song "Yiddishe Charleston," which asked: "Have you heard the latest noise/written by two Jewish boys?"

before stepping in front of the curtain, Brice happily created more and more grotesque Jewish characters to the delight of mainstream audiences. At one point Brice, feigning disinterest in "Jewish jingles," lamented to the press that she needed a "good coon song" like the ones she used to do.[7]

When it came to portraying negative Jewish stereotypes, Brice was hardly alone. Another Jewish comedienne, Rhoda Bernard, predated her. She produced "Jew" records from 1916 to 1918, including "Rosie Rosenblatt, Stop Your Turkey Trot," "Roll Your Yiddisha Eyes for Me," and Irving Berlin's "Cohen Owes Me Ninety-Seven Dollars." In 1916 she and Lester Bernard issued an English and Yiddish record, "The Delegate and the Shopgirl of Cloak and Shirtmaker's Union," for Columbia's Jewish catalog, making her the only comic performer to issue recordings in both the general and Jewish series.

As they steadily released authentic Yiddish music for the Jewish trade, major record companies increasingly presented stereotypical "hebe" recordings in their general record catalogs. One highly popular series of records was launched in England in 1914 with Monroe Silver's "Cohen on the Telephone," a dialect monologue of a Jewish tenant attempting to get his landlord to fix a broken window. The immigrant's inability to communicate, heightened by the novelty of early telephone technology, made for humor that is the audio equivalent of someone slipping on a banana peel.

Wildly popular, the "Cohen" concept spread to the United States, where it spawned a gaggle of "Hebrew" monologists including Joe Hayman, Barney Bernard, and Harry Marks, elbowing their way to the studios to make another of the fifty "Cohen" recordings that followed the original. In its wake the series inspired a host of "Cohen" character knockoffs: "Levinsky," "Goldstein," an "Einstein," and several competing "Levis."

Jewish performers like Willie and Eugene Howard (born Lefkowitz) also plied the stage "Jew" trade. Their 1910 song "That's Yiddisha Love" has a father advising his son to marry not a beautiful woman but one who can help out in the store and who "don't worry about clothes and a head full of fancy pompadoodles/but one who'll work and make gefilte fish and noodles." Willie Howard was also responsible for the first recording of Jack Yellen and Lew Pollack's "My Yiddishe Mama," in 1925, although it was Sophie Tucker who had the huge hit with her 1928 version in English with Yiddish on the flip side.[8]

Monologist Julian Rose recorded vaudeville-style skits and songs including "Levinsky's Jubilee," in 1917. Five years later came his

Sheet music cover for Eddie Cantor's Jewish knock-off of the 1920s' hit song "My Mammy."

"Yiddisher Jazz," about some Jewish musicians who sound better when they eat than when they play their instruments. Rose, who continued with his "Jew" portrayals long after the others had quit, felt the wrath of the B'nai B'rith, which organized protests in the 1930s in front of the venues in which he appeared.

Eddie Cantor also made several "Jew" recordings. A 1925 composition he co-wrote with Alex Gerber conflates Al Jolson's "Mammy" and Jack Yellin's and Lew Pollack's "My Yiddishe Mama," producing "My Yiddisha Mammy," who "don't play a banjo or a ukelele/But her lullabye is 'Eli, Eli.'" Cantor also weighed in with "(Lena is the Queen of) Palesteena" (1920). The song, about a portly girl from the Bronx who journeys to Palestine to shed her excess poundage by playing the concertina day and night, was a follow-up to the success earlier that year of an instrumental recording of the tune by the Original Dixieland Jazz Band. The dixieland band used the minor-key section of the popular klezmer melody "Nokh a Bisl" (Just a Little More) as its main theme and, in case the ethnic origins weren't clear enough, inserted sixteen measures of the ubiquitous Jewish melody "Ma Yofus" as a bridge. In Cantor's version, the Jewish mile-marker is a four-bar paraphrase of Mogulesko's "Khosn, Kale Mazl Tov," plopped into the middle of the arrangement.

Ted Lewis provided a parallel song in his 1931 "Egyptian Ella"— another overweight woman who journeys to Egypt because "she weighs 220 but she don't care/they like them a'plenty way out there." He concluded his recording with the opening phrase of "Hatikvah," the future national anthem of Israel.

Lewis, "the High-Hatted Tragedian of Jazz," was a consummate entertainer whose tag line "Is Everybody Happy?" became a catch-phrase in America. Born Theodore Leopold Friedman, Lewis grew up in Circleville, Ohio, where it is unlikely he ever heard klezmer music, let alone played it—although more than one listener claims to hear traces of it on his records. Lewis's band at the time of the "Ella" recording included soon-to-be-jazz-greats Benny Goodman, George Brunies, and Muggsy Spanier as well as trombonist Harry Raderman, who did double-duty on American and klezmer bandstands.

As soon as an American tune, dance step, or catchphrase came into vogue, Jewish recording artists almost instantaneously reinterpreted it for the Yiddish audience. One performer who developed a particular sweet tooth for recording Yiddish versions of English songs was comedian/singer Peisachke Burstein (1896–1986). Brought to the United States in 1923 by Boris Thomashefsky, Burstein struck it big—but first he had to be repackaged a little. Thomashefsky was unhappy with his protegé's first name, Pavlusha, and asked him to come up with something more "Jewish." When Burstein mentioned his mother's pet name for him, Peisachke, Thomashefsky slapped him on the back and cried "That's it!" And so it was.

As Thomashevsky had earlier misbilled Lebedeff as "Der Litvak Komiker," he now dubbed Burstein "Der Vilner Komiker" (The Comedian from Vilna), though he was really from Warsaw. No matter: when audiences got a load of Burstein's peppery delivery and characteristic whistling, it made no difference where he was from. By the mid-1920s records like "Yes Sir, Zi Iz Mayn Kale" (Yes Sir, That's My Baby), "Oh, Katarina," "Hallelujah, Ikh Bin a Bom," and "Sonny Boy"—his version of Al Jolson's lachrymose hit—made Burstein a hot-off-the-press Yiddish performer.

American tastes of another sort found their way into Yiddish songs in 1926, via Molly Picon's and Joseph Rumshinsky's "Hot Dogs," a paean to Brooklyn's Coney Island from their show *Dem Kleynem Mazik* (The Little Devil), and Lebedeff's culinary cross-cultural *Hot Dogs un Knishes*. Frank Silver and Irving Cohn's "Yes, We Have No Bananas" (Yes! Mir Hobn Keyn Banenez), sung by Gus Goldstein for Columbia in 1923—which featured a chorus performance in Litvak, Galitzianer, and Italian dialects—generated Joseph Tanzman's answer song "Gevalt! Di Banenez" (Yikes! The Bananas), by David Medoff. Even that most non-Jewish of symbols, Santa Claus, found his way onto a Yiddish disc by Joseph Tanzman and Anna Zeeman ("Der Yiddisher Santa Claus," Pathé, 1923).

Current events were constant inspiration for Yiddish songs. In 1911, after the tragic fire at the Triangle Shirtwaist Company, songwriters Anschel Schor and Joseph Rumshinsky composed "Elegy on the Triangle Fire Victims," recorded by Simon Paskal and also William Schwartz. The sinking of the Titanic the next year generated not only Smulewitz's "Der Naser Keyver" (The Watery Grave) but also an "El Mole Rachamim"—the prayer for the dead—sung by Yosele Rosenblatt, in one of his earliest American recorded performances.

The Great War was a good opportunity for every Jewish émigré artist to wave the flag. When it came to World War I songs, nobody beat singer Anna Hoffman for sheer output: "Der Yiddisher Volunteer" and "Vayber, Yente Geyt af Milkhome" (Ladies, Yente's Going to War) in 1916; Perlmutter and Wohl's "Yente Geyt Zich Registin" (Yente Goes to Register) the next year, when America entered the conflict; and later David Meyerowitz's "Tfiloh Milkhome" (War Prayer).

Isidore Lillian's 1918 "Goodbye Kaiser/A Gris fin di Trenches" (A Greeting From the Trenches), sung in Yiddish, is in a sprightly major key that includes a snatch of "Dixie." Less red-white-and-blue is the slightly subversive second verse: "As each nation now has a Jewish legion, let's go liberate our Jewish homeland." Clarinetist Naftule

American record companies capitalized on the ethnic music market. Above, Okeh's Statue of Liberty label release of Joseph Cherniavsky's "Dance, Song, and Wine."

Brandwein also got on the bandwagon, with instrumental discs "Der Yiddisher Soldat in di Trenches" (The Jewish Soldier in the Trenches) and "Tsurik fun Milkhome" (Back From the War.)

The outbreak of the Russian revolution in 1917 brought forth a slew of material commemorating the downfall of the hated czar. Louis Gilrod and Gus Goldstein wrote the vaudeville skit *Zar Nikolay un Charlie Chaplin* (Columbia, 1918), in which Chaplin, taking pity on the deposed Russian ruler, offers him a job taking pies in the face in Hollywood. There were paeans to the fledgling Soviet state—like Joseph Rumshinsky's 1922 "A Grus fun dem Nayem Russland" (A Greeting From the New Russia), sung by William Robyn—and more than a few pans of it, most notably Abe Schwartz and Morris

Tessler's "Lenin un Trotsky," which tells of a committed Communist who arrives in the United States, shaves off his beard, and runs a sweatshop worse than any capitalist's.

But the oddest song of this genre is "Meshiakh Kimt (Men Zogt Meshiakh Iz a Bolshevik)" (The Messiah Is Coming: They Say the Messiah Is a Bolshevik), the story of the Messiah's long-awaited arrival and his inability to get past Ellis Island, recorded in 1922 by Yiddish vaudeville star Jacob Jacobs. Jacobs was one of a bevy of entertainers who plied their trade in Yiddish vaudeville—a venue every bit as boisterous as its American counterpart—and the hundreds of records these performers made are an unparalleled glimpse of a typical Yiddish vaudeville show. These three-minute distillations of what Yiddish audiences clamored to see are dependably formulaic: a bit of a skit, a song, and some brisk closing music with which to dance off into the wings.

The quintessential Yiddish vaudeville routine was based on the age-old language tussle between Galitzianer (Jews from western Poland) and Litvaks (from the northern region of Lithuania). "Galitzianer versus Litvak" duels stood in for the dialect records found in non-Jewish circles and became a long-popular theatrical device used by recording artists for several labels.

Other topics for Yiddish vaudeville were broad, taking in all manner of daily events in the lives of contemporary Jews. "Froyen Nakht in a Terkisher Bod" (Ladies Night in a Turkish Bath; Victor, 1923), with Anna Hoffman and Betty Jacobs, was a ribald and earthy look at subjects from Litvaks and Galitzianer to men in general; "Lemel un Zayn Zeks Vayber" (Lemel and His Six Wives; Victor, 1922) is a surreal "laughing" record wherein the male character (Jacob Jacobs) tells the increasingly uproarious Anna Hoffman details of how each of his wives died—the last, of course, from laughing too hard.

But no theme was as popular or long-lived as the character Yente Telebende. Born in a series of newspaper sketches by the Yiddish humorist B. Kovner, Yente Telebende—and her husband, Mendel—leapt from the pages of the *Forverts* and onto the stage of the Yiddish theater. The phenomenal success of the strong-willed and argumentative Yente Telebende, who gave as good as she got, introduced a term into the Yiddish and English language: *yente*, supplanting the Yiddish word *yakhne*.

From 1916 to 1929, Yiddish vaudeville teams like Gus Goldstein and Clara Gold, Anna Hoffman and Jacob Jacobs, and Sam Silverbush and Sadie Wachtel wrote, recorded, and performed nearly one hundred "Yente Telebende" discs, which, like the "Cohen" records found in the general catalog, placed the character in a dizzying array of circumstances: "Yente Kholemt fin a Luft Shif" (Yente Dreams of an Air Ship), "Yente Telebende Loyft far Mayor" (. . . Runs for Mayor), "Yente Telebende Hot Faynt di Mener" (. . . Hates the Men), "Yente Hot a Good Time in Coney Island," "Yente Vert a Jeniter" (Yente Becomes a Janitor) and, of course, "Yente Blaybt a Yente" (Yente Remains a Yente).

The difference between the "Cohen" series' "Jew" humor and Jewish humor in the "Yente" records is clear in two 1922 recordings on the same subject. "Cohen Takes a Friend to the Opera" (Vocallion) centers on how Cohen can sneak from the cheap seats into more expensive ones. In "Yente Zitst in der Opera" (OKeh) the comic payoff is Yente musing on how the corpulent soprano can manage to sing with a spear sticking out of her chest.

Not everyone who sought the limelight crossed over into more mainstream popular culture. Some, like cantor Yosele Rosenblatt, loathed it. Joseph "Yosele" Rosenblatt (1882–1933) was born in the Ukrainian shtetl of Belaya Tserkov, where he was a *meshoyrer* under his father, a cantor. Rosenblatt himself became a star *khazn* and a composer before emigrating in 1912 to become the cantor at the First Hungarian Congregation Ohab Zedek in New York. Adored by his congregation, he was soon a favorite on records, making 78s for both Victor and Columbia.

In 1917 Rosenblatt was offered a thousand dollars a night to appear in the Chicago Opera Company's production of *La Juive*, but turned it down because he considered the singing of secular music incompatible with the role of the cantor. Moral rectitude was no longer an option by the early 1920s, however, when he was fleeced by a con man into coinvesting in a luxury *mikve* (ritual bathouse) and Orthodox Yiddish paper, and forced to enter vaudeville to pay back his debts.

This description of his act—one of the most poignant and telling views of the Jewish presence in vaudeville—is a firsthand account by the young professional vaudevillian Gypsy Rose Lee, who toured the circuit with the headlining Dainty June Company in the 1920s:

> Opening day in Cincinnati we scrambled out of the taxicab in front of the theatre. A man on a ladder was putting up the names of the acts on the marquee. A few letters of June's name were already up, but above it, in much larger letters, was the name Cantor J. Rosenblatt.

Yosele Rosenblatt, c. 1925

Mother repeated the name out loud, a look of bewilder-
ment on her face. "Why," she said, "I never heard of the
act." Other stars had been billed over us on the Orpheum
Circuit. Alice Brady had top billing when we worked
with her. Fanny Brice had headlined, and so had Sophie
Tucker and Olga Petrova. Mother didn't like it, but if the
act was, in her estimation, a real star act, she would
begrudgingly take second billing.

Gordon, the company's Jewish road manager, tried to explain the order of things to the fiery-tempered stage mother.

> "If anyone deserves top billing this man does. He's the most famous cantor in the world, Rose. He makes Victrola records; people come from miles around to hear him sing in a synagogue."
>
> "I don't care where he's played," Mother said evenly. "I've never heard of him and his name comes down, and June's goes up, or we don't go on."

Appeased with a higher quality dressing room, Rose finally relents. Then young Gypsy gets her first glimpse of Rosenblatt, who is pointed out to her by Gordon:

> I looked at the man again, then I looked at Gordon to see if he was looking where I was looking. I was sure Gordon meant someone else. The man I saw couldn't possibly be billed over us. His black suit was shabby and not even very clean. He was almost comical with his long, curly brown beard and the skullcap on the back of his head.

Later, at the matinee, she watches from the wings as Rosenblatt steps out onstage:

> With a drum roll and a cymbal crash the orchestra stopped playing. All the lights in the theater went on, not just the stage lights, but the house lights in the audience, too. The manager of the theater stepped through the curtain and said, "We are proud to introduce Cantor Joseph Rosenblatt." He pointed to the wings as he exited, and after a long stage-wait the man with the beard and the little skullcap walked slowly to the center of the stage. There was no music to bring him on, no spotlight on him. Before the show that day he had asked for this. Plain white lights, he had said, and no entrance music.
>
> The garish white lights made him look even more shabby. His suit was wrinkled and one trouser leg was caught up in the top of his high-laced shoe. The silence in the audience and the stillness in the orchestra pit were strange and untheater-like. He blinked his eyes at the

brightness, then suddenly, almost frighteningly, one note broke through the silence. It was a high, piercing sound like a wail. There was a sadness in it that choked me. The note faded away and I could hear the audience catch its breath almost as though it was one person.

The orchestra played softly as the Cantor began to sing. It wasn't a song I had ever heard before and I couldn't understand the Hebrew words but I knew he was singing about all the sadness in the world. He had the clearest, purest voice I had ever heard. There was a gentleness and strength, and warmth in it. I felt that if God were to sing to us, this is how His voice would sound.

Abruptly, and much too soon, it was over. The Cantor just stopped singing and without a nod or a bow he turned toward the wings and walked slowly off the stage. The cheap, coarse material of his coat brushed against my arm as he passed me. He walked straight toward the stage door and out onto the street. The stage door closed behind him.

The hushed silence in the audience broke as though someone had cracked a whip. Applause filled the theater. Then someone shouted, "More! More!" and someone else began to stomp his feet. Soon the theater rang with the noise of their shouting and stomping. The aisles began to fill with people rushing toward the stage. "Encore. Encore, more!," they yelled.

Backstage there was panic. The stage manager was shouting out orders, "I don't care where he went, find him! He's got to go out there and take a bow! Find him for God's sake before we have a riot on our hands!"

The applause and shouting from the audience were a deafening roar. The musicians crouched close to the wall in the pit away from the railing where the audience pushed and shoved as they shouted for the Cantor to come back. The moving-picture screen was quickly lowered behind the front curtain, the stage manager screaming into a phone to the front booth, "Get that newsreel on, hurry! We've got to quiet this mob!"

Then the orchestra leader tapped the stand with his baton and the musicians came to attention. "The Anthem," he said hoarsely, and as they played "The Star-

Spangled Banner" the audience quieted down, and in a little while they filed reluctantly out of the theater.

Before the show that night the stage manager told the Cantor that singing in a theater was different from singing in a synagogue. "You have to take bows," he explained. "You have to sing an encore or two—"

The Cantor listened patiently, nodding his head from time to time in agreement. But when he finished his act that night he walked straight across the stage and out the stage door. But this time the stage manager was prepared. The moving-picture screen was in position and the newsreel flashed on the screen the moment the Cantor exited. Every show that week, it was the same way. The newsreel would go on and the audience would applaud all through it, shouting and screaming for an encore, but the Cantor had gone back to his Synagogue.

Mother said it was the greatest piece of showmanship she had ever seen. Later, she agreed with Gordon that the Cantor had more than just showmanship. "He could be the biggest thing in vaudeville," she said, "if he'd just dress up the act a little."⁹

THE RISE OF THE MODERN KLEZMER ENSEMBLE

As the quality and quantity of performers in the cantorial and popular sections of the Jewish catalogs increased, labels began to seek klezmer-style musicians to fill out their instrumental sections. Israel J. Hochman, one of the earliest Yiddish song accompanists in the American recording arena, was also known for his klezmer recordings.

Hochman surfaced in 1916, recording an unsuccessful test record for Victor. Another test two years later, in which he directed the orchestra of fiddler Max Leibowitz, was again rejected by Victor. In 1919 Hochman had better luck at the Emerson company, then entering the ethnic music fray and looking for someone to accompany its small stable of Yiddish singers. He came on for a few sessions as an arranger/conductor for singers including Joseph Feldman, Clara Gold, and Simon Paskal.

Hochman also recorded three instrumental records for Edison. But they failed to find an audience, at least partly because—unlike Victor and Columbia records, which could be played on each other's machines—Edison records had to be played on a special Edison machine, an additional expense working-class record buyers were unwilling to make. And the records are characterized by the band's stilted, small sound, as if they are hemmed in not only by stiff arrangements but by the sonic limitations of the Edison disc.

Hochman recorded a range of material: Yiddish dance music, selections from Tchaikovsky and Liszt (Emerson, 1919), and several of his own compositions for Brunswick: klezmer tunes "Bessaraber Khosid'l" and "Kamanetzer Bulgar" and songs like "Ikh Hob Moyre Far Mayn Vayb" (I Fear My Wife), and "Tsiyon Mayn Heylik Land" (Zion, My Holy Land).

By mid-1916 an ensemble referred to alternately as the Jewish Orchestra and Orchestra Romaneasca was issuing discs for Columbia's Romanian and Jewish catalogs. By the next year a quintet under the name Oriental Orchestra recorded a pair of "Russian" tunes, a *sher* and a *bulgar*. This was the first offering of one of the most important klezmer bandleaders in recording history: Abe Schwartz (1881–1963).

As a child growing up just outside of Bucharest, Schwartz was actively discouraged from music-making by his father, a fine tinsmith

Bowling equipment manufacturer Brunswick also produced records, like I. J. Hochman's 1921 "Russian Sher," above.

who wanted his son to join the trade. "He went through hell to become a musician," his daughter Bebe recalled. "His father hated him to be one." Still, young Schwartz managed to develop his playing and composing skills.

In 1899, when Schwartz was eighteen, he and his parents emigrated to the United States, where he met David Nodiff, a part-time composer and artists and repertoire (A&R) man for Columbia. A&R men were the bridge between record companies and performers and, for the purposes of ethnic catalogs, to the general community. In 1917 Nodiff hired Schwartz to head up instrumental record performances and to act as his truffle hound, helping to sniff out Jewish talent for Columbia.

"[Nodiff] was very important to my father because he was the guiding factor in producing all those recordings," Bebe Schwartz said. And Nodiff and Schwartz went on to cowrite songs of their own, including "Di Bobe Ligt in Kempet" (Grandma's With Child) in 1924.

In 1917 Schwartz served as bandleader on three sessions producing a total of seven records, including "Tants, Tants Yiddlekh" (Dance, Dance Little Jews), originally known as "Ma Yofus," the early klezmer "hit" that had come to be regarded by non-Jews as a typical "Jewish" tune. It is not hard to understand why "Tants, Tants Yiddlekh" was so popular. The highly recognizable tune is energetic and expansive, a perfect dance record. Columbia re-released it several times, even targeting it for Latin American distribution under the title "Continua Bailando-Baile Nupcial Hebreo," credited to the "Orquestra Oriental." And non-Jewish renditions include the 1927 "Oj, Pidu Ja Szicher Wicher," subtitled "Zhidowska" (Little Jewish Girl), by the Ukrainian fiddler Pawlo Humeniuk.

It didn't take long for Schwartz to get into the world of Yiddish theater. By 1919 he had published his first song, "Dos Zekele Mit Koyln" (The Little Bag of Coals), and recorded it—thanks to David Nodiff—leading the orchestra behind Yiddish theater star and fellow Columbia artist Abe Moskowitz.

The same year Schwartz increased his recorded output at Columbia by adding several Polish and Russian sides as the Orkiestra Wiejska and Russky Narodny Orkestr. The Jewish records, meanwhile, finally began being credited to the Abe Schwartz Orchestra.

In 1920 Schwartz solidified his standing as a composer. Adapting traditional materials, he assiduously copyrighted more than thirty-five tunes, a feeding frenzy of *shers*, *bulgars*, *freylekhs*, and *khosidls* with assembly line titles like "Russian Sher no. 105" and "Hebrew Bulgars nos. 21, 24."[10] Some originals—"A Glezele Vayn" (A Glass of Wine)

and the folk song adaptation "A Yor Nokh Mayn Khasene" (A Year
After My Wedding) among them—were registered in anticipation of
their being recorded, during a series of sessions from March through
July of that year.

From this productive series came Schwartz's most personal set of
instrumental records. Usually, his fiddle playing was buried in the

PUBLISHED NOVEMBER 1st, 1920.

Bandleader Abe Schwartz and his reluctant accompanist, daughter Sylvia,
age twelve.

grand mix of instruments he amassed for his ensemble recordings, but in May 1920, he entered the studio with only a piano accompanist: his twelve-year-old daughter, Sylvia. "Sylvia was a wonderful pianist," Bebe Schwartz says of her sister. "And he couldn't wait to—you know, she was the firstborn: he couldn't wait. She practiced all the time and she was not too happy about it. In fact, she hated it."

Trained from age eight, Sylvia Schwartz (1908–1985) struggled as intensely not to be a musician as her father had striven to become one. Unlike her father, she lost. By the time of the 1920 Columbia sessions Schwartz, needing someone for his upcoming solo recording, pressed the girl into service, dressing her to look older for the publicity photo. In ruffled petticoats and with more than a touch of lip rouge, the preteen exuded the air of a twenty-year-old.

Billed as the "National Hora Parts One and Two" (the first side is in fact an extended *doina*), the recording evokes the scene of a restaurant. The disc opens with Nodiff ordering a bottle of wine and offering Schwartz $10 to play him a tune "on the two strings"—a popular trick wherein the fiddler switches the two inner strings on the violin, imparting a rich, bagpipelike effect.

The tunes are played with brio and relaxed enthusiasm as Schwartz leans into his fiddle, the pianist anticipating the twists and turns of her father's performance. An interesting throwback to a much older style of playing, Sylvia's piano stands in for the by-then-outdated *tsimbl*. The performance was so much a throwback that these records did not sell well at all and are among the rarest of Schwartz's recordings. Columbia did not release the likes of them again.

Columbia bolstered its klezmer arsenal with another émigré bandleader, Lieutenant Joseph Frankel (1885–1953). Frankel was born in Kiev and began studying music at age five. In 1896 he began his conservatory studies, graduating with honors at seventeen. Inducted into the czarist army, he was named bandleader of the 150th Infantry, the "Tomansky" regiment, which he headed up for three years. In 1904 he came to the United States on a concert tour as the head of the 14th Regiment military band.

World War I broke out while Frankel was on tour in South America with a Russian symphony orchestra. Stranded, he opted for American citizenship and was commissioned at the rank of lieutenant as bandleader for the First New York Field Artillery.[11] After the war, still sporting his rank in name if not in actual commission, Lt. Frankel began his very brief recording career. Pictured in the pages of the Columbia catalog in full military regalia, clarinetist Frankel cut a dashing figure.

Frankel's Yiddish-style instrumentals demonstrate a warm feeling for the music's varied textures. From the heated and energetic pace of compositions like "Fraytik Nokhn Tsimes" (Friday After the Vegetable Stew) to the introspective "Dem Rebin's Nigun (Oy Tate)" (The Rabbi's Tune; Oh, Daddy) Frankel's handful of Jewish records—eighteen side altogether—are little gems.

In 1919 he returned to Columbia's studios with some of his latest compositions: "Aheym, Kinderlakh, Aheym" (One Step), "Yiddelakh" (A Shimmy), and "Yiddishe Blues," conscious attempts to bridge Yiddish music with popular American dance forms. Stiff and clumsy, these records show that Frankel better understood what attracted the dance-hungry public than he did the music itself. He was the first in a series of Jewish bandleader/composers who attempted to cross over into American pop idioms only to be stymied by lack of insight into what made them tick. Given that his "Yiddishe Blues," for example, exhibits no trace of blues structure or hint of a blue note, it's perhaps merciful that another of his compositions, "Yiddishe Jazz," was never recorded.

Seeking to rival Columbia's stable of klezmer performers, the Victor company picked up a Philadelphia-based clarinetist/bandleader named Harry Kandel (1885–1943). Born in Lemberg to a family in the lumber business, Kandel had musical gifts that must have come as a surprise to his otherwise nonmusical family. Thanks to his talent, he was accepted to the Odessa Conservatory of Music. After serving a short stint in the czarist army, Kandel arrived in New York in 1905 and soon found work playing clarinet in the Great Lafayette Band, then touring the Keith-Orpheum vaudeville circuit, and later with Buffalo Bill's Wild West Show.

Just before World War I, Kandel moved south to Philadelphia, where Jewish cultural life was as varied as it was in New York. Several Yiddish theaters housed a variety of shows: the Arch Street Theater, a one-time vaudeville house saved from destruction by the incoming Jewish population; the Standard, at Twelfth and South Street; and the National, on the corner of Callowhill and Tenth. Each theater offered the local Jewish community a panoply of melodramas, musicals, and touring Yiddish acts that kept them up-to-date with the larger cultural center of New York. And each theater required large, adept orchestras to play for its constantly changing shows.

But Kandel's primary emphasis had become mainstream American music. He worked with John Philip Sousa's band in a series of concerts at Willow Grove Park and in 1916 led an Atlantic City dance band called Harry Kandel's Famous Inlet Orchestra. Then

Label of a Victor recording by the Kandel orchestra.

Victor's A&R department—familiar with Kandel from the Sousa band, which the label recorded in November 1915—targeted him to spearhead its emerging klezmer catalog.[12]

Victor reacted fast to the phenomenal 1917 success of Columbia's "Tants, Tants Yiddlakh" by staging a recording session before the year ended. Harry Kandel entered the Victor studios and recorded two sides, "A Freylakh fun der Khupe/Odessa Bulgarish" (A Lively Dance from the Wedding/*Bulgar* from Odessa). His full-bodied orchestra—two cornets, four violins, a flute, viola, trombone, tuba, piano, and Kandel on clarinet—stormed through these pieces. Victor had a winner.

In two weeks Kandel and company were back in the studio, this time doubling their output to produce, among other offerings, "Di Mama Iz Gegangen in Mark Arayn" (Mama's Gone to Market), quaintly subtitled "Old Hebrew Song from Odessa," and the first recording of "Der Shtiler Bulgar" (The Quiet Bulgar), a tune that twenty years later would put a new spin on American 78s.

The problem of identifying and naming songs, never before an issue, became almost epidemic. New titles needed to be thought up to be fitted to tunes just recorded. A letter to Edward King at Victor about some recently released Abe Schwartz discs points to the difficulty:

> We are enclosing an advertisement of the Columbia company showing that they have listed two Jewish wedding music records. It happens that these are the identical titles suggested by Mr. Kandel in his list . . . and [Kandel] asks if you want any of these wedding music records by him?[13]

Kandel, like so many klezmer musicians, plumbed other repertoires. In 1918 he recorded a polka and several mazurkas, releasing the records under the name Polska Orkiestra Tancowa.

Kandel's presence was magnetic and he soon became the hub of Philadelphia's Jewish music scene. Among the fine musicians who played in the Kandel orchestra over the years were percussionist Jacob "Jake" Hoffman (scion of a still-popular family of Philadelphia percussionists), clarinetist/bandleader Itzikl Kramtweiss, flute/piccolo player Israel Chazin, and multi-instrumentalist Kol Katz (uncle of Klezmer Conservatory Band director Hankus Netsky).

Kandel took great pains to get his performances right. His recordings show a leader's firm hand, with tight discipline in the various sections and rock-steady rhythms. His regular recorded output over a ten-year period came to be considered *the* Philadelphia klezmer repertoire, so unique that musicians who played jobs in nearby New York were obliged to learn a completely different set of tunes.

In May 1921, Kandel produced a dozen selections, including traditional wedding pieces like a *patsh tants* and *broyges tants*; the by-then "traditional" composition of Zelig Mogulesko, "Khosn, Kale Mazl Tov"; several tunes ascribed to the Hasidic repertoire; "A Yor Nokh Mayn Khasene" (a reworking of Abe Schwartz's disc for Columbia of the previous April), and a non-Jewish dance tune (a Russian *komarinska).* That year the assiduous arranger and orchestrator also composed tunes for the first time, including "Ba a Glezele Vayn" (A Glass of Wine) and "Azoy Fayft Min un a Shviger" (That's How We Fool a Mother-in-Law).

By the time Kandel had begun making records, standard discs were ten inches (approximately three minutes) or twelve inches

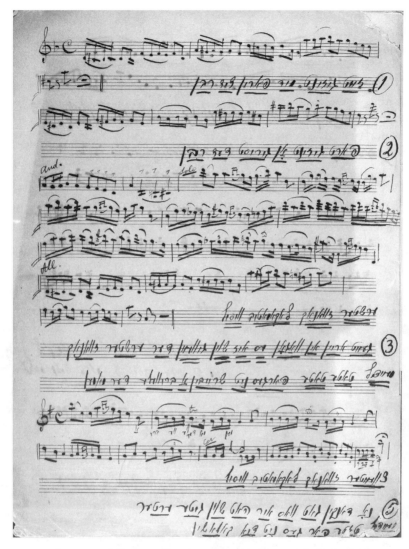

A page from Kandel's score for the 1924 Victor record playlet "Di Hasidim Forn Tsum Rebin" (The Hasidim Travel to Their Rebbe). (*Courtesy Doris Kandel*)

(approximately four minutes), the latter reserved for more prestigious performers or recordings deemed worthy of the longer running time—in the Jewish catalog mostly cantorials. The only klezmer record ever issued in twelve-inch format was "Di Hasidim Forn Tsum Rebin/A Yiddishe Khasene," a pair of old-world musical skits Kandel wrote that recreated a journey by Hasidim to visit their rebbe and an old-fashioned Jewish wedding, respectively. Seeing the concept's success, A&R men made "enactment" records a trend among other ethnic performers and, later, among blues and even country artists.

A score from the November 19, 1924, session that produced "Di Hasidim Forn Tsum Rebin" reveals Kandel's meticulous precision. The musical cues and script (performed by Philadelphia Yiddish theater personality Isador Meltzer) were penned in Kandel's firm, clear hand, and leave no room for error or misjudgment.

Though he periodically strayed from the Victor stable—in 1921 he recorded for OKeh and in 1924 for Brunswick—Kandel maintained a strong and close relationship with the company. By 1924, he had established himself as a Victor dealer and opened his popular People's Talking Machine Company store at 502 South Fifth Street. Three years later Kandel retired from recording to run his music

Harry Kandel's People's Talking Machine Company, on Philadelphia's south side, which he opened in 1924 after he quit recording Victor records in order to start selling them. Kandel was killed by a car outside his store two decades later. (*Courtesy Bill Tecosky*)

store—nearly a decade to the month after he had made his first disc. But he continued to give live concerts and to perform on the local radio station WRAX in shows sponsored by his store.

Back in New York, meanwhile, Abe Schwartz composed fifteen new tunes and songs in 1921, including "Got fun Avrohom" (God of Abraham). The song was a reworking of the traditional melody sung at the conclusion of the Sabbath that asks, "How long must our people be persecuted and driven from land to land?" Schwartz reunited with tenor Abe Moskowitz to make the record for Emerson.

The best known tune that year was Schwartz's most famous composition: "Di Grine Kuzine" (The Female Greenhorn Cousin). The song, a dirge about a beautiful young girl who "didn't talk but sang and didn't walk but danced," tells the story of how the cousin comes to America and works for years in a "millinery storke" until, with "cheeks like pomegranates now gone green," she curses the day she left her home. On December 2, Schwartz quietly copyrighted the song in a charming arrangement for violin, clarinet, and bass. Less than two weeks later the copyright office received music from another Yiddish composer, Hyman Prizant, for his song, "Mayn Kuzine" (My Female Cousin)—which was identical to Schwartz's "Grine Kuzine." While Schwartz and Prizant slugged it out, yet another composer, Yankele Brisker (the nom de plume of one Jacob Leiserowitz), published his version of "Di Grine Kuzine," listing himself as the lyricist and the music as "traditional."[14]

Leiserowitz may have the best argument for authorship of this evergreen song. In the February 16, 1917, issue of the Yiddish weekly *Miller's Vokhnshrift*, four years before Schwartz submitted his copyright, the song appears under the title of "Mayn Kuzine Dine" with the instruction that it should be sung to the folk melody of "Bayke." In unity there is strength, however. Settling their differences in March 1922, Schwartz and Prizant joined forces to copublish "Di Grine Kuzine"; dividing the spoils, Schwartz took credit for the music and Prizant for the text.

A bitter song of defeat that sounds as if it were composed sometime in the previous century, "Di Grine Kuzine" was a curious success, given the spate of wildly enthusiastic pro-America anthems then dominating record and sheet music catalogs. Odder still is its structure: unlike the standard popular songs of the day—verses capped by a snappy and memorable chorus—"Di Grine Kuzine" was relentlessly verse after verse after verse, with the last line repeated standing in for a chorus.

The song provoked tears, communicating the dehumanizing and debilitating effects of the shop system. Other songs had spoken eloquently of the sweatshop, most notably Morris Rosenfeld's "Mayn Rue Plats" (My Resting Place) in the late 1880s, but none were recorded in their time. "Di Grine Kuzine" even gained a second interpretation and came to be viewed as a parody, the tempo sped up and the tragic downfall of the heroine exaggerated.

Whatever the reason, the song became a huge hit. Schwartz—without Prizant—knowing he had an inside track at Columbia, quickly filed a separate copyright covering all versions for performances, recordings, and piano rolls and was in the studio almost immediately. The first record was sung by Abe Moskowitz at Columbia, and Schwartz adapted his trio arrangement to fit this session. Soon, it seems, everyone wanted to record the song: Abe Schwartz led the orchestra for Abe Rosenstein's disc for Emerson while

Vocalion's 1922 release "Di Grine Kuzine."

Joseph Feldman recorded it for Victor; Gus Goldstein for OKeh; and Morris Goldstein for Vocalion, Gennett, and Brunswick.

Much as the floodgate opened for "Brivele" songs in the previous decade, "Grine" songs took on a life of their own. You couldn't walk a Jewish street without hearing some new "Grine" song: be it about a male cousin ("Der Griner Kozin"), a woman named Lena ("Di Grine Lena"), a boy ("Di Grine Bokher"), even a janitor ("Der Griner Janitor"). Leiserowitz got back into the act too. If Schwartz and company had "Di Grine Kuzine," he would retaliate with "Di Royte Kuzine fun Russland" (The Red Female Cousin from Russia). In a reverse on her green cousin, she was hungry and worn out in the new Soviet state but, since coming to America, dances and sings.

All this was music to the ears of the newly formed J. and J. Kammen Publishing Company, which paid Schwartz one hundred dollars for the rights to "Di Grine Kuzine"—a deal Schwartz would soon regret. Twin brothers Jack and Joseph Kammen were an oddity in the hurly-burly world of Yiddish publishing. Starting out doing Yiddish adaptations of popular American songs, they had a very brief brush with recording: they produced one ho-hum 78 of "Velt Bakente Yiddishe Tents" (World-Renowned Yiddish Dances) on piano for four hands, made for Emerson in 1921. After deciding to publish their arrangement themselves, they issued a few more songs and cast about for other pieces to print. What they reeled in was "Di Grine Kuzine," which put Abe Schwartz on the map but did that and more for the Kammens.

The Kammen twins couldn't have chosen a better time to enter Yiddish music publishing: 1921–25 saw the greatest number of copyrights registered for Yiddish songs.[15] The Kammens' publishing output increased. Though there had been anthologies of klezmer music published earlier—most notably the *International Hebrew Wedding Dances*, put out by Nat and Wolff Kostakowsky in 1916—the brothers created a milestone publication with their *Kammen International Dance Folio* in 1924, a collection of fifty-six klezmer and Eastern European tunes rendered in easy-to-read arrangements. This book codified the standard material used by klezmer musicians and shifted it away from the earlier European-style repertoire. The Kammen books, as they've come to be called, remain in print to this day.

Besides making him a music store darling, "Di Grine Kuzine" put Schwartz in demand at various Yiddish theaters in New York, such as the Lyric, the Atheneum, and Brooklyn's Hopkinson Theater. The rapid turnover of shows meant composers needed to be working on new songs even as old ones were being played.

"My bedroom was right next to the music room, and I used to hear plunk, plunk, plunk because he used to compose on the violin," Bebe Schwartz recalled of her life in their eight-room apartment on Second Avenue. "Plunk, plunk, plunk and a little pause because he was writing and then plunk, plunk, plunk again. And I heard this for years and years and years. Because this was how I fell asleep. He used to work in the theaters and come home at eleven or twelve and then write until two, three o'clock in the morning."[16]

The Schwartz apartment housed a never-ending parade of singers, musicians, and producers—not a few of them hard-luck cases whom the big-hearted Schwartz would shore up with a place to stay, a meal, or a few bucks. "He helped everybody—he really did," his daughter says. "Without fanfare. He didn't go about and say, 'Oh, I helped him, and I helped him.' No. He did it. And everyone knew him and liked him. But they took advantage of him, but he didn't feel they were taking advantage of him. He was helping out."

Musically, that help took the form of promoting promising musicians. In his role as a sub-A&R man for Nodiff, Schwartz identified and then cultivated up-and-coming soloists, giving them a featured venue in his orchestra. The first of these was Naftule Brandwein.

If any musician personifies the klezmer scene in early-twentieth-century America, it is the clarinetist Brandwein. New York Yiddish music veterans have powerful and vivid memories of this man; nearly four decades after his death, tales of Brandwein abound, sounding as though they were written by a press agent with an overactive imagination.

People still talk of the time he appeared onstage wearing an Uncle Sam costume fashioned from Christmas tree lights and nearly electrocuted himself due to excessive perspiration; of his penchant for performing with his back to the audience so other clarinetists would not steal his fingerings; of how he would spontaneously drop his pants while playing at parties; the neon Naftule Brandwein Orchestra sign he wore around his neck as he played; how he was summoned to the Brooklyn headquarters of the notorious Murder Inc. mob to entertain the bosses; the sight of him drunkenly weaving up and down the median line of a busy Catskill Mountain highway while playing Brahms's "Lullaby."

It's much too easy to allow these fantastic stories to overwhelm the simple reality of his musical prowess. Let the needle slip into the groove of a Brandwein 78 RPM disc and that genius becomes abundantly clear. While popular folklore acknowledges his reputation as a roué and an alcoholic, he was forgiven everything when he replaced the bottle at his lips with a clarinet.

Brandwein, descended from the Hasidic dynasty of Rabbi Yehuda Hirsch Brandwein of Stratyn, was born into a musical family in the Polish Galician town of Przymyzl in 1884. The large Brandwein family was the primary source of musicians in the region. Naftule's father, Peisachke, who played fiddle and was a *badkhn*, produced thirteen children, five of whom became musicians: his sons Moishe (fiddle, French horn, and valve trombone), Mendel (piano), Leyzer (drums), and Azriel (cornet)—Naftule's first, most important music teacher.

Sadie Freeman, Naftule's daughter, remembered her father's stories of playing for and with Gypsies in the numerous inns that dotted the Polish countryside. "He played for everyone and everyone thought he was one of them: Poles, Gypsies, Jews." Pictures of him from this time, showing a dark-skinned young man with broad, high cheekbones, make it easy to understand how he could pass for one

The Brandwein brothers and their orchestra, c. 1925, including Azriel Brandwein (*bottom left*), Naftule Brandwein (*bottom center*), Louis Shuster (*bottom right*), and Louis Spielman (*top right*).

or the other of these ethnic identities. At what age he made the
momentous switch from cornet to clarinet is not known, but by the
time he boarded a ship for New York he sounded as if he had been
born playing clarinet.

When the nineteen-year-old Naftule left Poland bound for America in 1908, American Yiddish theater was in blossom. Its newborn
stars were the thespians who stepped out onstage, not denizens of
the orchestra pit at their feet; but Brandwein changed that quickly.
Engaging in an uncommon bit of public relations ballyhoo far more
typical of a vaudevillian than a klezmer, he set about promoting
what he did best. The self-appointed title "King of Jewish Music"
stuck: the professional Jewish music community of New York had
never before seen the likes of him.

Put on one of Abe Schwartz's hot band discs from around 1920
and you'll hear, way in the back, someone blowing an E♭ clarinet.
The E♭ is the runt of the clarinet litter, but this guy is back there
playing trills, harmonies, variations, and contrary melodies. He's
prancing, leading, following, swaying, and tantalizing—but he's kept
far in the background, because the recording engineers know if they
have him too close to the horn, he'll blow the needle out of the disc.
That's Naftule.

By September 1922 Brandwein was issuing records under his own
name at Columbia. On his first solo records he is backed by a muscu-
lar little band composed of a trombone, fiddle, and piano, allowing
him plenty of room to bob and weave with the melody. His recording
"Firn di Mekhutonim Aheym" (Escorting the Parents of the Bride and
Groom Home), copyrighted by Abe Schwartz in the old-fashioned
style of a *gasn nign* (street tune), allows Brandwein his full complement of improvisations, blinding scale runs, and back-from-the-brink
rhythmic turnarounds. It's a powerhouse performance that has lost
none of its punch since he recorded it in 1923. That same year,
Brandwein left Schwartz to become his own bandleader over at rival
label Victor. Columbia was out a clarinetist.

Brandwein was soon replaced by a far more genial and equally
dazzling reed player, Shloimke Beckerman (1883–1974). Born into a
professional music family in Rizish, in the Ukrainian region of
Poland, Beckerman came to the United States around 1910. His
father, a violinist, was his first teacher. The family story goes that
when the younger Beckerman played in the streets listeners used to
shower him with flowers. More family folkore has it that, clarinet
under his arm, he found work the very night his ship landed at Ellis
Island. He was, as his son, Sid, says, "a reader and a faker," meaning

Naftule Brandwein in knickers and tux.

he could improvise a part as easily as he could read it off a sheet of music. As such, Beckerman was the perfect transition between the era of the ear players and those who required the more demanding skills of sight-reading and instant transposing.

"He was never home," recalls Sid, today a prominent klezmer clarinetist. "He was constantly playing. During the day there were recording sessions, lunchtime restaurants, then steady jobs at night, be it theaters, movie houses, nightclubs, ballrooms, or more restaurants."[17]

In 1917 Shloimke Beckerman was working in a dance band at New York's Reisenwebber's restaurant the night the management debuted the Original Dixieland Jazz Band, introducing the New Orleans sound to the rest of the world. "Pop would be sitting there," Sid Beckerman recalls. "These guys would play the Dixieland and Pop says in Yiddish: 'Every trick he did I could do better!'"

By mid-1923 Abe Schwartz made two discs with Shloimke Beckerman—"Ot Azoy/Yismekhu" (That's the Way), an example of Beckerman's incredible stretch, and "T'kias Shoyfer Blozn/A Galitzianer

Shloimke Beckerman's 1923 recording of "Ot Azoy."

Tentsl" (Blowing of the Shofar/A Galitzianer Dance), a re-creation of a Yom Kippur celebration via a tour de force of themes, melodies, and shofar blasts played by the clarinet. Clearly something that would go over well in live performance, the "clarinet-as-shofar" trick was used by Dave Tarras with Abe Schwartz a few years later on a recording with the Boibriker Kapelle. Like Brandwein's "Firn di Mekhutonim," "A Galitzianer Tentsl" is an expansive melody master-fully played. Schwartz provides a solid framework of interesting and beautifully conceptualized harmonies that allow Beckerman to reach into the tune and come up with his dazzling interpretation. Becker-man's phrasing is breathtaking—literally: the first sixteen measures of the tune are played and then repeated on a single exhalation.

Shloimke Beckerman had established a solid reputation in the mainstream music world, playing with all the major New York bands. But something drew him to the old music. "When he started going back," Sid remembers, "my mother said to him, 'Shloimke, you're playing, you know, big shot, with all the big bands. Now you're going back to playing all this music with all the klezmer on the East Side again. What are you doing?' I think he enjoyed it. He really enjoyed it."

One of the big bands Shloimke Beckerman played with was the Paul Whiteman Orchestra, which began appearing regularly at New York's Little Club in 1923. It was only a matter of months before the bandleader Whiteman and his young pianist/composer would make American music history.

GEORGE GERSHWIN AND THE RISE OF JEWISH JAZZ

If one sound has come to symbolize the influence of klezmer on American popular music, it is the opening of George Gershwin's *Rhapsody in Blue*. Much has been made of that wailing clarinet cry, which for many writers and contemporary klezmer fans has become proof positive of Jewish music's presence in Gershwin's consciousness—and of the subsequent encoding of Jewish motifs in American popular song.

Some compare the opening to a shofar blast or to the plaintive prayer of the cantor on Yom Kippur, while others hear in it strong evocations of klezmer clarinet. Regardless, Gershwin emerged as a composer who had looked inside himself and found a sound that wedded the traditional Jewish modes of his past with the exciting jazzy sounds of his present. Like another famous Jewish musician, Benny Goodman, Gershwin became a Jewish-American success icon by seeming to bring the essence of Jewish music to Gentile society.

But nothing could be further from the truth. Examination of Gershwin's life and the composition of *Rhapsody* reveals that he did not create the famous opening and had even less to do with Jewish music. Gershwin's parents, neither of whom were particularly observant, did not encourage the presence of Jewish religion or culture in their New York home. (Only Ira, the younger of the two brothers, was bar mitzvahed.) Although his mother's friends included Yiddish theater professionals, the family did not attend performances, and as a child Gershwin exhibited no interest in music, Jewish or otherwise.[18]

By 1913 Gershwin, fifteen, had begun working at Remick's music store as a song plugger. Longing to be a composer himself—he would publish two songs before year's end—he sought outlets for his compositions. The Yiddish theater was a robust, secure place for a young go-getter to establish a foothold. In many ways, it offered a wider and finer array of showplaces and shows than its Gentile cousin uptown.

After three years of haunting the theaters, most likely exploiting his mother's contacts there, Gershwin came to the attention of the great Boris Thomashefsky. Thomashefsky had been coauthoring songs with several composers, including Joseph Rumshinsky and the team of former Goldfaden associate Arnold Perlmutter and Herman Wohl, with whom he had a big hit with his song "Lebn Zol Columbus" (Long Live Columbus). But Thomashefsky had bigger ideas. Perlmutter and Wohl were Old World, and he wanted to tap into the youthful energy that was America. So he agreed to see the young Gershwin.

But there was a catch: knowing of Gershwin's lack of knowledge about Jewish music and composing in general, Thomashefsky was going to match him up with another up-and-coming composer, the twenty-one-year-old Sholom Secunda. Secunda later recalled Thomashefsky's telling him: "We have a friend, a talented young man; we would like you to meet him. He's not as *Yidishlekh* as you are. He is American born and knows his jazz. I will fuse you together. Gershwin and Secunda. Together you should make a good composer."

Gershwin and Secunda eagerly accepted the famous actor's invitation to meet backstage during a matinee at his National Theater. But the *shidekh*, the match, did not take. Though impressed by Gershwin's adeptness at playing jazz, Secunda sniffed at the untutored and unpublished young pianist. Secunda had studied composition and arrangement at what was to become the Juilliard School of Music, while the young Gershwin, like his idol, Irving Berlin, still composed by ear. That, in addition to his complete lack of understanding of Jewish music ("Too much American and too little Jew," was how Secunda described him) left Secunda decidedly underwhelmed.

"I'm afraid, Mr. Gershwin, that nothing can come of Mr. Thomashefsky's plan for the two of us," Secunda said. "You see, I don't mean to hurt you, but I am a serious composer and have dedicated years to the study of music."

Thomashefsky returned to find the two sitting dejectedly at opposite sides of the room. Thomashefsky sadly accepted Secunda's assessment of Gershwin and retracted his offer. But Secunda didn't have much luck with Thomashefsky, either; the elder showman continued co-composing with his earlier partner, Rumshinsky, producing hit operettas like *Mazl Tov* in 1917, and *Di Khaznte* (Lady Cantor) in 1918, before they parted company in 1919.

For years afterward, whenever Gershwin would encounter Secunda on the street he would loudly proclaim him as being the man who saved him from the Yiddish theater: "When he saw me, he would stretch out his hand and with a big thank you would say, 'Sholom's the one I owe my present position to in the musical world. If he had agreed to become my partner I would now be a composer in the Yiddish theater.'"[19]

This then is the prelude to Gershwin's composition of the famous *Rhapsody*, in 1923–24. Conductor/impressario Paul Whiteman, the self-styled "King of Jazz," struck on the idea of commissioning a jazz concerto for a concert at New York's Aeolian Hall. From the start, he had Gershwin in mind.

Interestingly, the justifiably famous clarinet opening of the *Rhapsody* does not appear either in Gershwin's manuscript or in arranger Ferde Grofé's original orchestration. (Gershwin, though capable of reading and writing music, did not then arrange his own compositions.) What is clearly indicated there is not the famous glissando at all, not the plaintive cantor on Yom Kippur or hoary klezmer clarinet, but a rather bland, simple seventeen-note run up the scale. The opening came about due to the musical puckishness of clarinetist Ross Gorman. During rehearsals, to relieve the boredom and to amuse the other orchestra members, Gorman, a reed player of exceptional ability, played with the opening of the piece, substituting the clearly articulated run with an exaggerated glissando.[20]

More than likely the non-Jewish Gorman was also offering his fellow musicians a rather wicked take-off on the clarinetist/entertainer Ted Lewis, then at the height of his popularity. Lewis was a notoriously awful clarinetist. Jazz banjoist/guitarist and wag Eddie Condon said of him: "He made the clarinet talk and it usually said, 'Please put me back in my case.'"[21] The Whiteman band members must have been mightily amused by the left-handed tribute.

The substitution of a glissando for more precise incremental runs is a hallmark of inferior reed players, a lazy way of bridging the opening and concluding notes, and a device Lewis used regularly on his numerous 78s and in performance. It wasn't until the final rehearsals for *Rhapsody* were well under way that Gershwin even heard Gorman's opening glissando and, struck by the sound of it, encouraged him to keep it in. Following the work's enormous success, all performances and publications of *Rhapsody in Blue* included Gorman's opening.[22]

In 1929, following the fantastic stage success of S. Ansky's *The
Dybbuk* in Europe, financier Otto Kahn commissioned Gershwin to
write an opera based on it for the Metropolitan Opera. Though
Gershwin prepared some sketches and even considered traveling to
Europe to study Jewish music to add authenticity to the score, the
project faltered when the rights to the play could not be secured.
Rumor abounds concerning these supposed sketches, but they have
never surfaced. Gershwin biographer Isaac Goldberg claims not
only to have seen them but also that Gershwin played them for him.
But the late Ira Gershwin insisted that "no manuscript exists of, or
for, *The Dybbuk*."[23]

Fans and scholars have sifted through Gershwin's works over the
years, panning for nuggets of Jewish motifs to link the man to his
people. And though some similarities have been charted—the chorus
motif of Gershwin's 1927 song " 'S Wonderful" bears a curious
resemblance to "Noyakh's Teyve, lid Yitskhok," from Goldfaden's
operetta *Akeydes Yitskhok*, and "It Ain't Necessarily So" echoes a
Jewish prayer melody—they have less to do with Gershwin's understanding of Jewish music than with his enormous talent for appro-
priating a variety of themes.[24]

So despite having been "saved" from the Yiddish theater, Gershwin—the consummate improviser, the ne plus ultra recycler, the
quintessential American composer—continues to be associated with
Yiddish music after all.

The response to the Gershwin Aeolian Hall concert was tremendous.
Suddenly America—and the world—had become jazz crazy. The
frenzy extended into the world of Yiddish music.

Back in 1917, Kandel recorded "Der Shtiler Bulgar." The piece,
an uncharacteristic klezmer tune predominantly in a major key, sold
well enough to be covered by Abe Schwartz nine months later. In
July 1926 Kandel's Jazz Orchestra issued "Jakie, Jazz 'em Up" (as
the flip side of the equally surreal "Cohen's Visit to the Sesquicen-
tennial"), a newly retitled and rearranged version of the earlier tune.
Its only "jazz" element is a "do-wacka-do" trumpet break—already
hopelessly out-of-date given the brilliant jazz trumpet solos then
being recorded by greats like King Oliver, Louis Armstrong, and Bix
Beiderbecke.

Perhaps the most famous early Jewish-jazz pairing was the work of
composer/cellist Joseph Cherniavsky (1895–1959). A failed playwright (his 1919 work *Moishe der Klezmer* was never produced),

Cherniavsky was introduced to Yiddish theater by actor/director Maurice Schwartz in early 1920. The two agreed to collaborate on the first American production of *The Dybbuk*, with which Schwartz would open the 1921/1922 season of his Yiddish Art Theater. Cherniavsky set to work on a score for the project at once, and his first sketches were ready by the end of the year. His earliest offerings emerged as *Dybbuk Khasene*, an arrangement for string orchestra that he recorded in a stilted and bloodless performance for Columbia.

The much-anticipated *Dybbuk* was a hit, and the spotlight extended to the young émigré composer who had created the arresting music. When the play closed, Cherniavsky shrewdly decided to recycle the score into a Yiddish vaudeville act. Capitalizing on the seeming incongruity of Jews and jazz, he dubbed his ensemble Joseph Cherniavsky's Yiddish-American Jazz Band, also called the Hasidic-American Jazz Band and even the Oriental-American Syncopaters.

The idea was simple: get some of the most accomplished Jewish-style players, dress them up alternately as Cossacks or Hasidim, and

Joseph Cherniavsky's Yiddish-American Jazz Band, c. 1923, on the vaudeville circuit. Joseph Cherniavsky (*center*) with baton; Shloimke Beckerman (*second from right*); and Naftule Brandwein (*third from right*). (*YIVO Institute for Jewish Research*)

give them tight, sophisticated arrangements. Performing before a curtain painted with huge grotesque caricatures of klezmorim (influenced in no small way by Marc Chagall's famous 1920 painted curtains for the Moscow Yiddish Art Theater), Cherniavsky was a popular act on the East Coast Jewish and mainstream vaudeville circuit.

Handpicking his ensemble players, Cherniavsky used, among others, his wife on piano, reed players Shloimke Beckerman and Naftule Brandwein, and the percussionist Joe Helfenbein (1898–1989), whose earlier career came to include vaudeville, Broadway, and recordings. After more than fifty years off the road with Cherniavsky, Helfenbein remembered the act fondly.

"We had a number—Jewish—a beautiful number," he said. "The lights got dim, everybody wore *kapotes*, *peyes*, I'd give a roll on the big tom-toms and the fiddle started, you know. We had another Jewish number, good, like a *bulgar*, then an English number. We opened up in the Manhattan Center and most of the Jews were there. They used to love it, they used to eat it up."[25]

It wasn't all beautiful music. Naftule Brandwein, brilliant as a musician, could be socially discordant. First, he couldn't read music and Cherniavsky would have to have him memorize his parts. Then, as Helfenbein recalled: "When we would go on the road we would always have to double up—two guys in a room—sometimes three! And these were not big rooms. Somehow, I ended up with Naftule. Once was enough! He'd . . . you know, he'd get *shiker* and he was not a nice drunk: he was a nasty drunk. He had habits—terrible . So I went back to Cherniavsky and said: 'Please, Mr. Cherniavsky ,it's killing me. Let someone else take him for a while.' But by that time everyone had him and everyone complained."

Cherniavsky needed a replacement. Joe Helfenbein recommended a young man he had worked with recently: "I heard this guy play and I said, 'This guy is terrific.'" So I says, 'I played a job the other day and I worked with a player he plays Jewish beautifully. And a gentleman.' The clarinetist was Dave Tarras.

What with his experience in army bands and his family's orchestra back in the old country, twenty-six-year-old Dave Tarras knew a thing or two about being an ensemble player. In 1915 Tarras had been conscripted into the czarist army as a musician. But by 1917, the Russian Revolution destabilized the Allied Eastern Front in World War I and Russia pulled out. In the chaos and confusion, Tarras returned home to find the war, the Revolution, and the subsequent counter-revolution (all with their attendant anti-Jewish pogroms) overwhelming. In 1921, after having written to his older

Naftule Brandwein (*left*) and Louis Spielman on the road in Hurleyville, N.Y., 1923.

sister who lived in New York with her husband, he left for America, clarinet in his satchel.

Once here, however, he became disinclined to the notion of playing music. Instead, the recently married Tarras had his brother-in-law find him work in the fur trade. "I thought that in America to be a musician one has to have—he must be something; I didn't think I'm good enough to be a musician," Tarras said. "I went to work in a factory and I swept the floor. I got ten dollars the first week, I figured it was worth twenty rubles in Russian money. They taught me to be an operator; I got $15, $20, $50 a week with overtime I worked fifty hours. I was happy with it."[26]

Tarras worked at that job for almost a year before he bought a new clarinet and started taking small wedding jobs booked through his cousin, a trumpet player. One of the first small jobs he played was led by violinist Sam Ash, who in 1932 published Tarras's first composition and later opened a successful chain of New York-area music stores. Ash, no music talent, was however a real go-getter who led the house band at the Hopkinson Manor, a popular catering hall in Brooklyn. Impressed with Tarras's skill and learning that he still worked in a shop, Ash offered the émigré musician some advice: "*Yinger man, di arbetst in a shap? Farvus tiste nit vus ikh ti?* (Young man, you work in a shop? Why don't you do what I do?) I teach. I teach the boy for a year the mother says the teacher is not good, I say that the boy is not talented. So she gets another teacher and I get another sucker."

Word began to spread about the new clarinet player working weddings. Tarras's first important break came through drummer Joe Helfenbein. They worked a wedding together in 1923. Helfenbein and his brother Kulik, both drummers and members of the Progressive Musicians Benevolent Society, arranged for Tarras to play at their upcoming charity banquet—a high-visibility showcase for this newcomer. It was there that Cherniavsky heard him and agreed to an audition for Tarras.

"I had an appointment to see Cherniavsky," Tarras recalled. "His wife was a very fine pianist and I brought my clarinet and played for her. 'Very good. Could you read music?' 'I try.' So she put out a couple of songs and I swallowed it down. So Cherniavsky booked me for a job in Philadelphia with Cantor Yossele Rosenblatt."

Tarras replaced Brandwein as the principal clarinet soloist with the Cherniavsky band. The impact was immediate—and positive. "When we went to Philadelphia the first week he did the same thing what Brandwein did—the same number," Joe Helfenbein recalled. People looked up and said: 'Who the hell is this guy?' 'Where does he come from?' 'Where did you get him?' 'Terrific!' He went over after that."

Tarras's rapport with Cherniavsky was also a success. He was a fast and accurate reader who had a great command of Yiddish style as well as a clean "legitimate" sound, and he and Cherniavsky both

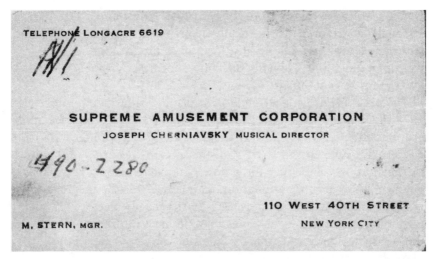

TELEPHONE LONGACRE 6619

SUPREME AMUSEMENT CORPORATION

JOSEPH CHERNIAVSKY MUSICAL DIRECTOR

110 WEST 40TH STREET

M. STERN, MGR.   NEW YORK CITY

Dave Tarras saved Cherniavsky's card from 1926. The other side reads: "Supreme Amusement Corporation owes David Terras [sic] $62.50 to be paid in future if and when possible within five months." He never got paid.

spoke Russian, making him a natural choice. At the conclusion of the concert Cherniavsky made Tarras, still working outside of music, an offer: "I have one week to play in the Bronx, next week—all I can pay you is $110."

"He thought I would ask for more, and when I heard $110 I nearly fainted," said Tarras. "So I accepted and saw that I can make a living here. I went to my brother-in-law and his two partners in the furriers and I said, 'Thank you very much for giving me a job—I'm quitting.' He was glad, too, to see that I'm doing good."

In April 1925 Cherniavsky got the opportunity to re-record his *Dybbuk* compositions with his Yiddish-American Jazz Band for the Victor company. These recordings give an excellent idea of the level of accuracy needed to play program music of this kind. But the music is only part of why these theatrical reworkings of "Hasidic" themes succeeded. Their popularity depended on the full effect of the show—the costumes, the lighting, the spectacle—and of course, the hype of "jazz."

Cherniavsky, like Shloimke Beckerman's other employer, Paul Whiteman, understood jazz's powerful pull. But unlike Whiteman, Cherniavsky didn't sprinkle his orchestra with jazz-literate players who could color the arrangements accordingly. This was not lost on Dave Tarras. "It was very nice theater music," he noted. "No jazz was played; it was what Cherniavsky called a Jewish jazz, a novelty."

The public seems to have agreed. After the band's last tour in 1925, its contract with the Keith-Orpheum Circuit was cancelled. Not long after this many of the members of Cherniavsky's orchestra—including Joe Helfenbein and Cherniavsky himself—drifted away from Jewish music.

The Jazz Age wasn't all tootling saxes and shimmying masses. In 1924 the United States government enacted the Reed Johnson Immigration Act, effectively shutting the door to further immigration from Eastern Europe. In the short run, this meant a dramatic downturn in the number of people for whom Yiddish was an everyday language, and an abrupt elimination of audiences for the theater, songs, and talent that would invigorate it. In the larger picture, it was the beginning of the end for a renewable Yiddish culture in America. Its more disastrous ramifications would not become clear until the rise of Adolf Hitler in 1933.

~ 4 ~

YIDDISH MELODIES
IN SWING: 1930s–1940s

TO READERS OF HENRY FORD'S WEEKLY, *The Dearborn Independent*, it was clear who was changing America's tune: Jews.

"Popular music is a Jewish monopoly," the crusading industrialist wrote in a 1922 edition of the paper. "Jazz is a Jewish creation. The mush, slush, the sly suggestion, the abandoned sensuousness of sliding notes, are of Jewish origin."[1]

The purported originators of the form would hardly have agreed. Yet Ford's lamentations over the displacement of traditional American music—the fiddle-driven square dance bands of his youth—found an odd consonance in the pages of the Yiddish press.

In "The Old-Time Real Jewish Klezmer Is Played Out in America," a 1932 article in the Yiddish newspaper the *Forverts*, a journalist named Isaac Pessler met a group of disgruntled intergenerational klezmorim at the local branch of New York's Musicians' Union. Bemoaning the rising popularity of *fleper djez* (flapper jazz), exemplified by the sax playing and crooning of Rudy Valle, the klezmorim crowded around this gentleman of the press and vented their disdain for everything from saxophones to "doublers" (musicians required to play more than one instrument on the job), but mostly for "djez." Then one player piped up.

> "The jazzers are the least of our problems," says a well-known old-time fiddler. "As bad as they are, why don't you tell your readers about our real problem: the Vitaphone [talking pictures]?"

What was once a reliable way for musicians to make a modest living, playing music for the movies, had been doomed to extinction by

Vitaphone, Warner Brothers' synchronized sound system that recorded sound on an oversize disc to be played in tandem with a running movie. The technological displacement was profound. Within a few short years, every theater in America was outfitted with some version of synchronized sound. Yet while sound films shut out musicians, they also opened a new, albeit narrower door.

Violinist Max Epstein was among the musicians who made the transition from silent movies to sound. Epstein, Brooklyn born and bred, played for silent movies from the age of twelve. But by his late teens he was on staff at the fledgling Warner Brothers Vitaphone Company in Brooklyn, making recorded accompaniments for popular stars.[2]

Most Vitaphone short-subject two- and three- reelers were of vaudeville and even operatic acts. These short features were so popular that the Warners, themselves children of Yiddish-speaking émigrés, branched out into other genres, eventually touching on the Jewish world. They filmed Molly Picon in a two-reeler called *Molly* in 1927 (singing a hokey song called "The Yiddishe Blues," which she composed with Joseph Rumshinsky's son, Murray), and a slightly surreal backstage featurette with Abe Ellstein called *A Little Girl with Big Ideas*, in 1933. Despite the Fanny Brice-ish "Jew" stage accent Picon affected for the two films, neither brought her the crossover audience she sought.[3]

Vitaphone made four featurettes with Cantor Yosele Rosenblatt, who was also enlisted to be part of what the company extolled as its "supreme triumph": *The Jazz Singer*. The 1927 film, based on Samson Raphaelson's short story "Day of Atonement," told of a fifth-generation cantor's son who yearns to sing in vaudeville while his father demands he serve the synagogue. Its themes of art versus obligation struck a resonant chord with young Jews beguiled by the promise of American acceptance.

The Jazz Singer was a smash on Broadway, starring George Jessel, but Al Jolson grabbed the screen role when Jessel, who had already appeared in several Vitaphone "Jew" featurettes, held out for too much cash. Jolson, like Jessel a cantor's son, was the model for Raphaelson's story and delivered a strong performance—stronger than Jessel would have, Jessel himself later admitted. Though daubed in blackface and sporting a wig, Jolson employs few of the accepted stage mannerisms of minstrel characters. Rather than relying on the broad, exaggerated speech of the "coon" character, his renditions of songs like "Swanee" and "Mammy" are actually more in the style of Irish tenors.

For a film centered on Yom Kippur—the holiest day of the Jewish year—*The Jazz Singer* has a fairly American-sounding score. Apart from "Orientalish" motifs supplied by Lou Silvers's orchestra and the obligatory Kol Nidre, the one recognizable Jewish refrain is the frequent use of the popular Nellie Casman song "Yosl, Yosl" when the comic character Yudelson appears onscreen.

However, some real Jewish music did creep into the film, in two set pieces featuring Yosele Rosenblatt. We hear him first in an uncredited rendition of Kol Nidre (lip-synched by actor Warner Oland, later known for his portrayals of Charlie Chan). Then we see him onscreen when the Jolson character ducks into a vaudeville house where the cantor is giving a concert. Seeing Rosenblatt simply and directly performing Peretz Sandler's Yiddish song "Yortsayt" brings Gypsy Rose Lee's description of him to life.

Part silent, part sound, part turgid romance, part novelty music feature, *The Jazz Singer*—premiered in a sly bit of public relations on October 6, 1927, just after the conclusion of Yom Kippur[4]—made film history, thanks to Jolson's ebullient persona and the visceral appeal of synchronized sound. Americans got their first taste of a new generation of technology and popular culture, brought to them by a new generation of children of immigrants.

The Jazz Singer was filmed and recorded at the Warner Brothers' Sunset Boulevard studios, far from the Brooklyn Vitaphone stages where violinist Max Epstein got his start. When not playing for Warner's, Epstein provided music for other film companies, including the animation studio run by Max and Dave Fleischer at 1600 Broadway in Manhattan. Recording for them at the Paramount sound studios on nearby Ninth Avenue, Epstein played music for a variety of shorts, including the mixed animation/live action Bouncing Ball series, and for Popeye and Betty Boop cartoons. Though he played all manner of music—and in some cases for stories that featured Jewish references—Epstein played no klezmer tunes for the Fleischers.

Though he had made good as a violinist, Epstein realized the instrument's place in popular music was diminishing fast. The syrupy sounds of Victor Herbert and Rudolf Friml were being drowned out by the bleat of brassier, reedier jazz bands. Violinists by the truckload were stumped as to what to do; many switched to saxophone, the easiest reed instrument and the musical symbol of the age. At twenty Epstein did too. "I quit my job and bought myself a saxophone and a clarinet, and ten days later I was working on a steady job," Epstein noted. "Playing saxophone and clarinet—that's right! Ten days I locked myself in a room!"

Composers, too, heeded the call to modernize their sound. Old-timers like Rumshinsky and Sandler were still influential, but new-generation composers were fashioning a firm link between tradition-al and American modern sounds. The greatest exemplar of the rising maturation of the new Yiddish theater was composer/violinist Alexander Olshanetsky (1892–1946). Dapper and urbane, Olshanet-sky brought to the Yiddish theater the kind of literate musical sophis-tication usually associated with Cole Porter or Noël Coward. His compositions and orchestrations made for smart, imaginative work in which old motifs were given an ear-catching turn.

Born in Odessa to a nonmusical family, Olshanetsky showed tal-ent early on at playing the violin. At six, he was enrolled at the Odessa Royal Music School, where he studied for nine years on a variety of instruments.[5] Leaving home against his parents' wishes, he joined the Odessa Opera and orchestra in 1911, traveling with the company throughout southern Russia and Siberia before quitting to become choral conductor for a Russian operetta troupe.

With the outbreak of the war, Olshanetsky was conscripted into the czarist army, where his musical skills got him appointed regi-mental bandleader. While stationed in Harbin, he encountered a Yiddish theater troupe under the direction of an old Goldfaden asso-ciate named Fishzohn. When the troupe's conductor, Peretz San-dler, left for America, Olshanetsky got permission from his regimen-tal commander to serve as his replacement. It was during this time that Olshanetsky began writing Yiddish music.

After the war, the situation deteriorated for Yiddish theater in Harbin, and Olshanetsky jumped ship and joined up with another Russian operetta troupe, with which he traveled through Japan, China, and India. By the time he returned to Harbin in 1921, Yid-dish theater was gone and he decided to emigrate to America.

An actor uncle of Olshanetsky's eased his introduction to the New York Yiddish theater. Within two years he had two shows under his belt: *Hayntike Meydlekh* (Today's Girls)—which he composed with lyricist Jacob Jacobs—up at Harlem's Lenox Avenue Theater, and *Zise Libe* (Sweet Love), downtown at Rolland's Liberty theater, co-composed with Louis Gilrod. Over the next few years he wrote or arranged music for some ten shows throughout New York.

In 1925 Olshanetsky befriended clarinetist Dave Tarras and hired him to play in his new show, *A Nakht in California* (A Night in Cali-

Alexander Olshanetsky in the 1930s.

fornia), Tarras's first job in Yiddish theater. Jacobs, Olshanetsky's lyricist partner, was also manager of the theater where the show opened, the National. Jacobs scored a coup by signing Aaron Lebedeff, the popular musical comedy leading man, for whom Olshansetsky had penned a successful song the previous year, to star in the show. And so Tarras met up with the temperamental and brilliant Lebedeff.

A Night in California was a big hit, and when the Vocalion company wanted Lebedeff and Olshanetsky to record it in September and October, Olshanetsky made sure Tarras was there too. The resulting 78, "I Like She/Petrograd," was as big a hit as the show. The success of *California* led to the reteaming of all the principals in new shows including *Paradise for Two* and *Goldene Teg* (Golden Days).

But it was the 1929 show *Der Litvisher Yankee* (The Lithuanian Yankee) that propelled Tarras to the forefront of popularity. "When

Olshanetsky had the idea for *Der Litvisher Yankee*, he came to me—
'Dave, I want you in the show,'" Tarras recalled. "But I was
approached already by Sholem Secunda for his new show, *Zayn
Vayb's Lubovnik* [His Wife's Lover]. Ludwig Satz was to star; that
was a big thing. But Olshanetsky had Aaron Lebedeff, so it was also
a big thing. I didn't know what to do.

"Several days later Olshanetsky called me and asked, 'If I write in
that you stand during your solo will you play for me?' He had a
song, 'What Can You Makh s'iz America?,' he wanted me to play
standing. To stand? Never did a musician stand, even if he played a
solo. And Olshanetsky was going to write it into the script! Of
course, I was honored."

But the star of the show was not so eager to share the limelight
with some young upstart playing in the pit. "We had one problem:
Lebedeff," Tarras said. "During rehearsals when he saw me get up
he suddenly says, 'I want to dance.' Yesterday there was no dancing,
but today suddenly there's dancing. Back and forth they argued. 'No
standing! I'm dancing!' Lebedeff was yelling. He didn't want me to
get any recognition."

Several of the Yiddish newspapers picked up on this bit of backstage wrangling and played it in their pages. At the premiere, Tarras
recalled, "I'm noticing people coming over to the orchestra pit and
looking in while I'm playing. And not just the first night."

Most working Yiddish musicians were worn to a frazzle trying to
keep up with the myriad jobs at their disposal. They were even kept
busy on Saturdays and religious holidays. Clarinetist Sid Beckerman
recalls what it was like growing up in the home of an in-demand
musician: "Know what time we used to have our Passover? Eleven,
eleven-thirty at night. Poppa had it after he played the last show in
the movies or the theater."

Sid began taking lessons from his father, Shloimke, in his early
teens, using both the standard published exercise books and *bulgars*
written out by his father. But mostly he learned from playing tunes
on the job.

The same was true for Howie Leess, another of Shloimke Beckerman's students. Leess started out studying violin with an uncle, but
his father, an amateur musician who had come to America from Bia-
lystok, felt that it would take him too long to master the instrument
and switched him to sax.

Leess's father tried to teach his son what he knew of Yiddish
music. "He taught me how to read, but basically he wasn't a

teacher," Leess said. "So he would pick up the guitar and play the melodies for me and I would imitate them."[6] At age nine, Leess began more systematic lessons with Beckerman, who switched him from sax to clarinet. For the next three years Leess stayed with Beckerman, learning *bulgar* after *bulgar*:

"Shloimke would write a *bulgar* every week for me, every time I took a lesson, as a present for me," he said. "He was very fast in writing by hand, and it took him two minutes to write and he would go over it with me and that's it."

At thirteen, Leess began working with older musicians, playing hotels in the Catskill mountains, north of New York City. American-born Jews going to these hotels demanded American music with a little bit of Jewish flavor. Leess was hired by musicians like Dave Tarras and Naftule Brandwein when American music was needed on their bandstands. "We young guys could play their music and they couldn't play our music, period," he said. "By the American bands I was the Jewish guy, and by the Jewish bands I was the American guy, same thing."

Leess played for second-line big bands like that of Artie Shaw imitator Jerry Wald, which, while prestigious, didn't pay as well as Jewish wedding bands. A standard job, called a club date, would be a four-piece group—usually a trumpet, sax/clarinet, drums, and piano—which for a wedding or bar mitzvah could get up to one hundred dollars, a good price. And while American music was making steady inroads into the standard Jewish ensemble, older audiences not entirely won over by popular American music still requested *bulgars*. "We had a job someplace on Pitkin Avenue [Brooklyn] and we took a stand out, we put some music out, and we played a foxtrot," Beckerman recalled. "And the people came over, knocked down the stand. '*Vus shpilste? Vus shpilste?* [What are you playing?]'"

Such scenes occurred less often at major catering halls like Burnside Manor in the Bronx or the Aperion and DeLuxe Palace in Brooklyn, which hosted more elaborate "affairs" for new-generation party-givers. And as they manipulated a three-ring circus of choreographed bridesmaids, gloved waiters, lavish spreads, choirs, and photographers, caterers figured out a way to make money on musicians, too: they took bribes to ensure that a bandleader's "orchestra"—any ensemble larger than a trio—would get the job. With the cost of the band already figured into the overhead of the party, party-givers never knew that they were paying for the band whether they hired it or not. This tradition of "buying a caterer" caught on as cannier—and more solvent—bandleaders cornered the club date market.

Modern Jewish weddings retained vestiges of early rituals, in modified form. The *badkhn* was gone, but the tunes that accompanied him remained, transformed into a dinner-music feature. A drumroll and then an announcement: "'Waiters, get off the floor. Get off the floor, waiters,'" Sid Beckerman recounts. "'*Mir shpiln a doina*. We're playing a *doina*. Don't serve.' In the middle of dinner. Right after the soup, before the main dish." The clarinet soloist would then walk to the middle of the floor and, microphone or no, play his pièce de résistance.

Some of the excessive pomp lavished on the wedding was finding its way into the bar mitzvah. Weddings required a cake-cutting, so bar mitzvahs began to see invented exercises like the pretentious "candle-lighting ceremony." These newly minted rituals demanded appropriate music to accompany the parade of relatives and friends asked to step up to the cake and light a candle.[7]

There had never before been bar mitzvah celebrations on this scale, so a suitable musical repertoire had to be invented. Though

Lavish bar mitzvah orchestras like the one pictured above (bandleader Al Glaser with baton) gained popularity in the 1940s. (*Courtesy Jeff and Bonnie Glaser*)

the repertoires for bar mitzvahs remained basically the same as for weddings, musicians scurried to add songs like Ilya Trilling's "Semele's Bar Mitzvah" (1938), Dave Tarras's similarly named "Simole's Bar Mitzvo" (Seymour at Confirmation) (1941), Chaim Towbera and Sholem Secunda's "Mayn Yingele" (1935), and other bar mitzvah-themed songs by Herman Yablokoff and Boris Thomashefsky.

The bible of the bandstand was still the *Kammen International Dance Folio*, billed as "The Most Useful Book of Its Kind." Simple and easy to read, it was a perfect way for non-klezmer players to survive on a Jewish job. Use of it, though, was a sure sign that the musician hadn't grown up playing the *bulgars*. Not quite a stigma, Kammen books were the equivalent of musical training wheels. As one old-timer said: "Admitting that you learned to play [Jewish] from the book was like admitting you learned how to have sex from a manual."

Beckerman and other players acquired notated tunes from job to job. "A *bulgar* would come out, a guy would like it, and he would write down the *bulgar*, and if you worked with this guy you learned that *bulgar*," he explains. "The other guy liked this *bulgar*, he would write it down, and you would pick them up, one by one by one." Though the Kammen book was ubiquitous, Beckerman says he didn't use it. "Those who needed the books couldn't play the music and those who could play the music didn't need the books."

AF DER LUFT: RADIO TO THE RESCUE

In mid-autumn 1929, the stock market wasn't the only show in town having its worst season. Early September had been a watershed period for Yiddish theater: in addition to *Der Litvisher Yankee*, Olshanetsky had *Di Eyntsiker Nakht* (The Only Night), starring Michal Michalesko, and *Hulye Kabstn* (Rejoice, Fool), with Lebedeff, at the National Theater; up in the Bronx at the Parkway Theater *Bublitshki* starred Peisechke Burstein; and at Kessler's Second Avenue Theater, Molly Picon appeared as *Dos Radio Girl*. But as theatergoers' and investors' discretionary spending dropped off, all these shows closed by year's end. The Yiddish theater never quite recovered.

It was still a reasonably good year for recording, though, with a handful of Jewish recording artists turning out some of their best work. Ever eager to capitalize on theater tie-ins, major labels rushed out 78s including Maurice Schwartz's monologues from his *Tevye der Milkhiker*, Lebedeff doing "What Can You Makh s'iz Amerika," from *Der Litvisher Yankee*, and Lebedeff rival Peisachke Burstein singing "Beygelekh" (from the show of the same name), of which Abe Schwartz and Dave Tarras did a hot cover the next year. And while Molly Picon took a hiatus from recording at this point, her former understudy Lucy Levin came out with a couple of songs from their recent *Radio Girl* show.

The record company policy of having Jewish bandleaders appear under nondescript non-Jewish names continued unabated. The Brunswick studios had cornetist Art Shryer doing triple duty: Art Shryer's Modern Jewish Orchestra produced Yiddish 78s; his Russky Narodny Orkestr made records for the Russian trade; and his Polska Orkiestra Narodowa played polkas, mazurkas, and waltzes. Columbia had Abe Schwartz making Jewish records under his own name but also as Polska Orkiestra Columbia (January 1929) and Russkij Orkester "Novinka" the next year.[8]

By 1930 the Depression had taken hold, and record companies needed to slash their offerings. Though every ethnic division was affected, Jewish recording was all but eliminated, not to be resumed in any meaningful way for another decade. The working-class customers this music was made for were not eager to spend seventy-five cents for a record when a ticket to the Yiddish theater could be had for a quarter. Plus, another competitor was encroaching on record companies' dwindling market share: radio. Company executives saw the threat radio posed to their monopoly on in-home mechanical entertainment.

In its frontier days, before the onslaught of the networks, radio was a casual, easygoing affair with myriad stations—public and private—elbowing one another for a slice of the ether. It was not uncommon to have a soporific broadcast of "Poetry at Sunset" interrupted by a hot jazz band broadcasting from the "Hotsy Totsy Club" muscling in on the frequency. This kind of hijacking encouraged the federal government to step in and appoint a "traffic cop" to assign and diligently monitor frequencies and rules of engagement. In 1927 the Federal Radio Commission was formed, headed by then Secretary of Commerce Herbert Hoover.

Soon the airwaves were sliced up like a kosher salami, with the bigger, juicier inside slabs going to the growing networks and the tougher, thinner outside slivers divided among small local entrepreneurs. It was only a matter of time before the clumsy wet-battery contraptions midwifed by "wireless" enthusiasts after World War I would blossom into the sleek, chic modern miracles of sound, the magnificent home radio. Radio stations sought out anyone who wanted to stand before the mike.

One of the earliest visionaries in Jewish broadcasting was news-paperman and socialist firebrand B. Charney Vladeck. As early as 1923 Vladeck, a committed and fervent leftist, understood the potential organizing power of radio. Just as his boss, *Forverts* editor Abe Cahan, had harnessed the press, Vladeck sought to tap the power of broadcasting. He saw the *Forverts*, the beacon of Socialist journalism, making its way into radio and envisioned a huge transmitter erected atop the roof of its building, already an imposing presence on the skyline of East Broadway. He interested Cahan in the idea and inaugurated a correspondence with the man who had made radio a household presence, RCA vice president David Sarnoff.

It certainly was a marriage of opposites: the capitalist Sarnoff and the socialist Charney Vladeck. Sarnoff was the one-time Marconi wireless employee who claimed to have been the first person to pick up the distress signals from the doomed Titanic, while Vladeck at that same time was a young revolutionary fleeing his homeland only steps ahead of the czarist police. But when it came to radio they were both idealists, and for the next few years Vladeck and Sarnoff were allied in the attempt to find a Jewish presence on the radio. At one point, Sarnoff asked Vladeck if he and his wife would accept a gift of a new RCA radio. Vladeck slyly declined by answering, "I would be very much embarrassed if a senatorial investigation in 1944 should find out that back in 1923 the Vice President and Manager of the RCA made a gift to the Secretary of the Interior."[9] Despite this seeming sure-bet liaison, the proposed Jewish station never came to pass. Disappointed but not discouraged, Vladeck put his broadcasting plans on the back burner. Other entrepreneurs did not.

Enterprising brokers approached owners of broadcast licenses to offer them entrée into the geographically dispersed Jewish communities. Like the record companies before them, radio station owners knew that ethnic communities would spend money to be entertained in their own language. Eager to cut their daily expenses, stations agreed to sell time to these brokers, who then went around to various Jewish stores offering the owners a way to be both smart advertisers and pint-sized patrons of the arts. Though this helped generate programming, its more direct result was a stampede of advertising, a malady greatly felt on Jewish radio shows. (A survey done at the time noted that for every fifteen minutes of programming—the usual running time—there were almost nine minutes of ads.)[10]

The first known Jewish broadcast in New York was *The Libby Hotel Program*, beamed from that hotel, located on New York's Lower East Side, and aired on station WHN. Long a favorite stopping place for émigré Jews from Eastern Europe, the Libby (named after the owner's mother) was an imposing multistory structure replete with *shvitsn* (steambaths), a synagogue, and a giant rooftop radio ballroom. The premiere show in 1926 featured the crème de la crème of the Jewish musical world, including cantor Samuel Vigoda; tragedian Jennie Goldstein; Yiddish musical-comedy stars Charlie Cohan, Peisachke Burstein, and Muni Serbarof; composers Abe Ellstein and Isidore Lillian; songstress Florence Weiss; and the new sensation, Dave Tarras. The mixture of music and pathos made for a sure combination that led other stations to seek out Jewish talent.

Soon dozens of small stations popped up throughout the New York City area, like WARD, WCNW, WFAB, WBBC, and WVFW, offering listeners some measure of Jewish entertainment. In the same way tenants of Lower East Side tenements took in "boarders" to help pay the rent, bargain broadcasters shared frequencies with several stations, each competing with the other for a slice of Jewish market share. This resulted in several stations sharing the same frequency, each limited to airing their shows a few hours a day.

Max Epstein described just how easy it was for a Jewish musician to play on many of the stations featuring Yiddish music. "I used to play five times a week, and that started right after Labor Day until June 30," he said. "You played in one studio, but you had two or three different stations coming in. One would go off the air, this one would go on the air. They used the same transmitters, see? So I played on almost all of them: WARD, WBBC, WCGU, WMIL, WCNW, all of them. It made no difference to me because I didn't have to go anywhere. I just stayed in the same studio in the downtown section of Brooklyn and that was it."

The tenement analogy holds true even for frequencies alloted by the Federal Radio Commission. The choicest slots were nestled comfortably in the middle of the dial, with their expansive transmitting power of 1,000, 2,500, and more than 5,000 watts. Penny-ante stations carrying Jewish and other ethnic programs were crammed onto the outskirts of the dial—in the lowest and highest frequencies eking out 50, 100, and 500 watts of power—and sometimes reached

Perry Voultsous and His AFM 802 Concert and Symphonic Jazz Orchestra, 1931. A so-called "concert symphonic jazz orchestra," the Voultsous band featured Izzy Drutin (*fifth from left*) on tuba and trombone, Isidore "Chizik" Epstein (*third from right*) on sax, pianist Beverly Musiker (*atop piano*)— sister of Sam and Ray Musiker—and Max Epstein on clarinet, saxophone, and violin (*kneeling, right*). (*Courtesy Ray Musiker*)

no further than the neighborhood from which they were transmitting. Jews tuned in from crowded apartment houses to hear shows radiating from crowded frequencies, low-power stations catering to politically and economically low-power listeners.

In 1927 Z. H. Rubinstein, editor of the Yiddish paper *Der Tog*, noting the popularity of the *Libby* program, decided a higher-quality Yiddish variety show was called for and threw the weight of his paper behind a new offering. Approaching a small station in midtown Manhattan, WABC, he launched *Der Tog Program* in September of that year. Maintaining the music and drama of the *Libby* show, which had since gone off the air, he added the kinds of features that made his paper popular: poetry, editorials, and dramatic serials. He also upgraded the orchestra, bringing in the finest conductors from the Yiddish theater, including Joseph Rumshinsky,

Alexander Olshanetsky, and Abe Ellstein. The most important inno-
vation was that he got his show aired at 11 A.M. on Sunday, a significant improvement over the *Libby*'s Wednesday night 10:00 P.M. slot.
Der Tog Program was an immediate hit.[11]

That same year the Socialist Party commemorated the passing of
Socialist leader Eugene Victor Debs with the newly formed Debs
Memorial Fund—and with the establishment of a radio station in his
honor. The fund featured many noted Socialist leaders of the day,
including Heywood Broun, Norman Thomas, Abe Cahan, and Charney Vladeck. Vladeck then revived his earlier idea for a radio station,
and in October 1927 WEVD was on the air. The nation's first listener-
supported station was given over to a mixture of didactic Socialist
programs in the evening and exceedingly nondescript shows by day.
Despite the presence of Vladeck and Cahan on the board, the only
programs with Jewish content during this time were an occasional
fifteen-minute slot by Jewish singer Shlomo Beinhorn and the
bizarrely titled seasonal show "Mrs. Rabinowitz's Xmas Tree."[12]

By 1930 William Paley, son of a Philadelphia cigar store owner,
had acquired a number of independent stations under the banner of
the Columbia Broadcasting System (CBS), with the intent of going
head to head with David Sarnoff's National Broadcasting Corporation, which RCA had recently launched. Casting about for a flagship
station, he acquired WABC, shows and all. For the next two years
Der Tog Program had the unique distinction of being the only Yiddish
show aired nationwide in the history of American broadcasting. By
1932, CBS produced enough of its own programming to fill its
broadcast day, and the quirky little Yiddish show was summarily
dropped.[13]

Things were not going so well for WEVD, either. By 1931 a series
of costly license appeals began to whittle down the station's finite
financial resources. Repeated entreaties to listeners for money were
doomed from the start: even had they wanted to, unemployed working-class listeners had little disposable income to help the ailing station. WEVD was on the ropes.

Realizing the dire circumstances for this beacon of Socialism, and
also sensing the loss of his long-held radio dream, Vladeck cajoled
Cahan to come to the aid of the faltering station. In 1932, the
Forverts dug into its pockets and came up with the necessary
$200,000 to bail out the station. It was not so long before that the
Forverts had ponied up nearly double that amount—$350,000—for

"The Manischewitz Radio Hour," with Ariel Rubestein's orchestra, on New York radio station WEVD, 1935.

the erection of their Lower East Side skyscraper headquarters. But the newspaper's largesse during the dark days of the Depression was a far greater expense, and a tremendous gesture of faith in the undertaking. WEVD was pulled back from the edge of the abyss, albeit now run commercially.[14]

The station came on the air in September 1932 with a slew of revamped programs. The jewel in the crown of the new WEVD was *The Forverts Hour*. Taking on the format and time slot of the recently cancelled *Tog Program*, *The Forverts Hour* rocketed to primacy in the Yiddish radio world, obliterating all competition and memory of shows before it. Though the stage was considered a higher calling than radio (theater was "legit," radio not), everyone and anyone in the Yiddish theater or the arts clamored for a chance to appear on the show. And its popularity reigned not just with performers but among its fervent listeners and studio attendees.

"Sunday afternoon in the springtime, every house—of course it was only Jewish people—every house had *The Forverts Hour* on," Sid Beckerman remembers. "Springtime, and people would be cleaning.

Sunday was for cleaning. You know, the windows would be open, the *betgevant* [bedclothes] would be aired out, and the floors would be mopped. But if you passed down my block, Longfellow Avenue in the Bronx, you wouldn't miss one note from *The Forverts Hour*."

But musicians playing for radio shows had to stay active in other venues. The Depression made it harder than ever for them to stitch together enough jobs to keep themselves and their families from being cast out into the streets, an increasingly common occurrence. The haphazard scheduling of jobs in the Jewish music world meant that willingness to travel and the ability to play various repertoires—those same skills learned in the old country—now came in handy.

Dave Tarras's description of a typical weekend from the mid-1930s illustrates how several small jobs could be thrown together by an enterprising musician in order to make a living: "I played with Olshanetsky a job for the Baker's Union in the Bronx till about five o'clock in the morning. So we went from that job to his hotel, where we showered and he had to finish one of the arrangements for *The Forverts Hour*. And we go straight to the radio to make rehearsal, and I got through with the job twelve o'clock. I went from the radio to the Paramount in the Bronx—I had an afternoon there—and at night to the DeLuxe Palace on Howard Avenue back in Brooklyn. See what I mean?"

During this period, Olshanetsky ran a booking office that took advantage of the growing hotel and catering hall trade, as Tarras recalled. "Olshanetsky got smart too. He opened up an office on Broadway and took on weddings, parties, the mountains. Took big prices—for back then, it was."

It was an Olshanetsky job that first took Tarras to the Catskills. Since the turn of the century the Catskill region of New York State had been home to numerous hotels from which Jews were restricted. Then Jewish farmers in Ulster and Sullivan counties began turning their properties into retreats for tubercular New York sweatshop laborers. From there it didn't take long for the Catskills to become one of the most developed (some would say overdeveloped) and influential resort areas in America.

Everyone who could—including Yiddish theater professionals—would escape to the Catskills during the hot summer months. But at the beginning there was no strong entertainment draw to a stay in the mountains. Gradually, it became more and more expected, and entertainers and musicians were in real demand.

By the 1920s, the "Borsht Belt," as it came to be called, boasted scores of hotels catering to Jewish clientele. Places like the Hotel

Majestic, the Pineview, the Normandie Hotel, and Echo Lodge were opened to bring the newly emerging Jewish leisure class all things cultural and culinary. Tarras describes his first Catskills booking:

"I get a call from Olshanetsky—'I booked us in the mountains!' 'Where?' 'Kiamesha Lake, ten men.' A big job for a hotel. We get there in the middle of the night. It's raining terrible. They got a new owner, and for him to have Alexander Olshanetsky is a big—so we are treated well, with respect. Later on, this little Kiamesha Concord, they turned into one of the biggest: the Concord hotel."

A Catskills gig required the rigor of playing for the theater plus the flexibility of playing a wedding reception, frequently offering the worst aspects of both. And while the repertoire grew to include more and more American songs, bands that played continued to cull material from the Yiddish theater.

By the early 1930s, the popularity of Yiddish songs on bandstands in Catskill hotels, weddings, on jukeboxes, and on radio caused Jewish composers to worry about massive lost royalty revenues. Aware that their colleagues on Broadway and in broadcasting were being taken care of by ASCAP (American Society of Composers Authors and Publishers), Yiddish tunesmiths sought the protection of the giant organization. For a variety of reasons, not least of which was the disdain it felt for non-mainstream performers, ASCAP refused to open its doors to composers in the Yiddish theater.

Reacting to this, Sholom Secunda, Alexander Olshanetsky, Joseph Rumshinsky, Abe Ellstein, Henry Lefkowitch, and Harry Lubin founded the Society of Jewish Composers (SJC) in 1932 to give themselves the kind of protection their popularity warranted. It wasn't until 1940, when Broadcast Music Incorporated (BMI) was founded to service artists rebuffed by ASCAP, that SJC found an established organization willing to offer a hand, which they happily accepted. By 1954, with the decline of Yiddish record and sheet music sales, SJC had outlived its usefulness, and surviving members were finally able to join ASCAP.

A MISS AND A HIT

A rich part of New York Jewish music lore concerns Yiddish theater composer Sholom Secunda and his brushes with American music greatness. First came his early rejection of George Gershwin as the collaborator chosen for him by his mentor, Yiddish theater giant Boris Thomashefsky. Then there was Secunda's bargain sale of his composition "Bay Mir Bistu Sheyn" (To Me You Are Beautiful). Simply put, it's the story of a tune from a failed Yiddish show, sold for a song, that went on to become one of the biggest crossover hits in American pop music history. The unabridged version is far more complicated.

The story begins deep in the Depression, as the Yiddish theater struggled to keep its head above water and turn out more shows. In the summer of 1932, Sholom Secunda composed a score for a new musical called *Men Ken Lebn Nor Men Lost Nisht*, or *I Would If I Could*, the English title its producers preferred over the literal translation: "You Could Live But They Don't Let You." Produced at Brooklyn's Rolland Theater, the show was an old-world romp written for the musical comedy stars Aaron Lebedeff and Lucy Levin. Together with lyricist Jacob Jacobs, Secunda crafted a powerhouse score designed to showcase the talents of Lebedeff and, not coincidentally, Dave Tarras.

As he had been the first time Tarras worked with him, Lebedeff was obstreperous; unlike the first time, it wasn't Tarras he was fighting. (They had since become friends.) Lebedeff was an energetic performer whose fleshy frame belied his sinewy stage presence. He was also full of himself and insisted that he help "fix" whichever songs composers offered him for his shows.

Secunda, who had never worked with Lebedeff before, was not amused. He stuck to his guns, refusing to allow the star to alter his compositions. Back and forth they fought until the audience's favorable reaction on opening night convinced them both of the rightness of Secunda's position. Lebedeff and costar Levin were called out for numerous encores. One song in particular, "Bay Mir Bistu Sheyn"—replete with a by then obligatory Tarras solo in the bridge—brought the house down.[15]

Secunda and Jacobs engaged in the not uncommon practice among Jewish composers of copyrighting and publishing their songs themselves and offering copies for sale as souvenirs in the theater lobby and in neighborhood music stores, like Metro Music on Second Avenue. Publishing ten thousand copies of the song—with Secunda's picture on the cover, not Jacobs's—over the next few years they sold out the printing.

Despite the sprightly score and enthusiastic response of the Depression-era audiences in the theater and on the road, it closed after the 1932–33 season. Secunda now looked to his next show for his meal ticket. That should have been the end of the story.

Fast forward to 1935. On a break from their songsmithing duties at Brooklyn's Vitaphone studios, two soon-to-be-famous composers,

Sammy Cahn and Saul Chaplin, went to see a show at Harlem's Apollo Theater that would come to have profound impact on American Jewish music. There they heard two black performers, Johnny and George, singing "Bay Mir Bistu Sheyn" in Yiddish. Stunned by the strongly favorable response, Cahn and Chaplin filed the tune away, figuring to write new English words for it.[16]

Two years later, with a suitcase full of songs—including "Bay Mir Bistu Sheyn"—Secunda headed to California to try to break into Hollywood and cross over into the mainstream. Fellow Yiddish composer Joseph Cherniavsky had taken the same trip in the early thirties with no success. Perhaps Cherniavsky and Secunda hoped that their composer skills plus their *landslayt* status with Jewish studio heads who were former New Yorkers would ease their way out west. But in their headlong scurry into assimilation, Hollywood producers from Samuel Goldwyn to Harry Cohn bent over backward to blunt overt references to or portrayals of Jews onscreen, contrary to revisionist film history.

A composer like Secunda, whose compositions were deeply hued with a sense of who he was and where he came from, touched a troubled nerve with the studio heads. There was no way these men would risk unmasking themselves to aid any composer, actor, or writer who exuded the Jewishness they had come to California to escape. Among those influential *landslayt* were Warner Brothers musical director Leo Forbstein and actor/singer Eddie Cantor, who proclaimed "Bay Mir Bistu Sheyn" too "Jewish." They had no idea how wrong they were.

Unbeknownst to Forbstein, the song was already on its way into the Warner Brothers pipeline. Secunda had returned to New York and had several shows running with his partner Jacobs, including *Lomir Khasene Hobn* (Let's Get Married) and *Pini fun Pinshev* (Pini from Pinshev), when Jack and Joe Kammen called about publishing some of their works. Surprisingly, the Kammens wanted not the team's fresh new pieces but the slightly stale "Bay Mir Bistu Sheyn." Secunda, figuring the song had achieved all it could, was sanguine about relinquishing the rights. Consulting Jacobs, he agreed to the sale, took the thirty dollars the twins offered him, and split the take with his partner.[17]

In what was either a carefully planned venture or a stroke of unimaginable coincidence, less than two weeks after buying the rights from Secunda and Jacobs, Jack and Joe Kammen turned around and licensed the song to the Warner Brothers subsidiary T.B.

Harms company. Though the exact amount the Kammens received in their arrangement with Harms is not known, it is safe to assume it exceeded the thirty dollars they paid for the song.

Within a month after its release Americans coast to coast were swinging to a deep-dish Yiddish song, albeit one masquerading under a German title. (The new songwriters retained the Yiddish pronunciation of "sheyn" but spelled it using the Germanized

Yiddish goes German goes French: Sholom Secunda's international hit.

"schön.") Considering the very recent vintage of the original Yiddish song, it is amusing to note how much of the press of the day insisted on referring to the original as an "old" Jewish song, displaying a common "Jewish equals old" bias that increased the song's exoticism even more.

Recorded by the Andrews Sisters in November 1937, the song was a hit by Christmas, producing an immediate cover by the Lombardo Brothers. The shellac on the Andrews Sisters' 78 was still warm when in December of 1937 Benny Goodman went into the studio to cover it. Its success was further enshrined when it was featured by Goodman in a concert at Carnegie Hall in January 1938.

Secunda was mortified. He had become the goat again. Now in addition to being the man who had sent George Gershwin packing, he was the guy who sold a million-dollar song for thirty dollars. Secunda had wanted to cross over into the American mainstream, but not this way! The irony is most clearly visible in a publicity photo of Secunda and the Andrews. There is Secunda, seated at the piano, hands poised over the keyboard, while the three beaming Andrews lean down around him, crosses dangling from their slender necks. While the Kammen brothers eventually agreed to give him a portion of their share of royalties, Secunda, for the most part, had been had.

The higher-ups at Warner Brothers woke to find that despite Leo Forbstein's decision to pass on it, "Bei Mir Bist Du Schön" was now the number one song in the United States. Deciding to capitalize on their latest acquisition, the studio rushed out a movie in January to exploit it. A two month writing and shooting schedule produced *Love, Honor and Behave*, directed by Stanley Logan and co-starring B-movie actors Wayne Morris and Priscilla Lane. An eminently forgettable boy-meets-girl potboiler, its raison d'être was Ms. Lane's very able performance of the new Warners' hit "Bei Mir Bist du Schön." The movie received justifiably tepid reviews and, mercifully, evaporated without a trace. (An anonymous reviewer for the *New York Herald Tribune* puckishly dubbed the film "Bei Mir Bist du a Shame.")

The success of "Bei Mir Bist du Schön" engendered a slew of songs aimed at capitalizing on the popularity of "Jewish" themes. Just a few months earlier Yiddish composers couldn't get the time of day from mainstream publishers or performers. Now it seemed no one could get enough of derivative Jewish tunes. Even ASCAP, which had sneered at welcoming in Yiddish composers, opened its doors to Secunda, but he declined the offer, citing allegiance to the start-up SJC.

The Andrews went back into the studio in February 1938, dusted off Nellie Casman's 1923 signature song "Yosl, Yosl," and rechristened it "Joseph, Joseph," hoping for another crossover hit. They even disinterred Adolf King's 1923 slightly risqué "Oy, Iz Dos a Rebetsin" (Wow, Is That a Rabbi's Wife!) and recast it as a song admonishing a bratty little brother in "Sha Sha, Jascha," with new lyrics by Jimmy Van Heusen. Jewish lightning did not strike twice, however.

Later that year Ziggy Elman (born Harry Finkelman), a trumpeter with the Benny Goodman Orchestra, reached back into his own

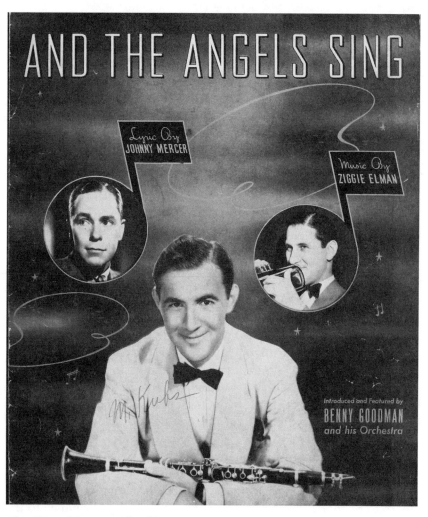

The King of Swing makes klezmer pop.

experience to record a klezmer tune. Brought in by Victor's budget label, Bluebird, to lead his own session, Elman's first records were some favorite klezmer tunes recorded years earlier by Abe Schwartz: "Beygelekh," which was renamed "Bublitchki," and "Der Shtiler Bulgar," which Elman renamed "Freilach in Swing (And the Angels Sing)."

The affection Elman had for these tunes is clear in that they were the first pieces he recorded when leading his own session, and he made no attempt to obscure the tunes' origins. With "Freilach in Swing," Elman rechoreographed the klezmer chestnut via an imaginative and thrilling arrangement that wove sophisticated, exciting swing trumpet with the driving meat-and-potatoes sound of Yiddish dance music. His experience in both genres shone through.

Beginning in a straight American-style arrangement, the tune makes a transition into a traditional up-tempo klezmer-style performance with the by then standard *bulgar* beat defined in the drums, and finishes with a return to an American-style performance. Elman's ABA form became the standard arrangement structure in all subsequent "Jewish-Jazz" recordings, including that of WHN's *Yiddish Melodies in Swing* and *Caravan of Stars*; the recording sessions of Sammy Musiker on the Savoy label; and, as late as the 1950s, Nat Farber's orchestrations for Mickey Katz.

In July 1939, Cab Calloway recorded a swing rendition of the folk song "Ot Azoy Neyt a Shnyader" (That's the Way a Tailor Sews) as "Utt-Da-Zay," followed the next month by scat singer Leo Watson's even hipper version. Calloway was soon back in the studio with another Yiddish crossover. That fall the new Molly Picon film *Mamele* had opened to rave reviews, and among its well-received songs was "Abi Gezint," written by Picon and Abe Ellstein. Calloway, borrowing just the title, recorded a tune called "A Bee Gezindt" in November.[18]

Singer/guitarist/pianist Slim Gaillard was another black performer who had a taste for Jewish-style songs, particularly those having to do with food. Gaillard recorded hot hep cat songs for Vocalion including "Vol Vistu Gaily Star" (1938), which uses the chord structure of "Yosl, Yosl," though not in klezmer style. The following October he recorded "Matzo Balls" which, ironically, was cut at the same session as the decidedly unkosher "Chittlin' Switch Blues." And in 1945 Gaillard served up "Dunkin' Bagel—Splat in the Coffee" one last offering of the kosher culinary kind.

This short-lived fad of using Yiddish material to create American popular songs did not constitute a trend in mainstream music. Aside

from the few songs that have survived in the standard swing repertoire there are no long-lived harmonic, thematic, or stylistic influences of Jewish music discernible in American popular music.

While the overall influence of Yiddish music on the American
landscape was slight, the effect of "Bei Mir Bist Du Schön" on the
American Jewish community was huge. Other Jewish songs had
made it across the ethnic boundary (most notably Peretz Sandler's
1896 "Eili, Eili"), but this was the first to be adapted and accepted
by the general public. Considering its enormous popularity and the
Yiddish music world's tendency to integrate pop styles quickly, it is
curious that neither Lebedeff nor any of the original interpreters of
"Bay Mir Bistu Sheyn" recorded a commercial "cover" version of it
themselves. Granted, there was a profound downturn in the number
of Yiddish records made in the 1930s. But even when recording did
resume in 1938, the Jewish entertainment world neglected to capitalize on the song until much later.

"Bei Mir Bist Du Schön" became the anthem of second-generation Jews, who saw the song's acceptance as a symbol of their own.
In baseball, that acceptance was personified by the Detroit Tiger
slugging star Hank Greenberg. In music, it was the King of Swing,
Benny Goodman. Their success meant Jews could make it in the
mainstream world on its terms without converting or even having to
change their names. For young Jewish clarinetists, Goodman
removed the necessity of playing Jewish repertoires altogether.

PLAYING AMERICAN

Born in 1909 to an immigrant family in Chicago's Jewish section,
Goodman started taking clarinet lessons at the local synagogue. He
progressed so rapidly that at nine he was studying with Franz
Schoepp, principal clarinetist of the Chicago Symphony Orchestra,
and by twelve he was a professional musician. Smitten by the energetic sound of jazz, at eighteen Goodman became a member, along
with Glenn Miller, of Ben Pollack's popular jazz band. Yet despite
his being Jewish and playing an instrument associated with Jews,
there is no hint in Goodman's fast ascent that he took part in or even
acknowledged the Chicago Jewish music scene.

Although Goodman knew as little about klezmer as Tarras knew
about jazz, Tarras was dubbed "the Jewish Benny Goodman," a
term he found bizarre but complimentary nonetheless. There is

only one tune Goodman and the Jewish Goodman both recorded: Romanian composer Dinicu's "Hora Staccato." While each displays the deep technical mastery demanded by this popular classical composition, Goodman plays it like a classical composition, betraying no evidence of a Jewish sound esthetic, while Tarras displays little but that. On "And the Angels Sing," which included Ziggy Elman on trumpet and singer Martha Tilton, Goodman has the perfect performance venue to assert his "klezmer" musicality. Yet he gives Elman the coveted spot to define the "color" of the piece: the record opens with his meaty and sure trumpet playing featuring his trademark "boyt'ya" ornament and his sensually oleaginous glissandos.

It's when Goodman comes in for a chorus after Tilton's vocal that we hear the strong contrast between the instrumentalists. Goodman's solo, while clean, elegant, and sophisticated, completely lacks the color, ornament, or phrasing of a klezmer background. In a piece signified by a strong Jewish-jazz identity, Goodman can't join in all the fun.

In other recordings like "My Little Cousin" and "Bei Mir Bist Du Schön," Goodman never takes any of the "Jewish" breaks; the few that appear were played by trumpeters Ziggy Elman and Jimmy Maxwell. Yet because he adapted some Jewish-themed tunes, he, like Gershwin, is widely credited with having forged the link between Jewish music and jazz.

The popularity of "Bei Mir Bist Du Schön" also fueled a craze for harmonizing siblings. The Jewish world came up with a few of its own: the Marlin Sisters (daughters of the famed cantor Samuel Malavsky), the Feder Sisters, the Pincus Sisters and, thanks to their stage-door mother, the Bagelman sisters, Merna and Claire.

After achieving early recognition on the "Feter Nahum (Uncle Norman) Program," a popular Jewish children's show on New York's WLTH (and later on WEVD), the Bagelman Sisters were quickly recognized as the valuable talents they were: young, attractive women who sang in a pouty Yiddish as homey as their slangy, unaccented English was up-to-date.[19]

They made their first records at Victor in 1939 with a quintet featuring Dave Tarras, playing improvised accompaniments, and the pianist/conductor Abe Ellstein (1907–63). These bouncy 78s, like "Abi Er Ken Tantsn" (As Long As He Can Dance) and the Joseph Rumshinsky/Chaim Towber classic "Sheyn Vi Di Levune" (As Beautiful as the Moon), were perfect little recordings: Ellstein's approach of interweaving the Bagelmans' close-as-the-air harmonies and Tarras's intuitive breaks was a winning formula.

The next year, the Bagelmans recorded with the diminutive tenor Seymour Rechtzeit, a former child star and popular matinee singer. Rechtzeit's glycerine-smooth voice epitomized the current crop of "microphone" singers, who relied on amplification to put forth their vocals rather than old-fashioned lung power. Their renditions of pieces like Ellstein's "Der Nayem Sher" (The New Sher) and "Der Alter Tsigayner" (The Old Gypsy) flew out of the record stores and in no time became de rigueur on Jewish bandstands, thanks to Tarras's masterful handling of the melodies.

These compositions were the handiwork of one of the youngest, brightest stars in the Yiddish music world. Abe Ellstein had begun his career as a *meshoyrer* and at nineteen began a six-year national tour with Yosele Rosenblatt, serving as arranger and accompanist. Considered one of the *yinge* (young ones), Ellstein, like his collaborator Molly Picon, was born in America but tried to keep a foot in both the Yiddish and mainstream music worlds.

Ellstein's recording stint at Victor began in 1939. He was peddling something called a "Jumpka," a watered-down polka with a light swing backbeat, under the name "Leon Steiner." Despite several recordings like "Jumpka Joe/Knock-Kneed Katie-Jumpka," the "Jumpka" never caught on.[20] What did, though, were recordings he made between his "Jumpka" sessions: klezmer tunes he wrote with his brother Harry, featuring Dave Tarras. Tending toward smooth, restrained music with an easy danceable beat, Ellstein represented the most perfect partnership Dave Tarras was to enjoy with any composer. From very early on Ellstein composed melodies that fit Tarras's style perfectly.

"Anything he had, a recording, a show, 'Dave, do what you want. Play the way you want it,'" recalled Tarras. "It didn't matter who was singing—Seymour Rechtzeit, Molly Picon, for the recording, for the theater. If I had to play ensemble, sure, I played what was written. But the solos? Anything I wanted."

Another composer/bandleader who let Tarras shine was pianist Sam Medoff (1915–90). His father was the popular Yiddish theater singer David Medoff (1888–1978), a prolific recording artist whose hundreds of 78s were aimed at the Jewish, Russian, and Ukrainian markets, each of which claimed him as one of their own. The younger Medoff wanted to achieve the same result in the American-Jewish market using the Jewish-jazz mix he learned as a pianist on club dates led by Max Epstein. Epstein called this potent mix "Jewish-American swing."

Medoff got the idea for a radio program that would feature swing arrangements of Yiddish songs and tunes, lively patter, and slick harmony singing. He scheduled an audition at WHN and asked Tarras to go with him.

"Dave could not make the audition," Epstein recalled. "So I went to the audition and Medoff got the job. After he got the job he didn't take me to play the job. He figured I might not be good enough for him. He wanted Dave Tarras to do it. Dave Tarras wasn't so familiar with Jewish-American swing as I was, but the name Dave Tarras meant a lot."[21]

Tarras *wasn't* familiar with American stylings, and Medoff had to work around that. His solution was to construct arrangements around Tarras modifying the ABA structure perfected by Ziggy Elman. Here, the A section would be carried by band members who could play jazz, leading into B, where Tarras would play the break in straight klezmer style, and then finish in A, with Tarras playing section parts. It was a tidily elegant solution that worked.

Next, Medoff needed a sister act. He first approached the Pincus Sisters, three singers—two also played accordion—who could deliver the rich three-part harmonies popularized by the Andrews. But due to disagreements among themselves, recalls Roz Pincus, the last surviving sister, the trio couldn't accept Medoff's offer. So he turned to the Bagelmans, who had recorded one of his songs at their premiere session in August 1939.

Each fifteen-minute *Yiddish Melodies in Swing* program offered "Yiddish songs played both *heymish* and hot." The typical roster included "those daughters of the downbeat" the Barry Sisters (none other than Merna and Claire Bagelman with new last names and the radio monikers "Pert" and "Gay"); a "thrilling young tenor" (Jan Bart, Nat Spencer, or Seymour Rechtzeit) for the soft-art music crowd; some comedy; and a solid swing accompaniment played by "Sam Medoff and the boys of the Yiddish Swingtette."

Though he was music director at a small Brooklyn station, WARD, Medoff signed a deal with station WHN for a thirteen-week series. Its premiere in September 1939, broadcast from atop the glamorous Loew's State Theater building in midtown Manhattan, featured a robust twelve-piece big band playing to a large studio audience. The tone was brisk and bouncy, as the announcer Lewis Charles cracked:

They do it to "Elimeylekh."
They do it to "Reb Dovid'l."
They even do it to "Yidl Mitn Fidl."
Who does what to which?
Yiddish Melodies in Swing takes old Jewish folk songs
and mixes them in the smart uptown fashion of Yiddish swing.

The audience loved it. It was sassy and modern, and it showed listeners that they could be Jewish and with-it Americans, too. Even the theme music was a combination of Yiddish and American sounds: Medoff's Jewish rearrangement of "When the Saints Go Marching In," with a little *dreydl* at the end, played by Tarras.

Each week Medoff wrote swing arrangements of everything from Moshe Nadir's "Rebbe Elimeylekh" (The Yiddish King Cole) to "Dayenu" (I'm Never Satisfied). He also produced a seemingly endless variety of *bulgars, horas,* and *freylekhs* with goofy names like "Blueberry Bulgar" and "Just a Little Bit North of South Fallsburg."

This trawling for themes in the sea of Yiddish songs ended as it began: with a crossover composition sold for virtually nothing. The victim this time was Abe Schwartz. Though he continued to play weddings and jobs in the Catskills, his career had slowed down precipitously. Having made his last record in 1938 and published nothing since 1926, Schwartz was approached in the spring of 1941 to sell the rights to "Di Grine Kuzine" for three hundred dollars outright, or a penny for every sheet published. (He coincidentally had renewed his copyright on the song in 1938.)

Schwartz asked his wife what he should do. "Take the money," she told him. "We need it for the rent." And so he did. Schwartz, unlike Secunda before him, failed to try and reclaim his forfeited royalties, though the family always wished he had, his daughter Bebe Schwartz noted.

Benny Goodman's 1941 reworking of Schwartz's ballad, "My Little Cousin," replaced the old-world beauty whose looks had faded from the harsh life in the sweatshops with a pretty young cousin whose only thoughts were of snaring the boy around the corner. The vocalist Goodman used on the track was Peggy Lee, who provided a slick pop reading of the text. Though nowhere near the hit "Bei Mir Bist du Schön" was, or even "And the Angels Sing," it made money for everyone but the original composers.

MEANWHILE, BACK IN EUROPE . . .

If change was a whirlwind for American Jews in entertainment, a breeze eventually reached even Rovne. The city was now a part of Poland, after country lines had been redrawn following World War I. Its rich Jewish community remained culturally active until the eve of its destruction. A *badkhn* at a wedding? No longer, and even though there were still plenty of people who could—and would—get up for a *sherele* when one was struck up by the band, they seemed to grow ever older as the bridal couples and their friends seemed to get younger.

Things hadn't been the same in Rovne since the end of the Great War, when the city became a battleground in the struggle between the rising tide of Communism and the Poles' national aspiration, fueled by the counterrevolutionary leader and *pogromtshik* Symon Petlura, who harnessed anti-Semitism in his goal to unify Poland. Some Jews had returned to their hometown—fiddler/*badhkn* Alter Getye's sons came back, and their klezmer band started playing again—but the deprivation and pogroms left little time for gaiety in the bitter postwar years.

Rovne was still the city of cantors, though. Zeydl Rovner continued to hold sway, as did the Koussevitsky Brothers—Moishe, David, Simche, and Jacob—who raised the level of cantorial and *meshoyrer* art. In the early '30s the famous cantorial performer Gershon Sirota came to Rovne to find choristers, his *geklibene shtimes* ("Chosen Voices"), with whom he traveled throughout Poland, bringing Jewish liturgy to the concert hall. One of those *geklibene shtimes* was my father, Zindel Sapoznik, who had previously sung with Moishe Koussevitsky.

The Yiddish community continued to balance inside and outside influences. "By then," my mother, Pearl, recalled of the 1930s, her teenage years, "you wouldn't have a *khasene* without a tango or a foxtrot." No, indeed. Still a majority Jewish city famous for its *khazonim* and klezmorim, Yiddish theaters, and performing troupes, Rovne, in its parlors and kitchens, experienced pomaded paramours serenading their beloveds with Yiddish translations of Polish pop songs while strumming on a *Havayski gitar*—a Hawaiian slide guitar! The crosscurrents of culture were strong in Rovne.

Radio was late in coming to the Polish city, and when it did old-time Yiddish music is not what Rovne's young people listened for as they spun the dial in search of broadcasts from Warsaw or Sofia. Only among the old did traditional songs still find resonance. My great-uncle Shmil, a successful teamster, was known for "entertaining" passersby on the street below by sitting out on his balcony playing cantorial and theater 78s upon his Pathéphone.

Yet in the headlong rush to modernity the old tunes persisted. My mother and her pals in the Gordonya Zionist group thought nothing of affixing an old melody to new *khalutz* (pioneer) lyrics. And when she and her friends got together to sew, they sang the latest Polish tangos interspersed with songs like "Ikh Hob Gekent a Meydele," a centuries-old murder ballad. There was no clear-cut beginning of one thing or ending of another. Traditions melded subtly, their edges softening.

Rovne was one of the cities that pioneering Soviet ethnomusicologist Moshe Beregovski (1892–1961) selected for his intensive Yiddish field collections of regional music. Remembered today thanks largely to the American music historian Mark Slobin, Beregovski was a critical figure in the history of Jewish culture, both for what he accomplished—the collecting, annotating, and preserving of thousands of Yiddish folk songs and klezmer tunes—and for what he was unable to complete: the history of klezmer music. If the press and various histories being published at the time remarked on nothing but klezmer music's sad demise, Beregovski was one man who knew its era had not passed.

Born in Kiev, Beregovski grew up surrounded by Jewish song. His father was a teacher at the Kiev Jewish music school, and from early on he himself showed great interest and aptitude for the art, studying at conservatories in Kiev and Leningrad. At age thirty-two Beregovski headed up the Ukrainian Academy of Sciences' Institute of Jewish Proletarian Culture, then home to the collections of ethnographer/playwright S. Ansky. Along with the earlier writings of pioneering Ukrainian musicologist Klement Kvitka, these collections fueled what would become Beregovski's lifelong passion.[22]

In a photograph taken with his colleagues in Kiev, Beregovski emits bespectacled earnestness, the kind of quiet enthusiasm and determination that allowed him to earn his doctorate during the dark days of 1944 and to persevere through the rigors of his mission. He could not have chosen a worse moment in which to conduct his research. But given the historical context of his work, carried out under the dual threats of Hitler and Stalin and despite the attrition of his subjects, what Beregovski achieved is nothing less than astounding.

Beregovski's 1937 research paper "Yiddishe Instrumentalishe Folks Muzik" proposed to place klezmorim within a musical, social, economic, and historical context. His goal was to collect, document, and disseminate music by "every teacher, administrator of libraries and clubs, cultural activist, every worker and farmworker."[23] He even planned to mobilize schoolchildren. "It is not hard to assign a special group of children to gather data on local klezmer," the historian noted. "Children in the upper grades who show great interest in folk art have sent us valuable data that they collected."

How sad, then, to read through this marvelous monograph and feel Beregovski's passion for his quest, knowing as he did not the extent to which it would become unrealizable. "Unfortunately, nowhere has anyone been interested in collecting the works of and data on the klezmorim in all the lands inhabited by Jews, where there were klezmorim in the nineteenth century and even to a great extent today," he lamented. "Is it still possible to accomplish this? Certainly! . . . One can find a great many klezmer in their fifties and sixties (and, not rarely, in their seventies and eighties) everywhere."

Beregovski assembled nearly one hundred detailed questions for interviewing the many older klezmorim he was determined to track down. The questionnaire—which marks the first use of the term "klezmer" to define the music as opposed to the people who make it—is a model of insight into how music works as a system and within a socioeconomic structure. The essay and survey are what remain, a gold mine of unasked questions. Unless something turns up among the Beregovski cylinders recently "discovered" in the post–Soviet archives, this may be the sum total of his work to chart the lives of European klezmer.

Beregovski's call to arms was fervent, enthusiastic—and too late. The scholar witnessed the destruction of the communities he so loved and to which he had dedicated his life, followed by the repression and denial of his work under Joseph Stalin's harsh postwar anti-Jewish purges.

With the post-war expansion of Communism, the largest concentrations of Yiddish-speaking Jews in Europe were now found in countries under its sway. Stalin's antipathy toward the Jews resulted in his wholesale elimination of the Yiddish intelligentsia, culminating in 1952's "Night of the Murdered Poets," the assassination of twenty-four of the greatest Yiddish writers and artists living in Russia.

The closing of Yiddish schools, theaters, and newspapers helped choke off any of the continuity that might have made Beregovski's work a part of the postwar Jewish cultural reanimation. In a way, the supression of the remnants of Yiddish life destroyed it yet again; nothing was meant to rise from the ashes of this cataclysm.

Imprisoned for a time in Siberia in 1949 at the height of these anti-Jewish purges, Beregovski was returned to a world that ignored his work and the existence of a community that had thrived until just a few short years before. In his final years Beregovski was reduced to begging emigrating scholars to smuggle out copies of his banned manuscripts, but none would risk it.[24] He died in1961, a sick and broken man.

YIDL MITN FIDL: JEWISH MUSIC ONSCREEN

While Beregovski was toiling to collect and document the old-time klezmer, a less authentic but ultimately more successful project was in progress: the 1936 feature film *Yidl Mitn Fidl*. Yiddish theater actor turned movie director Joseph Green, embarking on his first film, offered the starring role to the then-floundering Molly Picon. Picon, whose career had been stalled mainly by the tepid response that met her attempts to cross over into American venues like vaudeville and movies, accepted Green's offer.

Inspired by the old song of the same name, *Yidl Mitn Fidl* follows the exploits of Picon—in another of her trademark pants roles—and her fellow musicians across the roads and towns of Poland and, finally, to America. The film was shot in and around Kazimierz, Poland, a consciously picturesque town one hundred miles south of Warsaw that already boasted a robust American-Jewish tourist trade.

As in so many Yiddish theatrical productions, the best moment is the wedding sequence, a choreographed enactment featuring local residents as extras.

Molly Picon recalled:

> They thought they had been invited to a real wedding, and when one woman asked why so much food we explained to her that it wasn't a real wedding, we were just making a film. I don't think she had ever seen a film, but she said: "Why didn't you tell me this before? With so much food I could've brought my daughter to get married for real. She has a *khosn* but we have no money . . . to make a proper wedding."[25]

From the opening tune, "Oy, Mame Bin Ikh Farlibt" (Oy, Mama I'm So in Love), which tells of a young girl's infatuation with a klezmer, this movie crystallized the popular image of the romantic klezmer.

Green's presentation of the devil-may-care, down-at-the-heels, free-wheeling musicians, instruments aloft, hats askew, made filmgoers in Europe and America nod and say, "Aha! Now *that's* a klezmer."

But while the images were right, the music was not. *Yidl Mitn Fidl* features authentic costumes and locations but no traditional music. For *Yidl*, Abe Ellstein, brought in from New York together with lyricist Itsik Manger, created a smooth score that entirely misses the mark, considering the film supposedly portrayed klezmer musicians. Not a note of traditional music appears, a common problem in musical films.

In two exceptions, for his 1939 film *Fishke Der Krimer* (The Light Ahead), Yiddish and Hollywood movie director Edgar G. Ulmer cribbed music from a 1925 recording of Cherniavsky's Yiddish-American Jazz Band. And for *Moon Over Harlem*, a black musical film he directed that same year, Ulmer used a score by clarinet/sax player Sidney Bechet that accurately reflected the community being portrayed.

Yidl's denouement—a triumphant Picon on a boat bound for America following her rough passage from the dire poverty of klezmer music—fed the "success" myth klezmer music continued to hold out. From Gusikov to Heifetz, klezmer music was a bridge to a new and better world. The rise of Picon, and of Jewish music itself, from the street to the stage is implicit in this fairy tale ending. But, as the grim reality of Hitler became clearer, boats to America were the real fairy tale.

In film as in the theater, it was musicals people loved, and one of the first stars of Yiddish film musicals was Moishe Oysher (1907–58). Born in the town of Lipkon, in Bessarabia, Oysher was a *meshoyrer* who came from a long line of *khazonim*. Though he was a great talent at an early age, his success in America was far from overnight.

After arriving in New York in 1928, Oysher supported himself in less exalted ways, like washing dishes, in the nearly seven years it took him to break into the New York Yiddish theater. (The Hebrew Actors Union finally granted him his card after a four-year wait.)

A brilliant singer, he was however an indifferent actor, a problem that paled in comparison to his troubles with the Orthodox community. Oysher wanted to maintain his link with the synagogue by serving as a *khazn* while plying his trade as a popular performer. But unlike the prodigal son/cantor in *The Jazz Singer*, Oysher was met with angry congregants who railed against his presence in the *shul*, some to the point of staging a picket line.

The local film industry had no such qualms, featuring his magnificent singing voice in titles like *Dem Khazn's Zundl* (The Cantor's

Son, 1937), *Yankl der Shmid* (Yankl the Blacksmith, 1938), and in an inspired bit of casting, *Der Vilner Shtot Khazn* (The Cantor from Vilna, 1940)—an adaptation of the 1902 play *Der Vilner Balabesl*, based on the life of the cantor Joel-David Strashunsky. Oysher's Yiddish films were among the last major offerings of what had always been a somewhat minor branch of the film industry. The late thirties were alive with outstanding Yiddish *kunst* films like Edgar G. Ulmer's *Grine Felder* (1937) and Maurice Schwartz's *Tevye der Milkhiker* (1939), while Molly Picon was making popular musicals like *Yidl Mitn Fidl* (1936) and *Mamele* (1939).

Yet for every high budget *Teyve* there were films like *Bar Mitzvah* (1935), starring Boris Thomashefsky. Having fallen on hard times—the once great star was reduced to singing in a Lower East Side restaurant for a living—Thomashefky made this low-budget feature four years before his death. While the exteriors of what is supposed to be Vienna look oddly reminiscent of Brooklyn, it is Thomashefsky himself, too used to playing to the gallery to keep from looking directly into the camera, who underscores the sad end of a great career and of a medium: Yiddish film. Fade to black.

In March 1937 Dave Tarras was approached by the budget label Variety to put out some klezmer 78s. Though he assembled a fine band (trumpet, two fiddles, cello, piano, and string bass), the recordings were never issued.

Tarras's next recording offer came from bandleader Al Glaser (1898–1982), a classically trained violinist who had played music throughout the Far East before arriving in the United States in 1924, just before increasingly prohibitive anti-immigration laws made that virtually impossible. Glaser had contracted to put out some Jewish instrumental records with Decca, the upstart label that had had a hit with the Andrews Sisters' "Bei Mir Bist du Schön" in 1937. They issued four 78s under the name Al Glaser's Bucovina Kapelle, featuring Dave Tarras. Glaser stepped back and allowed Tarras to define the sound of the session. The recordings, elegant and restrained, demonstrate each player's keen knowledge of the music. Though the album set sold respectably, Decca did not follow up with more klezmer recordings.[26]

As if to make up for lost time, musicians like Tarras, Olshanetsky, and Ellstein seemed to be everywhere at once. The klezmer remained a viable motif for the popular representation of the mythic folk character, as proved by Olshanetsky's new hit show *Yosl, der Klezmer*. The recording of it by the show's star, Seymour Rechtzeit,

Aaron Lebedeff's "Roumania, Roumania," Columbia records, 1942.

featured the powerhouse ensemble of Joe Levitt on trumpet, Giuletta Morino on violin, Charlie Galazan on bass, Abe Ellstein on piano, and Tarras on clarinet.

From the end of 1939 throughout 1941, leading Yiddish theater stars like Seymour Rechtzeit, the Barry Sisters, and Aaron Lebedeff got busy again with recording sessions, at which Dave Tarras was always in demand. And why not? Tarras was at the peak of his powers, playing with a sureness born of fifteen years in the Yiddish theater and thousands of weddings. The Barry Sisters' "Dem Nayem Sher," Seymour Rechtzeit's "Belz," and Aaron Lebedeff's finest rerecording of "Roumania, Roumania" would not have had their strong sense of identity without the obligatory Dave Tarras solo.

By 1941 a kind of normalcy had returned to the recording world. Even Abe Schwartz returned briefly to the studio, playing a robust accompaniment to Yiddish comedy newcomer Fyvush Finkel singing

Rubin Doctor's "Ikh Bin a Border Bay Mayn Vayb" (I Board at My Wife's).

Dave Tarras exploded with a host of new compositions, most of which he recorded—including "Tants Istanbul," "A Pastukhl's Kholem," and "Shifra's Tants"—during sessions for Victor in April and December of that year. Owing to the decreased budgets allowed for recording, the large brass bands of old were replaced by a smaller, intimate trio comprising accordionist Sammy Beckerman (nephew of clarinet great Shloimke Beckerman) and Tarras's old drummer Irving Graetz. These trio discs exhibit a cool, pared-down sound that condensed the lusher feel of old into its basic components: melody (Tarras), harmony (Beckerman), and rhythm (Graetz). Bingbangbing: they went in and shot out the tunes one after another, a typical Tarras session.

Even more astounding was the unexpected return to the studio of Naftule Brandwein. Increasingly beset by his heavy drinking, Brandwein had been absent from the studio since 1927, but in April 1941, RCA Victor invited him back to record what would be his last session.

Made under the modernized moniker of "Nifty" Brandwein, the recordings—"Klayne Princesin," "Naftuli's Freylekh," "Freylekher Yontef," and "Nifty's Eygene"—trace Brandwein's development in his fourteen-year absence from the studio. His tone is edgier than before and his wind is cut down; nonetheless, he is still a powerful presence. Though no longer playing with the same fire, he demonstrates strong introspection and maturation. Gone are the rapier swoops and tears, replaced by gentler, no less impressive extended phrases. Most telling, however, are the rich lower-register passages, a popular hallmark of Tarras's style, now part of Brandwein's playing, in honor of his ascended rival.

One of the greatest things to happen to Tarras at this time was the addition to his group of ace musician Sammy Musiker (1916–64). A brilliant clarinetist and sax player, Musiker effortlessly moved from American to Jewish stylings as no musician had before him. As his name implies, Musiker came from a professional musical family: his father, a trumpet player, taught him and his younger brother Ray.[27]

Starting lessons as a child, Sammy quickly developed into a singular talent, able to run through any music put before him, though he preferred American and Yiddish styles. His reputation became so great that when drummer Gene Krupa left Benny Goodman to start his own band in 1938, he brought Musiker on as a tenor sax player. Musiker was with the Krupa band until 1942. Eagle-eyed fans of screwball comedy can catch a glimpse of Musiker when Krupa and the band play "Drum Boogie" in a cameo appearance in Howard Hawks's 1941 film *Ball of Fire*, with Barbara Stanwyck and Gary Cooper.

In 1939 drummer Irving Graetz introduced Dave Tarras to the twenty-three-year-old Sammy Musiker. "Dave Tarras came over to me one Friday and he says, 'Irving, I need a saxophone player, who can I get?'" Graetz remembers. "I says, 'Just a moment.' Sammy Musiker was in the hiring hall of Local 802 because he was that time with Gene Krupa, but they were off a couple of weeks, they were going to start at the New York Paramount on the stage.

"So I went over to Sammy Musiker and I said: 'Sammy, you got a job tomorrow? I can get you a job for tomorrow if you're not working.' He said: 'Irving, the only job I'm going to take is I want to hear Dave Tarras. If I could get a job with Dave Tarras, I will take it.' I said, 'You got it!' Just like that: 'You got it!'"

And he did. In the postwar years, Musiker worked with Dave Tarras regularly, developing a sound so like his mentor's that when he wanted, no one could tell them apart. But Musiker's ego would not let him merely imitate a style or a sound, and he pushed further to explore his own interpretations, incorporating all the lessons he had learned from both Tarras and Krupa. The results were extraordinary.

Sam Musiker got more than a musical education from his association with Dave Tarras. He also fell in love with and married Tarras's daughter, Branele (Brownie). Among the gifts they received was "Brana's Khasene," the 1941 disc Tarras composed and recorded to commemorate the wedding. Tarras was very proud of, and enthusiastic about, his new son-in-law, and proceeded to include him on as many jobs as he could. Young Sammy returned the favor.

In 1940 Alexander Olshanetsky's beautiful 1934 song "Ikh Hob Dikh Tsufil Lib," much played on Yiddish bandstands, attained general popularity as "I Love You Much Too Much," recorded by Bob Zurke and His Delta Rhythm Band. Not to be outdone, Krupa went into the studio the month following its release to cover it. Unlike Zurke, Krupa had someone in the band who could—and did—play the music as it was meant to be played: Sammy Musiker.

But just as the Jewish recording world was regaining its sea legs the bottom dropped out yet again. American Federation of Musicians president James Caesar Petrillo, incensed over the lack of royalties paid to members of his union, called for a complete ban on commercial recording. He felt that records being played on radio were denying union members much-needed work playing live music over the air. Though the ban didn't really hurt the popular mainstream name acts—many of whom were still making records for American soldiers on the so-called V-discs (or Victory Discs)—it wreaked havoc on smaller performers and labels.

Deprived of new records, lovers of Jewish music could hear top composers' latest offerings on radio and at the handful of Yiddish theaters still open for business. Alexander Olshanetsky, taking time from his flourishing Catskill booking agency, wrote the score for the show *Dos Goldene Land* (The Golden Land). It was staged at the Public Theater and starred Aaron Lebedeff, Leo Fuchs, and Goldie Eisman. Ilya Trilling wrote songs for *Meyer From Kentucky*, *Kinder on a Heym* (Children Without a Home), and *General Fishel Dovid*. Secunda, prolific as ever, composed scores for *Gimpl Nemt a Froy* (Gimpel Takes a Wife), *Der Raykher Feter* (The Rich Uncle), *Gliklikher Teg* (Lucky Days), and *Esterk* (Little Esther), for which he wrote "Dona, Dona," a sort of Yiddish "Git Along Little Dogies."

It may seem curious now that these everyday, almost banal shows were being peddled on Second Avenue while across the ocean Jews were being murdered at an industrial rate. And though some plays of the period reflected the situation in Europe—Joseph Ben-Ami returned to the Yiddish theater in 1944 to mount H. Levick's *Der Nes in Ghetto* (The Miracle in the Warsaw Ghetto") and David Bergelson's *Mir Veln Lebn* (We Will Live)—for the most part it was business as usual in the Yiddish theater, with its increasingly escapist fare.

After the war the Jewish music market was flooded with songs expressing the horror of the ordeal its people had endured. In 1947 publisher Leo Russoto issued a number of songs composed in the ghettos and camps, including Hirsh Glik's "Shtil di Nakht" (Quiet Is the Night), "Zog Nit Keynmol" (Never Say), and Leyb Rozenthal's "Tsu Eyns, Tsvey Dray" (To One, Two, Three) while several publishers rushed out the dirge "Ani Ma'amim" (I Believe). Hopeful postwar compositions like Leo Fuld's Zionist-themed "Vu Ahin Zol Ikh Geyn?" (Where Shall I Go?), also became favorites among Holocaust survivors.

Still, following World War II, active Yiddish culture was in a tailspin. During the war, the vast majority of radio stations featuring Yiddish programming like WBBC, WLTH, WCNW, and WARD went off the air, leaving just the Bronx-based WBNX and the clear leader in the field, WEVD. Soon, even WBNX could no longer compete with the *Forverts*-subsidized WEVD and it, too, went off the air in the late 1940s. After the demise of its longtime competitor, WEVD took over its motto, "The Station That Speaks Your Language."

The Yiddish theater was also mortally wounded, with even the great Maurice Schwartz forced to take bit parts in bad Hollywood B movies to compensate for drooping attendance at his Yiddish Art

Dave Tarras in the 1940s.

Theater. In addition to the absence of new talent and audiences from
Europe, young American actors were barred from attaining the
Hebrew Actors Union card, a prerequisite for playing Second
Avenue. That situation served to extend the tenure of aging ingenues
and septuagenarian juveniles, driving bright young actors and
actresses to the more welcoming venues of legitimate theater.

Klezmer musicians, meanwhile, were driven to far more prosaic
outlets. During the war, some, like Sid Beckerman and Howie Leess,
had joined the military. Beckerman was drafted and served in the
front lines in Italy. Leess had a less dangerous assignment more
befitting his musical talents. He served from 1941 until 1944 in the
Unit Band at a naval base in upstate New York, playing for the raising of the colors, in the officers' club, and for the troops when they
arrived and were shipped out. After the war Beckerman returned to
playing jobs but found few opportunities, and soon took a job with
the United States Post Office. Leess picked up playing with American orchestras but found that the big band era was over. The money
needed to support a wife and family was to be found in weddings
and bar mitzvahs.

Jewish jazz also had its last gasp in the postwar years. Tarras
remembered a call he got in 1946 from Savoy, the cutting-edge jazz
label. "Savoy came to me," he said. "They were *yidn* from Newark.
They wanted a band that mixed Jewish and jazz. And I arranged for
a big band and I made Sammy do the arrangements. He made beautiful arrangements."

The two sessions, in 1946 and 1947, produced ten sides. Musiker,
like Medoff before him, effectively constructed arrangements that
avoided Tarras's weaknesses—and emphasized his strengths. Knowing Tarras's jazz chops to be nonexistent, he had him play in the
ensemble, or sit out, until the arrangement blossomed forth in the
"Jewish" section, where Tarras soloed brilliantly.

Again, the Elman "ABA" form—jazz, Jewish, jazz—worked like a
charm. But as Tarras noted: "The stores said, 'It's a good record, it's
beautiful, but if jazz we want, we got Benny Goodman.' It's not Jewish 'cause it's mixing in too much jazz, and it's not jazz 'cause it's
mixing in too much Jewish. It's what killed it: too much jazz. They
had a contract with me for more records, but they stopped it and
they paid me a lump of money to get out of the contract. I really
loved the records, but I let them out of the contract."

They were just too late. "Hot" swing had finally surrendered its
place of honor to cool jazz, with its newfound edge, and to the

"sweet" bands, whose lush orchestrations became the pop music standard until the phenomenon of rock 'n' roll hit in the mid-1950s. The new rock craze would push Tarras and his klezmer peers further from the mainstream than ever before.

Max Kletter Orchestra, c. 1935. *Front row, right to left:* Ray Musiker, Paul Pincus, Max Epstein, Kletter in white jacket. *Second row:* Willie Epstein, trumpet.

~ 5 ~

"TWISTIN' THE FREILACHS"

The destruction World War II wrought on the communities in which Yiddish was born and had matured meant that America, once an outcropping of that culture, had become its unwitting home. And the prognosis for its survival in the New World was not good. In New York, enrollment in Yiddish day schools plummeted, theaters closed, major record labels all but abandoned Yiddish music, and all but one of seven radio stations featuring Yiddish programs went off the air.

Musicians like Sid Beckerman and Howie Leess coming back from the service saw that the market for the old *bulgars* was fading; the older people who wanted them were dying off. It was now common to play only one or two *freylekh* sets at weddings and bar mitzvahs, and requests for them came less and less frequently.

Then old-style music and culture got an unexpected boost from the arriving remnants of Europe's once-thriving Jewish population. Called *grine*, they came to America with little but their memories and a desire to start over. Among them were my family.

My father, Zindel Sapoznik, a master sergeant in the fallen Polish army, had been impressed into the Red Army when Eastern Poland came under Russia's control as a result of its 1939 nonaggression pact with Germany. Someone in the Russian chain of command must have heard him sing, because he was quickly made a featured soloist in the vaunted Red Army chorus, entertaining troops at the front until the war's end.

My mother, Pearl Steinberg, escaped Rovne with her mother, Rivke, father, Isaac, and sister Pepa on the eve of the Nazi occupation and destruction of the city and its inhabitants. Attaching themselves to the retreating Red Army, they made their way east, settling in the Ciscaucasian city of Derbent. There, living in a horse stall,

159

they worked for the Soviet war effort, bottling vegetables and sewing uniforms.

After the war, they eventually made their way back to Rovne, only to find that the city was devastated, the little that remained beyond repair. Worse still was the discovery made on the outskirts of the city. There, in the pleasant pine forest called the Sosnikes, returning Jews discovered the mass graves of 17,500 of their fellow Rovner machine-gunned to death, a gruesome dress rehearsal for the better-known killings carried out weeks later near Kiev's Babi Yar ravine.

In the months that followed, my grandfather haunted the train station, on the lookout for anyone from the old Rovne. He'd bring them to his home, where his wife and two remaining daughters had reestablished a warm, *heymish* atmosphere. One evening, Zeyde brought a demobilized Jewish soldier who won my mother's heart with his Russian version of the song "Oh, Marie." My parents were married soon after.

Unwilling to live under Soviet rule in Rovne, my family, heading west this time, was shunted from one displaced persons (DP) camp to another, finally arriving at the Vegscheid and then Bindermichl DP camps in Linz, Austria, in 1946 to await their turn to emigrate. While there, my father resumed his prewar occupation as a *khazn*, chanting the prayer for the dead at the numerous *troyer akademyes* (memorial services) held in surrounding DP camps. (The prayers were followed by blistering revenge speeches by future Nazi hunter Simon Wiesenthal.) Finally, in 1949 my parents, my mother's parents and sister, and my brother, Norman, then two years old, disembarked from Hamburg aboard the S.S. General Bulow for the choppy eleven-day transatlantic trip to New York. Upon arrival, they, like many before them, settled in Brooklyn.

Since the end of World War I, the Brooklyn neighborhood of Brownsville had been the place second-generation American Jews moved up to in their economic and social rise from the Lower East Side. But when World War II drew to a close, the destination of choice had become Long Island, and young Jews by the score were abandoning the Brooklyn neighborhood. By the time my family moved to Brownsville, it had begun its slide into dissolution, and mere vestiges of formerly active Jewish life remained. I was born there in 1953.

My father soon found work as a *khazn* at some of the old-time Orthodox synagogues like the Beys Hamedresh Ha'Godol, on the

Lower East Side, and the Stone Avenue Talmud Torah, near our family home in Brooklyn. Although press and popular acclaim for my father was great—he was billed as Der Letster Rovner Shtut Khazn (the Last of the Rovner Cantors)—his income was not. This was the tail end of an era that valued the time-honored skill and art of the cantor. Unable to eke out a suitable living in his trained profession, Zindel Sapoznik followed the footsteps of previous generations of émigré Jews: he found work as an unskilled tailor in the needle trades.

We, too, were soon able to leave Brownsville and headed west to Crown Heights. We took an apartment just down the block from 770 Eastern Parkway, the then recently founded headquarters of the Lubavitch Hasidim.

Before the war, in towns scattered throughout Eastern Europe, adherents of the various Hasidic sects had lived close together. With the destruction of their centers, most Hasidic groups transplanted themselves to the United States. As in Europe, Hasidim didn't have a vast resource of musicians of their own, so they sought players from outside the community to accompany their weddings and *simkhes*. The first of the younger klezmorim to reach out to the Hasidic world was pianist/accordionist Joe King. Starting in the late 1940s, King, who was Orthodox but not a Hasid, targeted this field and assembled other young players including clarinetists Rudy Tepel, Moe Begun, and Howie Leess. King played piano and accordion "very poor," Leess recalled, "but [he was] a gentleman and a nice man, very nice to work for. But I didn't want to spend the rest of my musical life working for him."

It was in King's band that Leess, brought in on sax, developed his trademark improvised accompaniment style of harmonies, contrary motions, doubling of melody, and rhythmic counterpoints—all played with his rich, meaty tenor sax tone. When King left the Hasidic music scene and moved on to the Orthodox "Young Israel" community, former sidemen like Tepel and the Epstein Brothers divided up the territory he left behind.

There were a few musicians in the Hasidic world, like fiddler Yidl Turner, but the first ensemble of its own came from the Stoliner community: the Klitnick brothers, Leyzer and Meyer (playing mediocre clarinet and sax, respectively), and the brilliant *badkhn* accordionist/fiddler Yomtov Ehrlich, who had been a renowned *badkhn* back in Europe. Even so, there weren't enough Hasidic musicians to staff the band, so non-Hasidim were routinely hired, like clarinetists Chizik and Max Epstein, who went on to eclipse the Klitnick orchestra.

By exporting their traditions, the Hasidim imported old rituals that had been abandoned decades earlier in America: Tuesday night *khupes*, *badkhonim*, and lengthy *sheva brokhas*, the elaborate post-nuptial festivities. At many Hasidic ceremonies, the band would set up during the first hour while the *tnoyim*—a ritual in which the bride breaks a plate for good luck and distributes the pieces to her friends—took place. Then the musicians would go out and fetch the groom and his pals, leading him in with music to the *khaboles ponem*, the veiling of the bride. Hasidim also revived the outdoor wedding ceremony, after which several long sets of *freylekhs* were danced. Guests were entertained during dinner with *doinas*, followed by the *benching* (grace after meals), led by a *badkhn*, whose words, while occasionally amusing, tended more toward erudition and wisdoms of the Torah than toward the more ribald rhymes of their non-Hasidic counterparts.

Although Jewish ethnographers and musicologists had taken interest in Hasidic music back in Europe, no commercial recordings had ever been made. That changed in America. Benedict Stambler, an Orthodox school teacher, founded the Collector's Guild label, dedicated to reissuing classic Jewish folk and popular music. His anthologies of performers like Aaron Lebedeff and Isa Kremer, remastered with great care and meticulous liner notes, have stood the test of time and remain among the greatest of Jewish reissues.

In early 1962 Stambler anthologized the current Hasidic repertoire as played by the best musicians in the field. Top of the heap was clarinetist Rudy Tepel, who had originally been an American club date leader in the Bronx, and retrofitted his playing to suit the rising interest in Hasidic music. He contracted other Hasidic-scene musicians, including Marty Bass on trumpet, Howie Leess on tenor sax, Walter Weinberg on piano, Peter Begelman on accordion, and Joey Ayervais on drums. From "head" arrangements (for which only the melody was written out), two LPs were made in a single session, testament to the playing skills of the musicians and to the tightness of the recording budget.

"Yeah, one take and out; next one, one take; next one," Leess recalled. "Unless there were tremendous mistakes, you know, quite noticeable. Otherwise, with mistakes and all, one take; next." The recordings, played in rock-solid classic style, document the last time klezmer and Hasidic music would sound so similar.

By the mid-1960s a new trend in Hasidic music appeared. Learning to play instruments like accordion and drums in summer camp, Modern Orthodox yeshiva students adapted Hasidic and Israeli tunes and played them in a contemporary American style. The first of these young bands was the Mark Three, cofounded by accordionist Sy Kushner, drummer Benjamin Hulkower, and saxophonist Jim Pankower. Challenging what was called the "Williamsburg" sound, after the section of Brooklyn that became home to the first American Hasidic enclave, the band brought a smoother, rock-oriented backbeat and simple melodies to the various prayer texts.

"The Hasidic music was written primarily by yeshiva boys who would fit the songs to the text of the Bible, and they had no musical talent," Leess noted. "They would sing it to a tape recorder and then have somebody copy down the tunes for them. They had less musical value than the klezmer musicians, who were pretty schooled in their own field and knew music and the amount of measures per song. The Hasidim knew nothing about that. And it would sound like that, too. So I thought it was a lower-grade than *bulgars*."

Similarly regarded were Israeli folk dance tunes. American klezmer musicians of the time looked down on these reconfigurations of the older music, but musicality wasn't the point. The folk dances, part of the Zionist political agenda, were used to help solidify the consciousness of the Jewish state and its allies throughout the world.

Halutz (pioneer) dances were introduced by the Socialist-Zionists during the Second Aliyah period of 1905–14, when the first *kibbutzim* were established in Palestine. The most famous tune from this period is the ubiquitous "Hava Nagila." Said to be based on a melody from the Sadegurer Hasidim in the Bukovina region, it was notated in Jerusalem by the musicologist A. Z. Idelsohn and published with a new set of lyrics to great acclaim in 1915.

Eventually, other folk dance tunes like "Mayim," "Kol Dodi," and "Harmonika" displaced the older Yiddish repertoire. "Heveinu Shalom Aleichem" obliterated "Reb Dovidl's Nign" and even "Khosn, Kale Mazl Tov" as "the" clearly identified Jewish tune.

This ascendancy of Israeli repertoire over Yiddish dances was furthered by numerous secular folk dance groups in the United States. The great proliferation of left-wing and recreational folk dance groups—young, often progressive people dancing to European "folk" musics—were among some of the earliest supporters of the Israeli folk dances. Into the 1950s you could find Israeli dances and remnants of the Yiddish dance repertoire, such as the *sher*, on the same dance schedule. But soon the Israeli *hora* in 2/4 replaced the older "Romanian" *hora* in 3/8 favored by Yiddish-speaking Jews.

These dances were generally accompanied not by live music but by records played on special folk-dance turntables called Caliphones, built with variable speeds so the dances could be taught at a slower tempo. "I remember hearing these records when I was at summer camp. They were very pretty—accordion, guitar, and clarinet played in a straight, clean style. Not Jewish, but very pretty." So recalls pianist and bandleader Pete Sokolow (b. 1940), who best exemplifies the style and esthetics of the previous generation of musicians. Though this was the era of bebop, rock 'n' roll, and folk music, there were still young Jewish musicians who found themselves gravitating to the Jewish music world. Chief among them was Sokolow.

Sokolow learned piano from his father, a professional pianist in the mold of George Gershwin and Zez Confrey. But after hearing his first Benny Goodman record, Sokolow knew he wanted to play clarinet. The youth trend at the time was toward rock 'n' roll, but Sokolow was a throwback—a "moldy fig," as young fans of old jazz were called—and became a swing and Dixieland devotee. With money he got from a state college scholarship, Sokolow bought himself a clarinet and a saxophone and got into playing tenor sax on rock 'n' roll jobs to support his real love: jazz.

In 1957 Sokolow got his first professional job playing at hotels in the Catskills with older Jewish club date musicians like trumpeter Ralph Kahn and accordionist Harry Berman. Here, for the first time, he was required to play Jewish music. Never having played it before, he picked up a copy of the *Kammen International Dance Folio*.

Working with these musicians got him into the older Jewish repertoire. In the person of one Harry ("He played more wrong chords than anyone in the business") Berman, Sokolow heard his first *doina* and *hora*, and through Ralph Kahn was introduced to Yiddish theater standards like "Sheyn Vi di Levone" and "Belz." They also introduced him to other veteran players like the clarinetist Chizik Epstein, whom Sokolow met at a nearby hotel while on a break from his own job. ("Nice to meet you," Epstein said. "What do you think of [Berman's] chords?") Because of the superior skill and influence of the Epstein brothers, this meeting "set up a path that

This contract for a 1953 Al Glaser job booked a seven-piece band that included trumpeter Willie Epstein and clarinetist Dave Tarras—all for $225. (*Courtesy Jeff and Bonnie Glaser*)

would govern what I do now," notes Sokolow. From that time he also started going out on midweek Hasidic jobs with Rudy Tepel in Williamsburg.

When Sokolow started playing, in the late 1950s, Jewish club dates were much the same as they had been before World War II.

The mix of tunes was eighty to eighty-five percent American, the rest Jewish. (One New York-area clarinetist, Marty Levitt, continued to play the old klezmer repertoire throughout the '50s and '60s.) Standards like "Arrivederci, Roma" were supplanted by the new craze for Latin music initiated in the '40s: merengues, cha-chas, and rumbas ("Bésame Mucho," "Perfidia"), which resulted in Yiddish numbers like "Ikh Hob Dikh Tsufil Lib" and "Mayn Yiddishe Meydele" being played as rhumbas.

The Jewish portion of the party consisted of Israeli tunes like "Hava Nagila," "Misirlou," and "Artza Alinu," *bulgars* having all but disappeared from the bandstand. The bands at bar mitzvahs were still ignoring the kids, playing primarily for the adults with perhaps one or two rock 'n' roll numbers the whole evening.

Drab New York–area catering halls with opulent names like Franklin Manor, Saratoga Mansion, Celian Mansion, and the novelty catering hall run by "the Twin Cantors" dominated the market. Caterers had made beachheads in the synagogues, too, like the Conservative upscale Brooklyn Jewish Center, where Sholom Secunda was musical director, all the way down the line to more modest neighborhood *shuls*.

The wedding and bar mitzvah biz was boosted by the coming of new *grine*. This influx of Holocaust survivors meant not only new customers for the music, but new musicians. One of these was the family band headed by drummer Al Peratin, who arranged for the majority of *landsmanshaft* parties held at the Hotel Diplomat on Forty-Sixth Street in Manhattan.

Sokolow recalls one especially memorable gig with Peratin, "absolutely the worst music I have ever played." A small man, Peratin was barely visible behind his big bass drum, while his wife played piano, one daughter played vibraphone ("She used to keep the sustain pedal down and the first note was still ringing at the end of the job") and the other daughter simultaneously played accordion with her left hand and an early version of the synthesizer with her right.

Bandstand attire was tuxedos with narrow lapels and tiny bowties. The other sax player that night came on the bandstand "with this double-breasted suit with airplane lapels, a long tie, and spats," Sokolow said. "He looked like he'd been taken out of a coffin. And he played that way too." Instead of achieving a vibrato as is normally done, by moving your mouth, this sax player would instead shake his instrument violently. After this job Peratin told the young Sokolow: "Kit, you're terrific. I give you all the chobs. I've got a terrific bent: wyolin and wibes."

Running counter to the general popularity of Israeli music and the simplified Hasidic tunes starting to come out, Sokolow began learning more and more *bulgars* at this time due to Dave Tarras. In 1959, three years after he had turned professional, Pete Sokolow played his first job with Tarras. They were co-occupants in the sax section of Ralph Kahn's band at the Hotel Astor.

"He was the absolute king of the Jewish world—an icon," Sokolow recalls. "People spoke of him in deferential tones. Kahn had him there to play a specialty: go out on the floor, play a *doina*, a *bulgar*. He introduced himself to me: 'I am Dave Tarras: I am teacher of clarinet.' As if I weren't intimidated enough!"

Tarras remained a name to be reckoned with and, at times, to be shamelessly exploited. Sid Beckerman tells of the time Ralph Kahn hired him to play a wedding and instructed him to tell the customers *he* was Dave Tarras!

The mid-'50s also saw the transition from 78 RPM discs to 33 $\frac{1}{3}$ RPM LPs, which meant that some of Tarras's older discs, like the ones he recorded for Seymour Rechtzeit's Banner label, could now be issued on LP, garnering new audiences and revenue. But here, too, Tarras had failed to look out for his own interests: he had no provision in his agreement with the label about royalties from reissues. And to add insult to injury, "it was 'Dave Tarras orchestra, Abe Ellstein piano'; but when these guys from Banner took the old records and made an LP, they changed it around: 'Abe Ellstein Orchestra, featuring Dave Tarras,'" Tarras recalled.

Tarras continued making records throughout the 1950s, however, with the petite Period and Colonial labels issuing some half-dozen albums between them. But Tarras's most important recording was yet to come.

In 1956 Epic records, then a budget label at Columbia, brought Tarras into the studios again to participate in the first major label recording of klezmer music since World War II: *Tanz!*, conceived by Sammy Musiker. Musiker's arrangements, with their foreshadowing of melodic elements and attention to interesting voicings, are matched by a unity of construction and theme. This highly sophisticated fusion of Yiddish and American music forms required the very best of musicians.

Since his "retirement" from full-time professional Jewish music, drummer Irving Graetz had not worked for Dave Tarras or Sammy Musiker. After he left Tarras in the late '40s and went independent, Tarras flexed his muscle and got Graetz blacklisted from other Jewish bandstands. Unable to find enough freelance music work to support his family, Graetz, in an ironic twist on Tarras's own story, entered the fur trade in 1950, retiring from that profession in 1967.

When this recording was being planned, Sammy contacted him. But as Graetz recalled, the problems that led him to stop working with Tarras cropped up again.

"When Dave played his *bulgars*, he always toned me down; I should play soft and soft," Graetz said. "So the engineer in there he stopped the orchestra and he says to Sammy—because it was Sammy's date—he says, 'Sammy, I cannot hear the drummer.' And Sammy knew why; because Dave. So Sammy says to me, 'Irving, I don't want you to listen to anybody; do anything you want. And let's hear the drums! Don't let anybody annoy you.' So that's how Dave stopped . . . and you were at least able, you know, to hear the rhythm, the drums. Naftule Brandwein wouldn't tell me how to play; Dave did."

Despite the presence of some of New York's top Jewish musicians ("Red" Solomon on trumpet; Seymour Megenheimer on accordion; Moe Wechsler, piano; Mac Chopnick, bass; Graetz, drums; and Sam and his younger brother Ray Musiker on clarinets and sax), Columbia did not pursue an aggressive publicity campaign for *Tanz!* and sales foundered. Within a few years it was impossible for the record-buying public to find a copy. Tapes of this greatest all-time klezmer recording languish in the vaults of the company to this day.

If people had trouble finding the good records, they had less difficulty locating the killer shlock—the 1960s "surf-guitar-meets-klezmer" LP *Twistin' the Freilachs* and the Latin-infused dance record *Raisins and Almonds Cha Cha Cha and Merengues*. Among the records that exemplify such music are the cocktail piano offerings of Irving Fields. Fields's *Bagels and Bongos* LPs were a vivisection of Yiddish and easy-listening music that created the monster of "Jew-zak." Even in the case of albums by quality musicians like Paul Pincus and Ray and Sam Musiker, you could count on the label to affix an incongruous album cover: a pseudo-Semitic beauty sprawled in a kitschy pose, or "Jewish" party guests resembling Episcopalians with yarmulkes perched on their heads.

In a diminutive coda of the crossover scare of the late '30s, pop artists in the '50s recycled Jewish tunes that were better left alone. Vic Damone weighed in with a misguided recording of "Calla, Calla" (Bride, Bride); Eartha Kitt purred "Yomme, Yomme"; Connie Francis and Dean Martin each saw fit to give forth renditions of "Ikh Hob Dikh Tsufil Lib" (I Love You Much Too Much); and the Weavers had a hit with "Tzena, Tzena."

These records never made their way into my family's home. The only recordings we had were of *khazonim*, except for one modern LP that somehow wound up alongside the hi-fi: *Mish Mosh*, by Cleveland-born entertainer Myron ("Mickey") Katz.

BORSCHT BELTERS

In the wake of Yiddish theater's self-immolation, the Catskills became the premier proving ground for the development of Jewish talent. The then numerous hotels like Brown's, the Concord, and the Nevele disgorged a seemingly endless number of comics, musicians, and entertainers. This was one place where old-fashioned Yiddish music still had an appreciative audience—provided you also gave them enough cha-chas.

In these hotels' twilight years—the mid-1950s to the late 1960s— my family traveled the Catskills circuit on holidays like Passover and Shevuous, when many hotels featured cantors and what were called double choirs. Old-time choirs still functioning included those led by Joseph Cohen, Mordechai Sukenig, Harry Laskin, and Morris Wolf. At age six, like my father and brother before me, I was impressed into these choirs and would sing accompanying my father.

Naftule Brandwein still "blowing like crazy" in the 1950s.

We made the rounds at the minor hotels, where my father found his place in the mountains. Working with different choir leaders, he would arrange to provide the needed religious services patrons required for their stay. The hotels, known for obsequious hospitality for paying customers, were as justly famous for active neglect of employees, and that included the cantor and the choirs. Given the central role of the cantor during the services, the status accorded us at these hotels was astonishingly low. We were paid poorly, put up in small, dirty rooms, and given extra duties when not conducting services; we were even expected to help out with the entertainment at night.

One horrific memory is of my father trying bravely but vainly to conduct a Passover seder. When the beginning of the seder was announced on the hotel public address system ("Dinner will be served at approximately 6:30 sharp"), the dining room filled with 1,500 ravenous and ill-tempered hotel guests in no mood for artsy ceremony. At one point, having been rushed for the umpteenth time, my father sarcastically asked whether instead of the usual four questions and ten plagues the assembled diners would prefer two questions and five plagues. He received an enthusiastic affirmation. Later, the basso in the choir stood and delivered a bathetic rendition of Paul Robeson's magnificent "Go Down, Moses." So much for tradition.

Over the years we also found ourselves working at the hotels like the Majestic, the Normandie, and the Blumenkranz, alongside former Yiddish theater stars like Molly Picon, Jacob Kalich, Jennie Goldstein, and Dave Tarras—my father conducting sacred music during the day and the entertainers conducting secular music at night, each guaranteed to be in one another's audience. I have hazy recollections of them playing in the sadly faded nightclubs of these faltering hotels.

Other veteran Yiddish performers were still making the hotel rounds. The comic Fyvush Finkel was working at the New Edgewood, along with Naftule Brandwein, clearly not in the best of health but "propped up in a chair and blowing like crazy," as clarinetist Howie Leshaw recalls.

But old-time acts were not what people really wanted. They loved the brash young comics who had made the transition from *tummler* (racket-maker) to "social director." From there it was an easy transition to the stage, one that former *tummlers* like Jerry Lewis, Buddy Hackett, Sid Caesar, and Danny Kaye made with aplomb.

But for every Sid Caesar, there were a dozen who didn't quite make it. Take Lee Tulley and Billy Hodes, whose only claim to fame

Advertisement for Dave Tarras and my father, the cantor Zindel Sapoznik, at the Majestic hotel in the Catskills for the holiday of Shevuous, 1956.

is their competing assertions that one and not the other is the sole genius behind the song "Essen" (Eating). The anthem of musicians playing in the mountains, it was a scathing skit about the never-ending appetites of Catskills hotel patrons replete with a machine-gun delivery of daily menus. Their competing 78s found small bands of adherents. (I, for example, prefer Billy Hodes's version.)

Slightly higher up the Borscht Belt food chain were the brothers Eddie and Joe Barton. In 1949 the tiny Apollo label issued their first 78

RPM, a takeoff of the kind of programming still being heard on the New York station WEVD. The song and skit were called "Joe and Paul," and in the hands of the Bartons—and fellow Borscht Belt alumnus Red Buttons (aka Aaron Chwat)—it became a classic of a kind. Originally a jingle written by Sholom Secunda in the 1930s for a men's clothing store of the same name (the store folded during World War II), the new "Joe and Paul," like "Essen," featured coarse and leaden double entendres rendered in garbled Yiddish and punctuated by clumsy klezmer-style playing. Unlike "Essen," it was a big seller and helped put Apollo on the map. At the time Apollo was also issuing other Jewish discs featuring comedian/singer Fyvush Finkel and monologues by comedian Sam Levenson, in addition to cantorial pieces and recordings of jazz, R&B, and country and western.

The Bartons followed up that record with others like "Minnie the Flapper" and "Cockeyed Jenny," the latter a spinoff from a line in "Joe and Paul" about a Lower East Side prostitute. (The tune itself was a reworking of Peretz Sandler's and Louis Gilrod's 1926 song "Zorg Nit Mame" [Don't Worry Mama], a hit for Aaron Lebedeff and a year later for Dave Tarras and Abe Schwartz.) The success of the Barton recordings caught the attention of one entertainer in particular, who took the formula and ran with it.

Mickey Katz (1909–85), born and raised in the Jewish section of Cleveland, studied clarinet as a boy and by age eighteen was playing with local society orchestras. Katz's onstage antics and comedic flair brought him to the attention of the novelty bandleader Spike Jones, whose wartime hit "Der Fuehrer's Face" and breathlessly rendered parodies of American popular songs catapulted him to a fame that continued into the 1950s. Jones hired Katz for the 1946 recording "Hawaiian War Chant," on which Katz can be heard making the "glug" sounds.

At a recording session with Spike Jones and his City Slickers, Katz confided in fellow bandmember Mannie Klein that he had composed his own Yiddish-English parodies in the Jones style. The casual remark bore fruit: in 1947 RCA issued Katz's "Haim Afn Range/Yiddish Square Dance." Thanks to its fresh approach and to the industrial strength of the RCA distribution machine, the little record sold some thirty-five thousand copies in the first few weeks, setting the Mickey Katz juggernaut in motion.

What made it so popular was Katz's plethora of funny voices and the comedic incongruity of Yiddish and English. (In typical Katz fashion he described the B side of the disc as "an Arkansas hog farmer calling a square dance in Yiddish.") His Yiddish, if not as pungent as that of a native speaker, contained enough veracity to satisfy even his foreign-born record audience, like my family.

Another reason for the 78's success was the high quality of his accompanists. Unlike the Barton Brothers' records, which used critically poor musicians, Katz, himself a passable clarinetist, wisely stocked his sessions with some of the top names in the Los Angeles music world, including jazz greats like trumpeter Mannie Klein, trombonist Si Zentner, Sam Weiss on drums, and Benny Gill on violin. He also employed the services of the arranger Nat Farber, who, taking a lead from earlier successes, employed the Ziggy Elman ABA structure of the late-1930s Yiddish crossover hits. In an interesting twist of fate, Ziggy Elman later became one of Katz's trumpeters, alternating with Klein.

In 1948, with the success of his RCA recordings, Katz decided to offer a live stage version of his music in the mold of Jones's shows. Dubbing it the *Borscht Capades*, he assembled a cast of performers including Hebrew singer Raasche, ventriloquist Ricky Lane (and his dummy "Velvel"), and Katz's sixteen-year-old son, Joel Grey.

Borscht Capades toured the country for two years. By the time it got to New York—one place Katz did not play, contrary to rumor, was the Catskills—Katz was handed a bit of show-biz irony. Having initially been inspired by the records of the Barton Brothers, Katz was shocked to find that Catskill entrepreneurs Beckman and Pransky had stitched together their own show of shtik called *Bagels and Yocks*, featuring none other than the Barton Brothers. Setting up shop two blocks from where *Borscht Capades* was playing on Broadway, the promoters even went so far as to hire away ventriloquist Ricky Lane and Velvel![1]

Katz had to react. He hired long-in-the-tooth Yiddish theater composer Joseph Rumshinsky to whip up a score for the show. Rumshinsky, at work on two shows with Molly Picon (*Mazl Tov Molly* and *Sadie Is a Lady*), took the additional job. But despite some favorable reviews, the Katz and Barton shows, like matter and antimatter, ultimately cancelled each other out.

Moving from RCA to Capitol, Katz continued to issue his popular parodies. One secret to Katz's success was that he never parodied Yiddish songs, only American, a funnier arrangement than vice versa. But his second LP was completely instrumental: *Mickey Katz Plays Music for Weddings, Bar Mitzvahs and Brisses* (1951). Played straight, this is Katz's homage to the klezmer repertoire he never played as a young man. "Every note of the album breathes the flavor of the old but little-known happy Jewish music of the old country," Katz wrote in his 1977 as-told-to autobiography, *Papa Play For Me*. "If I do say so myself, it was simply delicious music." The record, one of Katz's personal favorites, was his worst-selling album: no comedy. Listened to today these traditional and original compositions, written in "klezmer" style, demonstrate tremendous technical virtuosity, but the only whiff of authentic Yiddish styling comes from the trumpet playing of Ziggy Elman and Manny Klein.

Yiddish purists held their noses when it came to Katz's records. *"Prost!"* (common), they would say. "Cheap and vulgar." Sure, the jokes were blunt, and the same rhyming patterns are used in song after song. But like the occasional Yiddishisms sneaked into *Your Show of Shows* or the pages of *Mad* magazine, Katz's recordings were refreshing mainstream instances of Yiddish with a sense of humor.

I loved this record and delighted in sneaking Lubavitch pals up to my house to listen to it in a happy act of cultural subversion—nearly as much for me as for them. The frivolity of Katz's tunes were light years from the sort of Yiddish music that served as a backdrop of my young life. Constantly preparing for holiday services, the choirs I sang in from age six seemed to be in never-ending rehearsals. And rather than working with written music, parts had to be learned by ear and repetition, as my father had when he was a *meshoyrer* back in Rovne.

If that weren't enough, students in the Lubavitch yeshiva began to be drafted as part of the newly established children's choirs later known as *pirchei*. More than fifty of us would be coached in the latest Hasidic melodies to sing at special events, including the *rebbe's tish* at the Lubavitch headquarters at 770 Eastern Parkway, just down the block from where my family lived in Brooklyn.

In 1960 my mother had booked clarinetist Rudy Tepel to play my brother's bar mitzvah after hearing him at a Lubavitch *farbrengen* (celebration) near our house. Tepel double-booked himself and, without informing her, sent a vastly inferior player in his stead, hoping my mother wouldn't notice. She did and became livid (what in the club date business is delicately referred to as a "screamer"). "Don't worry," he told her. "For your next son's bar mitzvah, I'll be there." Unfortunately, he kept his word.

My bar mitzvah, six years later, was a typical "affair" of its time. Clad in a garish champagne-colored tuxedo jacket, I stumbled my way around Brooklyn's Kevelson Hall, amid fountains in which lions' mouths spouted blood-red punch, eating highly improbable continental renderings of *flanken* (boiled beef), and being hustled hither and yon by a photographer whose pictures wound up doing as much for our visages as the guillotine did for the French aristocracy's.

By this time, Tepel's music was so out of date it seemed as if he had crawled out of a time capsule to do the job. The only point of amusement for us kids was the occasional moment when Tepel's tux jacket would fan out, revealing the .38 revolver he wore, inexplicably, in a shoulder holster.

"Can't this guy play anything modern?" I whined, mortified, to whomever would listen. My parents had hired one of the top New York City klezmer clarinetists to play at the reception of my bar mitzvah, so there he was, blowing some of the best *bulgars* in the business—and all I wanted to do was to crawl into the nearest, deepest hole. He was playing klezmer music; I wanted rock 'n' roll. My assessment of the entertainment was that round men were playing square music.

At age fourteen, as my voice began to change, my father granted me a reprieve from the choirs until my vocal chords settled. Elated to be out, I vowed never to go back to performing Jewish music.

～ 6 ～

From the Catskill Mountains to the Blue Ridge Mountains (and Back!)

THE SIGN WELCOMING YOU to Mount Airy, North Carolina, reads: "Birthplace of Andy Griffith and Home of the World's Largest Open Granite Pit." It was also the home of the world-famous Siamese Twins Chang and Eng. Not the first locale you would think of for an epiphany in Jewish music, but for me, that's what it was.

Cutting loose from yeshiva and the choirs, by 1967 I had put my Jewish music in deep freeze and was careening through all sorts of American music from rock to folk-protest and, ultimately, to traditional music. I was introduced to the panoply of folk music by a young banjo player named Stuart Tursky. With his Mao hat and banjo—nicknamed "Big Red" and emblazoned, of course, with a bright red star—Stuie was my folk music rebbe, inaugurating me into the grassroots sounds of America. Soon I was busily replacing the medieval Rabbi Gamliel with Woody Guthrie, the gemorah texts of Baba Kama with the song texts of Bob Dylan, and employing my quick ear, so recently used to memorize the variant melodies for Adon Olom, to learn "Oh, Mary Don't You Weep."

Haunting the coffeehouses in Greenwich Village or heading to Washington Square Park, the Wailing Wall of folk music, we would play a host of antique American songs with other children and grandchildren of East European Jewish émigrés. Usually, it seemed, the deeper and twangier the drawl employed by whoever was singing, the more recently their family had come over from Eastern Europe.

177

It wasn't a quantum leap from the protest songs of Pete Seeger to the more rural music of his half-brother, Mike. Stuie's banjo was my ticket, and on those occasions he would leave it at my house, I'd puzzle out the mysteries of what the instrument could do. A fortuitous event then directed me to traditional music.

When I was sixteen a friend of my brother's who was moving away offered me the records in his collection. Among the rock and R&B recordings were some folk LPs, including a set for which I paid a dollar: *The Anthology of American Folk Music*, edited by Harry Smith. Pioneering the reissue of nonmainstream commercial recordings of the 1920s, Smith reintroduced a now nearly forgotten form to a new generation, effectively jump-starting the revival of old-time music and Delta blues as a viable urban performance genre.

What I thought was going to be a collection of nice, easy-to-assimilate songs turned out to be weird, almost surrealistic recordings. I had no idea what to make of them—I could barely figure out what the singers were saying—and the sound, so thin and faraway, like a really bad phone connection, didn't heighten their appeal. But as the recordings grew on me one piece at a time, starting with Chubby Parker's "King Kong Kitchee Kitchee Kaimeo," they all began to make sense. Even Smith's stream-of-consciousness liner notes, which distill country ballads into tabloid headlines ("Greedy Girl Goes to Adams Spring With Liar; Lives Just Long Enough to Regret It"), became meaningful. With the kind of fervor required back in yeshiva, I pored over them, trying to extract even greater meaning. The allure of 78s had taken hold.

By high school graduation, in 1971, I knew that traditional music—especially "old-time" music, played in Appalachia—spoke to me. Now traveling as "Hank" Sapoznik and sallying forth with my newly acquired ten dollar Japanese banjo, I was intent on embodying the hard-living, hard-traveling repertoire of rural Americans. Although my only riding of the rails to that point had been the D train to Coney Island, I was ready to learn. After a brief stint playing in a rock 'n' roll band cryptically named Debuh, I got helplessly hooked on old-time music.

Back then, it wasn't that hard to find teachers to learn from in the New York City area. The largest percentage of players of old-time music were Jews. (My first old-time banjo mentor, Bill Garbus, bore an unsettling resemblance to Rabbi Barnetsky, my fourth grade rebbe at Lubavitch.) The music scene was awash with fiddlers, banjo players, and guitarists, who, with their long stringy beards and intense gazes, looked like nothing less than students playing hooky from a *beys medresh*, the Jewish house of study. Playing century-old square dance tunes like "Soldier's Joy" or gospel chestnuts like "Hallelujah to the Lamb" came a tad too easy for this group of Kaufmans, Fingerhuts, Markowitzs, and Statmans, who sang earnestly of "corn likker stills in Georgia." Of course, I fit right in.

We children and grandchildren of European immigrants were glorifying a traditional music even dyed-in-the-wool fourth-generation Americans had rejected, an oddity not lost on us. (One of the bands I periodically sat in with was The Wretched Refuse String Band, whose name, taken from the famous Emma Lazarus poem, underscored the unintended irony of the music we played and the relatively recent émigré backgrounds of the musicians' families.) For me, the only Holocaust survivors' child in the bunch, the music advanced my Americanness more than my brief tour of duty as a Boy Scout.

The next three years were filled with listening to scratchy 78 RPM records of bands like Uncle Dave Macon and the Fruit Jar Drinkers, Dr. Humphrey Bates and the Possum Hunters, and my favorite, Charlie Poole and the North Carolina Ramblers. I quickly developed a voracious taste for these old records and for making the music they taught me alive, vibrant, and personal.

In 1972, guitarist/mandolinist Alan Podber and I formed the old-time band The Delaware Water Gap String Band, with Bill Garbus on fiddle and a lesbian Puerto Rican guitarist/singer named Myriam Valle. The Water Gap soon became a popular group in the bite-size universe populated by other urban revival old-time bands. Our personnel changed: we now had fiddler David Brody and bassist/banjoist Bob Carlin—all Jewish. The whirl of coffeehouses and folk festivals, fiddle contests and house concerts opened to us.

Our choice of music, from country dance tunes, early ragtime, and string swing, was a kaleidoscope of the music culture of America. Everything except, of course, Jewish music.

Our desire to be an activist part of the music scene encouraged Podber and me to open our own coffeehouse, Random Canyon (inspired by the song of the same name by the surreal old-time duo The Holy Modal Rounders), in the basement of a church in Brooklyn's Park Slope. We featured a wide variety of traditional music and square dancing. I had run another club several years earlier—also in a church basement; no synagogue ever seemed willing to sponsor one—but it was Random Canyon that gave me a nuts-and-bolts education in what it takes to make a living as a musician. The knowledge would come in handy.

At that time, I was attending various branches of the City University of New York, majoring in everything from archeology/ancient history to industrial arts. Only when I became passionate about old-time music did it occur to me that I could study music in college. I applied for and won admission to the CUNY Baccalaureate Program, an innovative degree curriculum that encouraged motivated and disciplined students to create their own course of study. With a team of academic advisors, I crafted a curriculum that led to a Bachelors of Arts degree in ethnomusicology from the City University in 1977. I now had a framework from which to pursue my interest in American traditional music.

Of all the members of the Water Gap, Bill Garbus was the only one who had actually gone down south to where this music was born and still being made. Bill fired my imagination with his anecdotes about visiting the old-timers, listening to them play, and talking with them about their music. Garbus's stories, to this nineteen-year-old Brooklyn boy, made North Carolina seem like an amalgam of Shangri-La and Tobacco Road, as remote and unapproachable as another world. My dream was to go as soon as possible.

The chance came in the summer of 1973, thanks to Garbus's friend Ray Alden, a New York City banjoist and music collector. For years they had been going to Mount Airy, North Carolina, home to two of the finest players of old-time music, Tommy Jarrell and Fred Cockerham. The CUNY advisory committee agreed to accept this field trip as part of my course of study.

Septuagenarians both, the irascible Tommy and the dryly self-deprecatory Fred made perfect teachers. They were generous, demonstrative, appreciative, accessible, and endlessly authentic. Between 1973 and 1977 I made a half-dozen trips to Mount Airy to visit with Fred and Tommy. Those visits are among my most wonderful memories.

On a trip during the summer of 1977, I was staying at Tommy's house. Earlier that year I had begun a vegetarian diet. One morning for breakfast he offered me scrambled eggs fried in bacon fat, the bacon itself, and biscuits drenched in bacon fat gravy. The only thing not made with bacon was the coffee. Politely demurring, I opted for coffee.

The genial Tommy pressed me with, "Come on, Hank. Eat up!"

"No thanks," I told him.

We parried and thrusted with Tommy acting more like a Jewish mother than a hillbilly fiddler until, getting more and more exasperated, he blurted: "What's the matter with you Hank? What're you, a damned Jew?"

Well *that* sure got my attention. I'm still not sure if I was more startled by Tommy's use of the term "damned Jew" or his unanticipated knowledge about pork products being taboo under kosher dietary laws. In any case, I stammered out: "Why, yes, Tommy. I am."

Hearing this, Tommy immediately launched into a story about a Mount Airy Jew named Cohen, who was approached on the street by a local anti-Semite leading a dog on a leash.

"Hey, Cohen," he yelled out. "This is my dog. He's half Jew and half son-of-a-bitch."

"Ah," Cohen retorted. "I see he's a little kin to both of us."

Jarrell got a kick out of telling that story. Suddenly, out of nowhere, here we were talking about Jews! Touched and impressed as he and Fred were by the boundless enthusiasm we had for their music and culture, they were still puzzled about the proliferation of Jews playing old-time music. After all, their own people took nearly no interest in their music, preferring the jazzier styles of bluegrass or more popular modern country music. Why should Jewish musicians from northern cities take such an interest? Though valiantly trying to learn the correct pronunciations of all the foreign-named students who descended upon their modest homes, Tommy and Fred never quite got it right. Both men attempted—and failed—to remember my last name, finally good-naturedly altering it to "Hank Snow," a popular country and western singer whose name they could easily remember.

From the framework of this experience, Tommy had a question: "Hank, don't your people got none of your own music?"

Until this moment I hadn't thought about it quite that way. Well, of course we had our own music: the *khazones* I sang with my father when I was a kid; the *zmires* we sang in yeshiva or at one of the Lubavitcher *rebbe's tishn*; the numerous melodies sung with gusto during Passover. There was the popular Israeli music, which I deeply loathed, and of course the music I remembered from my many years at the Catskills hotels and from my bar mitzvah. But where were the Jewish Tommys and Freds? Where was *my* traditional music? I didn't know, but I meant to find out.

When I returned to Brooklyn I asked my family these questions. They had barely tolerated my interest in old-time music, referring to what I was doing as *drimplen,* Yiddish for idle, incompetent strumming. They never saw my group play, since our standard venues—bars and coffeehouses in churches—were not places my parents would even consider visiting. But Yiddish music was something different. This they understood. This not only reflected their lives but glorified and perpetuated that which they had brought over with them.

On a warm night in June 1977, I took out a tape recorder and for the first time recorded my parents singing and talking about their lives in Rovne. I had recorded hours and hours of music of my friends down south, but nothing of my own family. Now I heard with new ears the stories and songs from my childhood. It suddenly became clear that I had sprung from a culturally rich environment but had missed it for my nagging desire to be more American. I was so busy trying to be my television idol, Beaver Cleaver, whose parents spoke with no accent, that I missed out on who I really was. It was a revelatory lesson: becoming a "stranger" to my own family, hearing those stories and songs anew, hearing the music, lore, and culture, in essence for the first time.

Next stop was Zeyde's house. My grandfather, Isaac Steinberg, was our family historian—for that matter the de facto historian for the entire Rovner *landsmanshaft*—and I made a beeline for his neat little Brighton Beach apartment. Zeyde, speaking a half dozen languages, to my good fortune drew the line at English, making our weekly visits a whetstone for my everyday conversational Yiddish. (At home I could get away with a mixture of Yiddish and English.) My timorous first questions about Yiddish culture were met with a torrent of facts, figures, and anecdotes. His recollections of Eastern European Jewish life opened like a tableau vivant presented as if he had been waiting for my questions all along. (Among other skills, Zeyde was a noted soapbox orator, a *deklamirer*, in his communities in Brighton Beach and Miami.)

Without hesitation Zeyde recommended—no, demanded—I go to YIVO, the Yiddish research institute then located along New York's Museum Mile on tony Fifth Avenue. Zeyde would regularly take the ninety-minute bus and subway ride from his home in Brooklyn just to sit and read in the library of the institute, the one tangible vestige of Eastern Europe as he knew it. Entering the building, Zeyde would breathe deep like a prisoner getting his first whiff of freedom. Except he took that deep whiff when he stepped inside, not out.

Founded in Vilna in 1925 by a dedicated group of linguists, folklorists, anthropologists, and historians, YIVO—its name is a translit-

Brandwein's grave, Progressive Musicians' Benevolent Society plot, Queens, N.Y.

erated acronym for *Yiddisher Visnshaftlekher Institut,* or the Jewish Scientific Institute—was the first research organization to study the civilization of the Jews of Eastern Europe and was one of the most important centers of Jewish intellectual learning throughout the 1930s. But like the people they documented, the institute's library and archives had fallen into grave danger of destruction with the outbreak of World War II. Looted by the Nazis for their planned "Institute for the Investigation of the Jewish Question," the materials were discovered by the United States Army and sent to America in 1947. (Remainders of the collection were also found in a church in Vilna in 1989.) In its original American incarnation, YIVO was housed in the old Hebrew Immigrant Aid Society (HIAS) building on Lafayette Street, current home of The Joseph Papp Public Theater; the institute relocated to Sixteenth Street between Fifth and Sixth avenues in 1999.

The YIVO I came to know was a place unhinged in time, the Yiddish version of the New York townhouse wherein quirky old scholars conduct encyclopedia research in Howard Hawks's 1941 film *Ball of Fire.* The YIVO academics were headquartered in a former Vanderbilt mansion across from Central Park. When YIVO acquired the lavish but now dowdy structure in 1955, its flamboyant interiors were muted to serve the needs of its current academic inhabitants. Renovators were instructed to paint all the walls battleship gray so the otherwise engaged scholars would not be distracted by the original goldleaf finials and tromp l'oeil painting that still graced its walls.

"*Di*," Zeyde told me with pride. "*Di kenst dort gefinen vus di zikhst.*" (You can find what you're looking for there.)

A phone call to YIVO soon afterward put me in contact with a scholar who would become one of my most important influences: the folklorist Barbara Kirshenblatt-Gimblett. It was she who uttered the Yiddish "open sesame" allowing access to the sound recordings that would focus my energies and change the direction of my life.

Down in the bowels of the YIVO building, amid perspiring steampipes, jumbled masses of decaying old newspapers, and voluminous deactivated files, lay a legion of 78 RPM records, stacked neatly in metal cabinets. In all the years YIVO archivists had grudgingly accepted the records like unwanted foundlings dropped at their door, no one had bothered to listen to the collection. Permitted in to examine the recordings, I found nothing on which to play them.

As much as I panted in anticipation of listening to the records, I had no way to subsidize my passion. No way, that is, until fate stepped in.

CETA: THE WOODSTOCK-ERA WPA

"Is this on the level"?

I was on the phone with Alan Kaufman, an old-time fiddle-playing pal of mine who was telling me something unbelievable.

"You mean the federal government is willing to pay *me* ten thousand dollars a year to study klezmer music?"

Difficult as it was to fathom, it was in essence true. Harking back to the dark days of the Depression, when the Works Progress Administration (WPA) acted as a safety valve and outlet for artists, writers, and photographers, in 1976 the Carter administration inaugurated CETA, the Comprehensive Employment Training Act, as its post-Aquarian equivalent. Nonprofit community-based agencies were eligible to apply for these funds, and the organization Kaufman knew of, the Martin Steinberg Center of the American Jewish Congress (AJC), had just gotten one. The timing couldn't have been better. Kaufman, who had written the hiring guidelines himself, encouraged me to go down and apply.

Among the experts on the panel was Yiddish music scholar Ruth Rubin, with whom I was to develop a close friendship. After cross-examination ("Do you know what the name 'Sapoznik' means?" I did: shoemaker), the panel approved me as director of the Jewish Music Research Community, which got to work bright and early on January 3, 1978. In addition to my own study of klezmer music, my colleagues' concentration included areas of Ladino music, field recordings of active Jewish communities like Brighton Beach, and the Hasidic enclave of Boro Park. It was a full plate.

Under the aegis of the Steinberg Center directors, Jeff Oboler and Chava Miller, the center was a short-lived oasis for young Jews who sought a means of self-expression and Jewish continuity through the arts. Musicians, filmmakers, writers, poets, painters, puppeteers, and playwrights made their way into the old carriage house on East Eighty-Fifth Street that housed the center. The first year at CETA was a dream come true, enabling me to chart a course of research, documentation, and study in a field that for all intents and purposes lay fallow and untouched.

With a mix of fear and exhilaration I took my first steps in the direction of that research. I perused all the standard texts of great musicologists, but beyond the work of A. Z. Idelsohn, Ruth Rubin, Alfred Sendry, and Joachim Stuchevsky, found barely a smattering of references to klezmer music. If there was anything more to study, I started wondering, wouldn't it have been done already?

Fortunately, YIVO was just around the corner. I decided to begin with those unlistened-to 78s, kicking off a daily ritual of shlepping in my own Garrard 40B turntable and plugging it into an antique tape recorder left behind by a visiting scholar. Days were thus given over to playing the 78s, taping them, cataloging them, and documenting what they were. The old recordings brought both a flood of recognition and the thrill of discovery. After having spent so much time perusing the scratchy 78s of American popular music from the early 1900s—the raw and vital first sounds of Appalachian fiddlers, banjo-playing blackface comics, and hot early jazz bands—the 78s were now surrendering to me the music of my forebears, the passionate and unfettered first American klezmorim.

Simultaneously new and old, these scratchy records were a passport to a vanished land. But the sort of face-to-face collecting and observation of continuity through which I'd researched old-time music was not possible for the study of this music; there was no old country to go back to, no Poland, Ukraine, or Romania where I might find Jewish old-timers tenaciously holding onto their repertoire against all modern influences. These delicate shellacs, these three-minute musical Rosetta Stones that unearthed a musical language, were my entrée to the klezmer tradition. These records, in effect, *were* the old country, a ticket back to that time and place. Almost immediately I resolved to get the records into circulation. Thinking back to how profoundly I had been affected by Harry Smith's *Anthology* and other subsequent old-time music reissues, in March 1977 I contacted Folkways, the label that had issued Smith's LPs.

Founded in 1948 by Moe Asch, the son of the controversial Yiddish writer Sholom Asch, Folkways was one of the first labels to give traditional music a platform. Asch, who began his career as a radio engineer at station WEVD in the 1930s, was a cantankerous iconoclast who put out music other labels would never touch, from political songs of blacklisted singers like Pete Seeger and Woody Guthrie to field recordings of tropical birds to the early work of the contemporary experimental composer John Cage. Moe doggedly kept in print every record he'd ever released. He was able to do this by using the simplest of record cover designs, keeping to low production budgets, and persistently resisting payments of artists' royalties.

Though Folkways had put out Jewish records in the past—a few LPs by Ruth Rubin and Mark Olf and a curious ten-inch 1951 LP by Yiddish singer "Prince" Nazaroff playing a guitar-like instrument he called an "octophone"—there weren't as many as you'd expect a Yiddish writer's son to have released.

I was ushered into an office full of African folk art, where Moe Asch, rumpled and grumpy, sat behind a desk piled high with papers. Like the great and powerful Oz, he attempted to humble his young visitor by responding to each question with an impatient outburst. After grilling me about my experience (I had none) and my willingness to work cheaply (I had plenty), Asch, in a well-honed performance, feigned a *weltzschmerzy* indifference and agreed to release an album, *Klezmer Music 1910-1942*.

Despite his initial disregard—"Who's gonna listen to this crap?" was his first retort—Moe later admitted he had decided in favor of the klezmer reissue almost immediately. It didn't hurt that I was already on another Folkways record. (I played banjo and autoharp on *Sweeney's Dream*, behind Irish fiddler Kevin Burke.) Once Asch agreed, I wrote to YIVO folklorist Kirshenblatt-Gimblett to get permission on behalf of the institute. She enthusiastically supported the project and I set to work.

Kirshenblatt-Gimblett was one reason young folks were showing up on YIVO's doorstep. Passionate, learned, and energetic, this folklorist, with her championing of Yiddish arts and lore, was a great inspiration and made up the ideological backbone of YIVO's new generation and of the resultant general Yiddish revival. Through her insistence on high standards, rigorous scholarship, and unceasingly top-drawer research, the Folkways reissue became a benchmark for scholarship in klezmer music.

Kirshenblatt-Gimblett notwithstanding, the Jewish musicology elite did not consider klezmer music an appropriate subject of inquiry. Indicative of the prevailing attitude was the discussion of klezmer music I initiated with the late great Jewish musicologist Dr. Albert Weisser, who must have felt like a master chef being asked about the sherbet he served between courses. The generous and thoughtful man was puzzled and tried to be helpful, although he could not. Weisser's assistance amounted to validating my sense that there was little documentation available. When he recommended I redirect my energies to an adjoining field—the turn-of-the-century Jewish Music Society of St. Petersburg—I respectfully declined.

GENERATION TO GENERATION: FINDING THE VETERAN PLAYERS

During this same period of time I undertook the study of the fiddle. Though an accomplished banjoist, I felt that the violin, more than any other instrument, embodied the essence of klezmer style. Though I'd never played it before and knew it was going to be an uphill undertaking, I made it my business to find a teacher.

The search for an instructor began with classical players who, while excellent in showing me the basics of tone production, bowing techniques, and scales, were at sea in their abilities to teach style and repertoire. Then, at a concert of Greek Gypsy music in early 1978 sponsored by the Balkan Arts Center, I encountered a violinist from the island of Epyrus named Achilles Halkias. His poignant playing bore such a profound similarity to the vocal sound of Yiddish music that I knew I must have him for a teacher. The concert's sponsors actively discouraged my approaching him, but I bypassed them and began studying with Halkias two months later. (I didn't know it then, but Halkias's father, Pericles, had given clarinet lessons to Andy Statman, a mandolinist I knew from the New York bluegrass scene who would go on to become one of the great klezmer clarinetists of our generation.)

With no common language but our love of music, Halkias and I entered into a wonderful student-teacher relationship. His request for payment was made in a scratched-out note accompanied by a look that said, "Of course, if this is too much . . ." It was not. But our happy association was not meant to last. With few concerts and even fewer students, Halkias, slowly starving in his little Hell's Kitchen apartment, was forced to return to Epyrus.

Bereft at the loss, I chanced to learn—through a fellow CETA worker, singer/researcher Carol Freeman—of an older Jewish violin-ist teaching classical music to children in his home in Sunnyside, Queens. Thanks to her, the contemporary klezmer world was graced with the presence of the wonderful *mentsh* and fiddler Leon Schwartz (1901–89).

Schwartz's passionate fiddling reflected Bukovina, the region of the Austro-Hungarian empire bisecting Romania and Ukraine in which he was born. Learning by ear as a child, he later took lessons with local teachers in classical music. But Schwartz's real love was for the traditional music—Jewish and non—that permeated the area.

On the eve of his bar mitzvah Schwartz was already leading his own fiddle band, which included his two brothers and local Gypsy musicians. They toured regionally until 1921, when Schwartz departed for New York. Though he worked a succession of day jobs throughout his life, it was music that anchored him. He often said it was the violin lessons that put bread on the table during the Depres-sion when his "regular" work dried up.

When we met in 1979, he was giving violin lessons to little Ortho-dox girls, teaching *haftorah* portions to imminent bar mitzvah boys, and serving as the *ba'al koyre* (reader of the Torah) at his neighbor-hood synagogue. Leon Schwartz's apartment, a cozy jumble of fid-dles, overstuffed furniture, and a myriad of paintings executed by his American-born wife, Charlotte, gave an immediate sense of the cou-ple's deep love for each other and for their religious and cultural heritage. And when Leon raised fiddle to chin, even the vanilla notes of a simple major scale exploded with the flavorful essence of Yid-dish music, marking him as one of the great interpreters of klezmer music. Here was my Jewish Tommy Jarrell!

Slightly amazed that anyone would be interested in studying klezmer music, Leon Schwartz agreed to teach me some at the con-clusion of our lessons, provided I had successfully run the gauntlet of classical exercises. I desultorily agreed. Weighed down with the full corpus of classical study books by Hrimaly, Sevczik, and Wolfhardt, I slogged through colorless exercises while trying unsuc-cessfully to keep my true enthusiasm in check.

Despite college experience in composition and arranging, I was never big on reading music—my *meshoyrer* and folkie experience was defined by aural transmission and repetition, not written music—and so I had a hard time with these books. During a lesson one day, Leon gave me a certain exercise to play. "Beautiful, wonderful," he said upon my completion of it. "Now please play what's written."

Despite this impediment, I tried to become a student worthy of Leon Schwartz. And as it happened, I wasn't the only American disciple of a Yiddish music master. In another instance of uncanny symmetry, fellow Brooklynite Andy Statman had come across some of Dave Tarras's 78s and learned the tunes on sax and mandolin. (He did not yet own a clarinet.) In the early 1970s he looked Tarras up in the American Federation of Musicians directory, called him, and went over to play for him.

Like Leon Schwartz, Tarras was amazed at the level of interest, and after a halfhearted attempt to talk Statman out of studying Jewish music, he gave the young student one of his own clarinets and took him on as his apprentice. Instead of practicing rigid paper exercises, Statman would watch Tarras play, record him, and go home and learn the style, asking questions the next time he came. Tarras clearly assumed Statman would succeed him and carry on his banner.

Renewed interest in Tarras's music combined with Tarras's own interest in playing out again led to the organization of a concert in November 1978, cosponsored by Statman and musicologist Zev Feldman, in conjunction with the Balkan Arts Center. Among others, the reunion concert featured the Dave Tarras Trio, which had recorded for Victor in the 1940s: Tarras, Sammy Beckerman on accordion, and Irving Graetz on drums. The event drew more than 700 people, with many turned away for lack of seating.

One outgrowth of the concert was Tarras's last recording, *Dave Tarras: Master of the Jewish Clarinet* (1979), a collection of traditional music from his youth as well as tunes he played during his first few years in America. If his tempos and trills had grown slower, his phrases less flowing, what hadn't changed was Tarras's deep intimacy with the music. The record is a capstone to Tarras's lengthy recording career. And while it memorializes the reprise of Tarras's trio with Beckerman and Graetz, Graetz explained that once again, Tarras had tried to bypass him.

"The record we made, the three-piece with Sammy Beckerman, Dave almost did not give me the job," Graetz explained. "Sammy

Beckerman, he told him he had this record and Sammy asked him who was going on the drums. So Dave wanted this drummer that he had with him in the mountains; a theater man. Fine. So Beckerman said to him: 'Dave, this is not a theater job. It's a three-piece band, you gotta take Irving.' Otherwise, Dave had no intention of giving me the date." Despite his initial reluctance, Tarras was greatly pleased with Graetz's smooth, intuitive playing.

The 1978 event generated publicity that helped draw older audience members, who recalled Tarras from their own experience. (Tarras would sigh and tell of the countless people who would come up to him and say, "Hello, Dave. You played at my wedding, remember?" He'd smile at them, nod, and think: "I played so many weddings. Who remembers?")

The concert also attracted a large number of young people, and was a tremendous breakthrough for me personally. During the intermission, I went up to Tarras and introduced myself. Besieged by other well-wishers, Tarras brusquely brushed me off until I told him I brought greetings from my father, *khazn* Zindel Sapoznik. His whole demeanor changed. *"Di bist Sapozhnik's zin?"* (You're Sapoznik's son?) Lacking the time and space to talk there, he encouraged me to call him at home and come visit.

Then, among the throng of audience members, I had the great good luck to meet Richard Spottswood. Spottswood, a pioneer of country and jazz discography (and a founding editor of the magazine *Bluegrass Unlimited*), had, along with other driven young music historians in the 1950s, used old 78s as a road map to locate the country and blues musicians who had recorded them in their youth. Venturing down south to reunite the players and their recordings, Spottswood segued past and present for an eager new generation of musicians and scholars.

When I played old-time music, Spottswood's name was as important to me as those musicians whose records I learned from. By wonderful coincidence, he was now living in New York, engaged in the research for his monumental *Ethnic Music in America*, a seven-volume catalog of 78s recorded in the United States from 1895 to 1942—a project in which I, too, would soon be knee-deep.

Another group of fellow researchers turned out to be not crosstown but cross-country. Kirshenblatt-Gimblett introduced me to her fellow academic Mark Slobin, who had recently switched his field of study from Central Asia to Yiddish music, along the way conducting some of the most important research in the field. In a May

1977 letter brimming with enthusiasm and research leads, Slobin alerted me to ongoing work in Berkeley, California, by a group calling themselves The Klezmorim.

I eagerly contacted the group's co-founder and leader, Lev Liberman, and over the next few years a vibrant correspondence ensued. His voluminous letters, filled with news of recent 78 RPM discoveries, reports of The Klezmorim's recent concerts, the travails of making a living as a klezmer musician, and his loopy but entertaining theories of Jewish cultural history, were a refreshing fountain of inspiration. Finding such a generous and eloquent colleague helped charge my batteries for the work I was doing in New York.

The Klezmorim's inspiration, meanwhile, and much of its repertoire came from their neighbor Martin Schwartz, a professor of Near Eastern languages at the University of California, Berkeley. An avid collector of Jewish and Greek 78s, the Bronx-born Schwartz was a native Yiddish speaker in whom the fluency of the culture was clearly discernible. For the Yiddish-challenged members of The Klezmorim, Schwartz was the closest they had come to someone for whom Yiddish and its attendant culture was easy and ongoing. Schwartz became the band's Yiddish coach and also came to take part in the robust correspondence and tape exchange Liberman and I had initiated. So Schwartz became, for me, a new piece in the evolving klezmer jigsaw puzzle.

Another came up during a visit to Tarras's home in which he described the time he played for the Progressive Musicians Benevolent Society, the fraternal organization of Jewish musicians. Was it still in operation? I asked. It was, Tarras said, though vastly diminished in size and now, perhaps not ironically, maintained by funeral director Jack Yablakoff, the son of the one-time Yiddish theater star Herman Yablakoff. I contacted his funeral home in Brooklyn and spoke to him. Yablakoff offered me a list of current members of the organization replete with phone numbers and addresses, and I set to work contacting as many as I could. Near the top of my list was violinist Louis Grupp, who also lived in Brooklyn, not far from me. Though we were neighbors, he insisted I come meet him at the headquarters of the AFM in Manhattan, where he still maintained an office.

I entered a tiny, time-stunted cubicle and found Grupp, a small, energetic man, seated beside a desk festooned with papers. Though retired, he was, among other things, the liaison between the AFM and the nearly moribund United Hebrew Trades, the one-time powerhouse amalgam of Jewish unions in the New York area. Before I could get my tape recorder out of my bag he asked if I was a musician. I quickly said I was.

"So, you belong to the union . . . ?"

Silence. I did not. For a moment I thought the interview was going to end before it began. Like my *zeyde* and his belief in Marxism, Grupp was a member of the generation that believed that the union cured all evils and that all professional musicians should be part of and support it. After a long moment's hesitation he granted dispensation. The meeting would go on.

At this meeting Grupp first told me about his uncle Alter Chudnover and the young apprentice musicians back in Volhyn, and of the early hard days of Jewish musicians in New York. At its conclusion he invited me to his home. I soon made regular Friday visits to Grupp's home, timed to coincide with his wife's beauty parlor appointments: she hated musicians and the music business. Our two-hour windows of opportunity allowed him to reach back and share his most treasured memories, albeit in truncated and segmented form.

During one meeting he excused himself and came back with a fiddle case under his arm. From where I sat the aroma of musty rosin-covered velvet reached me.

"It was my Uncle Alter's," he said. Somehow I already knew that.

"My wife wants me to give it to my sons, but they don't care about it." He hadn't played in many years, but the old tunes came out, haltingly at first and then with more verve. And just as he started getting going, his wife returned, freshly coiffed, and poured ice water on the proceedings. We decided to take a walk.

As we strolled along Kings Highway, he regaled me with stories of the combative personalities that populated the New York klezmer music scene of his youth. Every bitter dispute, every angry ego clash, every character assassination was retold in the kind of detail accessible only to this one-time officer of the Progressive Musicians' Benevolent Society. After hearing his stories I wondered how benevolent this society was. When it was time to head home, Grupp escorted me to the subway station. At the turnstiles he grabbed my hand with both of his and said, "Please don't forget me." I promised I wouldn't.

If my meeting with Grupp was deliberately sought-out, other encounters with pioneering klezmer players were strictly *bashert*, kismet. For example, one of my tasks in the CETA program was to give lectures on klezmer music at various senior centers and old-age homes in the New York City area. Translating some theater ads from vintage Yiddish newspapers, I came across a reference to an orchestra headed by cellist Joseph Cherniavsky and his "Hasidic-American Jazz Band." What a wonderful and incongruous name. I loved it! Who were they? Thereafter I made sure to mention the band name in all my lectures, including one on a spring day in the Bronx in 1978.

Seated before me were dozens of seniors: some listening, some dozing, some talking. One woman was seated in front, knitting furiously. When I mentioned the Cherniavsky outfit, without looking up she said aloud: "Oh, them. My husband used to play drums with them."

Fearing that she, like so many older women, was a widow, I asked: "Your husband: is he . . . all right?"

Again without looking up she replied: "He was when I left him in the back playing pinochle." Putting down her knitting Grace Helfenbein went into the back of the Bronx Senior Center to fetch her husband, Joe.

This was my first experience giving a lecture where I knew there was someone in the audience who had actually lived that life. Would he consider this the height of chutzpa? Of youthful hubris? I needn't have worried. The toothily radiant smile of Joe Helfenbein, sitting attentively alongside his still-knitting wife, was all I needed to assure me that I conveyed to him and to all assembled an accurate portrayal of their bygone world.

After the lecture Helfenbein and I made our way to the rear of the senior center. My tape recorder, only moments before expelling the sounds of antique recordings, was now turned on Helfenbein himself, to document his vital memories of the days when those recordings were new.

We settled down in a quiet corner with the tape recorder humming, the ambient sounds of pinochle players replaced by recollections of a faraway time in 1925.

"Did you make any records with the Cherniavsky band?"

"Yes," he said, turning inward. "Yes, we did. Of course, it's been a long time. I can't remember what happened to them."

Slowly, softly Helfenbein began to hum. The serpentine lines of a *doina* came out almost involuntarily, intensifying with each passing note. The tune took shape and became full and rich as he settled in, eyes half closed. Helfenbein's voice switching from throat to head tones clearly indicated which instruments in the orchestra were carrying the melody. The *doina* trailed off replaced by a robust *freylekhs*. He stopped suddenly: "I used a wind whistle here . . ." making the sound of the sirenlike instrument de rigueur in every percussionist's repertoire. He ended with a flamboyantly theatrical flourish and, opening his eyes again, murmured: "Of course, it was a long time ago."

Four years later, while on a visit to Martin Schwartz's home in Berkeley, Schwartz slipped the needle into the groove of one of his many 78s and my head snapped up. It was the Cherniavsky tune Helfenbein had hummed for me—an unerringly accurate re-creation, right down to the key! Though he hadn't played the tune in fifty years and had never heard the 78—and was a drummer—Joe still had it in him.

Of Cherniavsky, Helfenbein had much to say—all of it good. In fact, shy of his unfortunate run-in with a tempestuous Naftule Brandwein on one Cherniavsky road trip, he had nothing but happy recollections about his stint as one of the Jewish scene's top rhythm-keepers. Had his mother not pulled him off the road with Cherni-avsky, he might still be in the "Jewish line," he explained. Like so many Jewish musicians, Helfenbein made his way through the myri-ad of music venues: movie houses, vaudeville, cafes, hotels, radio, and theaters. He was a true professional who until his last days assiduously practiced his "paradiddles," the daily rhythm regimen of the serious drummer.

When I came to the Bronx to visit with him, he and Grace would lay out a lavish spread that culminated with my taping Joe as Grace sat by his side, smiling—and knitting. Once, years later, I brought drummer David Licht of a new klezmer group, The Klezmatics, with me, and Joe was elated. He took out his practice pad and proudly demonstrated his paradiddles for Licht, who expressed genuine admiration for Joe's limber acuity.

Facilitating this exchange between a veteran klezmer musician and an up-and-coming younger player delivered a joy and satisfaction I would come to experience again—in spades.

KLEZMER PILGRIMAGE

Due to funding cutbacks and labor/management problems within the AJC and CETA, my tenure at The Martin Steinberg Center ended at the close of 1978. Soon after, I was chatting with some friends about my current state of loose ends.

"Why not go to Israel?" one suggested.

Hmmm. No kind of Zionist, I realized I couldn't know what it was I was skeptical of unless I made the trip. Besides, I was told that libraries and archives there had materials on klezmer that were not available here. That settled it.

Staying with my brother's in-laws in the resort town of Netanya, I contacted several of the American expatriates who had set up shop there: clarinetists Dov Marienbach and Janet Elias, the woman who, with Barbara Kirshenblatt-Gimblett, had interviewed Dave Tarras in 1976.

Shortly after my arrival I met with major Israeli music researchers including Avigdor Herzog and Yakov Mazor at the Fonoteka, the Hebrew University's small but vital sound archives. Hospitable and welcoming, they spoke of establishing an international exchange of data on Jewish music and allowed me to set up shop there and to catalog their holdings of American 78s, the kind of work I had begun at YIVO.

The meetings with my Israeli colleagues were invigorating but also frustrating. Open as they were to my mission, these people also felt klezmer wasn't quite a suitable subject for research. "Why not study the music of a living Jewish culture, such as Israeli music?" they asked.

The Israeli researchers also considered the commercial 78 RPM recordings of the teens and twenties a funhouse-mirror reflection of what had actually gone on. Feeling that the recording studio created a sterile venue for documentation of this music, they favored the use of field recordings, made in the original social situation. So did I.

But there were no field recordings—or at least, none we were aware of, I explained, making this corpus of fleeting studio recordings eminently worthy of study. While not the candid snapshots we all wanted, the recordings were the equivalent of studio portraits taken of these master musicians shortly after their arrival in the New World. The truncated three-minute discs were a mere hint of the music's more lavish and wide-ranging sphere, but what could not be lost to technical limitation—or to these reluctant listeners—was its immediacy and vitality.

My Israeli colleagues encouraged me to go locate klezmer music as it is played today by Hasidim in Mea Shearim, in one of the oldest sections of Jerusalem. Decamping from Netanya, I traveled by bus to the city, taking a room at a hostel managed by the American Jewish Congress and named, by odd coincidence, The Martin Steinberg

House. Donning a plain white shirt, dark pants, and my father's old-fashioned *khazonish* yarmulke, I looked, with my full beard, like a regular resident of the quarter, able to mingle in mufti. With a tape recorder and a fistful of cassette transfers of klezmer 78s, I headed out to the old quarter.

Janet Elias had tipped me off to a Hasid named Ben Zion Kletzkin, a sign painter and clarinetist who played in the style of the Meron Hasidim, a sinewy amalgam of Eastern European and Middle Eastern sounds. The Meron Hasidim maintain a vital link with their departed rebbe by staging a yearly pilgrimage to the town of Sfat replete with music, trance dancing, and exuberant *nigun* singing. The story goes that their repertoire was inspired by the cache of klezmer 78s brought by an Ashkenazic Jew named Wallenstein, who emigrated to Israel in the 1920s.

I found Kletzkin in the cramped sign-painting studio he ran in the old Jewish quarter. Uninterested in discussing himself, he played me a tape of his son Gershon, also a clarinetist and a fine Meron stylist. Afterward, I headed deeper into Mea Shearim, seeking a place to buy recordings of these unique players. I located an appliance store filled to the rafters with tapes of this kind, including a CBS Israel LP of field recordings made by Messrs. Adler and Hajdu of Meron Hasidim. I was elated.

"This one is good too," a voice said in Yiddish. I turned to find at my elbow a small young Hasid whom I recalled seeing only moments ago in Kletzkin's studio. It turns out he, Yochanan, played drums with Kletzkin's son and was recommending a cassette of their band. Without hesitation I bought it. He was right. The recording had a biting energy unhindered by self-consciousness. Even the goofy-sounding electric piano had unique verve. When I mentioned I had some dubs with me of klezmer 78s Yochanan grabbed my arm with a strength not hinted at by his slight frame and led me back to his house. Leaving me alone, he returned with some fellow band members and had me play them my tapes, which elicited whoops and hollers with each new selection. No sooner did a record come on than they set to commenting in a rapid, nearly unintelligible fusion of Yiddish and Hebrew. With an extra tape recorder, I made transfers of the tapes for Yochanan and have since speculated on how many copies of copies of them must be floating around Mea Shearim.

Back at the hostel I had to change clothes quickly to attend a concert by the famous Israeli clarinetist Giora Feidman at Jerusalem's

Khan Theater. Claiming third-generation lineage of a family of klez-morim, Feidman had recently retired as bass clarinetist for the Israeli Philharmonic due to eyesight problems and had embarked on a career of reintroducing klezmer music to a new public. No matter where I went, his name was intoned with a mix of awe and admiration. Giora was considered the greatest living exponent of this music, a leader in the resuscitation of the rare and dying form. Having enjoyed hearing clarinetist Dov Marienbach play a few nights earlier, I prepared myself for a watershed evening.

Having arranged for some complimentary tickets, Elias and I went to the little theater. Filled with American tourists seeking authentic atmosphere, the hall buzzed with anticipation. The lights went low, and from the back of the theater came the sound of a clarinet, as Feidman, wearing a Greek fisherman's hat meant to evoke the little visored caps worn by Polish Jews, marched slowly toward the stage, playing his interpretation of a *doina*. He followed that with "Hava Nagila," melodies from *Fiddler on the Roof*, and an assortment of pasteurized klezmer tunes—what he referred to as "Jewish soul music." His playing, informed by a classical clarinet esthetic, replaced the dance music sound and the realism of the music I knew with a far-away spiritualism of overplayed subtleties.

The more the audience seemed to eat it up, the more disconcerted I became. Sensing my discomfort, Elias bravely tried to put a better face on it, but she knew what I knew: after hearing men like Dave Tarras and experiencing the grassroots sound of the music played by musicians raised in the culture, this was not klezmer.

Back in the United States, I excitedly continued researching the real thing. The Klezmorim had issued its first LP, *East Side Wedding*, for the California label Arhoolie, and I became a big supporter of the band, reviewing the album for the folk music magazine *Sing Out!*, for which I penned an old-time banjo column. Praising The Klezmorim's inventiveness and commitment to bringing back the music, I was nonetheless compelled to note their weak Yiddish pronunciation. Not having grown up with the music is one thing, but attempting to sing in a language you do not speak is a tougher obstacle and one that remained a real problem for the band in its early years.

In 1978 The Klezmorim issued what many (myself included) consider their best record, *Streets of Gold*, on which they hove to their mixed repertoire of instrumental music and vocals, importing standards like "Mayn Rue Plats," sung by the Bay Area fiddler Miriam Dvorin, a singer with more experience of the language. The album cover, by cartoonist R. Crumb, harkens to a mythic immigrant New York, turning the Lower East Side into a New Old World and relegating Eastern Europe to Old Old World status. That wasn't just Crumb's conception. Sometime before the band's first trip to New York, Liberman excitedly wrote me of his plans to look for old klezmer 78s "in attics on the Lower East Side." Amused by such naïveté of New York architecture, I remarked that the only attics he'd find on the Lower East Side were drug addicts.

In 1979 Andy Statman, Zev Feldman, and Marty Confurius released their seminal LP *Jewish Klezmer Music*, for the Bronx-based Irish music label Shanachie. This deeply felt, well-played anthology remains unique, even today, among the plethora of klezmer recordings. For the moment, these were the only young people playing klezmer in America.

Despite my departure from The Martin Steinberg Center, I maintained close ties with Chava Miller and Jeff Oboler, stopping by frequently. One day Miller told me of a synagogue in Providence, Rhode Island, that had contacted the center seeking a lecture demonstration on klezmer music. Until this point, I had been hesitant about forming my own band, partly because of my time commitment to the Delaware Water Gap Band, and because while I knew as much about the music as anyone playing it, I felt I had a lot to learn. But there was a place for what I wanted to do, for the kind of Yiddish music I wanted to play. The call from this Rhode Island synagogue was the push I needed.

Inspired as it was by my love for klezmer music, the band I sought to create also had to embody the range of Yiddish music, including folk ballads, labor and political anthems, and songs from the Yiddish theater. I didn't want the instrumental music yanked out of context but firmly placed in the same repertoire framework it had always been in, and performed by men and women who had grown up in the culture and could speak the language.

I approached singer/pianist Josh Waletzky, whom I had met in the late '70s at YIVO when he was editing his directorial debut, *Image Before My Eyes*, a film documentary on Jewish life in Poland between the wars. Waletzky had asked me to help with the music for the film, and I was quickly impressed by his knowledge of music and his easygoing, homey Yiddish. Josh's singing, albeit untrained, conveyed a warm sincerity that suited him well for the ensemble.

My next choice was also a singer: Michael Alpert, whom I'd met while working for CETA. Unlike Waletzky and me, Alpert didn't

Andy Statman (*left*) and the author, 1979.

come from a Yiddish-speaking home, but his facility with languages, familiarity with Eastern European music (he was involved in California's Balkan music scene before coming to New York), and ear-catching tenor made him another good choice. An added plus was his fiddle playing, which offered a good harmonic sense that made him a strong *secunda*, or second fiddle.

Through Alpert I was introduced to another Jewish member of the Balkan music scene, Lauren Brody, a gifted singer, accordionist, and pianist. No big fan of accordion music, I was initially unenthused at the prospect of adding it to the band. But Brody's pronounced musicality won me over to the instrument.

The all-important chair of clarinet proved difficult to fill, as I could find no young players of the style. So I cast my net wide, knowing I had to find and train someone. There was one clarinetist I had heard play Dixieland and whom I felt could acquit himself well if he could be induced to try his hand at klezmer. After numerous letters, cassette tapes dropped off at his house, and even a telephone call, I finally had to accept that Woody Allen was not interested in playing klezmer music. I turned to the veteran klezmer Pete Sokolow, who, though flattered, said he had given up playing clarinet for his career as a keyboardist.

A chance remark led me to the clarinetist Ken Maltz. Some mutual friends in the country music scene knew Maltz, who had grown up playing Jewish music at family events but had played orchestral jazz and club dates professionally. Currently a teacher seeking some sort of musical outlet, he immediately joined up.

For this band, unlike my previous band and most bands in general, I envisioned not a bass player but the more unique sound of a tuba. A banjo student of mine told me about a young jazz player named Dan Conte, who filled out the final chair in the band.

Though we tussled over names for the group, we settled on Waletzky's suggestion of Kapelye, which means simply "a band." Later, when promoters couldn't figure out its context, we added, "The Yiddish Klezmer Band."

In spring 1979 we began rehearsing. Waletzky contributed old songs learned at home, and Alpert his favorite pieces from the Yiddish theater. I brought in dubs of my favorite klezmer 78s from YIVO, which Maltz then transcribed. And so our modest sextet set itself the task of playing tunes originally arranged for fourteen-piece orchestras.

The Delaware Water Gap, meanwhile, embarked on its first European tour that summer, playing in Belgium, Switzerland, and France. While there I envisioned a tour for the newly formed Kapelye. A dream, for sure, but my notion was to force-feed Yiddish music back to the continent from which it had come.

At a festival in Switzerland, I came across an LP of Yiddish music by a German band called Zupfgeigenhansel. The album, *Jiddische Lieder ('ch hob gehert sogn)*—Jewish Songs (I once heard it said)—

played in an un-Jewish "folkie" style, was a hodgepodge of the usual suspects of Yiddish songs ("Dona, Dona," etc.) framed by photos from the Holocaust with cutesy illustrations of "Jews." (Why, I thought, are Jews in non-Jewish contexts pictured with beards and no moustaches, as if they were Amish?) If this was the state of consciousness of Yiddish music in Europe, I felt even more certain about our chances to make a splash.

The newly spawned world music movement was making its first foray into the folk festival circuit, and I envisioned a place in it for the kind of Yiddish music I was going to play. While in Europe, I cultivated interest among promoters who might prove sympathetic to bringing over a Yiddish band.

Kapelye's November 18, 1979, premiere concert at Providence's Temple Beth-El proved that there was an audience for traditional Yiddish music played in an authentic style. The show was everything I wanted, and the audience—a full house—seemed equally pleased. We returned to New York primed to expand our venues, and having been active in booking the Water Gap, I took on the role for Kapelye as well.

Nineteen eighty was a great year. Though I was now gainfully unemployed, Kapelye was heading into a regular schedule of rehearsing, and I began researching and collecting materials for the Folkways anthology of klezmer 78s. In May I got a phone call from Richard Siegel, program director at the National Foundation for Jewish Culture (NFJC), who was editing something called *The Jewish Almanac*, a collection of essays about aspects of Jewish life. I was asked to contribute an article about Jewish violinists. We met at the foundation's office in New York to discuss the essay.

Siegel told me the organization ran a variety of programs, but nothing relating to traditional Jewish culture. On the spot I asked if they might be interested in sponsoring a citywide folk arts event celebrating the ethnic diversity of New York's various Jewish communities. They were enthusiastic but wary, so I assured them of my background in mounting festivals (which was actually nil), and the Jewish Ethnic Music Festival was born.

Working with codirector Leslie Berman—also a veteran folk music scene participant—I organized an event along the lines of the successful and popular prototypes already at work at the Philadelphia Folk Festival, the National Folk Festival, and other mainstream regional events at which I'd performed. The three days were filled with workshops, lectures, films, concerts, and dances, while the evenings featured performers from the Jewish communities: Hasidic, Yiddish, Syrian, Egyptian, Sephardic, Soviet, and Indian.

What I hadn't anticipated was the almost complete lack of interest each community showed for the music of the others. For example, when the brilliant oud player and *hazzan* Vita Israel took the stage, scores of Hasidic music fans who had come to hear the Neginah Orchestra walked out. When Dave Tarras stepped up to play, the followers of Middle Eastern Pizmon left the room It was a sobering lesson about what was considered "Jewish" by different branches of the Jewish world.

It wasn't much different during the daytime workshops. My own curiosity had been piqued to set up panels that would explore the similarities and contrasts of prayer music within the mix of communities. I chose texts that were common to all and asked the various experts there to comment on them. What I learned was that while one community might have developed an ornate and tuneful melody for a particular prayer text, another community might ignore or speed through it.

Overwhelmed by the seemingly limitless demands of the festival, I found myself unable to take part in—or even observe—the planned workshops, including one I was to conduct with my fiddle teacher Leon Schwartz. I asked fellow Kapelye member Michael Alpert to fill in for me, resulting in his own apprenticeship with Schwartz.

After the festival, I convinced the NFJC to go through the numerous workshop and concert tapes to construct a public radio program. The four-part special, "One People, Many Voices," won numerous broadcast awards. Sadly, despite the success of the festival—nearly two thousand people turned out for the three-day event—NFJC never followed up with another like it.

DER YIDISHER CARAVAN:
KLEZMER MUSIC ON THE ROAD

In one of my meetings with festival advisor Barbara Kirshenblatt-Gimblett, she told me of a call she'd gotten from Joe Wilson at the National Council for the Traditional Arts (NCTA), sponsors of the National Folk Festival. No one who played traditional American music was unaware of the National Folk Festival. This event, founded during the heady days of the WPA, was the only coast-to-coast celebration of regional traditional music and crafts in America.

In addition to the festival itself, NCTA organized national tours of traditional musicians in the Irish and Franco-American communities. Nineteen eighty-one marked the centennial year of the beginning of peak emigration of Ashkenazi Jews to the United States, and NCTA associate director Bill Kornrich, seeking to organize a national tour to commemorate the anniversary, put in a call to Kirshenblatt-Gimblett. Not interested in running it herself, she recommended me for the job of project director.

I met in Washington with Kornrich, a seasoned veteran of these tours, who enthusiastically helped construct the most extensive national Yiddish touring company of the postwar era. First and foremost, the goal of the tour was to present Yiddish culture in all its diversity. To that end, I put together an intergenerational troupe. The first person I asked was my father, Zindel Sapoznik, in order to ground the shows in one of the musical underpinnings of Yiddish music—*khazones*. I then sought out an actor and actress from the Yiddish stage, interviewing several great ones, including monologist Herschel Gendel and film star Leon Liebgold, whose ill health made them unable to tour. Happily, an actor/comedian named David Ellin was excited about going back on the road, especially with a group of younger performers, and turned out to be one of the show's great highlights.

Kornrich introduced me to the actress Frieda Mariamova, a recent Russian émigré living in the Washington, D.C., area. Claiming to have been in the Moscow Yiddish Art Theater (it turns out she wasn't), Mariamova was a blustery and demanding diva who turned out good performances in spite of it. The last of our senior members of the tour was the singer Teddi Schwartz, best known for her translation of Sholom Secunda's song "Dona, Dona."

The younger players were much easier to find. Though I had wanted to bring Kapelye, school schedules prohibited clarinetist Ken Maltz and our new tubist, Eric Berman, from making the whole tour. Instead, I booked clarinetist Andy Statman and, on his advice, the Latin brass player Stan Schaffran.

Der Yidisher Caravan, as the troupe came to be called, booked a twenty-two-city East Coast tour designed to reach into the communities for which Yiddish was the historic culture. We traveled from places as far afield as the Ice Belt of Maine, where we opened on April 1, 1981, at the tail end of cabin fever season, to my hometown of Brooklyn, where we ended in mid-June.

To make the tour affordable for the communities, NCTA arranged for local hosts to provide the performers home hospitality. The best part was the idea that for every paid admission show we gave, we also gave a free show at a local old-age home—some of our favorite performances. There we met real carriers of the tradition for whom the music, songs, and language were as alive as when they were young.

The regular show ran about ninety minutes, split into forty-five-minute segments with a short intermission. After an introduction wherein I explained why we were called the Caravan (we travel in a car and a van), the houselights were dimmed and we showed a brief film compilation of footage culled from Eastern Europe from the YIVO archives. The first half of the program featured works from the region, including a wonderful reading of the Sholem Aleichem short story "Milkhiks" (Dairy), by comic David Ellin; Yiddish theater monologues by Frieda Mariamova; *khazones* my father learned from his teachers in Rovne; and of course, hot klezmer music interspersed throughout.

The second half of the show moved the action to America, featuring Yiddish theater songs from the 1930s and '40s; Ellin's masterful reading of satirist Moshe Nadir's hilarious story *Mayn Ershtn Depozit* about an ill-fated bank deposit; and of course, more *khazones*, folk songs, and klezmer music.

While on tour, I was also finishing notes for the Folkways klezmer reissue, having recently finalized choices of recordings from YIVO (and a few from Marty Schwartz's collection). Back in New York I asked Andy Statman and Zev Feldman to write additional commentary, and after locating some pictures in the YIVO archives—including what I used for the album cover, a stunning 1912 image of the Faust family *kapelye* from Galicia—the disc was complete. The klezmer scene now had a primary source, modeled after early country music and jazz anthologies that had helped modern musicians master a distant musical style.

Among the people I gave copies to was Woody Allen. Though rebuffed by his not having joined Kapelye, I somehow still fantasized that when he finally heard this music played by the greats, he would throw himself into klezmer as he had into Dixieland. I dropped a copy of the LP off at his apartment house—only a few blocks south of YIVO—but not surprisingly never heard from him. Imagine my shock two years later when, in Allen's film *Zelig*, the main character displays a photo of his family—the photo on the cover of the Folkways LP! The music hadn't gotten to him, but the image had.

HOLLYWOOD IN BROOKLYN : CHOSEN FOR "THE CHOSEN" AND "OVER THE BROOKLYN BRIDGE"

If Woody Allen passed on the klezmer bandwagon, other filmmakers did not. In spring 1981 an old Lubavitch pal of mine called me to say he'd been contacted by a production company doing an adaptation of

The Faust family *kapelye*, Rohatyn, Poland, 1912. Bandleader Moishe Faust (*seated left*) with sons on clarinet, trumpet, and fiddle behind him. The man with no instrument standing in back is a *badkhn*. (*Courtesy Annette Faust Heller*)

Chaim Potok's coming-of-age novel, *The Chosen*. The filmmakers were looking for literal "beards" to be extras in the group Hasidic scenes. He told me whom to contact, given that I was sporting a full growth at the time and might get some interesting side work.

While on the phone with the film contact it occurred to me to ask whether they had made arrangements for music. I was told that they had hired veteran film composer Elmer Bernstein and jazz pianist Dick Hyman, formidable choices. (I was friendly with Hyman's daughter, Judy, a wonderful fiddler in the New York old-time music scene.) Somehow I persuaded him that as great as Bernstein and Hyman were, a film about Hasidic life needed Jewish music and did I have a band for him! As easy as that, we arranged to meet with the film's director, Jeremy Kagan, a few days later. At the meeting I laid out ideas for the music, emphasizing my background in the Hasidic world. Though interested, he was not convinced and told me he would ask Hyman what he thought. I was worried that a profession-al like Dick Hyman, who later went on to score several Woody Allen pictures, might pooh-pooh the use of untested players. A few days of sitting on the edge of my chair and finally I heard: Hyman enthusias-tically agreed my idea was a good one.

Jeremy Kagan and his assistant attended a Kapelye rehearsal the next week, and as we played through our repertoire, Kagan picked pieces as though at a smorgasbord: "I'll have some of this, a little of that, some more of that . . ." What emerged was a seven-minute textured suite of tunes featured in the movie's wedding scene—a minor part of Potok's book, but in Kagan's film a major plot device that moves the action forward.

When it came time to go into the studio to lay down the tracks, which would then be synched during filming, we were a tad nervous: this was the band's first recording session. We became more nervous still when we found that we were to follow Hyman and his handpicked ensemble of top New York jazz players. Sitting through their wonderful swing set, we were fearful to have to follow, and made more so when they stuck around to listen. But we laid down the first take with no problem and were touched that as soon as the tape stopped rolling, Hyman and his players gave us a round of applause.

In August filming began in the Park Slope section of Brooklyn, with the principals Rod Steiger and Robby Benson. The weather, usually pretty unbearable at that time of year, was temperate thanks to a cool front that had settled in. We donned our layered *kapotes* and *peyes* and remained comfortable. The only hitch was that accordionist Lauren Brody, who had recorded the soundtrack, was in Bulgaria, so Pete Sokolow had to fill in the part.

Decked out in our Hasidic finery, we mimed playing to the music we had recorded, which poured out of massive speakers while Steiger, as the Hasidic rebbe, tried to dance. Time and again he couldn't get the rhythm and finally had to admit that when it came to dancing he was no actor. Undeterred, we played a live accompaniment for him, following his improvised twists and turns and trying to match our tempo to his gyrations. (In the final cut, part of Steiger's dance scene is rendered in slow motion, eliminating the tempo discrepancy completely.) Despite his inability to be choreographed, Steiger was a real *mentsh* and a pleasure to work with. After two nights of midnight to 6 A.M. filming, we finished our little seven-minute set. Apart from some additional shooting a few days later, we were done.

Another good thing about having worked on *The Chosen* was that now my name showed up in casting directors' Rolodexes when filmmakers were looking for Jewish-looking extras for their movies. I landed more film work, in *Once Upon a Time in America*, Sergio Leone's 1984 potboiler about Jewish-American gangsters. And that same year Kapelye was hired to do what we had done in *The*

Chosen—appear as Hasidim playing music at a wedding—for Israeli Menahem Golan's *Over the Brooklyn Bridge*.

Originally called *My Darling Shiksa*, the film starred Elliot Gould, Shelley Winters, Sid Caesar, Margaux Hemingway (the *shiksa* in question), and Carol Kane. You'd think that with these stars the movie would be superb, but that would not take into account the talents of producer-turned-director Golan, whose other artistic zenith was the ultraviolent *Death Wish* series, starring Charles Bronson.

In its attempt at humor *Over the Brooklyn Bridge* trades on the basest, most racist depictions of Jews. What's worse, it isn't funny,

Kapelye קאַפּעליע
A Yiddish/Klezmer Band

Kapelye, 1983 (*clockwise from center*): Ken Maltz, Lauren Brody, Michael Alpert, Eric Berman, Henry Sapoznik. (*J. J. Kriegsmann*)

merely insulting and blunt. A deeply sad spectacle was watching Sid Caesar, one of the funniest men in the history of television, take "comedy" direction from a man who lacked the trait so entirely. When the Kapelye clarinetist Ken Maltz went to see it in a local theater, a couple sitting in the row ahead of him took him to dinner after the show out of sympathy when they learned he was in the movie. This wasn't the only awful film to use a contemporary klezmer band for its soundtrack. Director Richard Fleischer hired The Klezmorim to play "Der Heyser Bulgar" in the unnecessary 1980 remake of *The Jazz Singer*, with Neil Diamond.

The Chosen was the best experience, not only because of its quality production but also for what it led to. Prior to the film, Kapelye had been looking to get a recording contract, and although I had a chance with Folkways, we wanted a label that offered wider distribution and a greater budget for production. During a break in the shooting of *The Chosen* I made a call to Bruce Kaplan, the founder/owner of the popular independent folk label Flying Fish. I told him we were interested in recording, and he asked if we were gigging much. We weren't, but when I said I was calling from the set of *The Chosen*, he agreed on the spot to release our album.

Timing is everything.

~ 7 ~

"FUTURE AND PAST" AND FUTURE

IN 1980 SOMEONE SHOPPING for contemporary Yiddish music would have had to flip through all manner of Jewish recordings to find The Klezmorim LPs, Statman's album, and the handful of discs born out of the New York Yiddishist scene in the mid-1970s. Among the latter was *Songs of Work and Struggle,* a collection of songs associated with the Jewish Labor Bund sung by young people who had grown up speaking Yiddish and sounded it. It was a well-intentioned record, but its chorus and piano were holdovers from the Workmen's Circle choirs of the interwar years. *Vaserl,* a collection of newly composed Yiddish songs played in a "modern" setting, was equally dated.

For Kapelye's first album, we wanted to meld the authentic Yiddish of these records with Statman's brand of fiery energy. The tunes we chose for *Future and Past* were an amalgam of mostly folk songs (*Vi Azoy Trinkt der Keyser Tey?*/"How Does the Czar Drink Tea?"; *Git Purim, Yidn*/"Happy Purim, Jews"); some theater songs, like *In Shtetl Nikolaev*; a labor ballad (*Motl Der Opreyter*/"Motl the Operator"); and of course, klezmer tunes. To cap it off, I sought a sort of *hekhsher*—the kosher thumbs-up—from the Yiddish author Isaac Bashevis Singer, whose endorsement in the liner notes reads: "I listened to the music of Kapelye and I enjoyed it because they have the flavor of the Yiddish of my roots. Every tune reminds me of something and brings me back to my past and people. . . ." Kapelye was in the running.

Klezmer groups around the world point to Klezmorim records as having been their impetus to play the music. The band had the same effect on klezmer that Virginia singer Henry Whitter had on country music back in the early 1920s. Whitter's playing was so accessible his recordings spirited hopeful musicians into the studio, feeling they could do as good or better. And they were right.

KLEZMER GOES TO COLLEGE: THE KLEZMER CONSERVATORY

By 1981, when Kapelye issued its first LP, klezmer music had begun to emerge as an American ethnic genre. Among the enthusiastic well-wishers at our March 5 record release concert at New York's Martin Steinberg Center was Hankus Netsky, down from Boston, where he had started up The Klezmer Conservatory Band (KCB) the year before.

Netsky's interest in the genre began in 1974, when he asked his uncle Sam to describe his exploits as a klezmer musician in Philadelphia during 1916–34. (Another uncle, Jerry, a clarinetist, was bitter about the klezmer music scene and tried to dampen young Netsky's interest in it; Uncle Sam did not.) Sam, a cornetist, had been witness to the Philadelphia klezmer scene as a sideman in the orchestra of local clarinetist and renowned character Itzikl Kramtweiss. Wistfully recounting his experiences, Sam played his nephew treasured 78s by Tarras, Brandwein, Abe Schwartz, and his one-time employer Kramtweiss. "You know," he told his young nephew, "you could do something with this stuff." Netsky did.

After giving long thought to playing a Brandwein composition for a masters recital at the New England Conservatory of Music in 1978—he lost heart and played a Greek tune instead—Netsky advertised locally for people to play klezmer music. To his great surprise, some twenty musicians turned up at the informal session.

A fundraiser for the short-lived Hillel chapter of the New England Conservatory brought the band and its music to the attention of the Boston Jewish community, and work offers began to come in. Now all they had to do was come up with a name. Like that of so many other klezmer bands, KCB's name began as a joke. After all, Netsky pointed out "Who'd ever heard of a klezmer conservatory?"

At this point Netsky's band consisted of cornetists Frank London and Ingrid Monson, Abby Rabinovitz (flute), Mimi Rabson, Greta Buck, and Marvin Weinberger (violins), Barry Shapiro (piano), Merryl Goldberg (baritone sax), David Harris (trombone), Jim Guttmann (bass), Judy Bressler (vocals), Charlie Berg (drums), and Netsky himself on alto sax and, for a time, oboe. For the highly visible clarinet chair, Netsky had the showman's instinct to hire the eccentric master clarinetist Don Byron.

Klezmer Conservatory Band publicity photo, 1984.

Byron was the first popular non-Jewish interpreter of klezmer music and, because of the success of the KCB, one of the most influential stylists of this modern period. His superior technical acuity aside, he has attracted more than his share of attention because he is also one of the few African-Americans playing the music.

One example of this "attention" occurred during a 1982 appearance of the KCB on a popular Boston public radio show, *Morning Pro Musica*. In what might have been an attempt to lighten up the interview portion of his show—or perhaps to demonstrate how "hip" he was—pompous host Robert J. Lurtsema asked Byron: "So Don . . . How did a *goyisher shvartzer* like you come to play klezmer music?" Aghast but gracious, Byron sidestepped the insensitivity of the question and talked instead about his desire to play great music. Not a few people have remarked that Byron's presence in the klezmer scene is some sort of "karmic" payback for all the Jews who have played black music. After leaving KCB, Byron went on to carve out another place for himself in the world of Jewish music by championing the novelty recordings of Mickey Katz.

Much of the success of the KCB's stage show has always been due to its massed grouping of enthusiastic and talented young musicians. Another was the contrast of Byron's studied surliness and the perky effervescence of singer Judy Bressler. Bressler, a granddaughter of Yiddish theater stars Lucy Gehrman and Menashe Skulnik, had

already crafted a smooth cabaret singing style before joining the
KCB in 1980. Not knowing Yiddish, she was coached in the lan-
guage by scholar Dovid Fishman, as shown in the 1988 film *A
Jumpin' Night in the Garden of Eden.*

When Netsky came to New York in 1981 to see the Kapelye show,
he was planning to go into the studios that spring to make his own
first record, *Yiddishe Renaissance,* and I told him about some of the
pitfalls we had encountered. Unlike Kapelye, he didn't have a regular label on which to release his record, so he bravely opted to make
it a vanity pressing under the whimsical name Kleztone.

One of the first big breaks The Klezmer Conservatory had was to
appear on *A Prairie Home Companion,* Garrison Keillor's popular
public radio show, on October 10, 1981—a broadcast I chanced to
miss, although on Saturday nights when Kapelye wasn't gigging, I
luxuriated by tuning in to the program. I had heard many of my
folkie friends perform and wanted to be on my favorite radio show.
So I bundled up a copy of our new record, shipped it out, and waited to hear back. Happily, it didn't take long until I heard from the
show's producer, Margaret Moos, and Kapelye trekked out to St.
Paul, Minnesota, for a special Hanukkah concert on December 11,
1982.

To appear on the show, I had taken time out of producing a festival in New York, called The Festival of Soviet-Jewish Traditions. An
old pal who had worked with me at CETA was now working at the
Federation for Jewish Philanthropies and brought me in to help con-
ceptualize a program that would combine social service (the Federation's raison d'être) and the arts. The recent large emigration of Russians to the United States offered a great chance for the kind of
grassroots fieldwork not usually possible in Jewish studies. Though
capable of bankrolling an event like this easily, the Federation was
steadfastly unwilling to hire sufficient staff. So I brought in some
friends—field-workers Carol Freeman (crafts), Michael Alpert
(music/dance), and Marion Sitomer (food)—who agreed as I did to
work for modest wages. And I got stuck with the administrative part
of the job, my least favorite.

It was hoped that the Soviet-Jewish Festival would unearth a rich
folkloric life in this understudied community. Sadly, what we found
were tenuous links with any kind of real folk literacy, especially in
the western Russian communites. (The continuity was much
stronger in Eastern communities like Bukhara, where Jews escaped
Stalin's purges more effectively.) It seemed a Soviet Jew younger

than fifty-five had little or no idea what Yiddish culture was, the effect of Stalin's effective cultural genocide against the Yiddish intelligenstia and his closing of Yiddish schools in the early 1950s. Of course, among the older émigrés there were some wonderful *folksmentshn*, none more vibrant than the singer and dancer Bronya Sakina. Bronya's delicate singing and evocative dancing were a treasure for all to see.

During the development of the Soviet-Jewish Festival I was called in to YIVO for a meeting with Sam Norich. The success of Josh Waletzky's film *Image Before My Eyes* had generated much popular interest. One potential donor, the Weinstein family, wanted to put up sixty thousand dollars for the production of another film like it, but Norich convinced him that while sixty thousand dollars itself couldn't fund a film, it could give birth to a sound archives of Yiddish recorded music. It seemed that an old proposal for the archives, thanks to Barbara Kirshenblatt-Gimblett's help, was coming to pass.

My one stipulation in accepting the job was the freedom to take time off to travel with Kapelye. This was immediately important, as Der Yidisher Caravan picked up the western end of its national tour, from St. Louis, Missouri, to Pomona, California, soon after the archives opened. The donors' stipulations were that the archives be named after their parents, Max and Frieda Weinstein, and that work to establish it begin immediately.

I knew I couldn't arrange to start up the archives and mount a complicated and richly textured festival at the same time, so I stepped down as the festival's director, bringing in several veteran festival colleagues to run the show. The result was a critically acclaimed and interesting event, which, although a hit with attendees and community, did not inspire the federation to allocate further funds to cultural continuity.

YIVO'S CULTURAL RECLAMATION

The night of June 8, 1982, a free concert was staged to celebrate the inauguration of the YIVO sound archives. As part of an area-wide evening of museum openings near the institute, nearly a thousand people jammed the corner of Fifth Avenue and East Eighty-Sixth Street to hear Kapelye play, the first of numerous concerts on this corner.

After the festivities, the difficult work of organizing the archives began. The room chosen, the fifth-floor garret of the old Vanderbilt mansion, had once been the servants' quarters. Like so many New York spaces, it only became available upon the death of the previous occupant, an elderly YIVO staffer. More a cell than an office, the six by twenty-one foot room was dark, cramped, and stuffy, with one tiny window that looked out directly onto an apartment house wall four feet away. Did I care? Not at all. To me the archive was well-lit, airy, and mine—the epicenter of the work I dreamed to do.

No rhyme or reason dictated where recordings would be found around the building. I soon consolidated the old commercial 78s, rare field recordings, and cassette tapes of lectures and oral histories and began a rudimentary cataloging project. With the acquisition of modest recording and remastering equipment, I was ready to hang out the shingle.

Now an effort to locate more records had to be mounted. At the time, ethnic 78s were not considered worthy of collecting; in fact, it was common practice for 78 dealers to use so-called foreign discs for packing when shipping a more valuable jazz or classical record. Flea markets, junk stores, and garage sales became my haunts; I once even found a wonderful Naftule Brandwein 78 at the Salvation Army! Frequently I would contact old-age homes and ask to go through the recordings in their social room. In most cases they agreed.

As I had done at CETA I continued to give lectures on Yiddish music, playing examples from the 78s I had collected. These presentations would occasionally result in someone offering me their old records, or, when I was especially fortunate, the chance to meet old-time klezmer musicians like Cherniavsky's drummer Joe Helfenbein.

I began hearing from people who had found old records while cleaning out their grandparents' house. ("What do I do with them?") Or a synagogue that was redecorating its Youth Room and found 78s scattered about. ("It seems a shame to throw them out.") Sometimes people would drop in with a box of records under their arm. When I would come into my office and see a new box sitting on the desk, it was like Hanukkah and my birthday rolled into one. Opening the box and discovering an unknown record amid the more popular ones ("Oh, no. Not *another* copy of 'Joe and Paul'") never stopped thrilling me; to be able to put it on the turntable and hear the sizzle of surface noise yield up another missing piece in the puzzle of Jewish popular culture in America. A song, a tune, a comedy skit, it made no difference: I played them all.

Each new record would be cataloged (performer, title, record label, and number) and given a special number. The disc was cleaned and transferred onto open-reel tape (for archival storage) and simultaneously cassette (for public listening). The disk was then stored in a special acid-free sleeve, the archival tape stored in a separate location, and the cassettes made available in the sound archives.

The mission to document the history of Yiddish recorded music was made easier by the fortuitous timing of the Ethnic Music in America project being conducted by Richard Spottswood, whom I'd met at Dave Tarras's concert three years before. Tracking fifty years' worth of American-made "foreign" records was a reasonably ambitious task, and even if you were the ever resourceful and methodical Dick Spottswood, you'd still need help—which is where I came in.

We combed 78 catalogs, record company ledgers, stray discs, and period newspaper ads to try and find out what had been recorded when. As folk-like songs backed by a lone piano gave way to the nimble orchestrations that accompanied the winks and struts of Yiddish comedy, a chronology began to emerge.

The discography was also a wish list. In addition to records of great performers like Aaron Lebedeff, Molly Picon, and Dave Tarras were quirky, mysterious listings that filled me with unending curiosity—the 1923 "Fifi, Fifi Azoy Heys Ikh" (Fifi, Fifi That's My Name), by the improbably named Mathilda St. Clair, or "Yidele Farlir Nit di Hofnung" (Jews, Don't Lose Hope), by a black cantor named Thomas LaRue. Their listing in a catalog or advertisement meant these records were out there somewhere and might someday turn up. Every time a box arrived at the sound archives I would wonder: "Fifi . . .?" Being paid to collect, study, and share the music I loved was a sound archivist's dream.

Once in a while I would get a call from someone whose parent had made records, wondering if I had a copy. In spring 1983 the daughter of a singer named Jack Kimelman came by and told me that her long-dead father had made a record in his younger years. The discography showed that Kimelman had indeed made a record, back in 1917, and amazingly, a copy of "Der Gambler"/"A Kholem" had recently turned up. We listened to it together—the first time this woman had heard her father since he died in the 1960s.

The same happened with klezmer bandleader Abe Elenkrig when his son Edward came by the archives to hear his father's music again. It was an honor to meet the son of the man who headed the first modern klezmer orchestra to record in America. And I was deeply moved by the exquisite moment when the record started and these children of pioneering Jewish recording artists heard their parents again. Taping copies for them, I felt more like a tracer of missing persons, a reuniter of long-lost relatives, than an archivist in a stuffy, cluttered garret.

THE ORIGINAL KLEZMER JAZZ BAND AND KLEZMER PLUS

Nineteen eighty-three was a watershed year for klezmer. *The Wall Street Journal* ran a front-page article on the music, with Kapelye featured in one of the *Journal's* signature line drawings by R. Webber. The Klezmorim had their Carnegie Hall concert, and their third record, *Metropolis*, was nominated for a Grammy. And Kapelye helped usher out an era by playing at the final World's Fair in Knoxville, Tennessee.

That spring I gave a lecture called "Jews, Blues and Jazz," sponsored by the Martin Steinberg Center. Joining me were bandleader/composer David Amram, jazz historian Nat Hentoff, and the late jazz pianist Stan Free. I invited Hentoff because since the beginnings of the klezmer renewal, Hentoff has provided some of the only consistently literate writing on Jewish music found in the popular press.

In our lectures, Hentoff and I sought to counter the catchphrase "Jewish jazz," so widely used to describe klezmer music. Despite the fact that the contexts for the two musics are completely different, and that they follow few if any of the same rules and have none of the same ornaments, this misnomer continues to find favor among critics and musicians alike.

Margo Bloom, then program director at the nearby Jewish Museum, had heard the lecture and asked if I would be willing to give it at the museum with Andy Statman, this time with a live band recreating the 78s. I jumped at the chance to customize an all-star group, with Pete Sokolow doing the arrangements and playing keyboards, Robert Weiner on drums, trumpet player Ken Gross, and bassist Marty Confurius.

When tickets sold out nearly as soon as they went on sale, another show was quickly added. Its success led to an invitation to play in the popular "Jazz at the Public" series at The Joseph Papp Public Theater, where interest in klezmer had been primed by The Klezmorim's appearance the year before. Here, too, we played to a full house. The crowd at the Jewish Museum regularly responded to our offerings with sighs of recognition, whereas for the younger, hipper

downtown crowd—brought in by the Public's avant-garde image—
the music was new, fresh, and revelatory.

Pete and I wanted to continue working with the ensemble, but
Statman's priorities were with his own band. Pete took his arrangements, added several new titles, and formed his own group, The
Original Klezmer Jazz Band (OKJB), a homage to the band that popularized jazz, The Original Dixieland Jazz Band.

Jeff Oboler, my old boss from the Martin Steinberg Center, came to
see our Jewish Museum show and asked if I would organize what was
to be the first klezmer music festival in America. With the American
Jewish Congress footing the bill, we got started right away. On March
4, 1984, Symphony Space, on New York's Upper West Side, filled to
its nine-hundred-person capacity for a show featuring The Andy Statman Klezmer Orchestra, Kapelye, and Pete's OKJB. The contrast
between the three bands was strong: Statman's dynamic clarinet and
mandolin soloing; Kapelye's rich diversity of songs and tunes; and the
hot big band sounds of OKJB comprised a unique primer to the various streams of the music. "The bands performing here tonight have
taken on the responsibility of learning, playing and teaching this
music to a new generation who never heard it in its strong days, by
making its strong days today," the program notes read.

The growing interest in klezmer music concerts began turning up
requests for our band to play at weddings and bar mitzvahs. Quietly,
the music was returning to its original context like an endangered
species bred in safe surroundings and re-released into the wild.

Fielding call after call to book Kapelye for these parties, I grew
uncertain about how to proceed. I felt if I accepted service-industry
jobs rather than higher-paying and more prestigious concerts
there'd be a problem. Ken and Eric, who had plenty of experience
playing these kinds of jobs, would want to do them because it would
launch extra work; but Lauren and Michael, the folkies in the group,
would look askance at having to play "The Girl From Ipanema" or
"The Hucklebuck." So imagine my shock when the band split down
the middle with Lauren and Michael enthusiastically wanting to
learn that new repertoire and Ken and Eric saying they didn't join a
klezmer band to end up back at the hors d'oeuvre table.

Not knowing what to do with this work, I started recommending
that people call Pete Sokolow, as he was the consummate club date
musician and could put together a top-notch klezmer band, too.
After a couple of years of these referrals, Pete called to say he was

thankful for all the work but puzzled as to why I wasn't taking it myself. I explained the situation with the band and also that, while I was familiar with some standard club date repertoire, I was not really conversant in it.

Quickly, he offered to teach me the repertoire and the business if I would continue bringing in the work. He knew all the old-timers in New York who could play this stuff, and they were barely if ever working. Leave that to him. Considering that this was strictly a commercial band, Pete dubbed it the utilitarian Klezmer Plus: klezmer plus everything else. Sure enough, he'd soon located a clarinetist to play with us: Rudy Tepel, the man whose music nearly ruined my bar mitzvah! Rudy, his salad days way behind him, was thrilled to be working.

With Pete running the bandstand, the jobs were smooth, the repertoire shifting easily from classic American popular music to klezmer to Latin to Israeli. Pete's dance-band skill—deftly mixing elements of musicology and group psychology—never failed to get people on the dance floor.

There was, however, one job Pete couldn't go on, a concert at a local college in honor of Sholem Aleichem's birthday. Constructing the show, I went as leader with Rudy on clarinet. I made him a set list and explained what we were going to do. He listened and agreed. Once we got onstage, though, it was an entirely different matter. Rudy started playing whatever he wanted, and I had to follow helplessly along. Like a low-rent Brandwein he launched into such antics as disassembling his clarinet and putting the bell half in his ear while playing the other half. I tried to stop him.

"Why should I listen to you?" he hissed. "I played at your bar mitzvah!"

I was horrified. Though he offered an apology about "spicing up the show," I knew I could never work with him again.

Pete now gave some thought to finding a clarinet replacement. To his everlasting credit, he came up with Sid Beckerman, who had recently retired from the United States Post Office, where he'd worked since returning from the army after World War II.

A perfect gentleman and professional with a unique personal repertoire, Sid was a dream come true. His tone, so unlike any of his contemporaries', showed no sign of American popular music's influence; as Pete said, "He plays as if Benny Goodman never lived." Just as important was his repertoire, a singular mix of tunes made popular by Dave Tarras and half-forgotten melodies taught him by his father.

Sid Beckerman, clarinet, Pete Sokolow, keyboard, and the author in the halls of KlezKamp 1987. (*Clemens Kalischer*)

Sokolow, sensing his mission, tucked his portable keyboard under his arm, went to Beckerman's house, and said, "Play me every tune you know." He taped them, transcribed them, and gave them their first cataloging. Being to klezmer music what Köchel was to Mozart, Sokolow compiled a complete catalog of Beckerman's repertoire—a gold mine of wonderful tunes and documentation of klezmer music in New York's interwar years.

Sokolow began introducing me to the fraternity of veteran klezmer musicians in New York, the men whose lives and careers showed that the music was never dormant. Players like Ray Musiker, Max Epstein, Howie Leess, Danny Rubinstein, Marty Levitt, and Paul Pincus—for all intents and purposes, none of these old-timers was even vaguely aware that any kind of klezmer "revival" was going on. Their sheltered world of weddings and bar mitzvahs had yet to feel the impact of the klezmer scene. Thanks to Sokolow, two generations—those who grew up with this music and those who were reanimating it—would finally meet.

In 1983 I was taking clarinet lessons with Sokolow, and when it came time to buy an instrument, he suggested we go to the Lower East Side to Blimpy Blank's.

Where?

Blank's Bargain Music Store had been a staple on East Second Street and Avenue B for more than sixty years, run by klezmer fiddler and trumpet player Shimele Blank. The Blank family was one of the most respected klezmer families, and Shimele's two sons, Manny (accordion/piano) and Blimpy (trumpet), were considered better than most musicians. Blank's small store, conveniently located across the street from the offices of the Progressive Musicians' Benevolent Society, was a popular meeting place for members of the Jewish music world. Here, they would talk, book work, leave and retrieve messages, try out instruments, and play new music that had just come out. Like other music stores, Blank's would occasionally publish music (sometimes Blank's own compositions). Unlike Metro Music, his large neighbor to the west that catered to a general trade in records and sheet music, Blank's clientele was strictly professional Jewish musicians.

Upon his death, Blank's inheritance, the store and all its stock, went to his two sons, who instead of combining their modest windfall and joining together as partners became heated rivals. The heat was turned up by Manny, who opened a store right next door to Blimpy. Haranguing customers from their doorways, loudly cajoling them with offers of better bargains and predicting dire consequences if they patronized the other, the Blank brothers effectively chased away as much business as they generated. Eventually, with the downturn of business in the Jewish music world and their inability to keep up with other music stores (like that of one-time klezmer fiddler Sam Ash) they fell on even harder times, but never reconciled. Soon, it was only Blimpy in the business.

By the time Pete and I went down to Blank's store, the block had long been turned into a bite-size Bosnia with burned-out buildings and cars, garbage-strewn streets, and an air of desolation. Among all this chaos and decay was Blank's. Barely able to see the storefront beneath the spray-painted graffiti on its gates, we went in. Upon entering the stuffy, cramped store my eye immediately fell upon a framed picture near the counter. A child's drawing, it showed the outside of Blank's store, but instead of the grim post-apocalyptic scene that existed, it was a large, airy house, surrounded by trees, grass, and a smiley face sun—a sad and ironic image given the reality.

Then there was Blank himself. Old and tired, he still proffered a clear explanation of his well-worn nickname: Blimpy was enormously fat. The store's shelves were a farrago of broken fiddles, fraying violin bows, and empty instrument cases covered in Eisenhower-era dust. While Pete rummaged around trying to find enough clarinet parts to make a single workable instrument, he asked Blank how he

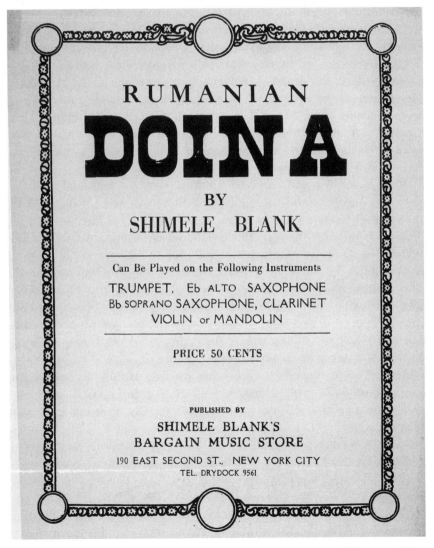

"Blank's Doina," published by Shimele Blank in 1929, was still being sold in 1983 by Blimpy Blank, who had dozens of copies left.

managed to stay in business. For some reason, Blank told us, the local junkies and other detritus took a liking to him and protected his store. It was true. Unaccustomed to seeing customers when we were there, Blank's neighbors would periodically poke their heads in and ask "Everything okay, Mr. Blimpy?" It was obvious someone was looking out for him; his was the only sign of retail life in this downtown lunar landscape.

Miraculously, Pete managed to put together a nice instrument for me, while for himself he found a little Albert-style E♭ clarinet just like the ones they used on early Abe Schwartz 78s. Counting out the embarrasingly modest sum Blimpy requested, we augmented the amount and left, two of the last customers at Blank's Bargain Music Store.

The opportunity to seat irreplaceable veteran musicians of Blank's generation on the Klezmer Plus bandstand was intensely rewarding, and it became clear that in doing so we had transcended being just a commercial band. That, combined with Sid and saxophonist Howie Leess's deep literacy and untouched repertoire, constructed an important musical bridge.

We applied for and received funding from the National Endowment for the Arts and the New York State Council on the Arts to record the greatest veteran players in New York, featuring Sid and Howie. Pete went through the Sid book, choosing repertoire with which Sid was most comfortable, and took to his second-nature task of arranging the music in its most authentic and professional sound. The resulting record, *Klezmer Plus!*, released on the Flying Fish label, was the first documentary recording of the classic Jewish music repertoire and style of the mid-twentieth century. Named a Library of Congress Outstanding Recording for 1991, it helped bring Sid out to a wider audience than ever before.

Though we'd played jobs from the Northwest Folklife Festival in Washington State to the National Folk Festival in Lowell, Massachusetts, one of our best and most unintentionally amusing gigs was when we were invited to take part in the prestigious Folk Masters concert series at Washington, D.C.'s Wolf Trap Farm on May 8, 1992.

Producer Nick Spitzer created a show that compared and contrasted jazz and klezmer. He chose two intergenerational groups, each headed by a young revivalist: New Orleans's Crescent City Serenaders, founded by clarinetist Michael White, and Klezmer Plus. The idea was to have each band play a set and then join forces for a jam at the end. Never a big fan of concert-ending "jam" sessions (they are invariably better performances than music), I nonetheless agreed.

In thinking about which tune both bands could jam on, the choice was clear: "Bay Mir Bist Du Schön." Assuming they knew it, I approached Michael White and the band and asked them what key they played it in. They looked blankly at each and told me that they'd never heard of it.

I couldn't believe that they did not know this famous piece, so I began to hum it. Their faces brightened.

"Oh, you mean 'The Bear Missed the Train'!" White said, upon which they started singing:

> The bear missed the train,
> Please let me explain.
> The bear missed the train,
> That's why he's walkin'.

"The Bear Missed the Train" indeed! And that's how we performed it—to a packed and happy house.

KAPELYE DOES GERMANY

Ever since The Delaware Water Gap toured Europe in 1979, I had tried unsuccessfully to locate an agent who would agree to bring Kapelye over. Some agents turned us down because they didn't know what klezmer music was; another quit after failing to convince festivals to book us because *they* didn't know what it was. It seemed nobody had the vision, taste, or courage to be the first to introduce this music. In several instances, when I'd located a willing agent and promoter, one of the then-common acts of random violence against Jews in France and Germany caused local promoters to get cold feet and cancel.

Finally, in 1984 I convinced a Belgian agent to book Kapelye in Europe. After a couple of months' silence I finally got a letter with the preliminary tour itinerary: England, France, Belgium, Holland, and—Germany. I stared at the letter awhile. Germany? Didn't that seem kind of ghoulish after all? What would I be going there for, some sort of traveling freak show—"Come See the Live Jews!"; "All Singing, All Dancing, All Living!"? It seemed too odd, a demented spin on the old criminology saw that the perp always returns to the scene of the crime. Yet off we went.

Thursday, July 26. From Belgium to Bremen is a six hour drive, so all through it we have a gallows humor attack about playing for the Germans: "Hi! We're the children of the ones you missed." When we arrive, I have an interview with a non-Jewish reporter from a local German paper, who asks some pretty lame questions. Whenever I mention the Holocaust she stops writing. I make it a game to see how often I can make her stop writing. Ken comes by a little later and she asks him if he'd ever been to Germany before. He says no, but his father had when he helped defeat it in the Second World War. That makes her stop writing too . . .

I go with Michael to a violin shop to get a bow fixed. On the way over I see my first gosh-darned real swastika in context. (I'm almost warmed by the sight of it—quite sentimental in a way.) After all, when I see one in the States I think, "What do these shmucks know about Hitler?" But here . . . they *know*!

The Schauberg is a very nice functioning movie house. When we get there our agent, Volker Steppard, who looks like a centerfold in Teutonic Monthly, pulls me over as we're going on to tell me sotto voce that he's sure he has some Jewish blood in his family and that the war was hard on everyone, including those unfortunate German soldiers who had to be away from home over Christmas! I agree with him, smiling wanly and thinking if I don't he may turn violent.

We have decided to do intros mostly in Yiddish with limited English because . . . because we're in Germany. We want our audiences to hear the language that their parents, grandparents, grandparents' neighbors, and friends nearly destroyed. During one of my intros, Ken eases up behind me, quietly playing "Springtime for Hitler," from the movie *The Producers*. It takes all the self-control I can muster not to burst out laughing. (Great idea: We will forgive any German who buys our record. Call it the Vinyl Solution. Amazing gaffe: During my intro, instead of saying *nokh di khasene* [after the wedding], I inadvertantly say *nokh di milkhume* [after the war]. We can barely keep from cracking up.)

At the conclusion of the tour we hit Berlin. The desire to play Berlin (and the Euro tour per se) overrode all other considerations (money, safety, etc.). I yearned to go, to be the first to flip out the Europeans with what they'd had in their midst and made disappear. England, France, Belgium, Switzerland, even Bremen did not have the same kind of macabre attraction for me as Berlin.

The car talk was very subdued, not at all like the trip to Bremen with its Nazi jokes and dark Holocaust humor. Driving into Berlin in the dead of night past the guards, the watchtowers, the Wall, and machine guns, we finally stumbled onto the place we're to play: the Cafe Einstein, on the Kurfürstenstrasse, the main drag. In a city whose rule seems to be drab postwar construction, the little mansion at number fifty-eight is a quiet exception. How this building survived the bombings is just dumb luck. Large windows, marble staircases, luxuriously high ceilings, and betuxed waiters in long white aprons made the place seem like another world (which it was, in a way).

> By 5 P.M. there is a line for the 7:00 show. I am heart-
> ened. There is a big media blitz (pardon the expression!)
> over our appearance here: TV, radio, newspapers, etc.
> Big house. But I've got a knot in my stomach. There's
> just something there: Berlin. Yiddish. Playing the
> "Happy Jews." This damned building. Should we make
> them squirm? Naw. Play hot, unself-consciously. Speak
> in Yiddish, translate into English. Let them hear the
> other elements of the East Euro world this came from.
> "Zog Nit Keynmol" (the Jewish partisans' hymn Never
> Say) will only mean something if they've learned to deal
> with their own history . . . Here we were, me in particu-
> lar, a son of "one of the ones who got away," standing in
> Berlin and flaunting *Yiddishkayt*. Who'dathunk?

Our shows were a success. We filled the club night after night with no fewer than three encores following our final set. People hadn't seen anything like it. Neither had we. This crowd was completely different than anything we'd ever played for. Mostly young, very hip. (The hippest wore the blackest clothing.) It became obvious that for the most part when there were young people in the house they'd be Gentile and when they were old, Jews. It was also strange to find we could do our show in Yiddish and it would be understood better here than back home. Even my quirky jokes in English were picked up by many in the crowd.

Some folks who came out had been introduced to "klezmer" through the German production of Israeli playwright Joshua Sobol's *Ghetto*, which had recently closed. This Holocaust revisionist musical about the Vilna ghetto—it should have been called "Hitler on the Roof"—featured clarinetist Giora Feidman as a ghetto musician, beginning his long close association in the German klezmer world.

The press was all over us in a variation of the freak show I had feared. One journalist, Stephan Wachwitz, kept peppering me with loaded questions: "How could you play here in the one-time international center of anti-Semitism?" I told him a story about a night a bunch of Jewish friends were over at my house and someone recommended going out for dinner. "Let's go to an ethnic restaurant whose population has never persecuted the Jews," I suggested. We ate in. The point? If you limit yourself to going to places where Jewish blood hasn't been spilled, you're going to spend a lot of time at home.

At the end of the run, we finally got the lowdown on the Cafe Einstein while having dinner with the chef. Built in the late nineteenth century by a successful Jewish manufacturer, in the 1920s the building passed into the hands of a second-tier German silent screen actress. By the thirties it had become the provisional headquarters of the Gestapo. "You see that there?" he asked, pointing out back to a grotesque cement block near a gazebo. "That's the bunker. Still intact." The *canard à la cérise* the chef made for us suddenly tasted like ashes in my mouth.

A few weeks after we got back to New York Wachwitz sent me a copy of his piece in the *Stuttgarter Zeitung* titled "The Klezmer's Revenge." Among other eye-catching segments, my favorite line was, "The grandchildren of the former subhumans entertained the grandchildren of the former mass murderers." Pithy though it was, Kapelye was never able to figure out a way to use that bit of press.

KLEZKAMP: THE YIDDISH FOLK ARTS PROGRAM

It was endlessly reassuring to know that whenever a Kapelye tour ended, my little job waited for me back at YIVO. The sound archives was basically a mom-and-pop operation; I had several part-time helpers including Dan Peck, from 1982 to 1984, and my longtime assistant Jenny Romaine, who began in 1987 and has headed the archives since my departure in 1994.

When I first started out there the musty timelessness that was the old YIVO, the shuffling and whispering you'd expect to hear in a reverential locale, still lingered. There were few young people. Though hobbled by a notoriously byzantine infrastructure and decades-old factional disputes, in the mid-1970s YIVO, through its Max Weinreich

Center, attracted the brightest and best grad students in the academic world. As if on cue, young people began turning up—first, students who used its unparalleled library and archives for school projects or papers, researchers doing work on books or documentaries, and by the 1980s artists and musicians. Some hung around long enough and became staff, like me.

Not since YIVO's founding days back in Vilna in the 1920s, with its attendant army of earnest and enthusiastic *zamlers* (collectors), had the institute housed such a passionate and vibrant environment. The fervent desire to escort or if necessary cajole Yiddish into the next century was at some level part of all our agendas—whether through film, literature, music, books, or museum exhibits.

The Max and Frieda Weinstein Archives' 78 RPM siren call attracted a steady stream of visitors, making the fifth floor a hub of activity in the building. While the administrative offices, library, and paper archives were located on the bottom two floors, the residents of our story quietly established a "Fifth Floor Autonomous Region." Across the hall from me was the film and photo archives, run by Josh Waletzky and Judith Helfand and, later, Roberta Newman. Down the hall over the years were historians including Jeff Shandler and Jenna Weisman-Joselit, and linguist David Goldberg. My favorite neighbors were the older YIVO staff, the wonderful actor and translator David Rogow and the late Polish historian Lucjan Dobroszycki. Projects were planned and perfected through the comings and goings between our offices, the institutional equivalent of the air shaft across which neighbors traded gossip and news in Gertrude Berg's radio program *The Goldbergs*.

Now that the Folkways klezmer anthology was out, the sound archives began attracting more donations, and its scope fast outgrew its space. When people would come to the sound archives for the first time they would look around the room and at me and say: "It's smaller than I imagined, and you're younger."

During the summer months I was teaching banjo at a camp in Ashokan, New York, run by fiddler Jay Unger, who went on to score Ken Burns's PBS documentary "The Civil War." Ungar's "Root Camp" taught traditional Appalachian music, dance, and song in a beautiful woodland setting. The music and people were great and provided a wonderful environment to learn and play this music. I saw again that the vast majority of teachers and students were Jewish, and though I surreptitiously tried to sneak in some klezmer music (I arranged "Freylekh fun der Khupe" for five-string banjo), mixing the music was not what I was after. Amid this gaggle of Jews playing old American music, I couldn't help recalling Tommy Jarrell asking whether we had any music of our own.

I was now pretty sure I wanted to start up a Yiddish music camp, but wanted to see how others were run. In 1983 the East European Folklife Center was sponsoring a Balkan music and dance camp at Ashokan, and I went as a student. Their camp was similar to Ungar's Fiddle and Dance camp in that the teachers for the most part studied the culture but were not necessarily of it—including Kapelye's Lauren Brody and Michael Alpert. And again, a majority of students and teachers were Jews, and there was no East European Jewish music. This puzzled me. I never really expected it in the old-time country music scene because folks there barely knew anything about any European music traditions. But the East European scene knew about the old-world Yiddish music traditions, yet did not present them alongside the other East European musics. Although there had been some talk among some of the staff at Balkan Camp on this subject, no one was doing anything. That nailed it for me; it was time to create an event that tied Yiddish tradition and culture to its music: klezmer.

What was missing in traditional music camps was a sense of transmission within a community context. They were almost all exclusively peer-driven, a vast departure from how music and culture traditionally gets passed on. I also sought a humanizing factor that would put a face on the folk music as opposed to treating the tunes as a mere commodity, another tune to play at some jam session. And much as I liked working with my peers, I wanted younger players to get the same experience I had had: learning from senior musicians, so they would get an honest take on what this music was about. This was music played by living, breathing people.

The other point of departure was to place the Yiddish music and dance within a larger context. We provided classes in Yiddish language, crafts, and the multitudinous aspects of the rich, diverse Yiddish culture. The program was called the Yiddish Folk Arts Institute, but with my weakness for nicknames (I would refer to the YIVO as "the 'Vo") my shorthand for the program was "KlezKamp," the name by which most people have come to know it.

The original idea of the Folk Arts Institute was to offer musicians, singers, and Yiddishists a place to learn, exchange, and create Yiddish music in a challenging intergenerational environment. It also came to serve as payoff for students who had just completed YIVO and Columbia University's rigorous six-week intensive summer Yiddish language program. For one week, these students would be able to use the language they learned with some of the leading lights of Yiddish music and folk art culture—and have a great time.

The camp was a way of making the sound archives—and YIVO itself—more activist. Instead of waiting for people to discover the institute and utilize its vast resources, KlezKamp would go out and find them, creating an easily accessible dynamic bridge to the institute. Underlying these more altruistic reasons for creating KlezKamp was my own selfish desire to assemble some of the world's greatest klezmorim and play wonderful music with them.

I presented the idea to Adrienne Cooper, then the assistant director of YIVO, and she immediately understood the import of the program and ran interference for it around the suspicious board. (Years later, after KlezKamp was an unqualified success, I asked a YIVO board member whether the event would have been allowed to happen had I gone through the usual channels. Her answer was a firm no.) By February 1984 Cooper and I were meeting with Becky Miller, hired to coordinate KlezKamp. We had already lined up Yiddish music veterans Ruth Rubin, Max Epstein, Leon Schwartz, Bronya Sakina, and younger players like Michael Alpert, Lauren Brody, Hankus Netsky, and dance ethnographer LeeEllen Friedland to serve as its staff.

After some looking around I had heard that a well-known summer Yiddish socialist camp in Dutchess County had fallen on hard times and had recently been sold to a New Age group. I went up to see the new owners and was surprised by how many of the original Yiddish accoutrements they'd preserved. "It's great karma," they said, that we were bringing a Yiddish camp back to this place. Being as big a fan of great karma as the next guy, I arranged for the first Yiddish Folk Arts Institute to take place August 4–10, 1984, at the newly opened Omega Institute in Rhinebeck, New York. With the help of mailing lists from YIVO and the East European Folklife Center, we sent out several thousand brochures and hoped for the best.

But as the Yiddish Folk Arts Institute started drawing more and more people, the New Age folks at the camp, in a decidedly Old Age kind of way, began gouging us for more and more cash. By the end of June it was clear that if this kept up, the bigger our success, the less money we'd make. I reluctantly canceled the program.

Disappointed but not stymied—the event had to happen—I shifted my focus. What was another large time slot that could accommodate a multi-day event like this? It occurred to me that the most readily available time slot in the Jewish world had yet to be tapped. Why not run the event over Christmas? No period in the calendar year alienates and marginalizes Jews as much as the week surrounding December 25.

In late August, Becky Miller and I made a grand inspection tour of hotels in the Catskills. We visited all the large resorts: the Concord, the Raleigh, the Nevelle. None had what we wanted: a warm, homey place reminiscent of the old-time hospitality the region had made famous. The final hotel on our list was the runt of the litter: the quirky little Paramount in Parksville. At its peak in the 1920s, the town of Parksville boasted more than fifty hotels; now all that was left was the Paramount. The last of the family-owned hotels, the place had somehow managed to avoid changing since the mid-1950s. It was like a time capsule with its round center lobby couch and walls covered in green carpeting reminiscent of Spanish moss, the thick red-and-amber water glasses on every dining room table, and the heavy kosher comfort food pouring from the kitchen. It reminded me of the hotels my parents used to shlep me to for Passover.

Built and expanded on over the years, the hotel is a crazy quilt of construction. The jumble of impetuous additions has resulted in some

Margot Leverett playing for dancing at KlezKamp 1987. (*Albert J. Winn*)

remarkably odd room numbering. For example, room 64 is down the hall from room 211, while 25 and 26 are at opposite ends of the hotel. The surest method of finding your way back to your room is to memorize the carpet pattern in your section of the hotel: like fingerprints, each is unique and never repeated. Even owner Fred Gasthalter's name was amusingly ideal: in Yiddish, *gasthalter* means "hotelier." Straight out of central casting right down to his ubiquitous cigar, Freddy, short and brusque, runs the Paramount like the Borscht Belt fiefdom it is, the last major employer in the area.

When Becky and I approached them with the idea of bringing in a Christmas trade they were elated. The place was seriously underutilized at that time of year, hosting only a tiny group of folk dancers and a B'nai B'rith Youth Organization convention of raging-hormone teenagers. The employees, usually tapped for funds to buy Christmas gifts, were thankful for this eleventh-hour burst of income.

Picking up where we had left off with the ill-fated summer KlezKamp, we sent out a new mailing, hoping to reattract some of the seventy people who had replied to our earlier announcement. To our amazement we exceeded the number, corralling some ninety people from around the country, most of them musicians. With the thirty staff members we hired, the first KlezKamp community comprised a nice, cozy 120 people. On December 21, 1985, the day before the event was to open, staff convened at the hotel, everyone pitching in. We ran roughshod through the Paramount, renaming rooms in Yiddish and posting signs drawn in the old-time "finger-pointing" style throughout the serpentine hallways.

The first KlezKamp was rough and clunky, but tremendously *heymish* and fun. The participants loved it; the staff loved it. YIVO, however, was less convinced of its worth. A few board members came up to see Kamp in action, like linguist Mikhl Herzog, who didn't want it to change a bit and wound up teaching a course for us four years later.

In the months after KlezKamp I put out a small short-lived KlezKamp newsletter and planned the second KlezKamp, with the help of Lynn Dion, a recent arrival at YIVO. A one-time ethnomusicology student at Brown University, Dion had been drawn to YIVO by her strong interest in Yiddish. Over the next few years, Dion and I would work on a variety of projects, she helping me edit and rework various articles, co-editing a special 1988 music issue of Aaron Lansky's *The Book Peddler*, and contributing essays to the *Klezmer Plus*

Folio (Tara Publications, 1990), a companion tune book to the Flying Fish recording. Her 1986 article on the klezmer "revival" for the *Jewish Folklore and Ethnology Newsletter* was in its day the single best-written article on the subject.

Meanwhile, since Becky Miller got kicked upstairs to work for Adrienne Cooper, my old Martin Steinberg cohort Chava Miller was brought in to help run KlezKamp. The following KlezKamp was bigger still, attracting almost 150 registrants, many of them returning participants and many bringing family members.

The best break for the future of KlezKamp happened in 1987, when Cooper hired Lorin Sklamberg. Already an accomplished singer and devotee of Yiddish music back in Los Angeles, Sklamberg was also a founding member of New York's newest klezmer group, The Klezmatics. Happily, as soon as he got settled in, Sklamberg started working with me on mounting KlezKamp 3. It didn't take us long to find that our work styles and temperaments were complementary.

By this time there had been a subtle but important shift in the event's constituency. For the first few years, the age of the registrants—mostly musicians—had mirrored the average age of the younger staff members. Though musicians still made up the bulk of staff and participants, their overall percentage was shrinking. We were now starting to attract more sixty- to eighty-year-olds and upward, many born in Europe.

There were all sorts of these older, mostly retired KlezKampers. Some had grown up within reach of this old culture and now basked in the delight of reclaiming it; others, either denied it by assimilated parents or having spurned it themselves, were experiencing Yiddish culture for the first time. And a precious few—like my own mother and father and Barbara Kirshenblatt-Gimblett's parents, Mayer and Dora Kirshenblatt—were those rare *folksmentshn*, people born and raised in Eastern Europe who retained crystal-clear access to that lost world and could transmit it to a new generation.

So KlezKamp was a win-win. For this older generation it offered not only a cultural coda but also the assurance that their stories, songs, accrued wisdom, and experience would be carried forward. For the younger participants, many of whom had never before even met a person with an Eastern European Jewish accent, let alone studied with one, it was their chance to experience people from the world that had produced the music they loved, to touch and be touched by someone who had lived in that vanished place, to become a part of that continuity.

Because the older participants were largely nonmusical, we began offering more and more general courses to our roster: more history, folklore, and "intro" courses. (My "Klezmology 101" class became a big draw for uninitiates and seasoned musicians alike.)

In another unanticipated shift in Kamp demographics, the positive word-of-mouth message that had helped solidify our base of support spread strongly throughout the long-disenfranchised Jewish gay and lesbian community, which by 1989 had come to represent a definable and defining portion of Kamp registrants and staff. Contemporary Jewish homosexuals had found themselves polarized between two worlds: in left-of-center groups they felt marginalized by cohorts who used anti-Zionism as a politically correct way to mask anti-Semitism; Jewish organizations and groups, meanwhile, often eschewed gays and lesbians because of their sexual preferences. KlezKamp, with its focus on Yiddish culture, gained the reputation of being gay- and lesbian-friendly, helped in no small part by Sklamberg's openly gay identity. But the active presence of *freylekhe*—as the community came to dub itself—at KlezKamp led several feature writers to emphasize that seeming incongruity at the cost of the true diversity of the event.

Non-nationals made up a third surprise element in our constituency. The first KlezKamp had only three people from outside the United States, and they were Canadians. The list of attendees from abroad quintupled the very next year, and by 1987, thanks to the growing number of European klezmer concerts, lovers of Yiddish culture from Germany, Switzerland, and England had become KlezKamp regulars. The continued growth of a European constituency—mostly German and the majority non-Jews—has been most telling. That the KlezKamp community is some fifteen percent non-Jewish is testament to the program's appeal. Eventually it was not unusual to have participants from Israel, South America, even Asia.

YIVO's sponsorship of KlezKamp came in the form of paying for my and Lorin Sklamberg's time, printing and mailing brochures, and not a lot more. The rest of the cash had to be culled from registration, which forced a dilemma. We knew that in order to attract people in the arts—who were usually young and broke—we'd have to keep the cost of Kamp low, but that if we did, the event would never pay for itself and wouldn't survive. If we charged a bigger fee we'd have a good fiscal buffer by drawing mostly retired and well-to-do older folks, but at the cost of young families or people in the arts. So we needed to find an equitable way of attracting all of these vital constituencies.

I sought the support of the folk arts divisions of the New York State Council on the Arts and the National Endowment for the Arts (NEA). Both agencies had supported YIVO projects in the past, in keeping with the limits of their modest operating budgets. To become eligible for funding we agreed to have auditors from the NEA and NYSCA come down and see what we were about. The auditor for the NEA, a devotee of East European culture then in the eighth month of her first pregnancy, arrived at Kamp just as an impromptu swaddling workshop was being conducted by my mother and the Russian émigré Bronya Sakina. That fortuitous bit of active folklore set the tone for our long-running relationship with the NEA, an undersung hero in the fostering and encouragement of America's folk communities.

By the fourth KlezKamp, in 1988, registration for the folklore class alone equaled the first Kamp's entire registration. And by 1989 the waiting list to get in to the event surpassed that number. But we had reached an impasse: with 350 attendees, KlezKamp had outgrown the hotel. We didn't want to move—the hotel staff had never

Sarah Gordon (*left*) and an unidentifed fiddling partner at KlezKamp 1988. (*Albert J. Winn*)

been anything less than helpful and supportive, and the Paramount's administration bent every which way to accommodate our growing needs, even letting us commandeer their kitchen to run classes on Jewish cuisine. The fact was that we filled the hotel, and they didn't want to lose us. So they started building again. And again. And again. We, meanwhile, found ourselves expanding in new ways.

Since the beginning of KlezKamp we had always made a schedule allowance for a children's program, at first a catch-as-catch-can affair, depending on the number and ages of kids who showed up and the resources we had at our disposal. But as more and more of our peers became parents, it became clear we needed to craft a multi-age-appropriate program for children. There were some models available; New York City's "Pripetshik" after-school program was one, but because it dealt with a regular group of children over the course of a school year and we met for just five days, it did not entirely serve. The more we tried to meet the needs of this community, the more kids showed up. By the third year, a full-time kid's staff was in place.

On the precipice of the 1990s, we looked back at our five years of KlezKamp to see a tremendous diversity of people totaling some 1,500 participants. "Community" no longer meant the physical limitations of region or neighborhood, but bespoke a shared literacy and cultural consciousness. During each event our near perfect mélange of kids and grandparents, musicians and artists, looked, acted, and reacted like a "real" community, coexisting in a way that evidenced a new method of jump-starting a near-moribund culture. So KlezKamp continued to find new participation, not just from the powerful word of mouth it had generated, but from its inclusion in two documentaries made about the klezmer scene.

THE KLEZMER DOCUMENTARIES: A JUMPIN' NIGHT IN THE GARDEN OF EDEN AND FIDDLERS ON THE HOOF

When the idea for KlezKamp was forming in 1984, a phone call came to my office at YIVO from a young Boston-area filmmaker named Michal (rhymes with "nickel") Goldman, who was making a documentary about klezmer music. Goldman had heard The Klezmer Conservatory Band play at her sister's wedding; transfixed by the music, she decided to do a documentary featuring them. The project, originally titled *My Uncle Sam*, in honor of Hankus Netsky's trumpet-playing relative, was her first film. Her call was to ask me to be the consultant on the project.

The film's final title, *A Jumpin' Night in the Garden of Eden*, was an improvement over its predecessor, although its relevance is not addressed in the narrative: Hankus Netsky is shown transcribing and performing the tune recorded in 1923 by Kandel's band as "A Freylekhn Nakht in Gan Eydn," but no mention is made of the fact that Netsky's uncle played on the original recording.

Much of the film had already been shot by the time I began work on it. Fortunately for Kapelye, sequences featuring us were filmed by the veteran documentary cameraman Boyd Estes. Estes's fine eye also captured KlezKamp; to amplify Goldman's desire to show klezmer music in its social context, I encouraged her to come film the event's premiere as an insider. These scenes of dance classes, music instruction, and a panel discussion on the image of the klezmer, featuring my mother and father and the parents of folklorist Barbara Kirshenblatt-Gimblett, are among the most compelling in the film.

Another film that came to KlezKamp was the BBC documentary *Fiddlers on the Hoof* (1989). As a contributor to a British world music series called "Rhythms of the World," director Simon Broughton came to the subject on assignment, bringing no knowledge of Yiddish music or its culture to the project, just his experience from a previous segment on Romanian music. After a visit to YIVO he retained me as a consultant on the program.

Unlike *A Jumpin' Night*, which focuses on just two klezmer bands, *Fiddlers* was an across-the-board who's who of the contemporary klezmer scene. Segments focus on Kapelye, The Klezmatics, Giora Feidman, and others in addition to the experience of KlezKamp, which opens the piece.

Fiddlers holds together more than *A Jumpin' Night* due to its consistently agile photography and strong internal structure. It gives first-time viewers of the scene highlights of the musicians out there and what they're doing. Yet for all that, it feels slightly rudderless. Broughton lets his talking heads make their points much like a debating society in evenly divided segments: accurate, but a bit clinical. Goldman, on the other hand, never lets you forget what it is about this music she likes and who she likes to hear play it. Her camera is more activist and partisan, and if she's less a craftsman than Broughton, her visceral approach better humanizes the personalities in her film.

SOUTH OF THE BORDER: KAPELYE IN MEXICO

In October 1988 Kapelye was invited to bring our music to Mexico to play for a bar mitzvah there. A rare-gems merchant from Mexico City had seen the band play at our annual Museum Mile concert and decided to import us to play for his son's *simkhe*. The Jewish community in Mexico were descendants of East European Jews whose trek to America while fleeing the Nazis was stopped south of the border. During their interminable wait to enter the United States they unintentionally became Mexicans themselves, deciding to stay.

Surrounded as they were by a dominant and largely antagonistic Catholic majority, these successful Jews took to housing themselves in luxury homes surrounded by imposing security walls, a strange inverted reprise of the walled ghettos imposed on their ancestors in medieval Europe.

Not knowing what to expect there, we found the bar mitzvahs to be more heartfelt yet as commercial as those in New York. This is a very tight-knit Jewish community, not hard to understand considering how "other" their neighbors make them feel. For bar mitzvahs, kids write, rehearse, and stage a kind of Jewish panorama to be presented during the party—a touching, homey offering, something that their north-of-the-border Jewish peers would probably be mortified to appear in.

Our Kapelye appearance was meant not only to put a stamp of "Jewishness" on the event, but also to demonstrate, as up north, the buying power of the bar mitzvah's family. We were a trophy, as most people (including our hosts) would rather boogie to the loud local rock 'n' roll band with whom we shared the bandstand. Over the next few years it became a "thing" among the nouveau riche Mexican Jewish families to bring Kapelye in to play a set for the guests as they ate.

When I had told Zeyde that the band was booked in Mexico City, he immediately became enthused and urged me to visit the mansion-cum-fortress Leon Trotsky had erected upon being exiled to Mexico as the Soviet ambassador. Although Zeyde had never been to Mexico, because he was a devoted follower of Trotsky he knew exactly where the house was: "*'s' nivint tsi Frida Kahlo's voyning* [It's near Freida Kahlo's home]." Zeyde then lovingly described the time in 1919 when he saw Trotsky's train pull into the Rovne railyard to raise troops to fight the Polish nationalists. Recalling the scene with his typical eye for detail, Zeyde repeated verbatim Trotsky's rallying speech on the flatbed railroad car and imitated his nervous, slightly hunched over to-and-fro walk with hands clasped behind his back. In the time leading up to the trip, Zeyde and I spoke of the trip and of the obligatory report I was to give upon my return.

But less than a month before my departure, Zeyde suffered a stroke and quickly died. He was ninety-five. Broken up, I resolved to visit the Trotsky house the first free moment I had. The former embassy was eerily forlorn, with its high walls, gun turrets, and abandoned, overgrown gardens. Though there were two caretakers looking after the place, it was left exactly as it was the day Stalin had Trotsky murdered in 1940.

Entering the house, the first thing I saw was a framed photo of a man standing on a flatbed freight car, hands clasped behind his back, addressing a crowd of thousands. The caption, typewritten in five languages, read: *"Leon Trotsky in Volhyn province, assembling troops to fight the counter-revolutionaries, 1919."* Seeing this picture and thinking of my *zeyde*, I burst into tears.

In Mexico City Kapelye enjoyed one of the rare thrills known to recording artists: discovering a bootleg version of one of our albums. While walking down a backstreet, we passed a store with recordings in the window and my eye was caught by a cassette with a cover faded by prolonged exposure to sunlight. On closer examination, however, the "faded" cover turned out to be a bad photocopy of the cover of one of our albums! Amazed that anyone would go to the trouble of pirating our record (especially in the back alleys of Mexico City), we did what any outraged artist would do whose work had been stolen from them: we went in and bought all the copies.

When it came to recording, Kapelye was never prolific. Groups like The Klezmorim and KCB could much more easily turn around a year after their previous record and produce a new one. Kapelye had trouble doing that. Bringing material into the band was a lengthy process. For tunes, I would make a tape of klezmer 78s I particularly liked, and pass it on to Maltz to listen to and transcribe.

Songs were the responsibility of the singers, Alpert and myself: you want to sing, you bring in the piece. Our tastes were becoming clearly defined; Michael hove to the flashy theater material in the style of Lebedeff and the occasional traditional song. I preferred quirky novelty pieces like the title song from our 1985 Shanachie record, *Levine and His Flying Machine*, and Abe Schwartz's post-Russian revolutionary send-up *Lenin un Trotsky*. For our 1987 album, *Chicken*, we came up with a novel performance idea. We always talked about ways of spanning the gap between the original function of klezmer music and the needs of a contemporary performance milieu. We decided to create a suite of traditional wedding tunes interlaced with newly crafted *badkhones* sung in alternating Yiddish (Alpert) and English (me). Basing our performance on the many mock-*badkhones* 78s made during the 1920s, we wove the contemporary and fast-paced medley "Der Badkhn," which gave most of our audience members their first taste of the indelible mix of klezmer music and singing.

After the successful release of *Chicken*, the band sank into an unexpected ennui. Though we were working regularly—in 1988 we toured Europe and played numerous domestic concerts (including the Democratic National Convention in Atlanta)—we were slowly drifting.

Despite Kapelye jobs, our schedule was breaking down, with rehearsals happening less and less frequently, usually only in preparation for a gig. The band began relying on material we'd already played many times, encouraging uncharacteristic lethargy. We also suffered from the periodic absences and eventual departure of accordionist Lauren Brody. Brody, who moved to California in 1988, was the first longtime member of the band to leave—Waletzky had moved on back in 1984 to pursue filmmaking full time—so the chair was filled by players including Hankus Netsky, Alan Bern, Zalmen Mlotek, and Lorin Sklamberg.

This downturn in Kapelye was edging me more toward other projects, including Klezmer Plus, lectures, my job at YIVO, and a growing desire to finish my work with Dave Tarras. In 1984 Tarras had received the National Heritage Folklife Award from the Smithsonian Institution, public acknowledgment of his status as a master folk musician. But his joy in winning it was undermined when, prior to performing onstage at the award ceremony in Washington, D.C.'s Ford's Theater, Tarras suffered a massive heart attack. If not for the quick thinking and CPR training of Andy Statman's guitarist, Bob Jones, Dave Tarras would likely have died that night.

In the "borrowed time" period that ensued, Tarras and I began serious work on a retrospective of his music. Though I had been visiting with him since 1979, he had always dominated our meetings, putting off looking at old music in favor of repeating choice, well-polished anecdotes. He felt that there was time and that we didn't need to worry about getting to everything right away—an attitude that changed after the terrifying occurrence in Washington.

Tarras was now much more willing to sit and listen to his old records and identify players and composers, or to look at photos and old sheet music. But the effort to document the great richness of his career was difficult. Sometimes Tarras remembered names but not places, sometimes just the opposite, and he could rarely recall exact dates. Tarras's vast popularity as an accompanist and soloist made it impossible for him to remember which record he made with whom. (It will probably never be known how many titles Tarras actually played on, both as a soloist and an ensemble player, though five hundred is a generally accepted conservative estimate.)

Still, Tarras shared his recollections of the myriad recording sessions in which he had taken part, his memory jogged by playing transfers of 78s he hadn't heard in fifty years. The recorded retrospective that emerged from these sessions, *Dave Tarras: Yiddish-American Klezmer Music*, was completed nearly a decade later and named an outstanding recording by the Library of Congress.

By the early 1980s Tarras's home, in the Coney Island section of Brooklyn, had become a klezmer mecca. It was not unusual for TV or documentary film crews to set up shop in his living room and record this last of the old-world klezmorim. Klezmer was in, and Tarras was its godfather. He made wonderful copy.

A steady stream of klezmer aficionados came to him bearing recordings, publicity kits, and videos of their groups, looking for insights from this man they had known through 78s or hard-to-find LPs. His influence, so powerful among an earlier generation, was once again transforming young musicians who this time arrived at klezmer via rock, jazz, country, or classical music. For them, Tarras was a 78 come to life; he was continuity. To be in his presence was to be part of the historic European transmission of the tradition, a chain growing more and more fragile.

Tarras was not a little amused by the whole klezmer upheaval. His most critical invective was reserved for those who anointed themselves "kings" of klezmer. For despite his bitter rivalry with one-time Jewish music "king" Naftule Brandwein, Tarras felt that none of the new royalty could carry Naftule's clarinet case (let alone his own).

Prior to Kapelye's departure for Mexico in 1988, I told Tarras about the death of my grandfather. He was visibly upset. While on the trip, and with Tarras in mind, it occurred to me that a Lifetime Achievement Award should be presented at KlezKamp to senior members of the Jewish community who had made outstanding contributions to the state of Yiddish culture. Tarras, deeply touched when I told him he was to be its first recipient, planned to come to KlezKamp to receive his award, but his ever-weakening condition kept him from making the trip. Dave Tarras died February 14, 1989.

In the months that followed, many events marked Tarras's passing. *The New Grove Dictionary of American Music* contacted me to write a biography of him for its inaugural edition. At the instigation of folklorist Kathy Condon, a series of concerts honoring Tarras was scheduled in Brooklyn with Klezmer Plus, featuring clarinetist Sid Beckerman, Pete Sokolow, drummer David Licht, and myself, on tenor banjo. Sokolow, a regular visitor to Irving Graetz, who was recuperating from a hip replacement, asked him to do a guest spot on drums as the concluding highlight of the concert; Graetz agreed.

The press was enormous for the first memorial concert honoring Tarras, and additional shows were added. These shows were the capping achievement of Graetz's life and career. On August 3, just a few weeks after another successful performance, Irving Graetz died—but not before finally getting to play Tarras's music without being "toned down."

The nineties were inaugurated with the death of my father Zindel Sapoznik in January followed by the loss of several of klezmer music's mightiest European giants: Tarras, Graetz, Joseph Cherniavsky's drummer Joe Helfenbein, my teacher Leon Schwartz, and drummer Ben Bazyler. Not since the passing in 1963 of Abe Ellstein, Sam Musiker, Abe Schwartz, and Naftule Brandwein had the klezmer world been so diminished.

～ 8 ～

The Emperor's New Klez:
The Future for a Music with a Past

WITH THE PASSING OF the European players for whom the meaning of "klezmer" was unamibiguous, a new generation of Jewish musicians, in inventing themselves, have redefined the term and the music. When klezmer music came to the fore in the late 1970s, some newspapers and magazines picked up on this "new" phenomenon and gave it wide coverage. Before too long, though, Jews playing Jewish music slipped into the domain of "Dog Bites Man." But now, with the music being played across North America, Europe—with Germany as the epicenter—and even as far as Japan, klezmer is once again big news indeed.

Amid this great popularization of the music, the meaning of the word "klezmer" itself is up for grabs. One of the most vexing avenues of discourse in the current klezmer universe centers not only on how the music is to be played, but on what the basic terms "klezmer" and "revival" mean. Webster's Ninth Collegiate Dictionary, published in 1980, did not list the word "klezmer." By 1996, however, there it is in Webster's Tenth, tucked neatly between "kleptomaniac" and "klieg light."

Webster's definition of "klezmer," "a Jewish instrumentalist esp. of Eastern European traditional music," is concise to a fault, but the real-world interpretation is far murkier. At this point in the development of the music, the term is highly unfocused. Embraced by record labels and performers as a new genre, it, like "folk" and "jazz" before it, has become a broad definer.

Two jazz musicians can get together and find they have nothing whatsoever in common because one plays 1920s New Orleans style and the other 1990s jazz fusion. With no shared repertoire, style, or technique, the word "jazz" makes little sense without a qualifier. Yet they're both considered jazz musicians. The same is true of klezmer.

And although modern musicians in both genres needn't know how to play traditional style, understand its inner workings, or even be able to quote from its rich literature in order to play widely accepted new forms of the music, the proof is still in the pudding.

"If someone says they're a jazz musician, everybody comes to the gig to pick them apart, and if they don't have the shit they're not really a jazz musician to the people who come," says the jazz and klezmer clarinetist Don Byron. "But the degree to which people can say they're klezmer musicians is based on a pretty short-term and not deep commitment to learning about it."

Klezmer pioneer Andy Statman agrees: "I don't think a lot of people who are playing 'klezmer' music today are really well trained in the style or really in fact even understand the style," he notes. "It becomes very easy for people to learn a melody of a Jewish song and text and superficial bits of ornamentation."[1]

Many bands subscribe to the word "klezmer" because the repertoire has always contained a wide range of music from inside and outside the Jewish community. In this way, they claim, the fact that klezmorim once played Gypsy music, classical, or polkas justifies inclusion of rock, jazz, Latin, or any other elements as being "in the tradition." The difference, of course, is that, back then, it was the Yiddish part of the musician's repertoire that sounded deeply rooted and the outside genres generally less so. Today it's exactly the opposite.

"Klezmer has gone from an underused term to being overgeneralized," the Klezmatics' trumpet player Frank London has observed. "A combination of self-serving commercial interests and basic ignorance has led many music critics, record labels, concert promoters, and even certain musicians to jump on the bandwagon and use klezmer as a buzzword that refers to anything that is remotely Jewish-identified or features a clarinet or sounds exotic or Oriental. . . . Music that functions as klezmer is klezmer."[2]

And Giora Feidman has found numerous adherents worldwide with his inclusionary assertion that all music is "klezmer." "People say klezmer music is Jewish music. It's not. Klezmer is the vessel, music is the language. . . . Music is sharing. Music never is the question. It's an answer. Take it. This is the meaning of klezmer."[3]

The move to deemphasize klezmer's Jewish roots may have begun with The Klezmorim. Though the notes to their first record clearly indicate the provenance of the genre, by their third record the music had become totally deracinated. London pointed out that The Klezmorim "never once mentioned Jews or being Jews; it was just klezmer, klezmer, klezmer." To achieve this distancing the band defined its music not as Jewish or Yiddish but as "Old World Cabaret Jazz." That policy was also evident in its renaming of tunes from their original Yiddish titles.

The Klezmorim based their promotion on the idea that the music had been "underground," and that by playing it they were uttering the abra cadabra that unearthed it. And the term "revival" had been affixed to the klezmer movement by the time I began my work in 1976, implying that the music had been dead and gone and brought back to life.

"'Revival' only makes sense in the case of Lazarus or in the giving of mouth-to-mouth resucitation," ethnomusicologist Mark Slobin notes. "Short of that, terms like 'reevaluation,' 'remembrance' or 'reenergizing'—as in lost battery power—are far more appropriate."[4] For those who stem from homes and communities where there was no Yiddish cultural continuity, the term "revival" might, in fact, apply. But affixing it to the active across-the-board performance of klezmer music denigrates the subtle and irrevocable process of continuity that is key to widespread renewal of the music.

As the route traced in this book exhibits, while the music did undergo a dramatic downturn, it was far from dead, as veteran players in the fifties and sixties always found creative ways to maintain its presence on the jobs they played. Klezmer was ailing, perhaps, but never dead.

An insightful summing up of the engine of today's activist Yiddish musicians—myself included—is "Klezmer Manifesto," a piece Klezmatics violinist Alicia Svigals wrote for the 1998 winter issue of the journal *Judaism*:

> [Some Yiddish speakers] used to deny that Yiddish was really a language, calling it a *dzhargon*. Similarly, journalists and music critics repeatedly emphasize the supposedly hodge-podge nature of klezmer, calling it a mix of everything from polkas to calypso. In fact, neither is true—Yiddish is a language and klezmer is an idiom with its own stylistic unity and integrity. Like any musical language klezmer needs to be studied and absorbed so it can be spoken with a native accent. . . .
>
> A corollary to the idea that this is our music is the notion that having inherited it, we can now do with it whatever we wish. . . . Every musical idiom constantly changes and interacts with other musics, and the 1920s were no

more "authentic" a period than any other. Rather, I believe in playing "authentically" in the sense of being true to oneself. My hope is that now that we're becoming fluent in our own language, we can go beyond simply reciting a received text to speak spontaneously in our own voices.[5]

The voices are increasingly myriad.

... BY ANY OTHER NAME

Dave Tarras once said that composing klezmer tunes was easy but naming them was the tough part. But many of today's fourth-generation klezmer bands' names are their most entertaining feature. Among the hundreds of band names worldwide are takeoffs of jazz bands (The Modern Klezmer Quartet, The Original Klezmer Jazz Band) or jazz standards (Take the Oy Train), and plays on the names of rock bands (The Beadles, Yid Vicious, Yehudi and the Gefilte Fish, KlezSka) or foods (Lox and Vodka, Garlic and Onions, Kreplakh, Hot Latkes Klezmer Band), or both (Hot Kugel). There are bands whose name may tip us off to their actual klezmer music ability, like Klezmokum (klezmer+"mokum," Dutch for Jews) or Close Enough for Klezmer.

Band names tell us who the musicians are (Di Goyim, Klezgoyim, Gay iz Mir), where they're from (Alaska Klezmer Band, Baltimore Klezmer Orchestra, Cincinnati Klezmer Project, the Prague Klezmerim, and Klezroym of Rome, Italy), and where Jews used to be from (Maxwell Street Klezmer Band, Bagg Street Klezmer Band, Hester Street Troupe). With so many groups, it was inevitable that there would be different bands with basically the same name: Ellis Island, Ellis Island/Old World Folk Band, Old World Folk Band; Klezmania (Australia), Klezmania (California), Boston Klezmania, Klezmaniacs; Clazzical Klezmer; Klezical Tradition, Mechaya, Klezmechaya, The Klezmer Conservatory Band, and The Conservatory Klezmer Band. Of course, a phalanx of "klez"-prefixed band names erupted in the wake of the Klezmatics, including Klezmos, Klezmotones, Kleztet, the Klez Dispensers, and Klezniks. And finally, my favorite name: the still underaged Klezminors.

A highly interesting spin on the new makeup of klezmer musicians has been the rise of all-women bands. The earliest group, formed in the mid-1980s, went by the prosaic name of The New York

Jewish Women's Band before redubbing itself Klezmeydlekh. More recent entries in this field include New York-based Mikveh (ritual bath) and KlezMs of Philadelphia.

THE EMERGENCE OF ORTHODOX, CONSERVATIVE, AND REFORM KLEZMER

The introduction to my 1987 tune book, *The Compleat Klezmer*, observes the striations of twentieth-century klezmer musicians:

- First generation: Musicians who were old-world born and trained and came to America in the first decades of the century. (i.e., Dave Tarras, Shloimke Beckerman, Leon Schwartz, Naftule Brandwein, and Abe Schwartz.)

- Second generation: American-born musicians who learned their music in the 1920s–50s from older European players. (Sid Beckerman, Howie Leess, Sammy and Ray Musiker, Pete Sokolow, etc.)

- Third generation: Musicians who began playing and recording klezmer music in the 1970s after exposure to older klezmorim and/or 78s: (i.e., Kapelye, Andy Statman, The Klezmorim, Giora Feidman, and Klezmer Conservatory Band.)

- Fourth generation: Musicians who in the 1980s–90s began playing after exposure to third-generation bands and/or 78 reissues (The Klezmatics, The Mazeltones, Maxwell Street, Nisht Gerferlach, Itzhak Perlman, and hundreds more . . .)

In the decade since this breakdown was published, third- and fourth-generation bands have subdivided into differing schools of ideological and esthetic interpretation uncannily like those of the Orthodox, Conservative, and Reform synagogues. And these very subdivisions continue to shift, as the rise of new "orthodox" bands make the work of original neo-klezmers sound like middle-of-the-road "conservative" interpretations, and anything-goes "reform" bands render everyone else traditional.

The players who can be thought of as "orthodox"—Kapelye, Klezmer Conservatory Band, The Klezmorim, and Andy Statman—at first defined a classical approach in which 78 RPM records served as a kind of *midrash*, with tunes played close to the vest and not veering far from their historic predecessors. The ultimate "orthodox" recording was one of the first: Andy Statman, Zev Feldman, and Marty Confurius's *Jewish Klezmer Music*, a collection of simple and powerful renditions of klezmer tunes that predated the 78s used as their source.

The Klezmorim intiated "reform" by de-emphasizing klezmer as Jewish music and by introducing ahistorical frantic tempos and faux cultural history as part of their stage show. They also made costumes key to their performance. Swaddling themselves in everything from thirties gangster outfits to czarist military uniforms, the band offered audiences a live cartoon history of the music.

The Klezmer Conservatory Band, meanwhile, upheld "orthodoxy" by remaining faithful to, and acknowledging, original source materials, but embraced "reform" with its multicultural, mixed gender makeup. The band also served as a kind of klezmer finishing school, sending forth graduates like clarinetist Don Byron, guitarist/mandolinist Jeff Warschauer, trumpeter/arranger Frank London, and accordionist/pianist Alan Bern to further reinterpret Yiddish music.

One major alumnus is Bern, who heads Brave Old World, which in its several incarnations has moved from staunchly "orthodox" to resolutely "reform." The band has its roots in an invitation-only jam session of KlezKamp staff headed by Joel Rubin in 1985. Then as now, Rubin, a student of classical clarinetist Richard Stoltzman, delivered an accurate, clean sound that reveals his former career as a bookkeeper: his voluminous knowledge of tunes is played with precision, every note in place and accounted for.

Rubin's playing gelled after KlezKamp 1986, with the launching of The Joel Rubin Klezmer Band, which supplanted The Old Country, a band he started in Portland, Oregon. Tapping Michael Alpert on fiddle, Stuart Brotman on string bass, Hankus Netsky on piano, Moishe Yerushalimsky on trombone, and his one-time Old Country bandmate Lisa Rose on *tsimbl*, Rubin produced a cassette under the brilliant title *Brave Old World*, probably his finest recording. For this vanity cassette, the ensemble lays down a punchy, athletic foundation inspired by Naftule Brandwein's 1923–26 Victor sessions.

Seeking to form his own permanent band, Rubin joined forces with former KCB and Kapelye accordionist Alan Bern in 1988, affixing the name of his recording to his new duo. By the time of Brave Old World's premiere performance at KlezKamp West in Santa Cruz, California, in 1989, the band had grown to its full four members, joined by moonlighting Kapelye member Michael Alpert and multi-instrumentalist wizard Stuart Brotman.

When Rubin departed from the band in, he was replaced by Chicago-area clarinetist Kurt Bjorling, who had turned to klezmer from jazz before coming to KlezKamp 1985.

Now under the ideological influence of former philosophy professor Alan Bern, Brave Old World staked out a higher intellectual and esthetic territory. In explaining their fusion of klezmer with jazz, rock, tango, Asian, ambient, gospel, world beat and new classical, the band has dropped the K word, switching instead to New Jewish Music. As Michael Alpert has noted: "We don't want to be confined by the label 'klezmer' and the kinds of things it suggests to people today. . . . it's a very pigeonholing kind of category, and it's associated in many people's minds with something less artful and less conscious than what we're doing."[6]

But it was another band that first ushered in a fusion take on the "reform" movement. Coming together in answer to an ad placed in New York City's *Village Voice* in summer 1985, the Klezmatics, originally known as Hotzeplotz, started out performing traditional klezmer music in the streets of New York City. The original members included Dave Lindsay on bass, Rob Chavez on clarinet, and Alicia Svigals on fiddle, and were soon joined by trumpeter Frank London, who began commuting between Brooklyn and his KCB gig in Boston.

Several talented young musicians came aboard in their wake. London brought in singer/accordionist Lorin Sklamberg, just in from Los Angeles, where he had been active in the folk music/folk dance scene. Avant-garde clarinetist Margot Leverett, from Bloomington, Indiana, also joined, as did the fringe rock drummer from North Carolina, David Licht. Though each had come to New York for individual reasons, they all became part of its burgeoning klezmer scene and of KlezKamp, which Leverett and Svigals first attended in 1986.

When Hotzeplotz learned there was another group of the same name, bassist David Lindsay jokingly suggested The Klezmatics as a substitute, a play on the then popular rock band The Plasmatics. It stuck. But personnel changes ensued. Lindsay left the band and was replaced by multi-instrumentalist Paul Morrissett on bass, a Colorado transplant. Then, not long after the band's first real gig in April 1986, Margot Leverett left, precipitating the Klezmatics' long-running rotating clarinet chair that would include Bjorling (from 1988 to 1989), who encountered the Klezmatics at KlezKamp 1987 and eventually left them to join Brave Old World; the classically trained David Krakauer (1989–94), who exited the band to start his own successful group, Klezmer Madness; and the band's current reed player, Matt Darriau, who also heads his own Eastern European/jazz quartet, The Paradox Trio.

Playing in the style of Abe Ellstein and Dave Tarras's records of the '40s and '50s, sophisticated, cool tunes that had found no other modern adherents, the Klezmatics had their first big break in 1988, when they, along with London's other group, the Les Miserables Brass Band, were invited to Germany to take part in the world music Heimatklänge (Sounds of Home) Festival. The record label Piranha, sponsor of the event, issued a CD of the band, the success of which catapulted the Klezmatics into the world music movement.

The Klezmatics' distinctive sound today is largely due to Borkowsky Akbar, founder of the Piranha label. Borkowsky, an early booster of world music fusion, encouraged the band to do for Yiddish music what other ethnic performers were doing: mixing traditional music with varied contemporary elements. With Licht's experience playing more "out" music in rock bands like Bongwater, London's intimate knowledge of free jazz, and Svigals's sweet tooth for metal bands like Led Zeppelin, the transition was remarkably smooth.

By 1989, billing themselves as "the planet's radical Jewish roots band," the group had taken off. But like American jazz musicians of the 1920s who found fame in Europe before being recognized at home, The Klezmatics slowly had to carve out an increasingly large share of the domestic performing market. And as they perfected their communal sound, band members continued to hone their personal klezmer skills. London continued performing with the KCB and playing some Hasidic jobs locally in New York; Licht began working with me, Sokolow, and New York's "old guys," in Klezmer Plus; and Svigals took gigs at a restaurant in Queens playing traditional and vintage pop Greek music. Svigals and Sklamberg got so into the Yiddish world—they had both taken the six-week summer YIVO Yiddish course—they, too, wound up working at YIVO: Sklamberg, among other functions, helping run Klez-Kamp and Alicia serving as personal secretary to then executive director Sam Norich.

A major contribution the Klezmatics made to the contemporary klezmer scene was the revitalization of the violin. When I first started playing fiddle in Kapelye in 1979, it did not take me long to realize that far from elevating the instrument to its rightful place in the pantheon of Yiddish music, my modest skills were in fact undermin-

The Klezmatics (*from left*): David Licht, Alicia Svigals, Frank London, Lorin Sklamberg, Matt Darriau, and Paul Morrissett. (*Lloyd Wolf*)

ing its reputation. By 1984 I had switched from fiddle back to an instrument I understood intimately: the banjo. Though the tenor banjo did have a modest place in Yiddish dance bands during the middle 1920s, it had never been associated with klezmer music. I crafted a new style that borrowed heavily from military drum press rolls, trombone lines, and tsimbl playing.

But when I heard Svigals play fiddle I realized she was doing what I had wanted to do all along. Though there had been other fiddle players ahead of her—Sandra Layman, David Skuse, and Miamon Miller on the west coast and Mimi Rabson in Boston—Svigals's gifts as a player and personal interpreter of Yiddish music placed her at the apogee of musicians revitalizing klezmer fiddle.

The Klezmatics fuse traditional motifs with contemporary interpretation. Proud of their Jewish identity, band members also celebrate their gay identity. For example, the title of the band's first record, *Shvaygn=Toyt* (a Yiddish translation of the popular AIDS slogan Silence=Death), made clear where the band stood on being gay and Jewish. (Silence about their Jewish identity equals death of the culture.) The group's original score for Tony Kushner's *The Dybbuk*, last performed in late 1997 at New York's Public Theater, re-created klezmer's European lineage. Yet by employing cutting-edge producers for their various CDs and inviting atypical guest artists to record with them—everyone from the trendy girl vocal group Betty to Israeli Yiddish chanteuse Chava Alberstein—they continue to surprise critics and fans.

With overheated tempos reminiscent of The Klezmorim and a predisposition for volume that bespeaks their rock influences, the Klezmatics evoke a feeling of youth that has spawned numerous imitators, inspired as much by their music as by their message. But for many newer musicians of the fourth generation, klezmer music has become a sort of democratizing genre allowing all sorts of meanings to be infused into its performance.

Like the Israeli Law of Return, which guarantees citizenship to Jews born anywhere in the world, klezmer music seems to extend that promise in a secular/cultural way. Espousing a "born to it" attitude, many musicians justify whatever they play by stating that they "have it in them" or "it's in their blood," as if cultural literacy can be passed on genetically like an aquiline nose or slate gray eyes.

This attitude has fostered the "reform" movement of klezmer music: the so-called Radical Jewish Music scene. Though in no way Yiddish or even klezmer, what is also called the "downtown sound" is actually the "*new* downtown sound," the first being the music as played by the immigrants and their kids in those New York City neighborhoods nearly a century ago. The current incarnation began as a series of 1994 klezmer concerts at the Lower East Side's hip music club the Knitting Factory that soon blossomed into a scene godfathered by composer John Zorn.

Zorn and I met in 1983 at the Pyramid Club, an alternative music spot on Avenue A co-run by a woman I'd met while working on Waletzky's film *Partisans of Vilna*. She'd heard klezmer music and thought that Zorn, a club habitué, would like it, so she invited me down to meet him. Zorn, who is Jewish, had never heard klezmer music, but he had heard about it and was enthused at the prospect of learning more. I made him a gift of my recent Folkways reissue, *Klezmer Music 1910–1942*, and we had an intense and animated discussion about the music, its history, and its function.

Since that time, Zorn, a prolific avant-garde composer, has explored his interest in interpreting Jewish music and historical themes by forging a link between art and identity rather than one of musical continuity. His performing ensemble Masada began attracting audiences at the well-attended Radical Jewish Music series held at the Knitting Factory and through records released on the Knitting Factory label. In 1995, Zorn spun off his own Jewish label, Tzadik. Zorn helped craft a music movement that lets composers and performers express personal/historical and political Jewish themes with little actual understanding of Jewish music. Zorn's close-knit group includes avant-garde composer/performers Mark Ribot, Roy Nathanson, Mark Dresser, Anthony Coleman, David Krakauer, and the Klezmatics' Lorin Sklamberg and Frank London. London, meanwhile, spreading his wings more broadly than he does under the aegis of the Klezmatics, produces music for films and theater and plays in new bands, including Les Miserables Brass Band, Hasidic New Wave, and Nigunim.

The "downtown sound" has become increasingly successful, finding fans not only in the United States but again, notably, in Germany, where in addition to the general interest in Jewish things per se, John Zorn and The Klezmatics have a strong following.

These downtown musicians, proud of being Jews, express that pride through the creation of "identity art" that pays scant allegiance to the klezmer style on which it is based—in neighborhoods where fifty years ago nary a musician *couldn't* play in the style. And the Radical Jewish movement has given impetus to a generation intent on melding a variety of genres.

An example of someone exploring fusion from the inside looking out is Massachusetts performer Wolf Krakowski, whose 1996 CD *Transmigrations* blends Yiddish song backed by a langorous Leonard Cohen–style rock accompaniment. On the album, whose title derives from the Y. L. Peretz story "A gilgul fun a nign" (A Transmigration of a Melody), Krakowski, one of the few children of Holocaust survivors on the Yiddish music scene, uses his command of the language and culture to update Peretz's story about how music changes in relation to its environment.

Numerous bands like the New Klezmer Trio and the New Orleans Klezmer All Stars actively subscribe to the fusion ethos. Boston's avant-garde band Naftule's Dream, a homage to Naftule Brandwein, features the brilliant trombonist and KCB alumnus David Harris, and suffuses klezmer with what they call "the exotic modalism of Eastern Europe, the improvising aesthetic of new jazz, hard-edged rhythms of rock, and Middle Eastern music." Donning more "traditional" hats as the ensemble Shirim, the bandmembers made klezmer music history by recording *Klezmer Nutcracker*, Tchaikovsky's Christmastime favorite reconfigured in minor and *freygish* modes.

Several of these intercultural meldings work. The majority do not. As clarinetist Ken Maltz has observed, "'Fusion' is short for 'confusion.'"

Just as a new generation of musicians virtually eschewed traditional klezmer music, a new or ultra "orthodox" faction emerged to balance the scales by playing the music as if it never intersected with the twentieth century. In a nod to the early music movement inspired by the 1960s formation of the New York Pro Musica, this new wing of "ultra-orthodox" players create a decidedly preindustrial sound without modern tonalities or repertoire and even, in several cases, twentieth-century instruments.

The Chicago Klezmer Ensemble, founded in 1984 by clarinetist Kurt Bjorling, lays its emphasis on delicate interpretations of klezmer tunes using original instruments like *tsimbl*, fiddle, and clarinet. Washington State percussionist Kim Goldoff has even gone so far as to attempt reconstructions of Michael Gusikov's *shtroyfidl*—with excellent results.

When Joel Rubin split with Brave Old World, he and accordion/*tsimbl* virtuoso Josh Horowitz formed a duo in August 1992. Rubin & Horowitz was dedicated to the performance of authentic, period klezmer music and issued one CD (*Bessarabian Symphony*). After that band split in 1994, Horowitz continued his dedication to the performance of antique klezmer music by forming Budowitz, named after a late-nineteenth-century accordion builder. The band played its first gig at Toronto's Ashkenaz festival in July 1995, and embarked on its first tour the following autumn. Thanks to Horowitz's musicological discoveries on period performance and the sizable contributions of Cleveland-area musicians Steve Greenman on fiddle and clarinetist Walt Mahovolich, the group quickly became the leading exponents of early klezmer music. Yet despite successful tours and a superior CD, Budowitz went through its own split in 1997.

Horowitz reformed the band later that year with Romany musicians and the inspired addition of the London-based clarinetist Merlin Shepherd. The Welsh-born Shepherd started playing klezmer music in 1988, and at the time of joining Budowitz he was earning his keep both as a classical musician in British national dance and theater companies and as a klezmer musician playing *simkhes* and concerts with several Jewish music bands for Jewish communities all over the United Kingdom. He also worked for the Royal Shakespeare Company as klezmer music advisor in their productions of *The Dybbuk*, in 1992, and as a clarinetist in "the little Jewish band," in its 1997 production of *The Cherry Orchard*.

Shepherd discovered klezmer music in London and started playing American-style klezmer with local bands. He became committed to developing the early European style after attending KlezKamp in 1992. He has since remained a member of Budowitz and a KlezKamp staffer, staking out a singular place in klezmer music performance with his keen ear for authentic nineteenth-century European style and nuance.

RECOGNITION AND REMEMBRANCE: THE HOLOCAUST RECORDINGS

"Did you see the papers today?"

I was waking up to a call from a friend in the recording business. "Have you seen the Grammy nominations?"

I hadn't, never really following those things. "Your record has been nominated." Indeed it had. And so in 1990 *Partisans of Vilna: Songs of World War Two Jewish Resistance* became the first Yiddish record to be nominated for a Grammy.

The previous year I had received an equally surprising phone call from Bruce Kaplan at Flying Fish records. Kapelye had left the label in a budget dispute after our first recordings and had found a happy home over at Shanachie. Yet despite my departure, I was pleased to speak with Kaplan again.

"I just saw this wonderful documentary on Jewish resistance to the Nazis and want to put out a soundtrack album of the music in the film," he said. "Can you find out who did the music for it?"

"You didn't stay for the closing credits?" I asked.

"No, I was so excited about my idea that I left to call you."

"It's your lucky day, Bruce. I did the music."

Partisans of Vilna, the second film I worked on with director Josh Waletzky, had come out the year before. Although the film was strong, it suffered the fate of bad release timing, coming out nearly simultaneously with *Shoah*, Claude Lanzmann's memorial to the Holocaust. Waletzky's documentary, which exploded the myth of Jewish passivity in the face of Nazi forces, made little headway in the public eye compared to *Shoah*. But Kaplan loved *Partisans*—and the music. His hope was that we had recorded full cuts in the studio that could easily be turned into a coherent sequenced recording. We hadn't. Rather, we had constructed exact-timing musical cuts to fit precisely into the film sequence. So to make a soundtrack recording, we would have to start from scratch. Kaplan agreed and offered me the producer's job and a very realistic recording budget. I invited Josh Waletzky to co-produce with me.

From the first, our idea was to create a sound portrait of the music played in settings that reflected the circumstances of the participants: the piano and trumpet of the ghetto cabarets; the accordion and *domra* of the partisans in the woods; the whispered a cappella singing of Jews in hiding. We wanted no part of lush orchestral arrangements or sweetly smooth choral singing, which, rather than transmit the immediacy and passion of the lyrics, would obscure the songs' intention and context. The idea was to deliver a spare but passionate reading of the cornerstone songs that, along with meager ammunition, were all the partisan fighters had to sustain them.

We brought together singers Adrienne Cooper and Michael Alpert, and instrumentalists including accordionist Lauren Brody, *domra* player Alan Zemel, and trumpet player Ken Gross. Waletzky and I both sang, and he played the piano accompaniments. He also brought in his young son, David, to sing the song of a street urchin ("Yisrolik") and arranged for Polish-born writer Irena Klepfisz to read the poems of partisan Abraham Sutzkever.

The sense of purpose and meaning behind the project assured a congenial working environment. Everyone involved knew how unique this was and dug inside themselves to minimize the usual wrangling that accompanies recording sessions. The peak moment came when we all sang "Zog Nit Keynmol," the hymn of the resistance fighters, in a small chorus fleshed out with friends from YIVO (including Jeff Shandler and The Klezmatic's Lorin Sklamberg, making one of his first Yiddish recordings). The plain unison rendition of the song, with its spare accompaniment, gave it a feeling of great immediacy, deepened by the fact that Irena Klepfisz, also singing with us, had been an infant in the Warsaw ghetto where the song was composed.

Once we finished the recording we divided up the postproduction work: Waletzky wrote the notes and I worked with graphic designer Jim Garber on the cover, which features a photo of the Jewish fighters, supplied by partisan Lazar Ran, against a backdrop of an original Yiddish street map of Vilna. One thing bothered me, however:

the title *Partisans of Vilna*. We wanted to use the name of the film but worried it wouldn't say anything to most people; so I added the subtitle: "Songs of World War Two Jewish Resistance."

The record was quietly released to favorable if few reviews followed by modest sales, and we all went on to our other projects. The call about the Grammy nomination was a complete surprise. My excitement at being at the Grammys ceremony, held that year at New York's Radio City Music Hall, was heightened by the presentation of a lifetime achievement award to Harry Smith. Harry Smith! I couldn't believe my luck: to meet the very man who had inspired me to reissue Jewish 78 recordings. Later, I went over to introduce myself and tell him what a thrill it was to meet him. A tad distracted and slightly disheveled, Smith nonetheless thanked me for my words and warmly shook my hand.

We, however, were not as lucky as Harry Smith. *Partisans of Vilna* lost in the Traditional Folk category to country guitarist Doc Watson. In the limited genres of the Grammys, which celebrates several rap categories, all so-called "folk" records are judged together. The material found on *Partisans* was anything but traditional. It was new music created in response to overwhelming circumstances, which, while tapping traditional sources, was as immediate as the circumstances these young Jewish fighters faced. Despite our disappointment at losing, being nominated was a wonderful thrill.

The following year brought another Holocaust recording, thanks to Israeli ethnomusicologist Gila Flam. Brought to the United States to head the music division of the soon-to-open United States Holocaust Memorial Museum in Washington, D.C., Flam's first job was to create audio presentations to complement the museum's exhibitions, as an outgrowth of her groundbreaking book *Singing for Survival: Songs of the Lodz Ghetto* (University of Illinois Press).

Conceptualizing a soundtrack to play in the exhibit area dedicated to the one million children consumed by the Holocaust, Flam expanded the idea to create a CD of songs about Jewish children during the war. *Remember the Children: Songs For and By Children of the Holocaust* was the Holocaust Museum's first public offering. Flam hired me as the producer, and we put together a recording featuring singers Adrienne Cooper, Eleanor Reissa, Lorin Sklamberg, the Yiddish theater actress/singer Rita Karin, Flam, pianist/musical director Zalmen Mlotek, mandolinist/guitarist Jeff Warschauer, and myself. The material, which primarily expanded on the songs presented in *Partisans,* included a reprise of the popular children's song

"Yisrolik" sung by Cooper's daughter, Sarah Gordon. Some of the songs had never been performed since the war and many had never been recorded.

The sessions were positive and productive. Flam, an extraordinary scholar and professional, established a working environment that maximized efficient and natural recording, as evidenced by "A Yiddish Kind," sung by Rita Karin. The song, about a Jewish mother forced to abandon her child with a Gentile family, was recorded without a hitch. Between takes, however, Karin, herself a Holocaust survivor, sobbed at the memories the song brought up.

Produced for the Holocaust Museum and only available there, this powerful and poignant recording never found an audience besides the museumgoers attending the exhibition. As of this writing, it is out of print.

ON THE AIR: WEVD AND "THE YIDDISH SGT. PEPPER"

In May 1985, a record-collecting pal passed on a hot tip: local broadcast personality Joe Franklin was leaving his long-occupied office overlooking Broadway and Forty-Second Street and was having what amounted to a yard sale of old recordings and memorabilia. Wasting no time, I called Pete Sokolow, and together we hotfooted it down to Franklin's office hoping to turn up some Yiddish records for the sound archives.

When we got there it looked as if the Visigoths had just finished redecorating the place: it was strewn with publicity photos of forgotten vaudeville headliners, unspooled reels of film, stacks of old newspapers, and broken 78s. Under a pile of ancient movie fan magazines, I found a batch of records that were larger than any I'd ever seen; I was used to ten- and twelve-inch discs, but these were sixteen inches. At first, I thought they might have been meant to play with early synch-sound films like the Warner Brothers' Vitaphone films. But on examining them closely I found they were not: they were radio transcription discs, and there were hundreds of them.

Ever the flea market denizen, I plopped myself down on the floor and started methodically going through the records one at a time, passing up shows with titles like "Omar the Mystic" and "Stop the Music" in favor of *American Jewish Hour: Yiddish Melodies in Swing*, *Life Is Funny* with Harry Hirschfield sponsored by Tuxedo Brand Cottage Cheese, and *The Molly Picon Maxwell House Program*. The bulk of the records were aluminum, others vinyl, even a few World War II-era glass. Many were broken but a substantial number were not, and as I separated the discs I wanted, the pile grew to more than two hundred.

When Joe Franklin came into the office to see what was being taken, he removed a few records he wanted to keep—some Fanny Brice and George Jessel shows—and began to bargain.

I told him I represented a not-for-profit institution that could give him a sizable tax deduction, but he cut me short. Franklin wanted cash and he wanted it now.

Having no idea what these materials were worth, I asked him how much he wanted. "How much do you have on you?" he replied. Doing a quick search of my various pockets I came up with just under forty dollars including loose change. He quickly agreed. When I once again repeated my offer for the tax deduction, he held out his hand for the cash. He got it and we left, shlepping the heavy trove of discs. (Fortunately, I'd withheld five dollars for cab fare to the sound archives.)

YIVO raised funds to preserve the collection. My assistant Jenny Romaine and I cataloged and organized the materials, and had the discs cleaned, transferred to fresh tape, and housed in archival-quality acid-free boxes. Once completed, there they lay.

The idea of doing something with the materials was engendered by public radio producer Andy Lanset, who came to YIVO to do a piece on Yiddish culture. After showing him the commercial 78 collections, in passing I mentioned the radio materials. Andy, a devotee of historic radio, perked right up and asked to see them. When he did, his eyes approximated the size of the discs themselves, and he told me they could form the foundation of an important radio documentary. That enthusiasm ignited a fifteen-year research and fundraising journey through which, as coproducers and good friends, we have endeavored to bring the story of Jewish broadcasting to the airwaves.

Beginning the research into Yiddish radio, I found the same dearth of materials and general lack of interest in the subject that I had encountered earlier with klezmer music. There was little period documentation and no historical materials from which to derive a point of departure. In fact, documenting the radio materials was even more difficult than the Yiddish recordings. The 78s were pressed in the multiple thousands of copies, so if one broke there was always the chance another might someday turn up. The radio transcription discs, however, were one-of-a-kind, highly fragile, irreplaceable recordings.

Fortunately, situations like these are both upsetting and energizing. Also fortunately, generous and helpful people arose to help the work along—most notably Sholom Rubinstein, whose father, A. Z. Rubinstein, editor at the New York daily *Der Tog*, produced the pioneering Yiddish radio shows *Der Tog Program* from 1929 until 1932. Yet for every Sholom Rubinstein there were people like the curmudgeonly and bitter one-time Yiddish theater actor who hoarded his cache of radio shows as if he had figured a way of taking them with him to the next world. For every Isaiah Sheffer—the artistic director of New York's Symphony Space who made available the remarkable archives of his prolific uncle, Zvee Scooler (and who also eloquently shared his own hilarious and insightful Yiddish radio experiences)—there was the WEVD *tummler* who, upon hearing of my interest in old shows, proudly said, "We threw that crap out years ago!"

Almost immediately, Lanset, a born investigative reporter, sent in a Freedom of Information Act request to the Federal Bureau of Investigation on station WEVD. Figuring on the FBI's antipathy to anything remotely politically progressive, Andy knew to expect a paper trail. But we couldn't have guessed it would take nearly eight years for us to receive some fifty pages detailing the expurgated exploits of FBI informants who worked at the station and of the informants who also secretly informed on them.

We next sent scores of letters to the editors of Jewish newspapers around the country telling of our project and recruiting input from people who had either been on Yiddish radio themselves, had relatives who were, or simply wanted to share their memories of listening to the broadcasts. Lanset and I went on to conduct more than fifty interviews with veteran Yiddish radio performers and children of radio stars who for the first time in their lives could proudly record the story of their moment in the limelight. Their stories, family anecdotes for so long, were now going to become history.

We were also lucky enough to discover the records of a now-forgotten organization called The Common Council for American Unity, an ethnic-language radio advocacy group founded in the late 1930s by a German-Jewish refugee named Jacques Ferrand. Ferrand, a one-time broadcaster in Germany, fled the Nazis and came to the United States, where he found that antisedition legislation had thrown a chill on all non-English radio programs in this country. Ferrand founded the organization to help those with marginal language and political skills maintain access to the airwaves. He almost immediately became one of the first targets of the newly minted House Un-American Activities Committee.

In order to bolster his case for the efficacy of foreign language programs, Ferrand and his little group conducted a massive survey of radio stations nationwide to ascertain how much ethnic radio existed. The resultant files, newspaper clippings, court records, and correspondence comprise the largest repository of ethnic and Yiddish radio documentation to date. Thanks to Ferrand's work of fifty years before, we had a clue as to what we were looking for.

Armed with this data, we pitched our tent in the archives of the Federal Communications Commission and assiduously went through every file, looking for stations around the country with any quantity of Jewish programming and compiling folders of our own. We augmented this by combing the microfiche of all Yiddish newspapers of the era and collecting data about programs and stations from radio listings, ads, and occasional articles.

Materials continued to turn up. We got a call from a woman whose late husband had been a Yiddish on-air personality and producer at the Brooklyn station WLTH and later at WEVD. Victor Packer had died ten years previously, and his widow was finally moving and wanted her husband's materials to go to a good home. When Lanset and I arrived at her house in Queens, it was like time turned back. The basement was crowded with scores of sixteen-inch discs, photos, theater posters, listener correspondence, catalogs, and many more artifacts of this rich tradition.

But the materials to document this forgotten chapter of Jewish history were coming in far faster than support for the research. Neither Lanset nor I was terribly proficient in raising money for a project most funders found too abstract to understand. Except for the helpful people at New York's Littauer Foundation and several other vest pocket funders, we were treated to a smorgasbord of form rejection letters about our project. But far from being distanced from Yiddish radio, I was poised to be pulled even more deeply into that world than I ever imagined.

ADVENTURES AT "THE STATION THAT SPEAKS YOUR LANGUAGE"

By the late 1960s WEVD, "The Station That Speaks Your Language," the once proud voice of progressive politics, had, like its parent, the *Forverts*, greatly receded in importance, suffering one demeaning retrenchment after another. *The Forverts Hour* radio show was uprooted from its nearly sixty-year-old time slot on Sundays at 11 A.M. and moved to the netherworld of 5 P.M., while the paper went from broadsheet to tabloid by 1976, and from five issues per week to weekly in 1983. In 1989, in order to raise capital needed to launch the much-vaunted English language edition, the Forward Association sold WEVD's highly desirable FM frequency for cash, real estate, and the station's new home: a low-power AM frequency (1050 kc, the former WHN).

The following year I was invited by WEVD to host and produce two segments a month of the down-at-the-heels weekly *Forverts Hour*. The other weeks were alternately hosted by older program regulars: Seymour Rechtzeit and the late Miriam Kressyn, Emil Gorovets and Michael Barron. The show, which first aired in 1932 (making it the longest-running show in broadcast history), had been steadily losing listeners for years. It was hoped I would bring a youthful presence to this moribund series and possibly attract a new audience.

After Manhattan's Hotel Claridge was torn down in the 1960s, WEVD moved its studio and office to a bland downtown space at 770 Broadway, near Cooper Union. (Coincidentally, the new building had had its own brush with broadcast history: in its day, 770 Broadway was the annex to Wanamakers' department store, on whose top floor in 1912 the distress signals of the doomed HMS Titanic were supposedly monitored by the young David Sarnoff, thus ushering in the modern era of radio.) The new studios and offices still housed tiny remnants of the station that was. As if initiated into some sort of secret religious order, I was solemnly shown these relics of the past: a broken bust of Eugene V. Debs, a nonworking RCA microphone circa 1945 with the WEVD call letters on top, and the most wonderful contraption I had ever seen: a sound effects wagon built for Nahum Stutchkoff's dramatic shows. Its squat, four-feet-by-four-feet wheeled body ingeniously housed a screen door, a double-hung window, a doorbell, a telephone, and a car horn.

Here was the tiny fifteen-by-ten-foot studio B, from which we would be recording and into which had been shoehorned both the six-foot Steinway grand piano and the Hammond organ from the old station. I intended somehow to work them both into the act.

Eschewing the services of WEVD's in-house engineers, I brought in veteran NPR producer/reporter Jon Kalish to facilitate a much-needed updating of the show. The week before going into the studio to record the first program the station manager took me aside. "Two things you must always remember," he told me solemnly. "Always do the show in Yiddish and *never* announce what the call letters EVD stand for." Puzzled by this odd directive, I shrugged it off as some sort of surreal, obscure joke. It was no joke, but an insight into the strange world of WEVD. After all this time, the station still feared the socialist stigma of being named for Eugene Victor Debs.

The show needed a hook, a sound that both evoked the old days but was distinctly our own. The fates intervened as I arrived at the studio that night: there, peeping out from a dumpster in front of the building, was a set of little chimes—the very chimes that had sounded the WEVD station IDs for some fifty years. (The keys even had the number sequence scratched into them to ensure the proper rendition.) I rescued the still undamaged instrument from the trash and used it for that show and every show thereafter. It was not the last time I had to snatch shards of Yiddish radio history from the WEVD garbage.

Sporting *noms de luft*, Kalish ("Shmuel Biederman") and I ("Der Ba'al Radio" or "Master of the Radio") aired our first show on April 22, 1990, dedicating it to the memory of my late father. My homey Yiddish was perfectly acceptable, but since it was being broadcast on the station that had broadcast the likes of Nahum Stutchkoff, Zvee Scooler, and Ben Basenko, it needed to be better. So I enlisted the aid of my YIVO colleague and friend David Rogow, and my mother, to help me hone a mix of folksy and erudite Yiddish for the program.

The shows from the first several months were stiff, no doubt about it, but our ideas were new and appealing. Our listeners had never heard contemporary public radio and so had no idea how fresh and accessible it could be. We introduced elements long familiar to public radio listeners, like "buttons" (musical interludes between segments), and produced off-site stories, magazine format pieces, etc. We had regular features like "Today in Jewish Music," where I would play 78s recorded on that same date in the era extending from the 1910s to the 1950s and talk about the performers and the songs; we ran a contest called *der mysterye disk*, where we would play a 78, tell something about the song, the composer or person singing it, and then ask listeners to write in with their guesses about who it was. The promise of a free recording for the correct entry—usually a Kapelye cassette—made this one of our most popular segments. This correspondence not only put us in touch with our listeners but gave us a rough idea of who was out there, since the station wouldn't pay for an Arbitron survey to gauge how many listeners were tuning in.

Although there wasn't much fan mail, what did come in was exponentially more than what had preceded it. Plying listeners with requests for *proste bild postkartlekh* (tacky picture postcards), we received all manner of funny and odd cards registering their words of praise, requests, and of course, *kvetshes*. Even the *spodek dreyer* (complainers) appreciated our attempts to find a new and active audience for Yiddish culture.

On the anniversary of the birth of William Shakespeare we featured YIVO colleague Jeffrey Shandler reading Yiddish translations of the Bard's sonnets accompanied by lute music. On another occasion, Shandler read Yiddish poems about the subway. To accompany this reading, I rode the IRT with tape recorder in hand, at Kalish's recommendation, capturing ambient sound.

As the collection of old Yiddish radio shows grew, we took to rebroadcasting many of these programs in full, sometimes on the date they had originally aired. It was a real thrill to be able to reunite the shows with both the station and with the old listeners. Fans loved it. I would ask listeners to write in if they remembered these shows, and some would respond with memories about the old programs, their performers, and even the show's sponsors—all of which came in handy for the ongoing Yiddish radio research. *The Forverts Hour* also featured guest appearances of known and up-and-coming Yiddish cultural personalities, premiered new Yiddish record releases, and reviewed films, recordings, books, and concerts.

I had really wanted to do a live Yiddish show, a cross between the old *Forverts Hour*, with its poetry and deep *Yiddishkayt*, and *A Prairie Home Companion*, with its hot musical elements and humor. I was refused, I was told, because the studios were too small and the budget too big. So, in an effort to entice a new spate of listeners, I tried to sneak in some English for people whose Yiddish was not so fluent yet who loved the culture. Again, the idea was squelched, with the insistence that the show had always been and always would be in Yiddish. (That the show had once been live with a twenty-piece orchestra and a four hundred–person audience was somehow immaterial.) I was puzzled: Why bring in a new, young producer to develop contemporary Yiddish cultural programming and then put the kibosh on every idea put forth? It was like being hired as a race car driver but ordered not to exceed sixty M.P.H.

Within a year our airtime was slashed in half. On orders from the Forward Association board, the show was cut down because a *Forverts Hour* colleague resented having his airtime given over to what he deemed a *smarkatsh* (a snot nose). The elderly *Forverts Hour* hosts found their audience base eroding, while Kalish and I were bringing in new listeners. Never mind. The "Old Boychik" network had kicked in.

As if this weren't enough, during winter sports season *The Forverts Hour* would regularly be preempted to rebroadcast second-string hockey and basketball games. At that time of year and with the multiple host rotation, it was not uncommon for six weeks to pass between our shows—not the best way to build and sustain a loyal listening audience.

Coming into the studios one day in 1993 Kalish and I found the fine old Hammond organ gone, and realized it might not be long before the piano was also taken. We asked Pete Sokolow to come in and play Yiddish songs and klezmer tunes during the show. It was a nice touch that added a sense of liveness to this taped program. Listeners got into the spirit of it by sending in requests for him to play—also on *proste bild postkartlekh*—which he loved honoring.

Yet despite my love for radio and for the program, in July 1994, I quit. One spring day I had come in to find the Steinway gone too, moved, like the Hammond, to the Siberia of the Workmen's Circle Home in the Bronx, never to be played again. The rotation period between our segments was becoming longer and longer, and since the beginning of the year I was obligated to submit a written script for approval weeks in advance. Plus, there was a new directive for the show we were to produce: the same dull format I was asked in to change in 1990. No thanks. The idea was to bring Yiddish into the next century, not bury it along the way. Our final show aired on July 17. WEVD's attempt to bring Yiddish programming into the future was over.

As one of WEVD's last Yiddish shows, *The Forverts Hour* had fallen into a state of not-so-benign neglect. Under a new station manager an attrition policy was in effect: as older Yiddish on-air personalities died, they were not being replaced. The station was now filling those slots with leased time (read: paying) rather than the sustaining (read: subsidized) programs, so new listeners could get their fill of medical, sport, and investment talk—a stark contrast to WEVD's 1928 appeal for survival to the Federal Radio Commission:

> This station exists for the purpose of maintaining at least one channel of air free and open to the uses of the workers. We admit without apology that this station has no deep concern with reporting polo matches . . . [or] the broadcasting of fancy dress receptions in Fifth Avenue ballrooms.

For the first time in the history of the station WEVD was making money: by repudiating its "red" origins, the station was no longer in the red. That humming sound you hear is not radio static, but WEVD's socialist founders spinning in their graves.

My work at WEVD reinforced my resolve to do something to honor Yiddish radio. I had been thinking of an idea for the next Kapelye recording that would place Yiddish music within the context of radio. The concept was to create a series of suites as a tone poem to Yiddish radio, its variety, its immediacy, and its presence at almost every major Jewish event of this century. A medium that had been so omnipresent in Jewish life was now completely forgotten. It has become common-place for performers and musicians to place Yiddish music within its old-world, theater, and 78 RPM recording contexts while overlooking its concurrent radio history. I wanted to change that.

In 1993 Michael Alpert had left Kapelye, and the subsequent addition of Pete Sokolow and Adrienne Cooper greatly facilitated the project. I set myself to the task of researching, conceptualizing, and designing this audio tone poem.

Structured to sound as if you are turning the dial on an old-fashioned radio, the piece mirrors the lifespan of Yiddish radio beginning bright and early one morning in the 1920s and concluding its broadcast day at the end of the week in the late 1950s. I used band crawl—the static between stations—as a kind of theme signaling the transition from segment to segment, inspired by Mussorgsky's use of the "Promenade" in *Pictures at an Exhibition*.

The more than fifty minutes of music took about thirty hours to record and another twenty to mix. The introduction of other sound elements—band crawl, period radio spots, sound effects—added twenty minutes to the running time and required an additional thirty hours of mixing, making this record the most labor-intensive project Kapelye had ever done.

I spent the summer of 1994 writing the twenty-seven-page accompanying CD booklet, the first article ever published on the history of Yiddish radio:

> Imagine a radio powerful enough to pick up not only large and small stations across America, but even those across time—reaching back to the earliest days of broadcasting. Welcome, then, to *On the Air*, Kapelye's homage to the rich and exciting story of Yiddish-American radio. By blending authentic period music and broadcasts with

> newly written and arranged material, Kapelye offers its own unique insight into important yet neglected chapters in both Jewish history and American broadcast history.

Throughout the creative giddiness, though, an unhappy thought nagged at me: the knowledge that recordings interspersing music with talk are demanding to listen to, and notoriously bad sellers. Flow can become impeded, and the listener, distracted, loses interest and does not relish repeat plays of the disc. Plus, for the scope of its subject to be fully appreciated, this recording begged to be heard in one seventy-minute sitting without distractions—a lot to ask of listeners in today's world. The recording was more a radio show than a CD.

We were somewhat bolstered by members of the press, including writer Joel Lewis of *The Forward*, who took a passionate interest in the disc, calling it "the Jewish *Sergeant Pepper*"—an astute comparison to the Beatles' nod to the English musical styles that preceded them. Although we garnered good press elsewhere, it did not translate into dollar figures. The artistic success but commercial failure of the recording led to a distinct demoralization within the band. Banking on the CD to offer us a renewed entry into the mainstream of klezmer music, we were instead stymied by the lack of interest among our fans and colleagues.

I took to trying to rewrite what was in essence a radio show into something I hoped would be stageworthy. I sought the advice of playwright Herb Gardner, whom I met at Kapelye's 1992 Museum Mile concert on Fifth Avenue. His earlier Jewish-tinged play *I'm Not Rappaport* led him to compose the semi-autobiographical *Conversations With My Father*, for which he hired me as music consultant for the Broadway opening in 1992.

Gardner, whose plays move confidently from broad comedy to humanizing drama, saw the humorous and historical *On the Air* as too one-dimensional and encouraged me to build a dramatic narrative that would act as a structure for the takeoffs and cultural allusions that abound in the piece. Numerous rewrites and rehearsals led me to the understanding that even if I could accomplish this kind of writing, there were only two members of Kapelye with any stage experience at all, and that I was neither a playwright nor a director. As we could not interest any playwright or director to come in and help with the piece, I erred on the side of easy access, adapting the CD to a straight-ahead version of the recording replete with sound effects and commercials.

Within a few months of the release of the CD we were invited to Holland to perform our stage version of the show. Making sure our sponsor understood that this was in fact a stage show and not a concert, we were assured they wanted our performance as billed. Mounting the stage in the Dutch city of Utrecht, we began our show, which included all the spoken intros, announcements, and sung jingles. Within minutes, a stagehand appeared onstage and embarrassedly slipped us a note that read, "Please stop all this talking. People want to dance"—an insulting breach of professionalism sharpened by the fact that the tightly seated theater made dancing out of the question. Subsequent performances of the show in Germany and the United States were far more successful.

Back in the States, my other radio project also seemed to be on the rocks. After years of fundraising, Andy Lanset and I had barely a drop in the bucket of funds necessary for the research, preservation, and cataloging that would create a broadcast-quality documentary on Yiddish radio. After a particularly grueling experience with the National Endowment for the Humanities, Lanset, disspirited, resigned as coproducer. Though I didn't feel like quitting I knew that without him there was no way the program would get done.

A few months later, Steve Zeitlin, director of the innovative New York-based urban folk arts organization CityLore, introduced me to David Isay, a talented young award-winning radio producer. After producing the music for *Julius Knipl: Real Estate Photographer*, Isay's short-lived NPR "radio cartoon" series based on the brilliant Ben Katchor strip, Isay and I became friends. Like Lanset before him, he immediately recognized the singular worth of the old Yiddish programs and of the project itself. Through his production company, Sound Portraits, he reactivated the project, reconfigured its structure, and raised the critical funds necessary to realize our dream. There was even enough money to bring Andy Lanset back in. As of this writing, the multi-part documentary program is scheduled to air on flagship station WNYC New York and National Public Radio in 2001.

KLEZKAMP AND THE RISE OF YIDDISH CULTURAL LITERACY

Since its creation, KlezKamp, the Yiddish Folk Arts Program, has served as a yardstick on many levels—of itself, of the klezmer scene, and of Yiddish cultural literacy. The event continues to grow, and though we've been courted by numerous larger hotels to bring our business there, we still like the size and slightly frayed ambience of the Paramount.

The process of organizing KlezKamp, though straightforward, is time-consuming, requiring some nine months of preparation for Lorin Sklamberg, Dan Peck, and members of our setup staff. Working with a cadre of dependable top-drawer teachers, we continue to craft diverse programs, interesting themes, and challenging combinations of offerings.

The goal of KlezKamp was to create a community in which every aspect of Yiddish culture, from music to movies and from folklore to forklore, was given equal recognition and focus. By avoiding overemphasis on one aspect of the culture over another, we were able to broaden our community from one of primarily musicians to a deeply textured and varied population encompassing senior and toddler, Jew and Gentile, straight and gay, religious and secular.

The most singular evidence of the resonance of KlezKamp in the extended Jewish community has been the explosion of registrants wishing to celebrate life-cycle events at Kamp. Over the last few years, participants have opted to share these very personal and community-based events in the context of KlezKamp. Over the years we have hosted baby namings, *opsherns* (the ritual haircutting of a three-year-old boy), even a wedding.

But the most profoundly moving event was when KlezKamp veteran Lincoln Shnur-Fishman asked to have his bar mitzvah at KlezKamp in 1995. His family had been coming since he was a child, and his world view was shaped by the regular place of KlezKamp in the yearly calendar that informed his Jewish identity.

"If KlezKamp didn't exist, I don't know what I would do," Lincoln said in his bar mitzvah speech. "It's like a *shtetl* where you hear and play music all week and you go to classes. I wanted my bar mitzvah to feel like I'm surrounded by *Yiddishkayt*. KlezKamp, for me, means doing my part to carry on, keeping alive the souls of my grandparents' grandparents . . . I wouldn't have done my bar mitzvah here if it didn't really mean something to me. I've chosen to have the most important milestone in my life here because I'm saying, 'I'm committed.'"

We are now beginning to see the fruits of our many years of labor at KlezKamp. The sign of our success is not the bands we've inspired and which have formed at Kamp, the numerous people we've inspired to learn Yiddish, or the multitudes who have carried back the essence of *Yiddishkayt* to their communities around the world.

The real measure is the kids who grew up coming to KlezKamp and have come to see it as just another event, like Passover, Rosh Hashona, and Hanukkah, in the firmament of the Jewish calendar— a new generation that assumes the mantle of cultural heritage with great aplomb and for which Yiddish and its culture is no revival but simple continuity.

Another big bonus are the myriad instances of people who came to the Yiddish Folk Arts Program as registrants and worked their way up to staff and from there to worldwide prominence. This includes musicians like fiddler Alicia Svigals, clarinetists Margot Leverett, Merlin Shepherd, and Sherry Mayrent, and drummer David Licht; dance instructor Steve Weintraub; and standup Yiddishist Michael Wex.

Further evidence of KlezKamp's success is in the explosion of events that borrow its format, content, and even its staff. Events like the late Buffalo on the Roof, the Workmen's Circle's Mameloshn, or the Los Angeles-based *Yiddishkayt* festival, billed as "the West Coast's largest festival of its kind," have their roots at KlezKamp: all were inspired and founded by one-time KlezKamp staff or attendees.

Several years ago we were visited by a doctor from Montréal, who, though he had never been to KlezKamp, knew of it and wanted to run a similar event in Canada. Because of its cachet, he sought the use of our name for an event he wanted to call KlezKamp Kanada. I demurred. First, I told him that we wouldn't allow the name of our program to be used without having input into its operation— which he refused—and second, that unless he sought an unwanted clientele, it was unwise to run an event whose initials were KKK. He changed the name to KlezKanada.

Another Canadian event inspired by KlezKamp is the weeklong Ashkenaz festival, held every other year in Toronto. After attending KlezKamp for several seasons, Ashkenaz founder David Buchbinder reasoned that a modified version of KlezKamp would work well in his Eastern Canadian city. Since its founding, Ashkenaz, like its model, has been a focus of international interest among fans and performers of Yiddish music and culture.

The influence of KlezKamp has extended beyond North America. When Dutch poet and playwright Mira Rafalowicz came to KlezKamp in 1995, she took back with her what she learned there to found Amsterdam's International Yiddish Festival, which she ran for two years until her recent death.

In 1996, when our theme was Jews of Russia, we hosted several Yiddish activists from St. Petersburg. Unacquainted as they were

Merlin Shepherd leading a dance band at KlezKamp 1998. (*Albert J. Winn*)

with the kind of open environment within which America's Yiddish culture has been created in the past few decades, these young people came away with a fervent desire to replicate at home what they experienced in the Catskills. In 1997, the St. Petersburg-based KlezFest was born, with the assistance of KlezKamp staff Adrienne Cooper and Zalmen Mlotek, who helped the Russian Jews mount their modest program, which has continued as an annual event in the Russian Yiddish renewal.

By recontextualizing Yiddish culture, KlezKamp has itself become a context.

THE YIVO HEAVE-HO AND
THE BIRTH OF LIVING TRADITIONS

In its first nine years, KlezKamp, unlike any other of the organization's events, continued to bring in new and renewed members for YIVO. But YIVO's board had always been ambivalent about the program. There was a mistaken belief that the popularization of Yiddish culture would dilute "true" Yiddish literacy and defeat the goals of the institute.

In late January 1994, after taking a few days off following KlezKamp, I returned to the Fifth Avenue building to discover that I had quietly been fired, along with Lorin Sklamberg, and that the lock on my office door had been changed. If this sort of occurrence is common in cold-blooded corporate America, it was unheard of in the cozy world of *Yiddishkayt*.

Out but not down, Sklamberg and I resolved to get KlezKamp back on its feet as soon as possible. Thanks to the Jewish Community Relations Council and the pro-bono policy of its legal staff, Sklamberg and I set about establishing our own not-for-profit organization. By March, less than two months after our firing, we had submitted paperwork to the IRS for nonprofit status and moved into our new office in Greenwich Village.

Dubbing the organization Living Traditions, we managed to jumpstart the fledgling outfit with a small but helpful government grant: our unemployment insurance. Our dismissal from YIVO was indeed the best thing that could have happened to the event. Living Traditions' KlezKamp continues to attract increasing and increasingly varied participants from throughout the United States, Canada, South America, Europe, Asia, and Israel. While it is not surprising that an activist Yiddish culture would spring up in this country and find passionate practitioners, the rise of interest outside the United States—most notably in Israel and Europe—has created particular and peculiar spins on what constitutes klezmer.

↜ 9 ↝

The Sound Heard 'Round the World

HAD ANYONE A GENERATION AGO predicted that klezmer music would be enthusiastically revived in Germany and largely ignored in Israel, he or she would have been laughed out of the room. But that is just what has happened.

What's nearly as surprising is that Ashkenazic music and culture have found champions in Israel at all, in light of the country's historic adamant anti-Yiddish bias. The few stars of Yiddish culture in Israel in the 1950s were the comedy team of Dzigan and Shumacher—exceptions to the Film and Theater Censorship Board's 1951 edict banning native performance in Yiddish—and American entertainers Peisachke Burstein and Lillian Lux.

Touring the nation extensively with shows like *The Megilla of Itzik Manger*, the Bursteins became known as the "First Family of Yiddish" in Israel. The lineage continues with their son, Mike, an Israeli star in his own right as a singer and actor in the low-budget/low-comedy *Kuni Lemel* movie series of the 1970s. (In America he has played in Broadway shows including *Barnum* and *Jolson*.) These days, it is the rare and courageous performers like Chava Alberstein and Soviet émigré Nekhama Lifshifta who sustain Yiddish song alongside its younger Israeli cousin.

Historically, Yiddish song and theater has had higher visibility than klezmer music in Israel. Klezmer in the Jewish state can be traced back to the mid-nineteenth century, via Hasidic emigration to the upper Galilee, but the music all but died out until it was repopularized in the mid-1930s by clarinetist/drummer Avraham "Avreyml Shpiler" Segal (1908–93). The son of an Eastern European klezmer musician who continued to play in Israel, Segal passed on his musical legacy to clarinetist Moshe "Musa" Berlin (b. 1937), Israel's finest exponent of klezmer music.

Yet it was not Berlin who came to epitomize klezmer music in Israel, but a more recent convert to klezmer music: the one-time Israel Philharmonic clarinetist Giora Feidman. Primarily a bass clarinetist, Feidman, who switched to standard B♭ clarinet when he began playing klezmer music, generated a host of sound-alikes in Israel and beyond such as Shmuel Achiezer and Israel "The Philharmonic Klezmer" Zohar. Compared to Israeli counterparts like these, the music of Musa Berlin, deeply redolent of the sound of the Meron Hasidim, is an oasis of restraint and introspection.

Since 1987, evidence of a klezmer consciousness has centered on the annual klezmer festival in the city of Safed. Performers from around the world converge on this Galilean hill city to take part in the festival and to vie for the title of "best" klezmer musician, awarded at the event. The festival directors' hopeful assertion is that "only klezmer soul music can bridge the gap in Israeli society and repair the fissure that has appeared in her terribly fragile social structure." The nation itself hardly calls upon Yiddish culture as a balm, however; presentations in the language are not permitted at national Yom Ha'Shoa or Holocaust Memorial Day ceremonies.

Yet Israel is rich in world-renowned Yiddish talent. The scholar Dov Noy leads the way in the world of Yiddish folklore and song research, as did his late brother, Meir. Gila Flam, director of the national sound archives at Hebrew University in Jerusalem, continues to enrich the literature of Jewish music in the Holocaust. Yiddish theater lives on through actors like Nosn Gilboa and impresario Shmuel Atzmon in Jerusalem, while the Yiddish poet/Holocaust survivor and partisan Abraham Sutzkever still publishes the poetry journal *Di Goldene Keyt* (The Golden Chain), in print since 1938. There is even a modest annual Yiddish music festival called Freyd af Yidish, founded in 1988, which brings together singers, activists, and teachers from around the country. And in a move that may foster more such efforts, the Ministry of Education has granted funding for the National Council for Yiddish sanctioned by the Knesset in March 1996.

The official coolness toward *Yiddishkayt* in Israel makes it even more macabre that the culture should be championed in the nation that engineered its near destruction. The earliest postwar Jewish performers in West Germany were the Israeli team Esther and Abi Ofarim. In the 1950s, they recorded highly popular hit *schlager*—the tackier equivalent of Muzak—in several languages, including Hebrew and Yiddish. They were followed in the 1960s by Peter Roland, the first German to release an album of Yiddish songs in

West Germany. Roland, like the Ofarims, had issued albums in several languages, including one with some Yiddish folk songs.

By 1968 roomfuls of student protesters were singing Yiddish songs. Driving this short-lived trend and the German hippie movement in general was the question students posed to their elders: "What did you do during the war?" As part of their barrage against the nation's resolute lack of response, young Germans used Yiddish songs to remonstrate against their parents, their community, and their country. Manfred Lemm, a singer from that period, concentrated on the music of Mordechai Gebirtig, a Yiddish composer murdered in the Krakow Ghetto by the Nazis. The band ESPE focused not only on Gebirtig and Yiddish pop and vaudeville but may also have been the first postwar European band to use klezmer tunes in their repertoire.

Yiddish music found its way into the consciousness of the Left through the popularity of Paul Robeson. Robeson's great political integrity and his love for Yiddish music (his rendition of "Zog Nit Keynmol" still ranks as one of the best) gave the music a significant boost among German progressives. The first group to emerge from the Left was the group Zupfgeigenhansel. Playing German folksongs in a naive American "folkie" style, in 1979 Zupfgeigenhansel issued a record of Yiddish songs called *Jiddische Lieder ("'ch hob gehert sogn")*. Extremely popular among young people and students in West Germany—the record sold more than thirty-five thousand copies—Zupfgeigenhansel was also considered useful by the East German officials who invited them to perform at political song festivals in East Berlin. The band's record label, Pläne, was run by West Germany's Communist party at the time (interestingly, now Giora Feidman's label), making their records easy and politically correct to purchase in the East.

Once the record was released on the other side of the Wall, it soon made the rounds via numerous bootleg tape copies and went on to influence one of the founders of Germany's first traditional-style klezmer band, Aufwind. While serving in the German Army in 1982 band cofounder Hardy Reich began singing Yiddish songs learned off this record.

Other than that, the only serious attempt to represent Yiddish culture in the East came from Dutch Holocaust survivor Lin Jaldati. Jaldati grew up in Amsterdam, and, though she knew nothing of Yiddish culture as a child, she picked up some of the language in Auschwitz, where she was deported in 1943 and is said to have befriended the doomed Anne Frank. After the war, Jaldati, a Communist, settled in Germany and used Yiddish music as a political tool to bring Germans closer to a culture they had very nearly destroyed. Beginning in 1952 Jaldati, together with her husband, Eberhard Rebling (a pianist and a member of the former East German Parliament), gave recitals of Yiddish music to appreciative audiences. These concerts were most significant because most performers East and West considered Yiddish culture dead.

In the 1960s a Canadian-born banjo player named Perry Friedman founded a hootenanny club called Oktoberklub in East Berlin. Friedman used Yiddish songs to demonstrate his credentials as a leftist, a Westerner, and a Jew. Thanks to him and his very popular club, many Yiddish songs were introduced on both sides of the Berlin Wall. Oktoberklub was also where Lin Jaldati's younger daughter, Jalda Rebling, gained further popularity performing Yiddish songs.

Things changed in 1981 when non-Jewish performers of Yiddish music like Karsten Troyke started out, followed in 1984 by the formation of Aufwind. At that time, young people had a different approach to Yiddish music. According to the German klezmer musician Heiko Lehmann, they tried not only to discover a culture quashed by their parents and grandparents but to look at it as a whole. Troyke, a gravelly voiced singer, specialized in cabaret songs, while Aufwind tried to bring a wedding repertoire to the stage, a near impossibility considering the lack of information on the topic in East Germany. (Non-Jewish singers like Troyke, Aufwind's Hardy Reich and Claudia Koch, and Andreas Rohde actually learned to speak Yiddish in order to sing the songs correctly; Jewish-born performers like Jalda Rebling and the recent Russian émigré Mark Aizikovitch have not.)

In the East, the klezmer boom set in immediately after the Berlin Wall came down. And as American performers came East, Aufwind took off to tour West Germany extensively. There are now at least one hundred klezmer bands in Germany, by far the largest number in Europe. Part of the reason was the formation of the organization Klezmer Gesellschaft e.V., founded in Berlin in 1990, and its klezmer orchestra, founded in 1995. Inspired by the music and inclusionary philosophy of Giora Feidman, the Gesellschaft meets for weekly jam sessions in bars around Berlin.

Despite the rise of consciousness of Yiddish culture in Germany, Kapelye had plenty of disconcerting experiences performing Jewish music there. Jewish imagery is still fraught with racist stereotypes, even among Jewish performers. And many of the Holocaust songs have been changed, through slick pop renditions, into nothing more than romantic ballads—the antithesis of social-protest music.

But these spectacles pale when compared to what we experienced in a Berlin bar in 1994, where after a Kapelye concert we first met with the ethnomusicologist Susan Bauer. As we talked, our attention was suddenly diverted by the sound of klezmer music. Sure enough, a German documentary on Giora Feidman chanced to be playing on the television above the bar.

As we watched Feidman leading classes and explaining that "all music is klezmer," the scene switched to a slow pan across a barbed wire fence. Quietly at first, we heard the indistinct playing of a clarinet, growing stronger as the camera continued its measured movement. As it pulled back to reveal Feidman standing under an iron gate framed with the words *Arbeit Macht Frei* (Work Will Set You Free), we came to the sinking realization that the Israeli clarinetist stood at the entrance of Auschwitz and that the music he was playing was that of the notoriously anti-Semitic composer Richard Wagner, Hitler's personal favorite. People at the bar laughed while we sat in our booth dumbstruck.

THE CLASSICAL WORLD TAKES NOTE

If Giora Feidman was among the first classically trained musicians to take up klezmer music, today a large percentage of klezmer musicians come from a classical music background—a historical inversion of the original route followed by the klezmer. The turn of the century afforded a generation of child prodigies from Europe the golden opportunity to move from *shtetl* to stage by embracing classical music. Musicians at the turn of the twentieth century like Efrem Zimbalist, Fritz Kreisler, and Mischa Elman found that reapplying the skills they had learned in the service of Jewish music could build a bridge to the outside world.

These musicians could not wait to shake loose the dust of their little *shtetlekh*—and the repertoire and style of Yiddish music they were trained in—to play for the masses on the stages of the world's great concert halls. A previous generation would have had to convert to enter the prestigious music academies; but this generation did not renounce its Jewish identity or faith, bringing to their classical interpretations some of the warmth and sound of their upbringing.

Other than Yiddish composers like Lazar Saminsky, who along with Joel Engel and others cofounded the Society for Jewish Folk Music in St. Petersburg in 1912, few composers sought to meld traditional Yiddish music with the higher-toned classical esthetic that characterized the new century.

It wasn't until the current renewal of interest in Yiddish instrumental music that a new generation of composers schooled in classical music began penning works inspired by the lure of the klezmer and of Yiddish music. A contemporary composition that trades on the genre is Osvaldo Golijov's *The Dreams and Prayers of Isaac the Blind* (1994), written for the Cleveland Quartet and Giora Feidman. Conceived for klezmer clarinet and string quartet, the piece was performed in concert several times before it was eventually recorded by the avant-garde Kronos Quartet, with David Krakauer on clarinet. A comparison of the performances shows up how Krakauer, with his insightful underplayed ornaments and nuances, gives the work the authority of authenticity. Krakauer's gifts of technique, fidelity to his original sources, and passion for updating sources with new and innovative influences, also informs his band, Klezmer Madness.

Successful Jewish/classical compositions also come from the Belgian composer Marc Henri Cykiert (b. 1957). His *Capriccio Hassidico*, for violin and piano, among his other Jewish-themed works, is a contemporary counterpart to Joseph Achron's classic 1932 *Stempenyu Suite*.

In the current klezmer field the bulk of leading players—fiddlers Alicia Svigals, Deborah Strauss, Mimi Rabson, and Steve Greenman, and clarinetists David Krakauer, Ken Maltz, Merlin Shepherd, and Margot Leverett—come from a classical music background. In fact, other than Andy Statman, no great current players come out the klezmer music continuity, as did the generation of Sid Beckerman and Ray Musiker.

By the end of the twentieth century classically trained musicians such as Giora Feidman and Itzhak Perlman have crossed back over the line from the comfort and security of the world of classical music to explore klezmer. Several years ago I received a call from the cellist Yo-Yo Ma. Asked to play at the bar mitzvah of a friend's son, he was looking for tunes and wanted a copy of *The Compleat Klezmer*. Sending him a copy, I included a note saying that as long as he was horning in on my bar mitzvah business, the least he could do was assume a Jewish name. I suggested "Yo-Yo Maskowitz." He wrote back thanking me, signing his letter in that way.

It is no exaggeration to say that the 1995 public televison special "In The Fiddler's House," together with Itzhak Perlman's two subsequent tie-in CDs and periodic national concert tours, did more to introduce klezmer music to a wider audience than anything before. The first CD born of the project, *In the Fiddler's House*, sold over 250,000 copies by 1998, more than every klezmer recording ever made combined.

What with the fundraising success of Michal Goldman's *A Jumpin' Night in the Garden of Eden* and Simon Broughton's BBC production *Fiddlers on the Hoof*, the Public Broadcasting System (PBS) was on the lookout for another Jewish music special to air during annual fundraising drives. It was clear that if they wanted to appeal to the Jewish community they would do well to combine two highly successful subjects: klezmer music and high-profile PBS booster Itzhak Perlman. Rather than have to depend on programs produced outside the PBS sphere, the station commissioned the proven production team at *Great Performances* to create a program showcasing this winning combination.

The concept devised was to show Perlman interacting with top klezmer bands including The Klezmatics, The Klezmer Conservatory Band, Brave Old World, and Andy Statman, ending in Perlman's mastery of the form and an Emmy for PBS. Perlman signed on to the the project, despite the fact that his previous foray into Jewish music, an album called *Traditions*, with orchestrations by Israeli composer Dov Seltzer and clarinet by Giora Feidman, had met with modest reviews. The *Great Performances* crew got busy, seeking out klezmer scholars to help shape the work.

When the producers were casting about for Jewish celebrities to ornament the program, I suggested Fyvush Finkel, the Yiddish theater veteran who had recently gained national popularity thanks to his Emmy–award winning performance on the ABC drama series *Picket Fences*. The plan was to have him recreate his first recording, a 1947 Apollo release of Rubin Doctor's '20s-era comic hit *Ikh Bin a Border Bay Mayn Vayb* (I Board at My Wife's).

For Finkel's performance of the song I wrote a new singable English translation and a short little script set in a period radio station broadcasting the ersatz Fyvush Finkel Show. Dancing onto a set replete with potted palms, an old piano, and the art-deco microphone built for the Kapelye *On the Air* cover in the foreground, Finkel charmed in Yiddish and in English.

In conjunction with the TV special, Angel, Perlman's label, issued a companion CD. The wild success of the first record led to an immediate follow-up disc, *Live from the Fiddler's House*, a recording of a concert at Radio City Music Hall. Sales were far more modest, ending the series.

Regardless, "The Fiddler's House" project was a major boost for the popularity of klezmer, providing a solid platform for bands featured in the show and a general imprimatur to the music. Though diffident at the outset of the project because of his unfamiliarity with the music, by the end, Perlman confidently asserted in the booklet accompanying the CD that "the music is in my blood." Many listeners—and music professionals alike—agreed.

"Itzhak takes it very seriously," Andy Statman told the *Detroit Free Press* in November 1997. "He's got the chops and the ears, and he's studied transcriptions and listened to hours and hours of tapes."

The Klezmatics's fiddle player, Alicia Svigals, coached the violin virtuoso in the techniques of the klezmer. "Perlman understood that it takes time to learn a musical idiom," she notes. "After hearing the old 78s and the new players, he created a fusion style—something evocative of the new sounds he learned." Svigals adds that she was surprised by the level of improvisation "from a lifelong classical player who normally works close to a score."

MANDY PATINKIN: "MAMALOSHEN"

If Perlman's approach to Yiddish music is pragmatic, Mandy Patinkin's is ecstatic. When Patinkin first contacted me in spring 1996 to assist with his Yiddish music recording, he had recently left his successful role on TV's *Chicago Hope* to devote himself to personal projects, this being the most important.

His interest in Yiddish music developed in the late 1980s, when his mentor, the late theater impresario Joseph Papp, was chairing a theater benefit for the YIVO Institute. Papp recruited various performers to do star turns for the evening event, and he tapped Patinkin. The proviso was that the music had to be sung in Yiddish, something Patinkin had never done. Papp introduced him to the wonderfully energetic Nellie Casman hit "Yosl, Yosl," which also just happened to be Papp's Yiddish name.

Patinkin performed that night accompanied by Kapelye, who were also on the bill. And in 1990 Patinkin recorded "Yosl," featuring Don Byron on clarinet. Not long before Papp died, Patinkin played him the recording. "You have to do this music," he recalls Papp telling him. "This is your job."

By the time I came aboard on the project, Patinkin had already worked with Moishe Rosenfeld and Zalmen Mlotek to locate songbooks and recordings. But he needed a repertoire scout, someone who could bring the songs to him, translate them, and coach him toward his own interpretation. Surprisingly, although he possesses a wonderful instrument Patinkin was primarily concerned with text, not melody. He wanted, above all, songs he could act, ones with great characters, place, or imagery. This made the search more interesting.

I broke down the genres of Yiddish songs, giving examples of each: political anthems, Yiddish theater hits, folk songs, parodies. When I suggested a song I had recorded several times, Chaim Tow-ber's "Motl der Opreyter," it was like proffering a precious family heirloom, something very personal and meaningful.

What ensued was a stimulating and creative months-long process. It was a treat sitting in Patinkin's little music room and having him serenade me with his latest woodshed offering. Patinkin is a diligent and maniacally focused worker, and when he believes in some-thing—and he believed in this project—he is completely energized. At our first meeting he handed me a small business card. It read: THIS IS TO CERTIFY THAT MANDY PATINKIN IS A MEMBER IN GOOD STAND-ING OF THE OVER THE TOP CLUB. And so he is.

Many ideas were generated, though not all realized. Because of his experience singing with soprano Judy Blazer, I thought he could recreate some of the marvelous duets made famous by Moishe Oysh-er and Florence Weiss or Peisachke Bursteyn and Lillian Lux, reper-toires that have never been adequately revived. Another idea was to have Patinkin perform the songs as they were done originally—for example, to accompany theater songs with a big orchestra and folk songs with a small ensemble or even perform them a cappella. He disagreed, performing each selection as he does all his music, as massive "over the top" theater pieces.

Apart from Yiddish materials, Patinkin said he wanted transla-tions of songs. I assumed he was referring to English renderings of Yiddish songs, which would give his Yiddish-challenged listeners a frame of reference. With this in mind, I came to an early meeting with examples of my translation work from Kapelye, like "Chicken," "Levine, the Big Man," and my recent "Ikh Bin a Border . . .," writ-ten for Fyvush Finkel. No, Patinkin said, he didn't want English translations of Yiddish songs; he wanted no English on the record. Rather, he wanted Yiddish translations of English songs written by Jewish-born but non-Yiddish American tunesmiths.

The vagaries of the languages make going from Yiddish to Eng-lish much simpler than the other way around. Given the quirky ver-nacular of the composers he favored—from Stephen Sondheim to Leonard Bernstein to Paul Simon—I knew I could not do this job alone. I brought in the finest Yiddish/English translator around, Toronto's Michael Wex.

I had first met Wex when he came to KlezKamp as a registrant in 1987. The initial indication of his creative genius was when he got onstage and performed a Yiddish version of Louis Jordan's "Caldonia" as "Kuldunya" (Kuldunya was a character in a Goldfaden operetta). It was devastatingly funny. Wex's cultural literacy, his intimate knowledge of Yiddish, Hebrew, and Talmudic texts, and gimlet-eyed view of American popular culture as evidenced in his 1992 faux-memoirs *Shlepping the Exile* make him a Yiddish national treasure. And although he is not credited in the *Mameloshen* CD liner notes, he was a critical part of that recording's success.

As Patinkin and I went through tune after tune looking for English-language material that would suit him, songs were translated and then discarded, like "Brother, Can You Spare a Dime?" (Brider, Host Far Mir a Dime?) "As Time Goes By" (Fun Tomid On), and "Somewhere Over the Rainbow" (Ergets Iber Sambatyon). Some of Patinkin's ideas struck Wex and me as slightly off-kilter, such as Irving Berlin's "White Christmas," our translation of which was ultimately passed over. After we had left the project, Patinkin added other translated songs like the "Hokey Pokey" and "Supercalifragalisticexpialidocious"—the nonsense song from *Mary Poppins*.

One English-to-Yiddish song I suggested spontaneously was a cute translation of the 1908 baseball anthem "Take Me out to the Ballgame" I had done while scoring Aviva Kempner's 1999 film *The Life and Times of Hank Greenberg*, a documentary about the 1930s Detroit Tiger home run king. I was pleased with the little couplet *keyf mir di nislekh un kreker jek/vil ikh keynmol fin dort geyn avek* (Buy me some peanuts and Cracker Jack/I never want to leave and go back), and Patinkin flipped over the song, using it in live performances and exhorting the audience to sing along. (People especially like the *eyns, tsvey, dray strikes bist oys*.)

If Perlman had to be talked into the klezmer project, in Patinkin's case it was his label, Nonesuch, that was uneasy about the idea, humoring their star warily. Patinkin proved them wrong, with six-month sales of the CD exceeding seventy-five thousand units—as many as any of his earlier recordings had sold in total.

Mamaloshen, like Perlman's *In the Fiddler's House*, has garnered wide praise from critics and fans alike, acclaimed as Patinkin's best work to date. An August 16, 1998 *New York Times* article by Barry

Singer even goes so far as to assert that "a Yiddish-music renaissance . . . has found its fullest expression in Mandy Patinkin's album
Mamaloshen."

So Perlman and Patinkin, stars in the classical and popular music
worlds, are paradigms of yet another aspect of the inverted route
Jewish-American musicians have followed. While immigrant musicians, in order to "pass," submerged their Jewish sound, Perlman
and Patinkin subtly color their mainstream aesthetics in order to
evoke that sound. And the insecurity that led the previous generation
to abandon Jewish music was as strong an impetus as the security
the current generation seeks in attempting to join its roots to its own
mainstream identity. In both cases, the artists' efforts were buttressed by a market previously defined and developed by a generation of grassroots practitioners.

OLD WORLD 1989

The device PBS used in *In the Fiddler's House* to underscore Perlman's sense of Jewishness was a scene in which he returns to his
family's Polish *shtetl*—a motif popular in a spate of recent films
including *Shoah*. Such a return proved far less cinematic in real life.

Until his death, my *zeyde* used to divide his time between his neat
little apartment in Brighton Beach, a rooming house in Miami, and
a frowsy hotel in his hometown of Rovne. Dragged unwillingly from
the city of his birth after the war, he returned as often as he could to
commune with the few living *landslayt* and the thousands of ghosts
in this once great regional Jewish city.

How many times did he implore my mother and me to accompany him, and how many times did we decline? It wasn't until he was
gone that my mother understood the import of his request.

In 1989, on the eve of the Soviet going-out-of-business sale, my
mother, my Aunt Pepa, my cousin Rochelle, and I packed our bags
for this somber homecoming. Though the clumsy Intourist office
demanded we visit other Soviet cities in order to spread around our
Americanskaya dollarskis, our attention was focused on the middle
of the trip when we boarded the night train in Kiev for a dawn
arrival in Rovne.

In the compartment next to mine I heard my mother and aunt
talking all night: they were too excited to sleep, and their excitement
was infectious. My aunt, ten years younger than my mother, had dim

memories of the city, while my mother, ever her father's daughter with her unerring recall, retained crystal-clear images of the city she hadn't seen in fifty years. Staring out into the weak gray dawn, my mother strained to catch a glimpse of her hometown as the train lurched into the station.

We were met by the remnants of the Rovne Jewish community with flowers in their hands and tears in their eyes. My mother kept repeating *"Dus iz nisht mayn Rovner vagzal"* [This is not my Rovne train station] as I looked into the faces of these poverty-stricken survivors. I knew none of them, in their ill-fitting, boxy Soviet suits, but when Jascha Gehrman, a retired Jewish Rovne archivist, spoke his chewy, familiar Rovner Yiddish, I felt at home.

Checking into the seedy Hotel Mir (Peace), my mother quickly renamed it *Hotel de Vance*, or "The Hotel de Bedbug." It was like the rest of the city: grim, sad, and not a little depressing.

Olga, our Intourist guide, was a reservoir of useless propaganda whose revisionist blather was like rouge on a cadaver. For every retrofitted fact she offered up in broken English, my mother would quietly counter with a contradicting and far more meaningful fact in Yiddish: "On this corner Comrade Stalin addressed our workers"/*Du hot geshtanen di shnaydershe shil* [This is where the tailor's synagogue stood]." It went on like that all day.

A trip to the Rovne Museum revealed a fact that my mother neglected to share with me: Rovne never had any Jews. How else to explain the complete absence of references to the Jewish city that once thrived here? How can you go home again if there's no proof you ever lived here? What Hitler began with bullets, the postwar Soviet state completed with its historical whitewashing.

In a city overrun with memorials to the Great Patriotic War (World War II) and its victimized "Soviet Citizens"—plaques, monuments, statues, tombs, flags, banners, and bas relief on every building, street corner, wall, and park—no mention is made of the destruction of the Jews. Once home to twenty-one thousand Jews among a population of thirty thousand, Rovne now had a population of more than a million, with maybe one thousand Jews. We knew where the rest were, and we wanted to visit.

Intent as we were on going to Di Sosnikes, the forest on the outskirts of town and site of Rovne's infamous mass murder, our Intourist guide blandly refused to take us. "It's not on the approved list," she said. "How about the pencil factory?" Wrong answer.

"Either you take us to the Sosnikes or we walk there!" my mother retorted in fluent Russian.

Our flummoxed guide was out of her league. Rovne was not the usual choice of visitors, so the Intourist apparatchiks only assigned grade B tour leaders. Unsure of how to handle the situation, Olga removed herself to confer with her boss. Left to cool our heels, my mother would accept nothing less than what she wanted. And bless her, she got it. Shamefacedly, our rosy-cheeked tour guide returned in a tiny smoke-spewing Lada station wagon, offering us a driver to take us wherever we wanted to go. Satisfied that we had won this battle, we quickly organized a memorial service, and our sad little caravan headed out to the bucolic Sosnikes.

"No monument stands over Babi Yar," says the opening stanza of Yevgeny Yevtushenko's poem. True when written, that is no longer the case. Thanks to Yevtushenko's powerful postwar verse, an imposing memorial now marks the spot of this dread event. When we posed for a picture before this monument on the day before we left for Rovne, my mother had already resolved that her hometown would be similarly memorialized.

Nothing at the Sosnikes hints of the infamy that will forever inform this spot. Seventeen thousand five hundred Rovner, including nearly one hundred members of my mother's and father's families, lay tangled in a mass grave beneath the sod of the quiet woods. A prayer for the dead was concluded, the first offered for my family since the end of the war. As I stood on the periphery, a participant/observer with a *makhzor* (prayer book) in one hand and videocam in the other, I chose to stop filming to be part of the memorial. A few years earlier, one of my mother's Rovner friends had also returned and for his memorial service played a tape of my father singing the El Mole Rachamim, the prayer for the dead. In a city once famous for its cantors, this was as close as they could get to hearing one.

Back in town, armed with family photos and pictures of Rovne from the YIVO archives, we tooled around trying to identify surviving places. Mama points to an empty lot off the Chechegomaya (Third of May Street), the main drag, and identifies it as the site of her old house. Down another street she points to a large brick wall and pegs it as Pisjuk's brewery. Here is a building, now an apartment house, that before the war was a cinema where my Aunt Rukhl worked as a film editor. But I and my cousin Rochelle (who is named after our murdered aunt) can't look through our mother's eyes, so we must take all these things on faith. We see a tawdry city, and past their teary, sepia-streaked recollections, so do they.

Later, as honored guests at a banquet, we were fêted with speeches, vodka, heavy familiar food, and more speeches. And tears. Every speech was laden with tears invoked by the memory of this shocking moment in the history of this lost Jewish city. The most profound moments were when a small woman named Manya Bilenko delivered a painful and moving memoir about how she and her sister survived the machine gunning at the Sosnikes and crawled out of the pit to safety. Another speaker, the secretary of the recently formed Yidishe Kultur Farband, told of the time after his release from the Red Army in 1946 when he traveled the countryside around Rovne quietly and brutally murdering ex-members of the Ukrainian fascist groups.

After four days, our stay was over. There was no catharsis for my mother or Aunt Pepa, no real feeling of release or closure. Yet we did win a minor victory. We learned later that due to our visit, the Sosnikes was put on the Intourist tour list. And a monument? As of 1997, thanks to the unflagging effort of Jascha Gehrman, a tall, handsome black obelisk stands at the Sosnikes on whose sides are carved thousands of names of the dead at rest beneath the soft green earth.

We're happy we went. And happier never to go again.

YIDDISH AT THE SMITHSONIAN

Back home, klezmer was about to gain an imprimatur that had eluded it thus far. In 1998 the Smithsonian Institution included the genre at its annual Washington, D.C.–based Folklife Festival, marking American-style klezmer music's first appearance in the event's thirty-three-year history.

The seeds for this concert had been sown in 1980, when Kapelye played at the American opening of A Precious Legacy: The Wonders of the Prague Museum, at the Smithsonian. The exhibition, which displayed some of the artifacts scheduled to be shown in the Nazi's planned Museum of the Disappeared Race, made its first stop in the United States in the capital, and the concert reacquainted Ralph Rinzler, founder of the Folklife Festival, with the music his family had once known.

Famed for his pioneering introduction of bluegrass and old-time music to urban audiences, Rinzler was a member of the popular Greenbriar Boys bluegrass band, a cofounder of the Newport Folk Festival, and the one-time manager of Bill Monroe, the father of bluegrass music. He was also a field collector, performer, and producer of records of rural American music for the Folkways label. Yet despite his passion for traditional music of all sorts, under his watch there was never any Yiddish-American klezmer at the Smithsonian Folklife Festival.

After his death in 1995, his widow, Kate, made it a personal mission to include klezmer among the musical forms associated with his memory, hiring clarinetist Sherry Mayrent, accordionist Lorin Sklamberg, and me to play that autumn at a private memorial ceremony at Kate Rinzler's family estate on Naushon Island off New Bedford, Massachusetts. Our performance, combined with her attendance at KlezKamp '95 in late December, spurred Kate to feature klezmer music at the 1998 Smithsonian Folklife Festival, on the newly launched Ralph Rinzler stage.

As curator of the program, I wanted to show the process of the culture's continuity by assembling two bands: one of seniors and one of the next generation. I had Pete Sokolow on keyboards lead the classic veterans ensemble Klezmer Plus: Sid Beckerman on clarinet, Paul Pincus on tenor sax, me on banjo, and drummer Michael Spielzinger, a second-generation klezmer musician whose very name—"playsinger" or "musician"—makes him eligible.

We contrasted the classic bandstand sounds of the '30s and '40s with a younger band, Freylakh! Freylakh!: Margot Leverett on clarinet, Lauren Brody on accordion, fiddler Steve Greenman, Mark Rubin on tuba, and myself on banjo. We demonstrated how the renewed interest in the music honored the previous generation, our teachers, and also jumped back over their heads by reviving an older repertoire already abandoned by the time they started performing.

Playing a cross-section of tunes like Brandwein's "Yidisher Soldat in di Trenches" and Sammy Musiker's "Der Heymisher Bulgar," the young band fervently advocated the traditional music and its performance, but also happily broke with traditions like the tacit agreement that the music be played solely by men. Leverett's emerging status as one of the great klezmer stylists today is also bound up with her status as Beckerman's greatest student. In many ways she represents a perfect symbol for the coming generation of the music.

A trained classical player who had moved on to the genre's more avant-garde incarnations, Leverett had never played klezmer music when the Klezmatics invited her to join them in 1985. Her playing coalesced when she attended KlezKamp for the first time the next year. Hearing Sid Beckerman at Kamp, she immediately took to his playing and convinced him to take her on as a student. Learning his repertoire was the easy part; Leverett then tackled the more difficult task of internalizing the tone, color, and phraseology of the music, achieving what only a few players—Statman, Krakauer, and Shepherd among them—have ever achieved. By going into the music, executing a fresh series of subtle variations, she expands the music's structure and shape while adhering to the stylistic and tonal core that gives it its identity. It is a risky and iffy thing, yet audiences and peers alike can sense it when it happens. Leverett's playing is passionate and exciting.

Among the more than five hundred people who turned out to hear us were some of the most important people in my development as a traditional musician, including John Cohen, cofounder of the pioneering old-time music band The New Lost City Ramblers, and Dick Spottswood, with whom I had coproduced two klezmer reissues—*Klezmer Pioneers: European and American Recordings* (1993) and *Naftule Brandwein: King of the Klezmer Clarinet* (1997). The audience that day heard two Yiddish bands that complemented each other, each exemplifying the vigor and ease the players felt about the music. The final part of the Smithsonian program was the joining of the two bands to play for dances taught by Steve Weintraub, an Atlanta-based instructor of Jewish dance.

This was not the only honor through which the federal government recognized surviving veterans of the old klezmer world. In 1998 the National Endowment for the Arts for the second time bestowed its august National Heritage Folklife Award on klezmer musicians: The first had been for Dave Tarras; now, it was the Epstein Brothers—Max (clarinet), Willie (trumpet), and Julie (drums).

The Epstein Brothers owe this grand resurgence to Pete Sokolow. After years of Sokolow's coaxing Max Epstein to come to KlezKamp, the veteran clarinetist finally attended as a teacher in 1991. There clarinetist Joel Rubin, also on staff, met Epstein for the first time, beginning his multiyear research project on the elder musician's music. With Rubin's bringing Max and his brothers to Germany, the old players scored a series of great successes, filling concert halls and generating columns of laudatory reviews. A movie about the

Epsteins, *A Tickle in the Heart*, was released to European acclaim. It is not a great documentary by any means—even the Epsteins dislike it—yet they understand how it enhanced their refound popularity.

Sadly, a car accident in November 1996 brought about the quick decline of Max Epstein, who survived but can no longer play clarinet. He was replaced by Ray Musiker, the band then comprising Willie, Julie, Paul Pincus (tenor sax), and the long-time "fifth Epstein": Pete Sokolow on piano. Then, in July 1999, Willie died of a heart-attack, spelling the end for the veteran ensemble. But no musicians deserved a second helping of fame more or relished it with greater enthusiasm than the Epstein Brothers.

RITES OF PASSAGE

By the time Sokolow inaugurated me into the once proud world of the club-date musician, its glory days were long gone. Left in its wake were musicians who, in order to enter lavish dining rooms, pass through the sticky kitchen floors and endure the snubs of out-of-work-actor waiters.

Musicians of Pete's generation make no distinction between concerts and club dates. They came up with a service-industry mentality that a job was a job and that was it. You got hired, you did it, you went home. Though some younger musicians who have come up in the klezmer scene take wedding and bar mitzvah work in stride, not all professional klezmer musicians want to play parties. The Klezmatics' Lorin Sklamberg, for example, will rarely go on such a job, regardless of the money.

Another is Don Byron, who accurately sums up what many younger concert klezmer players feel about parties. "Playing weddings is kind of mean little work in a lot of ways," he told the ethnomusicologist Susan Bauer. "It's hard work people don't necessarily like to pay for . . . and maybe the people who ask you want to hear it but a lot of other people don't. At a concert, everybody who's there wants to hear what you're playing."

The most recent scourge of the club date world are "party planners," the majordomos of the event. With more knowledge of hors d'oeuvres than *horas*, the party planner attempts to do for the affair what Mussolini did for Italian trains—and in the final analysis succeeds as well. Weddings and bar mitzvahs are more than ever overproduced, with precise schedules constructed around contrived rituals. Part director, part dictator, the party planner has had the scepter of power passed on by the caterers of old, who inherited theirs from the long-absent *marshalik*.

Musicians and caterers, meanwhile, have become like the mongoose and hooded cobra that fight to the death in "Rikki-Tikki-Tavi." The antagonism, which centers on the issue of food, has worsened in recent years. Certainly none of the old-timers can recall when such a vehement disdain for musicians by waiters and caterers existed. "There was never a time when you weren't fed," Sid Beckerman, a veteran of thousands of weddings, mused about the parties of old.

The feud may have at its roots the demise of the Waiters Union in the early 1970s, when Local 2 in Brooklyn was compelled by caterers to let in nonunion workers. Until then, professional waiters and musicians were comrades and allies, respectful of one another's picket lines. The replacement of career waiters with actors or actresses "temporarily between shows" created ill feelings between the waiters and the musicians. Most veteran musicians are professionals, whereas most wait staff are not.

Musicians' and waiters' best interests were often at odds even during the golden days, however. The musicians' contract is booked for a period of four hours, and once that period is passed, overtime is charged; but no such provision exists for the wait staff, who must hang around unrecompensed, while the musicians make extra money.

Clients, taking a clue from the party planner or caterer, are encouraged to avoid paying additional cash to feed musicians. As has happened to me several times, musicians may be offered sandwiches, leftover hors d'oeuvres, or nothing at all. Of course, not every caterer sees musicians as the bar mitzvah bane. But as the cost of parties continue to skyrocket, live music becomes a less-and-less-frequent option altogether.

If the party planner/caterer is the *marshalik*, assuring that all the necessary phases of the party are adhered to, then the central MC, the *badkhn*, is now the DJ. Unlike the *badkhn* of old, who was hobbled by the necessity of having a band back him up, the DJ has a milk crate full of records and thousand-watt amps and speaker columns to accompany him.

Once the last option for families of modest income who couldn't afford live music, DJs are increasingly overshadowing bands at bar and bas mitzvahs, into which they've spread from their first appearances—sweet sixteens—like South American fire ants. For the moment, their progress has been largely stopped at weddings, but who knows for how long.

At one bar mitzvah I worked, a DJ, after learning that I was part of Kapelye, played a cut from one of our records. Although he meant well, it chilled me with realization that for all intents and purposes I could easily be replaced—by me.

But DJs are only one small shift in the movement of the party venue from synagogue to catering hall, from catering hall to amusement park, and from there to places like the aircraft carrier USS Intrepid. With the introduction of themes—be they baseball or rock 'n' roll—the context of the bar and bas mitzvah seems to be becoming a thing of the past. More than ever, the party reflects the economic arrival of the parents rather than the ritual arrival of the child.

Yet a small number of Jews are going in the opposite direction, using the milestone event to make a statement about their connection to community and continuity. Some demonstrate this through good works or by asking that instead of gifts guests make a donation to charity.

Some insist on the active presence of klezmer music at their receptions. One parent, booking us for their boy's bar mitzvah, told us to play just klezmer music. When I suggested that he might want some contemporary American music for the thirty or so kids who would be there, he cut me off. "This is my party," he said. "At my bar mitzvah my parents chose the music they wanted, and my son can do the same when he throws a party for his kid."

It is one thing when a couple asks for klezmer music at their wedding, but when a young bar/bas mitzvah makes that request—or even joins in to play, as happens occasionally—it is far more meaningful and hopeful. The desire of these new members of the adult Jewish community points to the future of an applied Yiddish culture.

Among klezmer musicians, this reforged link manifests in various ways. For some it is a chance to play wonderful old-time music for its own sake. Others consider cultural continuity to be as or more important than technical prowess. And avant-garde players plug klezmer's odd tonalities, curious rhythms, and exotic context into their passion for multicultural music fusion.

Whatever the reasons, klezmer has emerged from its exile in a Siberia of Jewish consciousness to enjoy a new and unexpected coda. In the final analysis, Yiddish culture and music today can be an overt political act, a show of resistance to Jewish homogeneousness, American "kulturzak," and the artificial monolith of Israeli=Jewish. It is a partisan hymn with a *bulgar* beat.

The drive to renew Yiddish cultural literacy is clearly, meanwhile, at odds with mainstream Jewish society, which is intent on erecting inanimate monuments to the Holocaust rather than rekindling the culture the Holocaust nearly extinguished.

Still, klezmer pulses on. Where don't you encounter it now? Selections are featured in in-flight entertainment. I once heard a Muzak version of "Der Heyser Bulgar" in a restaurant. And a friend recently sent me an ad for a bagel bakery in Canada that used the story of klezmer music—and, as it happens, the anecdote of my seminal visit to old-time fiddler Tommy Jarrell—to sell rugelakh.

How long the current wave of interest will continue to crest is anybody's guess; this "revival" has already outlived the most pessimistic predictions. But once it ebbs, the sound of klezmer will reverberate through the body of performance, research, and personal expression it inspires in new generations of musicians—from ultratraditionalists to new-music denizens. The music also echoes in the awareness of the growing community for which this historical reconnection has been as meaningful as finding a long-lost relative.

Yiddish music may never again achieve the widespread, energetic popularity it enjoyed a century ago. Yet rumors of its death, in the words of Mark Twain—the Gentile Sholom Aleichem—have been greatly exaggerated. Klezmer's resurgence has allowed it to exit the twentieth century as proudly and buoyantly as it entered.

APPENDIX I[1]

MODES AND SCALES

"D minor is the saddest of all keys."

NIGEL TUFNEL OF *SPINAL TAP*

"To you, D minor is a key. To me, it's a living."

SID BECKERMAN

AS SIMPLE AND STRAIGHT AHEAD as Beckerman's assessment of the infrastructure of Yiddish music is, it's actually not that simple. When people first hear Yiddish music they are struck by its apparent sadness. After all, didn't we all learn in school that "minor keys are sad and major keys are happy?"

This kind of oversimplification points to the Western music bias under which non-mainstream music has labored. After all, how could a music that is "sad" find most of its outlet in a form called *freylekhs* (happy)?

Yiddish music is a combination of modes, scales, and keys. Any tune can have within it any one of a number of major, minor, or modal keys.

One of the hallmarks in the current renewal of klezmer music is the increased emphasis placed on *dreydlekh*, the ornaments and grace notes that are part of klezmer tunes. When clarinetist Max Epstein taught at KlezKamp in 1991, he repeatedly advised his young students that melody comes first and that the *dreydlekh* always follow.

Despite his sage advice, many young players currently overornament the music with excessive glissandi, chirps, and *krekhtsn*, using them as a signifier of style and authenticity. Loading the tunes with these ornaments is somewhat akin to a hypochondriac who figures that if one pill is good, then five must be five times better. Careful listening to the old records reveals an exquisite restraint on the part of the classic stylists who merely hint at the battery of colorations they have at their disposal rather than giving an endless display of them.

What follows is a shorthand insight into the modes (or *shteyger*), the veritable DNA that makes up the inner workings of Yiddish music. For simplicity's sake, all illustrations will use the starting note of D. Keeping in mind that modes are transposable—any mode can begin on any pitch—it is the pattern of the mode rather than its starting note that defines it.

MELODIC AND HARMONIC MODES

Major

Perhaps the least used mode in Yiddish music is the major scale. The half steps fall between the third and fourth degrees and the seventh and eighth degrees. This last interval is especially important in the Western music system because it provides the mode with the "leading tone," the seventh note, which has a strong melodic tendency to pull toward the upper tonic note. This also means that the dominant (V) chord will be major, since the third of this chord is the leading tone. These features are key in defining tonality.

Note that all the primary chords—tonic (I), subdominant (IV), and dominant (V)—are major in this mode. The secondary chords ii and vi, which are minor, are used as variants for the primary chords, especially in the internal sections of a tune, where the emphasis may temporarily shift away from the primary key toward a related key.

Minor

The primary difference between the major and minor modes lies in the position of the third degree of the scale. In the minor, the half step falls between two and three. In the upper half of the scale, some variation occurs according to one of the three forms of minor: natural, harmonic, and melodic.

Natural: This form has no alterations away from its usual whole and half step pattern. In the key of D, it would run as follows: D E F G A B♭ C D.

Harmonic: This is the most common in music of the tonal period (c. 1600–1900). It raises the C to C# in order to obtain the important leading tone and the major quality of the dominant chord.

Melodic: This form further alters the basic minor interval pattern in order to "correct" the large interval of the augmented second that occurs when the seventh degree is raised to C# and the sixth degree becomes B♮. This correction is deemed necessary in Western usage when the scale is used in certain melodic passages.

Of the three, it is the Harmonic minor that is almost universally used in Yiddish music. The tonic (i) and the subdominant (iv) chords are minor and the dominant is major due to the chromatic alterations of the basic scale.

The remaining three modes are those that are characteristic of Ashkenazic and other East European musics. A. Z. Idelsohn, in his seminal book *Jewish Music in Its Historical Development*, has named these modes after their cantorial equivalents: *Ahava Raba* (A Great Love), *Mi Sheberakh* (He Who Blesses), and *Adonoy Molokh* (The Lord is King).

Ahava Raba

This mode is commonly known as *freygish* among modern klezmer musicians. The *Ahava Raba* mode is characterized by its third step being major, thus creating a wide interval of a step and a half between the second and third intervals. The seventh may be major or minor according to the melody.

For reasons of convenience, pieces in this mode are usually written in the key of the subdominant minor (iv) because most of the notes fall in that signature. The tonic (I) chord is major and the subdominant (iv) is minor. The chord that is usually used in cadences in place of the dominant is the minor seventh, a whole step below the tonic, which is a minor triad. The *Ahava Raba* mode is referred to in Soviet musicologist Beregovski's work as altered Phrygian.

A cousin of *Ahava Raba* called *Hijaz* is widely used in Arabic music.

Mi Sheberakh

Also referred to as *Av Harakhamim*, this *shteyger* is like the *Ahava Raba* in that it is also characterized by an augmented second, this time occurring between the third and fourth degrees of the scale; the sixth degree is natural and not flatted.

This minorlike configuration in the first three notes and the natural sixth degree likens this mode to the medieval Dorian mode. Although Beregovski refers to it in his writings as altered Dorian because of its popularity in Ukraine, Idelsohn dubs it Ukrainian Dorian. Idelsohn goes on to state that the mode is not prominent in Jewish usage except in the prayers of *Mi Sheberakh* or *Ov Horakhamim*, the implication being that its presence in Yiddish music is strongest in regions where non-Jewish usage reinforces it. Mark Slobin, in *Tenement Songs*, infers that the most frequent occurrence of the mode is in the areas of heavy Jewish population of Romania and Ukraine.

Mi Sheberakh presents interesting problems and possibilities of harmonization, because of its raised fourth degree. First, there can be no normal subdominant in the functional sense, which is built on the fourth. In the Romanian usage, and particularly in the frequent use of this mode for the Romanian *doina*, the major II chord is often used in this subdominant-like function.

In later American settings, a diminished chord with a distinctive "bluesy" sonority is generated on the tonic chord using the first, third, and fourth degrees of the scale (or, in D: D, F, and A♭ as the enharmonic equivalent of G#). Very often passages in the *Mi Sheberakh* mode are harmonized only with the tonic minor chord, allowing the fourth, sixth, and seventh notes to act as passing tones, or making the triad a four-note minor seventh or added sixth chord. A less frequent harmonization uses the major II triad to lead to the V minor.

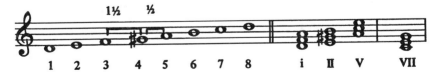

Adonoy Molokh

The scale of this mode follows the medieval Mixolydian. It is essentially a major scale, except for its seventh note, which is a minor interval a whole step below the tonic. The I and IV chords are consequently major and the V should be minor. For some reason, in virtually all known pieces in this mode, a major V chord is used and a major leading tone seventh is used below the tonic.

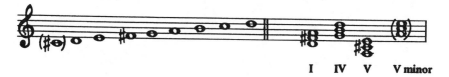

I   IV   V   V minor

Harmonic Phrase Structure

Within a given klezmer piece there are usually two, three, or even more individual sections. Often, there will be a related key change from section A to B or B to C or C to D, etc. For example: if section A is in minor then section B or C may go into the relative major, the major key a minor third above the tonic.

Conversely, if the piece begins in major, the move would be to the relative minor, a minor third below the tonic. If section A is in the *Ahava Raba*, the usual transition is to the IV, subdominant minor. A subsequent change could be to the dominant (VII minor) sections in major and minor or vice versa in the same key. It is also common for a piece beginning in harmonic minor to move to relative major (D minor to F major) and from there into D *Ahava Raba* before returning to the original key. And it is not uncommon to have a tune that is played primarily in the harmonic minor employ cadences from the *freygish* mode.

A major difference in the harmonization of melodies between klezmer and Hungarian, Romanian, and Rom (Gypsy) musicians is that the latter group tends to use transitional chords, such as diminished triads and sevenths, ii and iv minor chords, and secondary dominants, whereas the early klezmer recordings show a simpler and more basic concept that allows raised fourths, major sixths, and minor sevenths to act as passing tones over a basic tonic or dominant chord. This changed with second-generation American klezmorim who incorporated the Romanian and American dance band practice of secondary chords and chromatic countermelodies.

And finally, the standard ending for all klezmer pieces (what in American country music is referred to as "Shave and a haircut: two bits") is a chromatic run, or glissando, into a three note 1-5-1 pattern. The player substitutes the run or glissando for the penultimate measure; the 1-5-1 may be three short notes, or short note-rest, short note-rest, long note.

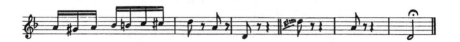

The chords are I (major or minor), V (major), I (major or minor).

APPENDIX II

TANTS NIT, YIDDLAKH: DANCE MUSIC WITH NO DANCERS

WHAT SETS THE KLEZMER SCENE APART from any other traditional music movement is its near absence of a contemporary dance component. In most every other music scene—old time, Balkan, Irish—there is a parallel and equally robust dance scene that exists on its own apart from the musicians. It has its own stars, teachers, and champions. Not so in the Yiddish world. Except for the pioneering research of traditional East European Jewish dance by LeeEllen Friedland and Jill Gellerman and the people whom they inspired (like Michael Alpert and recently, Steve Weintraub) there is no commensurate interest in the Jewish dance world. That world is overcrowded with modern dancers—who inspired by *shtetl* themes have not recognized the value of actually learning the dances of those *shtetlekh*. That, and the fact that Israeli dance still dominates the Jewish dance world, makes Yiddish dance one of the least explored and realized forms in traditional dance. The klezmer universe is a robust dance music scene with virtually no dancers. One of the only places to experience Yiddish dance with dependable regularity is KlezKamp.

This absence of dance in the Jewish world is manifested time and again at the non-Orthodox parties I've played with Kapeleye and Klezmer Plus.[1] When the band begins a Jewish dance set, most of the guests will join the amorphous gyrating circle sharing in the spirit of the moment. But soon, you start to see the effect of people dancing dances they don't know with other people dancing dances they don't know either. They lose interest.

Inevitably, someone will remember The Chairs. Interest will peak with the placing of the bride and groom in chairs held aloft. The popularity of The Chairs has become so great it has also become a staple ritual at bar and bas mitzvahs.

As the dance begins to lose its exotic appeal, the majority of dancers will stop, standing on the periphery of the circle, clapping in time. When this happens the band knows it's inevitable that the circle will quickly dwindle, inhabited only by family or close friends. What finally brings the dancing to a careening halt is the arrival of the

299

caterer to tell us that they're ready to serve the first course and to announce that everyone should find their seats.

This lack of veteran dancers has created a profound shift in the sound and performance of the music. When musicians play for knowledgeable dancers, the tunes unfold in a way that makes clear how to phrase them and how they should really sound. Klezmer music never sounds as good as when it's played at the more moderate and old-time dance tempos. It is with the disappearance of the dance tradition and the subsequent popularity of klezmer as concert music that these tempos have nearly been lost. Most bands playing today take the music at a pace geared more to theatricality than musicality, casting aside the unique subtleties that are impossible to play at those speeds.

The notes are the same, but with the real moderate dance tempos the tunes take on what musicians call its "lift." Buoyant, graceful, and exuberant, the lift is the secret ingredient that gives this music its infectious power. Without it, musicians and audiences alike miss a profoundly elemental aspect of the music.

Far fewer scholars are interested in Yiddish dance than in Yiddish dance music. Shy of the few publications by scholars like LeeEllen Friedland, only one booklet, "Jewish Folk Dances," by Nathan Vizonsky has been issued in America. This rare out-of-print slim volume was published by Chicago's American-Hebrew Theatrical Alliance in 1942.

Sadly, there were no dance instructions given out along with the hundreds of klezmer records made in the 1920s, when the dances were still accessible. What if Arthur Teichman had used his revolutionary dance instruction method of placing numbered footprints on the floor to teach *freylekhs* instead of fox-trots? What may well have happened is he would have remained Arthur Teichman and not become Arthur Murray, the ballroom dance instruction king.

Our loss is the cha-cha's gain.

DANCES AND DANCE RHYTHMS[3]

Bulgar

This dance was popular with Jews from Romania and south Ukraine and came to America with the large-scale immigration around the turn of the century, subsequently overwhelming all previous Jewish dance forms.

The name for the tunes and the dance are derived from the Moldavian-Bessarabian line dance called *bulgaresti* or *bulgareasca*. Whether this has anything to do with Bulgaria per se is a matter of pure speculation, even though a reasonably sizable Bulgarian population was living in southern Ukraine at this time. It is also conjectured that there was contact between Moldavian Gypsies and Jews back in Bulgaria.

The *bulgar* is a circle dance played at a moderate to lively tempo. The rhythmic uniqueness that gives this tune its lift is its subdivision of the beats in its 8/8 meter: two groups of three and one group of two played (<u>1</u>23 <u>1</u>23 <u>1</u>2). When the drums or rhythm section plays this beat against the bass playing a steady "oom-pah" the truly unique character of the inner rhythm emerges, not unlike the clave beat in Latin music, which, like the *bulgar*, is inferred even if not actually played throughout.

Freylekhs

Meaning "lively" or "happy," this ubiquitous dance also goes by a myriad of other names including *redl*, *redele* (circle or little circle), *karahod* and *hopkele*.

Honga

Also called *onga* or *Hangu* this line dance is very popular among Romanians and Jews from the East Romanian region of Bessarabia and probably derives from the Turkish form *hangi* (meaning "line"). Though played in a moderate 2/4, *hongas* are melodically busier than other tunes normally played for Jewish dances, making them seem faster than they really are.

Khosid'l

Stemming from regions in East Galicia and Bukovina where Hasidism was popular, this dance in the style of the Hasidim has a moderate 2/4 tempo that moves slowly enough to invite embellishments by both musicians and dancers.

Kolomeyke

Stemming from the East Galician Ukrainian town of Kolomyja, *Kolomeyke* (as it's pronounced in Yiddish) is a brisk couple dance in 2/4 meter to which rhymed couplets are commonly sung. Popular among both Jews and their Gentile neighbors at the turn of the century, the dance can still be found among older Poles and Ukrainians.

Sher

Sher or *sherele* is a figure set dance (also called *runde* in some regions), and is a first cousin to the Russian *kadril* and even to the American square dance. The tune is usually played in a moderate 2/4 tempo somewhere between a *bulgar* and a *khosidl*.

The derivation of the name *sher* provides a bit of a mystery. According to some accounts, *sher* (scissors) is a description of the dance movement itself with its scissorslike back-and-forth motion. Others claim it was a popular dance among tailors and thus its scissors associations.

One of the few Yiddish dances to be part of the American international folk dance scene of the 1930s, it had great longevity here and was displaced only by Israeli dances after World War II.

As LeeEllen Friedland points out, although there are specific steps to every one of these dances, they are really venues for the individual dancers to use personal steps.

NOTES

Chapter 1

1. Joshua Horowitz, "Gusikov in Wien," *Jüdische Traditionelle Musik in Oesterreich* (Vienna, Oetserreichische Volksliedwerks Vienna, 2001).
2. Felix Mendelssohn to Lea Saloman, *Briefe aus Jahren 1833–1847, von Felix Mendelssohn Bartholdy*, ed. Paul Mendelssohn Bartholdy and Carl Mendelssohn Bartholdy (1865), 121.
3. A.Z. Idelsohn, *Jewish Music in Its Historical Context* (New York: Schocken Books, 1967), 459.
4. Martin Schwartz, personal communication with author, January 18, 1981.
5. Alfred Sendry, *Jewish Music in the Diaspora (Up to 1800): A Contribution to the Social and Cultural History of the Jews* (New York: Thomas Yoseloff, 1970), 353.
6. Itzik Schwartz, "Lautari evrei din Moldova," *Revista Cultului Mozaic* (1974), 10. Trans. Joshua Horowitz.
7. Idelsohn, *Jewish Music*, 457.
8. Ibid.
9. Schwartz, "Lautari evrei din Moldova," 12.
10. Robert A. Rothstein "Klezmer-loshn" *Judaism: A Quarterly Journal of Jewish Life and Thought* 47, no. 1 (issue no. 185, winter 1998), 24.
11. S. Weissenberg, "Die klesmer Sprache," *Mitteilungen der anthropologischen Geselleschaft in Wien* 3, no. 13 (1913), 134.
12. E. Lifschultz, "Merrymakers and Jesters Among the Jews, Materials for a Lexicon," *YIVO Annual for Jewish Social Science VII* (New York: 1952), 61.
13. Ibid., 62.
14. Lulla Rosenfeld, *Bright Star of Exile Jacob Adler and the Yiddish Theater* (New York: Thomas Crowell Company, 1977), 50.
15. Mark Slobin, personal communication with author, 1977.
16. Schwartz, "Lautari evrei din Moldova," 12.
17. Idelsohn, *Jewish Music*, 459.
18. Moshe Beregovski, "Evereiske narodnye pesni," Moskva: Sovetskii kompozitor (1962). Trans. Michael Alpert.
19. Walter Zev Feldman, "Bulgareasca/Bulgarish/Bulgar: The Transformation of a Klezmer Dance Genre," *Ethnomusicology* 38.1 (winter 1994).

Chapter 2

1. Dave Tarras, interview by Barbara Kirshenblatt-Gimblett and Janet Elias, September 1975.
2. Robert Snyder, *The Voice of the City: Vaudeville and Popular Culture in New York* (New York: Oxford University Press, 1989), 5.

3. Charles Stein, ed. *American Vaudeville as Seen By Its Contemporaries* (New York: Da Capo, 1984), 71.

4. Ibid., 109.

5. *The Dearborn Independent*, January 7, 1922.

6. Michael Corenthal, *Cohen on the Telephone: A History of Jewish Recorded Humor and Popular Music, 1892–1942* (Milwaukee: Michael Corenthal, 1984), 29.

7. Ibid., 35.

8. Joe Smith, interview by Morton Tankus, Actor's Fund Home, Englewoood, N.J. June 1978.

9. Louis Grupp, interview with author, April 1978.

10. Kevin Brownlow, *Behind the Mask of Innocence: Films of Social Conscience in the Silent Era* (London: Jonathan Cape, 1990), 374.

11. Max Epstein, interview with author, winter 1995.

12. Moses Rischin, *The Promised City: New York's Jews 1870–1914* (New York: Harper Torchbooks, 1970), 272.

13. Hutchins Hapsgood, *Spirit of the Ghetto* (New York: Funk and Wagnalls, 1902), 134.

14. Jenna Weisman Joselit, *The Wonders of America: Reinventing Jewish Culture 1880–1950* (New York: Hill and Wang, 1994), 25.

15. Irene Heskes, *Yiddish American Popular Songs 1895–1950* (Washington, D.C.: Library of Congress, 1992), xv.

16. Morris Clark, "America as the Cradle of Jewish Music," *Musical America* (June 28, 1913), 25.

17. Nahma Sandrow, *Vagabond Stars: A World History of the Yiddish Theater* (New York: Limelight Editions, 1986), 102.

18. Mark Slobin, "From Vilna to Vaudeville: Minikes and *Among the Indians*," *The Drama Review 3*, 24. no. 3 (September 1980), 17–26.

19. Rosenfeld, *Bright Star of Exile*, 327.

20. David S. Lifson, *Yiddish Theater in America* (Cranbury: A. S. Barnes, 1965), 128.

21. Jim Loeffler, "Di Russishe Progresiv Muzikal Yunyon No. 1 Fun Amerike: The First Klezmer Union in America," *Judaism: A Quarterly Journal of Jewish Life and Thought* 47, no. 1 (issue no. 185, winter 1998), 33.

22. Rick Kennedy, *Jelly Roll, Bix and Hoagy Gennett Studios and the Birth of Recorded Jazz* (Bloomington: Indiana University Press, 1994), 5.

23. Heskes, *Yiddish American Popular Songs*, xxi.

24. Ibid., xx.

25. Frederic William Wile, *Emile Berliner: Maker of the Microphone* (Indianapolis: Bobbs-Merrill, 1926), 187.

26. Roland Gelatt, *The Fabulous Phonograph* (New York: Collier Books, 1977), 60.

27. Richard Spottswood, *Ethnic Music on Records: A Discography of Ethnic Recordings Produced in the United States 1894–1942* (Urbana, Chicago: University of Illinois Press, 1990), vol. 1, xxxi.

28. Wile, *Emile Berliner*, 235.

29. *The Gramophone Company Limited Corporate History* (London: unpublished), 4.

30. Bob Ziering, Rabbi Sidney Silberg, and Alan Bigora, "Gershon Sirota (1874–1943)" (Hertfordshire: Symposium 1147, 1993), 5.

31. Gramophone Company Riga office to Fred Gaisberg, EMI Archives, London.

32. Paul Brumberg to Herr Vogel, September 20, 1911, EMI Archives, London.

33. Jeffrey Wollock, "European Recordings of Jewish Instrumental Folk Music 1911–1914," *ARSC Journal* 28, no.1 (spring 1997), 38.

34. "Turist," *Grammofonii Mir* (June 25, 1912), 39, quoted in Wollock, "European Recordings," 39.

35. Wollock, "European Recordings," 40.

36. Ricky Jay, *Learned Pigs and Fireproof Women* (New York: Villard Books, 1986), 85.

37. Zalmen Zylbercweig, *Leksicon fun Yidishn Teater* (New York: 1934). 2:909–10.

38. Spottswood, *Ethnic Music*, 3:1388–91.

38. *Talking Machine World* (January 15, 1905), 3.

39. Russell Sanjek and David Sanjek, *American Popular Music Business in the 20th Century* (New York: Oxford University Press, 1991), 12.

40. Spottswood, *Ethnic Music*, 1:xvi.

41. Ibid., :1:xxxviii.

42. Spottswood, *Ethnic Music*, 3:99.

43. Sales of ethnic records were not charted in the mainstream or even ethnic press at the time. In my thirteen years as the director of the sound archives at the YIVO Institute in New York, I was able to gauge these period records' popularity by how frequently they turned up in donated collections. When I note the popularity of a particular record, it is generally based on this informal survey.

Chapter 3

1. Gelatt, *The Fabulous Phonograph*, 190.

2. Samuel Vigoda, *Legendary Voices* (New York: MP Press, 1981), 285.

3. Zylbercweig, *Leksikon fun Yidishn Teater*, 2: 1133–35.

4. Victor Greene, *Passion for the Polka: Old Time Ethnic Music in America* (Berkeley: University of California Press, 1992), 103.

5. "Picon Bows in New Yiddish Musical," *Variety*, October 9, 1925.

6. Barbara W. Grossman, *Funny Woman: The Life and Times of Fanny Brice* (Bloomington: Indiana University Press, 1991), 191.

7. Grossman, *Funny Woman*, 189.

8. Corenthal, *Cohen on the Telephone*, 76.

9. Gypsy Rose Lee, *Gypsy: A Memoir* (New York: Harper, 1957), 80–81, 82, 84–86.

10. Heskes, *Yiddish American Popular Songs*, 150–62.

11. Columbia record catalog, May 1920, 16.

12. Jim Smart, *Sousa: A Discography* (Washington, D.C.: Library of Congress, 1970), 65.

13. F. Rous to Edward King, Victor offices, New York, April 10, 1919.

14. Heskes, *Yiddish American Popular Songs* 181, 188, 190, 191.

15. Ibid., 163.
16. Bebe Gould, interview with author, May 12, 1995.
17. Sid Beckerman, interview with author, April 19, 1984.
18. Charles Schwartz, *Gershwin, His Life and Music* (New York: Da Capo Press, 1979), 5–7.
19. Sholom Secunda, "The Melody Remains," *Forverts*, May–June 1969. (Oddly, there is no mention of this Gershwin-Secunda *shidekh* in Boris Thomashefsky's kiss-and-tell 1937 autobiography, *Mayn Lebn's Geshikhte* (The Story of My Life)—curious for someone who otherwise never missed an "I told you so" during his long career.)
20. Schwartz, *Gershwin*, 81–82.
21. Eddie Condon and Hank O'Neal, *Eddie Condon's Scrapbook of Jazz* (New York: St. Martin's Press, 1973), 24.
22. Schwartz, *Gershwin*, 83.
23. Ibid., 292n.
24. Ibid., 29.
25. Joe Helfenbein, interview with author, spring 1979.
26. Dave Tarras, interview with author, fall 1975.

Chapter 4

1. Henry Ford, "Jewish Jazz Becomes Our National Music," *The International Jew: World's Foremost Problem*, vol. III, chapter 11, 1922.
2. Max Epstein, interview with author, December 23, 1991.
3. J. Hoberman, *Bridge of Light: Yiddish Film Between Two Worlds* (New York: Museum of Modern Art/Schocken, 1991), 152.
4. Michael Freeland, *The Warner Brothers* (London: Harrap Ltd., 1983), 38.
5. Zylbercweig, *Leksikon fun Yidishn Teater*, 1:434.
6. Howie Leess, interview with author, fall 1986.
7. Joselit, *The Wonders of America*, 33.
8. Spottswood, *Ethnic Music on Records*, 3:1501.
9. Correspondence between B. Charney Vladek and David Sarnoff, March 21, 1924.
10. *Brooklyn Israelite*, July 12, 1932.
11. Sholom Rubinstein, interview with author, May 1984.
12. Petition for license renewal, 1930, WEVD file, FCC Archives.
13. *Der Tog*, 1930–32.
14. Nathan Godfried, "WEVD: The Working-Class Station," *Journal of Radio* (spring 1990), 23
15. Victoria Secunda, *Bay Mir Bist Du Schön: The Life of Sholom Secunda* (Weston, Conn.: Magic Circle Press, 1982), 131.
16. Saul Chaplin, *The Golden Age of Movie Musicals and Me* (Norman: University of Oklahoma Press, 1994), 79.
17. Secunda, "The Melody Remains," August 1969.
18. Brian Rust, *Jazz Records 1897–1942* (New Rochelle, N.Y.: Arlington House, 1978), 1:259.
19. Claire Barry, interview with author, winter 1989.
20. Spottswood, *Ethnic Music on Records*, 3:1324.

21. Max Epstein, interview with author, winter 1994.

22. Mark Slobin, *Old Jewish Folk Music: The Collections and Writings of Moshe Beregovski* (Philadelphia: University of Pennsylvania Press, 1982), 1.

23. Moshe Beregovski "Yiddishe Instrumentalishe Folks Muzik," Farlag fun der Visnshaft Akadamye fun USSR (Kiev, 1937), 19.

24. Eleanor Mlotek, review of *Old Jewish Folk Music: The Collections and Writings of Moshe Beregovski* (Philadelphia: University of Pennsylvania Press, 1982), in *Jewish Quarterly Review* 78, nos. 3 and 4 (January–April, 1988), 321.

25. Hoberman, *Bridge of Light*, 241.

26. Spottswood, *Ethnic Music*, 3:1339.

27. Ray Musiker, interview with author, fall 1997.

28. Irving Graetz, interview with author, spring 1988.

Chapter 5

1. Joey Adams and Henry Tobias, *The Borscht Belt* (New York: Bobbs-Merrill, 1959), 100.

Chapter 8

1. Susan Bauer *From the Khupe to KlezKamp: The Process of Change and Forms of Reinterpretation of Klezmer Music in New York* (Berlin: Piranha, 1999).

2. Frank London, "An Insider's View: How We Traveled from Obscurity to the Klezmer Establishment in Twenty Years," *Judaism: A Quarterly Journal of Jewish Life and Thought* 47, no. 1 (winter 1998), 41.

3. Ibid.

4. Mark Slobin, personal communication with author, March 1999.

5. Alicia Svigals "Why Do We Do This Anyway: Klezmer as Jewish Youth Subculture," *Judaism: A Quarterly Journal of Jewish Life and Thought* 47, no.1 (winter 1998), 47.

6. Seth Rogovoy, "Klezmer Band Reveals a New World Amid Old World Yiddish Traditions," *The Eagle*, March 13, 1998.

Chapter 9

1. Yaakov Mazor, liner notes for *Klezmer Traditions in the Land of Israel*, Anthology of Musical Traditions in Israel, 11, 1998.

2. Heiko Lehmann, private correspondence.

Appendix I

1. This section is adapted from the chapter written by Peter Sokolow on modes and scales, which appears in Henry Sapoznik and Peter Sokolow, *The Compleat Klezmer* (Cedarhurst, N.Y.: Tara Publications, 1987).

Appendix II

1. The absence of Jewish dance is not an issue at Orthodox weddings. There, the issue is the absence of klezmer music.
2. Descriptions of dances are derived from publications by LeeEllen Friedland and materials developed for classes taught at KlezKamp by Michael Alpert.

BIBLIOGRAPHY

BOOKS

Aleichem, Sholem (Rabinowitz, Sholem). *Stempenyu: A Yiddishe Roman* (1888). New York: Sholem Aleichem Folksfund Oysgabe, 1919.

Anonymous. *Di Vunderlikhe Geshikhte fun Reb Shmelkeli der Klezmer*. Warsaw: Farlag Oster, 1911.

Bauer, Susan. *From the Khupe to KlezKamp: The Process of Change and Forms of Reinterpretation of Klezmer Music in New York*. Berlin: Piranha, 1999.

Brownlow, Kevin. *Behind the Mask of Innocence: Films of Social Conscience in the Silent Era*. London: Jonathan Cape, 1990.

Chaplin, Saul. *Golden Age of Movie Musicals and Me*. Norman: University of Oklahoma Press, 1994

Condon, Eddie, and Hank O'Neal. *Eddie Condon's Scrapbook of Jazz*. New York: St. Martin's Press, 1973.

Corenthal, Michael. *Cohen on the Telephone: A History of Jewish Recorded Humor and Popular Music*. Milwaukee: Yesterday's Memories, 1984.

Erdman, Harley. *Staging the Jew: The Performance of an American Ethnicity 1860–1920*. New Brunswick: Rutgers University Press, 1997.

Freeland, Michael. *The Warner Brothers*. London: Harrap Ltd., 1983.

Gelatt, Roland. *The Fabulous Phonograph 1877–1977*. New York: Collier Books, 1977.

Gold, Michael. *Jews Without Money*. New York: Horace Liveright, Inc., 1930.

Greene, Victor. *Passion for Polka: Old Time Ethnic Music in America*. Oxford: University of California Press, 1992.

Grossman, Barbara W. *Funny Woman: The Life and Times of Fanny Brice*. Bloomington: Indiana University Press, 1991.

Hapsgood, Hutchins. *The Spirit of the Ghetto*. New York, London: Funk and Wagnalls, 1902.

Heskes, Irene. *Yiddish American Popular Songs 1895–1950*. Washington, D.C.: Library of Congress, 1992.

Hoberman, J. *Bridge of Light: Yiddish Film Between Two Worlds*. New York: Museum of Modern Art/Schocken Books, 1991.

Howe, Irving. *World of Our Fathers*, New York: Harcourt Brace Jovanovich, 1976.

Idelsohn, A. Z. *Jewish Music in Its Historic Development*. New York: Schocken Books, 1967.

Jay, Ricky. *Learned Pigs and Fireproof Women*. New York: Villard Books, 1986.

Lee, Gypsy Rose. *Gypsy: A Memoir*. New York: Harper, 1957.

Joselit, Jenna W. *The Wonders of America: Reinventing Jewish Culture 1880–1950*. New York: Hill and Wang, 1994.

Katz, Mickey, and Hannibal Coons. *Papa, Play for Me*. New York: Simon and Schuster, 1977.

Kennedy, Rick. *Jelly Roll, Bix and Hoagy: Gennett Studios and the Birth of Recorded Jazz*. Bloomington: Indiana University Press, 1994.

Levine, Lawrence W. *Highbrow/Lowbrow The Emergence of Cultural Hierarchy in America*. Cambridge: Harvard University Press, 1988

Lifson, David S. *The Yiddish Theater in America*. New York, London: Thomas Yoseloff, 1965.

Nulman, Macy. *Concise Encyclopedia of Jewish Music*. New York: McGraw-Hill, 1975.

Rischin, Moses. *The Promised City: New York's Jews 1870–1914*. New York: Harper Torchbooks, 1962.

Rosenfeld, Lulla. *Jacob Adler and the Yiddish Theater*. N.Y.: Thomas Crowell, 1977.

Rubin, Ruth. *Voices of a People: The Story of Yiddish Folksong*. New York: McGraw-Hill, 1963.

Rust, Brian. *Jazz Records 1897–1942*. New Rochelle, N.Y.: Arlington House, 1978.

Sandrow, Nahma. *Vagabond Stars: A World History of the Yiddish Theater*. New York: Harper and Row, 1977.

Sanjek, Russell, and David Sanjek. *American Popular Music Business in the Twentieth Century*. New York: Oxford University Press, 1991.

Sapoznik, Henry, and Pete Sokolow. *The Compleat Klezmer*. Cedarhurst, N.Y.: Tara Publications, 1985.

Sapoznik, Henry, Pete Sokolow, and Lynn Dion. *The Klezmer Plus! Folio*, Cedarhurst, N.Y.: Tara Publications, 1992.

Sárosi, Bálint. *Gypsy Music*. Budapest: Corvina Press, 1978.

Schwartz, Charles. *Gershwin, His Life and Music*. New York: Da Capo Press, 1979.

Secunda, Victoria. *Bay Mir Bist Du Schön: The Life of Sholom Secunda*. Weston, Conn.: Magic Circle Press, 1982.

Sendry, Alfred. *The Music of the Jews in the Diaspora (up to 1800): A Contribution to the Social and Cultural History of the Jews*. New York: Thomas Yoseloff, 1970.

Slobin, Mark. *Tenement Songs: The Popular Music of the Jewish Immigrant*. Urbana: University of Illinois Press, 1981.

————ed. and trans. *Old Jewish Folk Music: The Collections and Writings of Moshe Beregovski.* Philadelphia: University of Pennsylvania Press, 1982.

Smart, Jim. *Sousa: A Discography.* Washington, D.C.: Library of Congress, 1970.

Snyder, Robert. *The Voice of the City: Vaudeville and Popular Culture in New York.* New York: Oxford University Press, 1989.

Spottswood, Richard K. *Ethnic Music on Records: A Discography of Ethnic Recordings Produced in the United States, 1893–1942.* Urbana: University of Illinois Press, 1990.

Stein, Charles, ed. *American Vaudeville as Seen By Its Contemporaries.* New York: DaCapo, 1984.

Vigoda, Samuel. *Legendary Voices.* New York: M.P. Press, 1981.

Vizonsky, Nathan. *Ten Jewish Folk Dances: A Manual for Teachers and Leaders.* Chicago: American-Hebrew Theatrical League, 1942.

Wile, Frederic William. *Emile Berliner: Maker of the Microphone.* Indianapolis: Bobbs-Merrill, 1926.

Zylbercweig, Zalmen. *Leksicon fun Yidishn Teater.* New York, 1934.

Zylbercweig, Zalmen, Harry Lang, and Abraham Babitz, eds. *Elia Tenenholtz Yubl Bukh.* Los Angeles: Elia Tenenholtz Jubilee Committee, 1955.

ARTICLES

Beregovsky, Moshe. "Yiddishe Instrumentalishe Folksmuzik Program tsu Forshn di Musikalishe Tetikayt fun di Yiddishe Klezmer." Kiev: Kabinet far Derlernen di Yiddish Sovetishe Literatur, Sprakh un Folklore Sektsye (1937).

————."Evereiske narodnye pesni." Moscow: Sovetskii kompozitor, (1962).

Clark, Morris. "America as the Cradle of Jewish Music."*Musical America,* June 28 (1913).

Dion, Lynn. "Klezmer Music in America: Revival and Beyond." *Jewish Folklore and Ethnology Newsletter* (1986): 8.1–2.

Feldman, Walter Zev. "Bulgareasca/Bulgarish/Bulgar: The Transformation of a Klezmer Dance Genre." *Ethnomusicology* 38.1 (winter 1994).

Friedland, LeeEllen. "The Search for Klezmer Music in Context: The Reconstruction and Revival of a Folk Dance Tradition." (unpublished) Conference on Jewish Folklife in West Orange, N.J., 1983.

Godfried, Nathan. "WEVD: The Working-Class Station." *Journal of Radio* (spring 1990).

Goldin, M. "A Kapitl Verk 'Vegn Yiddishn Muzikaln Folklor.'" *Sovietish Heymland,* no. 1 (January 1983).

Horowitz, Joshua. Liner notes for the CD *Mother Tongue: Music of the 19th Century Klezmorim* (Koch, 3-1261-2), 1997.

———. "Gusikov in Wien." *Jüdische Traditionelle Musik in Oesterreich.* Vienna Oetserreichische Volksliedwerk Vienna, 2001.

James, Patterson. "Off the Record." *The Dearborn Independent* (January 7, 1922).

Loeffler, James. "Di Russishe Progresiv Muzikal Yunyon No. 1 Fun Amerike: The First Klezmer Union in America." *Judaism: A Quarterly Journal of Jewish Life and Thought* 47, no. 1 (winter 1998).

London, Frank. "An Insider's View: How We Traveled from Obscurity to the Klezmer Establishment in Twenty Years." *Judaism: A Quarterly Journal of Jewish Life and Thought* 47, no. 1 (winter 1998).

Lifshultz, I. "Merrymakers and Jesters Among the Jews." *YIVO Annual of Jewish Social Science* 7, 1952.

Pessler, Isaac. "Der Alt Modishe Ekht Yiddisher Klezmer iz Oysgeshpilt in Amerike." *Forverts*, May 1, 1932.

Rothstein, Robert A. "Klezmer-loshn." *Judaism: A Quarterly Journal of Jewish Life and Thought* 47, no. 1 (winter 1998).

Sapoznik, Henry. "Dave Tarras." *New Grove Dictionary of American Music.* Edited by H. Wiley Hitchcock and Stanley Sadie. New York: Stockholm Press, 1986.

———. "From Eastern Europe to East Broadway: Yiddish Music in Old World and New." *New York Folklore Quarterly* 14, nos. 3–4 (summer/fall 1988).

———"Klezmer Music: The First 500 Years." *Musics of Multicultural America.* Edited by Anne Rassmusen and Kip Lornell. New York: Schirmer Books, 1997.

———"Yiddish Music." *Encyclopedia of American Jewish Culture.* Edited by Sanford Pinsker. New York: Garland Publications, 1990.

Schwartz, Itzik. "Lautari evrei din Moldova." *Revista Cultului Mozaic* (1974).

Schwartz, Martin. "Klezmer Music 1908–1927." (Arhoolie 7034) 1997.

Sholom Secunda. "The Melody Remains." *Forverts* (May 1969–December 1970).

Slobin, Mark. "Jewish-American Music." *New Grove Dictionary of American Music.* Edited by H. Wiley Hitchcock and Stanley Sadie. New York: Grove Press, 1986.

———"From Vilna to Vaudeville: Minikes and *Among the Indians.*" *The Drama Review 3* 24, no. 3 (September 1980).

Svigals, Alicia. "Why Do We Do This Anyway: Klezmer as Jewish Youth Subculture." *Judaism: A Quarterly Journal of Jewish Life and Thought* 47, no. 1 (winter 1998).

Trivaks, Avrom-Yitskhok. "Di Yiddishe Zhargonen: Kley-Zemer Loshn." *Bay undz Yidn.* Edited by M. Vanvild. Warsaw: Pinkhes Graubard, 1923.

Weissenberg, S. "Die Klesmer Sprache." *Mitteilungen der anthropologischen Gesellschaft in Wien* 13 (1913).

Wollock, Jeffrey. "European Recordings of Jewish Instrumental Music, 1911–1914," *ARSC Journal* 28, no. 1 (spring 1997).

GLOSSARY

Underline indicates where stress is placed on the word.
Kh = as in "Bach"

Ba'alTfile Reader of the Torah.

Badekn Veiling of the bride.

Badkhn Improvisatory wedding poet (pl. badkhonim).

Badkhones the rhymes performed by a badkhn.

Bar Mitzvah Confirmation of a thirteen-year-old (fem: Bas mitz-vah).

Baraban Drum.

Bulgar Bessarabian dance tune popular among Jewish musicians during the first half of the twentieth century that forms the basis of modern klezmer music.

Doina Improvisatory free-metered melody based on music of Romanian shepherds.

Dreydl Turning; also familar term for ornament in klezmer music (pl: dreydlakh).

Fleyt Flute.

Freylekh (Lit: happy) Yiddish dance and tune type.

Gemorah A commentary on the Mishna forming the second part of the Talmud.

Grine Greenhorn.

Hasid Ultra-Orthodox Jewish sect founded by the Ba'al Shem Tov in the eighteenth century (pl: hasidim).

Haskalah Enlightenment movement founded by Rabbi Moses Mendelssohn in eighteenth-century Germany.

Kaboles ponim (Lit: Welcoming a face) The greeting of guests by the bride.

Kale Bride.

Kapelye Band.

Kapote Calf-length coat worn by Hasidim.

Khazn Cantor (pl. khazonim).

Khazones Music sung by *khazonim*.

Kheyder Religious primary school.

Khosidl Dance based on those done by Hasidim.

Khosn Groom.

Khupe Wedding canopy.

Kiddush Blessing made over wine; also small celebration held after sabbath services.

Klezmer Eastern-European Jewish musician; also modifier (e.g. klezmer music).

Krekhts Sigh or moan; also ornament in klezmer music.

Kunstler Artist.

Landsman (also **landslayt**) Fellow countryman.

Landsmanshaft Organization of expatriate Jews from the same town.

Marshalik Master of ceremonies at a wedding.

Meshoyrer Apprentice cantor (pl. meshoyrerim).

Musikant (**Musiker**) Musician.

Nigun Wordless song sung by Hasidim (pl. nigunim).

Patriot Fan (pl. patriotn).

Peyes Sidecurls worn by Hasidic Jews.

Purimshpiel Folk play depicting the triumph of Mordechai and Esther over the evil Persian Haman.

Rebbe Hasidic rabbi.

Secunda Second fiddle, usually playing chords.

Shabbos Sabbath.

Sher (also **sherele**) (Lit: scissors) Yiddish square dance.

Shul Synagogue.

Shtetl Small town (pl. shtetlekh).

Shteyger Mode.

Shtrayml Round brimmed beaver-trimmed hat worn by Hasidim.

Simkhe Celebration.

Tats Cymbal.

Tsimbl Hammered dulcimer.

Zeyde Grandfather.

INDEX

Page numbers in *italics* indicate illustrations or musical examples.

A COMPANION CD

KLEZMER!

Jewish Music from Old World to Our World

featuring 23 selected examples of historic recordings mentioned in this book, is available from Shanachie Entertainment.

Send check or money order for $15.00, plus $3.00 postage and handling to:

Living Traditions
430 West 14 Street, Suite 409
New York, NY 10014

You may also order it from our website, henry@livingtraditions.org, or ask for it at your local record store.

A percentage of your purchase benefits Living Traditions, Inc., in its work of popularizing and disseminating traditional Yiddish culture.